Mirror for Humanity

A Concise Introduction to Cultural Anthropology

Ninth Edition

Conrad Phillip Kottak
University of Michigan

Mc
Graw
Hill
Education

MIRROR FOR HUMANITY: A CONCISE INTRODUCTION TO CULTURAL ANTHROPOLOGY, NINTH EDITION

Published by McGraw-Hill Education, 2 Penn Plaza, New York, NY 10121. Copyright © 2014 by McGraw-Hill Education. All rights reserved. Printed in the United States of America. Previous editions © 2012, 2010, and 2008. No part of this publication may be reproduced or distributed in any form or by any means, or stored in a database or retrieval system, without the prior written consent of McGraw-Hill Education, including, but not limited to, in any network or other electronic storage or transmission, or broadcast for distance learning.

Some ancillaries, including electronic and print components, may not be available to customers outside the United States.

This book is printed on acid-free paper.

1 2 3 4 5 6 7 8 9 0 DOC/DOC 1 0 9 8 7 6 5 4 3

ISBN 978-0-07-803505-0
MHID 0-07-803505-8

Senior Vice President, Products & Markets: *Kurt L. Strand*
Vice President, General Manager, Products & Markets: *Michael J. Ryan*
Vice President, Content Production & Technology Services: *Kimberly Meriwether David*
Managing Director: *Gina Boedeker*
Director: *Matthew Busbridge*
Brand Manager: *Courtney Austermehle*
Director of Development: *Rhona Robbin*
Brand Coordinator: *Ryan Viviani*

Development Editor: *Emily Pecora*
Marketing Manager: *Philip Weaver*
Content Project Manager: *Bruce Gin*
Senior Buyer: *Laura M. Fuller*
Design: *Tara McDermott*
Cover Image: © *Jim Zuckerman/Alamy*
Content Licensing Specialist: *Shawntel Schmitt*
Media Project Manager: *Mahalakshmi Vijay*
Typeface: *10/12 Times*
Compositor: *Aptara®, Inc.*
Printer: *R. R. Donnelley*

All credits appearing on page or at the end of the book are considered to be an extension of the copyright page.

Library of Congress Cataloging-in-Publication Data

Kottak, Conrad Phillip.
  Mirror for humanity : a concise introduction to cultural anthropology / Conrad Phillip Kottak, University of Michigan.
     p. cm.
  Includes index.
  ISBN 978-0-07-803505-0 (alk. paper)
  ISBN 0-07-803505-8 (alk. paper)
  1. Ethnology. I. Title.
  GN316.K66 2014
  306—dc23

2013019763

The Internet addresses listed in the text were accurate at the time of publication. The inclusion of a website does not indicate an endorsement by the authors or McGraw-Hill Education, and McGraw-Hill Education does not guarantee the accuracy of the information presented at these sites.

www.mhhe.com

To my daughter,
Dr. Juliet Kottak Mavromatis

Also available from McGraw-Hill by Conrad Phillip Kottak:

Window on Humanity: A Concise Introduction to Anthropology, 6th ed. (2014)

CULTURE, 2nd ed. (2014) (Lisa Gezon and Conrad Phillip Kottak)

Anthropology: Appreciating Human Diversity, 15th ed. (2013)

Cultural Anthropology: Appreciating Cultural Diversity, 15th ed. (2013)

On Being Different: Diversity and Multiculturalism in the North American Mainstream, 4th ed. (2012) (with Kathryn A. Kozaitis)

Assault on Paradise: The Globalization of a Little Community in Brazil, 4th ed. (2006)

Brief Contents

Contents

Anthropology Today Boxes

Preface

Mirror for Humanity (MFH) is intended to provide a concise, readable, lower-cost introduction to cultural anthropology. The combination of shorter length and lower cost increases the instructor's options for assigning additional reading—case studies, readers, and other supplements—in a semester course. MFH also can work well in a quarter system, for which traditional texts may be too long.

As a college student, I was drawn to anthropology by its breadth and because of what it could tell me about the human condition. Cultural anthropology has compiled an impressive body of knowledge about human similarities and differences. I'm eager to introduce that knowledge in the pages that follow. I believe strongly in anthropology's capacity to enlighten and inform. Anthropology's subject matter is intrinsically fascinating, and its focus on diversity helps students understand and interact with their fellow human beings in an increasingly interconnected world and an increasingly diverse North America.

Anthropology remains exciting, even as profound changes affect the people and societies ethnographers study. In cultural anthropology it's increasingly difficult to know when to write in the present and when to write in the past tense. Yet many texts ignore change—except maybe with a chapter tacked on at the end—and are written as though cultural anthropology and the people it studies were the same as they were decades ago. While any competent text must present cultural anthropology's core, it should also demonstrate anthropology's relevance to today's world.

Like the world itself, anthropology seems to change at an accelerating rate. I see no reason an introductory text should confine itself to subject matter defined more than a generation ago, ignoring globalization and the pervasive changes now affecting the peoples, places, and topics traditionally studied by anthropologists. MFH thus includes discussions of ethnicity and nationalism in a global context and of diversity and multiculturalism in North America. Also highlighted are anthropology's increasingly transnational, multilocal, and longitudinal perspectives.

Rapid change notwithstanding, anthropology has a core—the subject matter, perspectives, and approaches that first attracted me when I was an undergraduate. Even the briefest text must expose anthropology's nature, scope, and roles as a science, a humanities field, and a mirror for humanity. Anthropology is a science—a "systematic field of study or body of knowledge that aims, through experiment, observation, and deduction, to produce reliable explanations of phenomena, with reference to the material and physical world" (Webster's New World Encyclopedia, 1993, p. 937). Clyde Kluckhohn called anthropology "the science of human similarities and differences." His statement of the need for such a science still stands: "Anthropology provides a scientific basis for dealing with the crucial dilemma of the world today: how can peoples of different appearance, mutually unintelligible languages, and dissimilar ways of life get along peaceably together?" (Kluckhohn 1944, p. 9).

Anthropology also has strong links to the humanities. Cultural anthropology may well be the most humanistic of academic fields because of its fundamental respect for human diversity. Anthropologists listen to, record, and represent voices from a multitude of nations and cultures. We strive to convince our students of the value of local knowledge, of diverse worldviews and perspectives. Cultural anthropology brings a comparative and nonelitist perspective to forms of creative expression, including art, narratives, music, and dance. Cultural anthropology is influenced by and influences the humanities. Adopting a view of creativity in the context of cultural, social, and power differentials, recent approaches in the humanities have mirrored anthropology in paying greater attention to mass and popular culture and to local and subaltern creative expressions.

Anthropology's final basic role is as a mirror for humanity—a phrase derived from Clyde Kluckhohn's metaphor, expressed in his book *Mirror for Man* (1944), which suggested the title of this text. By looking at other cultures we can see ourselves more clearly:

> Ordinarily we are unaware of the special lens through which we look at life. It would hardly be fish who discovered the existence of water. Students who had not yet gone beyond the horizon of their own society could not be expected to perceive custom which was the stuff of their own thinking. Anthropology holds up a great mirror to man and lets him look at himself in his infinite variety. (Kluckhohn, 1944, p. 16)

This point reminds me of one of my own teachers, Margaret Mead, who is remembered for her unparalleled success in demonstrating anthropology's value and relevance in allowing Americans to reflect on cultural variation and the plasticity of human nature. Mead represented anthropology so effectively because she viewed it as a humanistic science of unique value in understanding and improving the human condition. This book is written in the belief that anthropologists should remember and emulate Dr. Mead's example.

Content and Organization

No single or monolithic theoretical perspective orients this book. My e-mail, along with reviewers' comments, confirms that instructors with a wide range of views and approaches have been pleased with MFH as a teaching tool.

The chapters are organized to place related content close together—although they are sufficiently independent of one another to be assigned in any order the instructor might select. Culture, ethnography, and language are covered in Chapters 2–4. "Political Systems" (Chapter 6) logically follows "Making a Living" (Chapter 5). Chapters 7 and 8 ("Families, Kinship, and Marriage" and "Gender," respectively) also form a coherent unit.

The chapter on religion (9) covers not just traditional religious practices but also contemporary world religions and religious movements. It is followed by four chapters (10–13) that form a natural unit exploring sociocultural transformations and expressions in today's world. This concluding unit represents one of the key differences between this text and others. These four chapters address several key questions: What role should anthropology play in studying, understanding, and potentially changing today's world? How are ethnicity and race socially constructed and handled in different societies, and how do they generate prejudice, discrimination, and conflict? How and why did the modern world system emerge? How has world capitalism affected patterns of stratification and inequality within and among nations? What were colonialism, imperialism, and Communism, and what are their legacies? How do economic development, globalization, and climate change affect the peoples, societies, and communities among which anthropologists traditionally have worked? How do people today actively interpret and confront the world system and the products of globalization? How does globalization as ideology differ from globalization as fact? What factors threaten continued human diversity? How can anthropologists work to ensure the preservation of that diversity?

Let me focus here as well on two chapters present in *Mirror for Humanity* but not found consistently in other anthropology texts: "Ethnicity and Race" (Chapter 10) and "Gender" (Chapter 8). I believe that systematic consideration of race, ethnicity, and gender is vital in an introductory anthropology text. Anthropology's distinctive four-field approach can shed special light on these subjects. Race and gender studies are fields in which anthropology always has taken the lead. I'm convinced that anthropology's special contributions to understanding the biological, social, cultural, and linguistic dimensions of race, ethnicity, and gender should be highlighted in any introductory text, as they are in this one. Ever since the writings of Franz Boas, a founder of American anthropology, issues of race, language, and culture have been central to anthropology. I make every attempt to illuminate them in this book.

New in the Ninth Edition

All chapters of *Mirror for Humanity* have been updated, with charts, tables, and statistics based on the most recent information available. Of the 13 end-of-chapter boxes, 7 are new to this edition. These "Anthropology Today" boxes are intended to bring home anthropology's relevance to current issues and events in today's world. With the revised Chapter 13, "Anthropology's Role in a Globalizing World," and other changes, the focus on global themes, trends, and issues has been strengthened even further in this edition.

Chapter-by-Chapter Changes

Chapter 1: What Is Anthropology?
This chapter has been updated.

Chapter 2: Culture
This chapter has been updated, with a rewritten section on globalization.

Chapter 3: Doing Anthropology
This chapter has been updated throughout.

Chapter 4: Language and Communication
This chapter has been updated and contains a new "Anthropology Today" box on California accents.

Chapter 5: Making a Living
Chapter 5 has undergone a major revision and rewrite. Specific changes include the following:

- A new introduction clarifying the huge importance and transformational nature of food-producing (Neolithic) economies.
- New material on foragers in South Asia.
- A new hunter-gatherer distribution map.
- A new section on the cultivation continuum.

Chapter 6: Political Systems

Chapter 6 contains a new "Anthropology Today" on contemporary politics in rural Thailand.

Chapter 7: Families, Kinship, and Marriage

This chapter has an informative new "Anthropology Today" on American family life in the 21st century. The section on gifts at marriage has been substantially revised. All charts, figures, and statistics have been updated.

Chapter 8: Gender

Chapter 8 has been updated and revised substantially. It now includes the following:

- A discussion of Margaret Mead's pioneering work on gender.
- An updated section on gender in industrial societies.
- Revised material on transgender and gender identity (as distinguished from sexual orientation).
- A new "Anthropology Today" on the Global Gender Gap Index.

Chapter 9: Religion

Chapter 9 has been revised substantially, with new sections on

- Protestant values and capitalism.
- Religion and cultural globalization, including subsections on Evangelical Protestantism and Pentecostalism; homogenization, indigenization, or hybridization; antimodernism and fundamentalism; and the spread of Islam.
- A substantially updated and revised section on world religions.

This chapter also contains a new "Anthropology Today" on "baseball magic."

Chapter 10: Ethnicity and Race

This chapter has been updated and revised substantially. It now includes the following:

- A new section on minority groups and stratification.
- A new section on changing American demographics.
- New material on evolving Brazilian racial classification.
- A revised and updated section on multiculturalism.
- A new "Anthropology Today"—the AAA Statement on Race.

Chapter 11: Applying Anthropology

This chapter has been updated throughout.

Chapter 12: The World System and Colonialism

Chapter 12 (formerly Chapter 10) has been moved next to the final chapter, where they form a coherent unit. Updates and other revisions to this chapter include the following:

- A major new section on neoliberalism and NAFTA's economic refugees.
- A new discussion of skewed wealth distribution in the contemporary United States (including the Occupy Movement).

Chapter 13: Anthropology's Role in a Globalizing World

A substantially revised section on globalization begins this chapter, which has been updated throughout. Specific changes include the following:

- A section on energy consumption and industrial degradation, moved here from the previous chapter.
- A major new section on emerging diseases.
- Substantially revised sections on global climate change, environmental anthropology, and cultural imperialism and indigenization.
- A new concluding discussion of anthropology's key lessons.

Pedagogy

This ninth edition incorporates suggestions made by users of my other texts as well as reviewers of previous editions of *Mirror for Humanity*. The result, I hope, is a sound, well-organized, interesting, and user-friendly introduction to cultural anthropology.

MFH contains seven new "Anthropology Today" boxes. Placed consistently at the end of each chapter, "Anthropology Today" is intended to give students a chance to consider anthropology's relevance to today's world and to their own lives. Some boxes examine current events or debates. Others are more personal accounts, which add human feeling to the presentation of anthropology's subject matter. Many boxes illustrate a point with examples familiar to students from their enculturation or everyday experience.

End-of-chapter summaries are numbered, to make major points stand out.

Boldface key terms in each chapter are defined in the glossary at the end of the book. A bibliography contains references cited and relevant reading.

Supplements

Visit our Online Learning Center website at www.mhhe.com/kottakmfh9e for robust student and instructor resources.

For Students

Student resources include self-quizzes (multiple-choice, true or false, essay), Internet exercises, and additional chapter study aides.

For Instructors

The password-protected instructor portion of the website includes the instructor's manual, a comprehensive computerized test bank, PowerPoint lecture slides, and a variety of additional instructor resources.

Create

Design your ideal course materials with McGraw-Hill's Create: www.mcgrawhillcreate. com! Rearrange or omit chapters, combine materials from other sources, and/or upload any other content you have written to make the perfect resource for your students. You can even personalize your book's appearance by selecting the cover and adding your name, school, and course information. When you order a Create book, you receive a complimentary review copy. Get a printed copy in three to five business days or an electronic copy (eComp) via e-mail in about an hour. Register today at www.mcgrawhillcreate. com and craft your course resources to match the way you teach.

CourseSmart eBook

CourseSmart is a new way to find and buy eTextbooks. At CourseSmart you can save up to 50 percent of the cost of a print textbook, reduce your impact on the environment, and gain access to powerful Web tools for learning. CourseSmart has the largest selection of eTextbooks available anywhere, offering thousands of the most commonly adopted textbooks from a wide variety of higher-education publishers. CourseSmart eTextbooks are available in one standard online reader with full text search, notes and highlighting, and e-mail tools for sharing notes between classmates. For further details contact your sales representative or go to www.coursesmart.com.

Acknowledgments

I'm grateful to many colleagues at McGraw-Hill. Emily Pecora has been a wonderfully helpful and supportive Developmental Editor. I thank her for synthesizing and summarizing the prepublication reviews, helping me plan and implement this revision, and working with me to complete and submit the manuscript. I always benefit from Emily's careful reading of my new writing, of which there was a lot in this edition. Thanks, too, to Courtney Austermehle, Brand Manager for anthropology (along with sociology and women's studies), to Marketing Manager Philip Weaver, and to Brand Coordinator Ryan Viviani. I'm grateful as well for the support of Managing Director Gina Boedeker and Michael Ryan, Vice President and General Manager, Products & Markets.

Thanks to Bruce Gin for his work as Content Project Manager, guiding the manuscript through production and keeping everything moving on schedule. Thanks as well to the entire K4 team. Laura Fuller, Buyer, worked with the printer to make sure everything came out right. Thanks, too, to Emily Tietz, freelance photo researcher, and to Geoffrey Hughes for his work on the Instructor's Manual and to Geoffrey Williams for his work on the PowerPoints, Test Bank, and student supplements located on the Online Learning Center website. I also thank Debra DeBord for copyediting, Lauren Timmer for proofreading, and Tara McDermott for executing the design.

Shawntel Schmitt also deserves thanks as content licensing specialist, as does Mahalakshmi Vijay, media project manager, who created the OLC. I also thank Wes Hall, who has handled the literary permissions.

I'm very grateful to a long list of reviewers of this and previous editions of *Window on Humanity* and *Mirror for Humanity:*

The names and schools of the reviewers contracted by McGraw-Hill to review the 5th edition of *Window on Humanity,* in preparation for the 6th edition, or the 8th edition of *Mirror for Humanity*, in preparation for the 9th edition, are as follows:

Beau Bowers
Central Piedmont Community College

Margaret Bruchez
Blinn College

Richard Buonforte
Brigham Young University

Beverly Chiarulli
*Indiana University of
Pennsylvania*

Ricardo Fernandez
Ball State University

Peter Gardner
University of Missouri

Jamon Alex Halvaksz, II
University of Texas at San Antonio

Fred Heifner
Cumberland University

Jon Holtzman
Western Michigan University

Jayne Howell
*California State University –
Long Beach*

Alana Jolley
Saddleback College

John Michels
University of Illinois

Jason Miller
University of South Florida

Alan Mock
Lakeland College

John Napota
University of South Florida

Thomas Pearson
University of Wisconsin–Stout

Holly Peters-Golden
The University of Michigan

Kendall Roark
Drexel University

Deborah Rotman
University of Notre Dame

Richard Sattler
University of Montana

Michael Simonton
Northern Kentucky University

Michael Uzendoski
Florida State University

Jack Wynn
North Georgia College and State University

The reviewers of previous editions of this book and of *Window on Humanity* are as follows:

Terri Aihoshi
Grant MacEwan College

Sue L. Aki
University of Texas at San Antonio

Linda Allen
Kirkwood Community College

Ari N. Ariyaratne
College of DuPage

Diane Everett Barbolla
San Diego Mesa College

Joshua Barker
University of Toronto

Jeffrey P. Blick
Georgia College & State University

Beau Bowers
Central Piedmont Community College

Jim Brady
California State University, Los Angeles

Larisa Lee Broyles,
California State University, San Bernardino

Stephen Childs
Valdosta State University

William L. Coleman
University of North Carolina, Greensboro

Garrett Cook
Baylor University

Leslie Dawson
Grant MacEwan College

Connie Deroche
Cape Breton University

Barbra E. Erickson
California State University–Fullerton

Charles R. Ewen
East Carolina University

Jason M. Fancher
Washington State University

Les W. Field
University of New Mexico

Elizabeth Fortenbery
Pierce Community College

Elizabeth Fuller-Tarbox
State University of New York–Potsdam

Dan Gardiner
Mohawk College

Maidie R. Golan
Kennesaw State University

David B. Halmo
University of Wisconsin–Parkside

Christopher Hays
University of Wisconsin–Washington County

Marc Healy
Elgin Community College

Katherine Hirschfeld
University of Oklahoma

Patricia Jolly
University of Northern Colorado

Hilary Kahn
Indiana University–Indianapolis

Patricia Kelly-Spurles
Mount Allison University

Yin Lam
University of Victoria

Jami Leibowitz
East Carolina University

William Leons
University of Toledo

Daniel Maher
Westark College

Susan Meswick
CUNY Queens College

Garry Morgan
Northwestern College

Martin Oppenheimer
Kansas State University

Mary Patterson
The University of Melbourne, Australia

Megan A. Perry
East Carolina University

Gerald F. Reid
Sacred Heart University

Carolyn Rock
Valdosta State University

Rita C. Rodabaugh
Central Piedmont Community College

Eugene E. Ruyle
California State University, Long Beach

Carleen Sanchez
University of Nebraska Lincoln

Jon A. Schlenker
University of Maine at Augusta

Pete Sinelli
University of Central Florida

Andris Skreija
University of Nebraska–Omaha

Betty A. Smith
Kennesaw State University

Shannon Speed
University of Texas at Austin

Emily Stovel
Ripon College

Ted Swedenburg
University of Arkansas

Susan Tanner
University of Georgia

Mark Tromans
Broward Community College

Helen Vallianatos
University of Alberta

Salena Wakim
Orange Coast College

Thomas Williamson
St. Olaf College

I'm grateful to all these reviewers and professors for their enthusiasm and their suggestions for changes, additions, and deletions (sometimes in very different directions!).

Special thanks to Michael McCrath of the Seattle Community Colleges for his excellent suggestion for a change in the chapter "Families, Kinship, and Marriage," which I have implemented in this edition.

Students also share their insights about *Mirror* via e-mail. Anyone—student or instructor—can reach me at the following e-mail address: ckottak@bellsouth.net.

As always, my family has offered me understanding, support, and inspiration during the preparation of MFH. My son, Dr. Nicholas Kottak (himself an anthropologist) regularly shares his insights with me, as does Isabel Wagley Kottak, my companion in the field and in life for more than four decades. This book is dedicated to my daughter, Dr. Juliet Kottak Mavromatis, who continues our family tradition of exploring and writing about human diversity and diagnosing and treating the human condition.

During my long academic career, I've benefited from the knowledge, help, and advice of so many friends, colleagues, teaching assistants (graduate student instructors—GSIs), and students that I can no longer fit their names into a short preface. I hope they know who they are and accept my thanks. I do especially thank my co-authors of other books: Kathryn Kozaitis (*On Being Different*), Lara Descartes (*Media and Middle Class Moms*), and Lisa Gezon (*Culture*). Kathryn, Lara, and Lisa are prized former students of mine. Today they all are accomplished anthropologists in their own right, and they continue to share their wisdom with me.

I'm very grateful to my Michigan colleagues who've shared their insights and suggested ways of making my books better. Thanks especially to a 101 team that includes Tom Fricke, Stuart Kirsch, Holly Peters-Golden, and Andrew Shryock.

Feedback from students, faculty, and GSIs keeps me up-to-date on the interests, needs, and views of the people for whom *Mirror* is written, as does my ongoing participation in workshops on the teaching of anthropology. I continue to believe that effective textbooks are based in the enthusiastic practice of teaching. I hope this product of my experience will continue to be helpful to others.

Conrad Phillip Kottak

Seabrook Island, South Carolina

ckottak@bellsouth.net

About the Author

Conrad Phillip Kottak, who received his AB and PhD degrees from Columbia University, is the Julian H. Steward Collegiate Professor Emeritus of Anthropology at the University of Michigan, where he served as anthropology department chair from 1996 to 2006. In 1991 he was honored for his teaching by the university and the state of Michigan. In 1999 the American Anthropological Association (AAA) awarded Professor Kottak its Award for Excellence in the Undergraduate Teaching of Anthropology. In 2005 he was elected to the American Academy of Arts and Sciences, and in 2008 to the National Academy of Sciences. Professor Kottak has done ethnographic fieldwork in Brazil, Madagascar, and the United States. His general interests are in the processes by which local cultures are incorporated—and resist incorporation—into larger systems. This interest links his earlier work on ecology and state formation in Africa and Madagascar to his more recent research on globalization, national and international culture, and the mass media.

The fourth edition of Kottak's popular case study *Assault on Paradise: The Globalization of a Little Community in Brazil,* based on his continuing fieldwork in Arembepe, Bahia, Brazil, was published in 2006 by McGraw-Hill. In a research project during the 1980s, Kottak blended ethnography and survey research in studying "Television's Behavioral Effects in Brazil." That research is the basis of Kottak's book *Prime-Time Society: An Anthropological Analysis of Television and Culture* (updated edition published by Left Coast Press in 2009)—a comparative study of the nature and impact of television in Brazil and the United States. Kottak's Brazilian media research is being updated through a new (2013) NSF grant titled "The Evolution of Media Impact: A Longitudinal and Multi-Site Study of Television and New Electronic/Digital Media in Brazil."

Kottak's other books include *The Past in the Present: History, Ecology and Cultural Variation in Highland Madagascar* (1980), *Researching American Culture: A Guide for Student Anthropologists* (edited 1982) (both University of Michigan Press), and *Madagascar: Society and History* (1986) (Carolina Academic Press). The most recent editions (15th) of his texts *Anthropology: Appreciating Human Diversity* and *Cultural Anthropology: Appreciating Cultural Diversity* were published by McGraw-Hill in 2013. He also is the author of *Window on Humanity: A Concise Introduction to Anthropology* (6th ed., McGraw-Hill, 2014) and of this book—*Mirror for Humanity: A Concise Introduction to Cultural Anthropology* (9th ed., McGraw-Hill, 2014).

Conrad Kottak's articles have appeared in academic journals, including *American Anthropologist, Journal of Anthropological Research, American Ethnologist, Ethnology, Human Organization,* and *Luso-Brazilian Review.* He also has written for more popular publications, including *Transaction/SOCIETY, Natural History, Psychology Today,* and *General Anthropology.*

In other research projects, Kottak and his colleagues have investigated the emergence of ecological awareness in Brazil, the social context of deforestation and biodiversity conservation in Madagascar, and popular participation in economic development planning in northeastern Brazil. With the support of the Alfred P. Sloan Foundation, Kottak and his colleague Lara Descartes investigated how middle-class American families in a midwestern town draw on various media in planning, managing, and evaluating the competing demands of work and family. That research is the basis of their book *Media and Middle Class Moms: Images and Realities of Work and Family* (Descartes and Kottak 2009, Routledge/Taylor and Francis). Kottak currently is collaborating with Professor Richard Pace and several graduate students on research investigating "The Evolution of Media Impact: A Longitudinal and Multi-Site study of Television and New Electronic/Digital Media in Brazil."

Conrad Kottak appreciates comments about his books from professors and students. He can be reached by e-mail at the following e-mail address: **ckottak@bellsouth.net.**

Chapter 1

What Is Anthropology?

"That's just human nature." "People are pretty much the same all over the world." Such opinions, which we hear in conversations, in the mass media, and in a dozen scenes in daily life, promote the erroneous idea that people in other countries have the same desires, feelings, values, and aspirations that we do. Such statements proclaim that because people are essentially the same, they are eager to receive the ideas, beliefs, values, institutions, practices, and products of an expansive North American culture. Often this assumption turns out to be wrong.

Anthropology offers a broader view—a distinctive comparative, cross-cultural perspective. Most people think that anthropologists study nonindustrial societies, and they do. My research has taken me to remote villages in Brazil and Madagascar, a large island off the southeast coast of Africa. In Brazil I sailed with fishers in simple sailboats on Atlantic waters. Among Madagascar's Betsileo people I worked in rice fields and took part in ceremonies in which I entered tombs to rewrap the corpses of decaying ancestors.

However, anthropology is much more than the study of nonindustrial peoples. It is a comparative science that examines all societies, ancient and modern, simple and complex. Most of the other social sciences tend to focus on a single society, usually an industrial nation such as the United States or Canada. Anthropology offers a unique cross-cultural perspective, constantly comparing the customs of one society with those of others.

To become a cultural anthropologist, one normally does *ethnography* (the first-hand, personal study of local settings). Ethnographic fieldwork usually entails spending a year

1

or more in another society, living with the local people and learning about their way of life. No matter how much the ethnographer discovers about that society, he or she remains an alien there. That experience of alienation has a profound impact. Having learned to respect other customs and beliefs, anthropologists can never forget that there is a wider world. There are normal ways of thinking and acting other than our own.

Human Adaptability

Anthropologists study human beings wherever and whenever they find them—in a Turkish café, a Mesopotamian tomb, or a North American shopping mall. Anthropology is the exploration of human diversity in time and space. Anthropology studies the whole of the human condition: past, present, and future; biology, society, language, and culture. Of particular interest is the diversity that comes through human adaptability.

Humans are among the world's most adaptable animals. In the Andes of South America, people wake up in villages 16,000 feet above sea level and then trek 1,500 feet higher to work in tin mines. Tribes in the Australian desert worship animals and discuss philosophy. People survive malaria in the tropics. Men have walked on the moon. The model of the starship *Enterprise* in Washington's Smithsonian Institution symbolizes the desire to "seek out new life and civilizations, to boldly go where no one has gone before." Wishes to know the unknown, control the uncontrollable, and create order out of chaos find expression among all peoples. Creativity, adaptability, and flexibility are basic human attributes, and human diversity is the subject matter of anthropology.

Students often are surprised by the breadth of **anthropology,** which is the study of the human species and its immediate ancestors. Anthropology is a uniquely comparative and **holistic** science. *Holism* refers to the study of the whole of the human condition: past, present, and future; biology, society, language, and culture.

People share **society**—organized life in groups—with other animals, including baboons, wolves, mole rats, and even ants. Culture, however, is more distinctly human. **Cultures** are traditions and customs, transmitted through learning, that form and guide the beliefs and behavior of the people exposed to them. Children learn such a tradition by growing up in a particular society, through a process called enculturation. Cultural traditions include customs and opinions, developed over the generations, about proper and improper behavior. These traditions answer such questions as: How should we do things? How do we make sense of the world? How do we tell right from wrong? What is right, and what is wrong? A culture produces a degree of consistency in behavior and thought among the people who live in a particular society.

The most critical element of cultural traditions is their transmission through learning rather than through biological inheritance. Culture is not itself biological, but it rests on certain features of human biology. For more than a million years, humans have had at least some of the biological capacities on which culture depends. These abilities are to learn, to think symbolically, to use language, and to employ tools and other products in organizing their lives and adapting to their environments.

Anthropology confronts and ponders major questions of human existence as it explores human biological and cultural diversity in time and space. By examining ancient bones and tools, we unravel the mysteries of human origins. When did our ancestors separate from those remote great-aunts and great-uncles whose descendants are the apes? Where and when did *Homo sapiens* originate? How has our species changed? What are we now, and where are we going? How have changes in culture and society influenced biological change? Our genus, *Homo*, has been changing for more than 2 million years. Humans continue to adapt and change both biologically and culturally.

Adaptation, Variation, and Change

Adaptation refers to the processes by which organisms cope with environmental forces and stresses, such as those posed by climate and *topography* or terrains, also called landforms. How do organisms change to fit their environments, such as dry climates or high mountain altitudes? Like other animals, humans use biological means of adaptation. But humans are unique in also having cultural means of adaptation. Table 1.1 summarizes the cultural and biological means that humans use to adapt to high altitudes.

Mountainous terrains pose particular challenges, those associated with high altitude and oxygen deprivation. Consider four ways (one cultural and three biological) in which humans may cope with low oxygen pressure at high altitudes. Illustrating cultural (technological) adaptation would be a pressurized airplane cabin equipped with oxygen masks. There are three ways of adapting biologically to high altitudes: genetic adaptation, long-term physiological adaptation, and short-term physiological adaptation. First, native populations of high-altitude areas, such as the Andes of Peru and the Himalayas of Tibet and Nepal, seem to have acquired certain genetic advantages for life at very high altitudes. The Andean tendency to develop a voluminous chest and lungs probably has a genetic basis. Second, regardless of their genes, people who grow up at a high altitude become physiologically more efficient there than genetically similar people who have grown up at sea level would be. This illustrates long-term physiological adaptation during the body's growth and development. Third, humans also have the capacity for short-term or immediate physiological adaptation. Thus, when lowlanders arrive in the highlands, they immediately increase their breathing and heart

TABLE 1.1   Forms of Cultural and Biological Adaptation (to High Altitude)

Form of Adaptation	Type of Adaptation	Example
Technology	Cultural	Pressurized airplane cabin with oxygen masks
Genetic adaptation (occurs over generations)	Biological	Larger "barrel chests" of native highlanders
Long-term physiological adaptation (occurs during growth and development of the individual organism)	Biological	More efficient respiratory system, to extract oxygen from "thin air"
Short-term physiological adaptation (occurs spontaneously when the individual organism enters a new environment)	Biological	Increased heart rate, hyperventilation

rates. Hyperventilation increases the oxygen in their lungs and arteries. As the pulse also increases, blood reaches their tissues more rapidly. All these varied adaptive responses—cultural and biological—achieve a single goal: maintaining an adequate supply of oxygen to the body.

As human history has unfolded, the social and cultural means of adaptation have become increasingly important. In this process, humans have devised diverse ways of coping with a wide range of environments. The rate of cultural adaptation and change has accelerated, particularly during the past 10,000 years. For millions of years, hunting and gathering of nature's bounty—*foraging*—was the sole basis of human subsistence. However, it took only a few thousand years for **food production** (the cultivation of plants and domestication of animals), which originated some 12,000–10,000 years ago, to replace foraging in most areas. Between 6000 and 5000 B.P. (before the present), the first civilizations arose. These were large, powerful, and complex societies, such as ancient Egypt, that conquered and governed large geographic areas.

Much more recently, the spread of industrial production has profoundly affected human life. Throughout human history, major innovations have spread at the expense of earlier ones. Each economic revolution has had social and cultural repercussions. Today's global economy and communications link all contemporary people, directly or indirectly, in the modern world system. People must cope with forces generated by progressively larger systems—region, nation, and world. The study of such contemporary adaptations generates new challenges for anthropology: "The cultures of world peoples need to be constantly rediscovered as these people reinvent them in changing historical circumstances" (Marcus and Fischer 1986, p. 24).

General Anthropology

The academic discipline of anthropology, also known as **general anthropology** or "four-field" anthropology, includes four main subdisciplines, or subfields. They are sociocultural, archaeological, biological, and linguistic anthropology. (From here on, the shorter term *cultural anthropology* will be used as a synonym for *sociocultural anthropology*.) Of the subfields, cultural anthropology has the largest membership. Most departments of anthropology teach courses in all four subfields.

There are historical reasons for the inclusion of four subfields in a single discipline. The origin of anthropology as a scientific field, and of American anthropology in particular, can be traced to the 19th century. Early American anthropologists were concerned especially with the history and cultures of the native peoples of North America. Interest in the origins and diversity of Native Americans brought together studies of customs, social life, language, and physical traits. Anthropologists still are pondering such questions as: Where did Native Americans come from? How many waves of migration brought them to the New World? What are the linguistic, cultural, and biological links among Native Americans and between them and Asia? (Note that a unified four-field anthropology did not develop in Europe, where the subfields tend to exist separately.)

There also are logical reasons for the unity of American anthropology. Each subfield considers variation in time and space (that is, in different geographic areas). Cultural and archaeological anthropologists study changes in social life and customs (among many other topics). Archaeologists use studies of living societies to imagine what life might have been like in the past. Biological anthropologists examine evolutionary changes in physical form, for example, anatomical changes that might have been associated with the origin of tool use or language. Linguistic anthropologists may reconstruct the basics of ancient languages by studying modern ones.

The subfields influence each other as anthropologists talk to each other, read books and journals, and meet in professional organizations. General anthropology explores the basics of human biology, society, and culture and considers their interrelations. Anthropologists share certain key assumptions. Perhaps the most fundamental is the idea that sound conclusions about "human nature" cannot be derived from studying a single population, nation, society, or cultural tradition. A comparative, cross-cultural approach is essential.

Early American anthropology was especially concerned with the history and cultures of Native North Americans. Ely S. Parker, or Ha-sa-no-an-da, was a Seneca Indian who made important contributions to early anthropology. Parker also served as Commissioner of Indian Affairs for the United States.

Cultural Forces Shape Human Biology

Anthropology's comparative, biocultural perspective recognizes that cultural forces constantly mold human biology. (**Biocultural** refers to the inclusion and combination of both biological and cultural perspectives and approaches to comment on or solve a particular issue or problem.) Culture is a key environmental force in determining how human bodies grow and develop. Cultural traditions promote certain activities and abilities, discourage others, and set standards of physical well-being and attractiveness. Physical activities, including sports, which are influenced by culture, help build the body. For example, North American girls are encouraged to pursue, and therefore do well in, competition involving figure skating, gymnastics, track and field, swimming, diving, and many other sports. Brazilian girls, although excelling in the team sports of basketball and volleyball, haven't fared nearly as well in individual sports as have their American and Canadian counterparts. Why are people encouraged to excel as athletes in some nations but not others? Why do people in some countries invest so much time and effort in competitive sports that their bodies change significantly as a result?

Cultural standards of attractiveness and propriety influence participation and achievement in sports. Americans run or swim not just to compete but to keep trim and fit. Brazil's beauty standards have traditionally accepted more fat, especially in female buttocks and hips. Brazilian men have had some international success in swimming and running, but Brazil rarely sends female swimmers or runners to the Olympics.

Brazil rarely sends female swimmers to the Olympics. One exception (shown here) is Fabiola Molina, who competed in the 2000, 2008, and 2012 Summer Olympics. How might years of competitive swimming affect phenotype?

One reason Brazilian women avoid competitive swimming in particular may be that sport's effects on the body. Years of swimming sculpt a distinctive physique: an enlarged upper torso, a massive neck, and powerful shoulders and back. Successful female swimmers tend to be big, strong, and bulky. The countries that have produced them most consistently are the United States, Canada, Australia, Germany, the Scandinavian nations, the Netherlands, and the former Soviet Union, where this body type isn't as stigmatized as it is in Latin countries. Swimmers develop hard bodies, but Brazilian culture says that women should be soft, with big hips and buttocks, not big shoulders. Many young female swimmers in Brazil choose to abandon the sport rather than the "feminine" body ideal.

When you grew up, which sport did you appreciate the most—soccer, swimming, football, baseball, tennis, golf, or some other sport (or perhaps none at all)? Is this because of "who you are" or because of the opportunities you had as a child to practice and participate in this particular activity? When you were young, your parents might have told you that drinking milk and eating vegetables would help you grow up "big and strong." They probably didn't as readily recognize the role that *culture* plays in shaping bodies, personalities, and personal health. If nutrition matters in growth, so, too, do cultural guidelines. What is proper behavior for boys and girls? What kinds of work should men and women do? Where should people live? What are proper uses of their leisure time? What role should religion play? How should people relate to their family, friends, and neighbors? Although our genetic attributes provide a foundation for our growth and development, human biology is fairly plastic—that is, it is malleable. Culture is an environmental force that affects our development as much as do nutrition, heat, cold, and altitude. Culture also guides our emotional and cognitive growth and helps determine the kinds of personalities we have as adults.

The Subdisciplines of Anthropology

Cultural Anthropology

Cultural anthropology is the study of human society and culture, the subfield that describes, analyzes, interprets, and explains social and cultural similarities and differences. To study and interpret cultural diversity, cultural anthropologists engage in two kinds of activity: ethnography (based on fieldwork) and ethnology (based on cross-cultural comparison). **Ethnography** provides an account of a particular community, society, or culture. During ethnographic fieldwork, the ethnographer gathers data that he or she organizes, analyzes, and interprets to develop that account, which may be in the form of a book, an article, or a film. Traditionally, ethnographers have lived in small communities and studied local behavior, beliefs, customs, social life, economic activities, politics, and religion (see Wolcott 2008).

The anthropological perspective derived from ethnographic fieldwork often differs radically from that of economics or political science. Those fields focus on national and official organizations and policies and often on elites. However, the groups that anthropologists traditionally have studied usually have been relatively poor and powerless. Ethnographers often observe discriminatory practices directed toward such people, who experience food shortages, dietary deficiencies, and other aspects of poverty. Political scientists tend to study programs that national planners develop, while anthropologists discover how these programs work on the local level.

Cultures are not isolated. As noted by Franz Boas (1940/1966) many years ago, contact between neighboring tribes always has existed and has extended over enormous areas. "Human populations construct their cultures in interaction with one another, and not in isolation" (Wolf 1982, p. ix). Villagers increasingly participate in regional, national, and world events. Exposure to external forces comes through the mass media, migration, and modern transportation. City and nation increasingly invade local communities with the arrival of tourists, development agents, government and religious officials, and political candidates. Such linkages are prominent components of regional, national, and international systems of politics, economics, and information. These larger systems increasingly affect the people and places anthropology traditionally has studied. The study of such linkages and systems is part of the subject matter of modern anthropology.

Ethnology examines, compares, analyzes, and interprets the results of ethnography—the data gathered in different societies. Ethnologists use such data to compare and

TABLE 1.2   **Ethnography and Ethnology—Two Dimensions of Cultural Anthropology**

Ethnography	Ethnology
Requires fieldwork to collect data	Uses data collected by a series of researchers
Is often descriptive	Is usually synthetic
Is group- and community-specific	Is comparative and cross-cultural

contrast and to make generalizations about society and culture. Looking beyond the particular to the more general, they attempt to identify and explain cultural differences and similarities, to test hypotheses, and to build theory to enhance our understanding of how social and cultural systems work. Ethnology gets its data for comparison not just from ethnography but also from the other subfields, particularly from archaeological anthropology, which reconstructs social systems of the past. (Table 1.2 summarizes the main contrasts between ethnography and ethnology.)

Archaeological Anthropology

Archaeological anthropology (more simply, "archaeology") reconstructs, describes, and interprets human behavior and cultural patterns through material remains (see Fagan 2012). At sites where people live or have lived, archaeologists find artifacts—material items that humans have made, used, or modified—such as tools, weapons, campsites, buildings, and garbage. Plant and animal remains and ancient garbage tell stories about consumption and activities. Wild and domesticated grains have different characteristics, which allow archaeologists to distinguish between gathering and cultivation. Examination of animal bones reveals the ages of slaughtered animals and provides other information useful in determining whether species were wild or domesticated.

Analyzing such data, archaeologists answer several questions about ancient economies: Did the group get its meat from hunting, or did it domesticate and breed animals, killing only those of a certain age and sex? Did plant food come from wild plants or from sowing, tending, and harvesting crops? Did the residents make, trade for, or buy particular items? Were raw materials available locally? If not, where did they come from? From such information, archaeologists reconstruct patterns of production, trade, and consumption.

Archaeologists have spent considerable time studying potsherds, fragments of earthenware. Potsherds are more durable than many other artifacts, such as textiles and wood. The quantity of pottery fragments allows estimates of population size and density. The discovery that potters used materials that were not available locally suggests systems of trade. Similarities in manufacture and decoration at different sites may be proof of cultural connections. Groups with similar pots may be historically related. Perhaps they shared common cultural ancestors, traded with each other, or belonged to the same political system.

Many archaeologists examine paleoecology. *Ecology* is the study of interrelations among living things in an environment. The organisms and environment together constitute an *ecosystem,* a patterned arrangement of energy flows and exchanges. Human ecology studies ecosystems that include people, focusing on the ways in which human use "of nature influences and is influenced by social organization and cultural values" (Bennett 1969, pp. 10–11). *Paleoecology* looks at the ecosystems of the past.

An archaeological team works at Harappa, one site from an ancient Indus River civilization dating back some 4,800 years.

In addition to reconstructing ecological patterns, archaeologists may infer cultural transformations, for example, by observing changes in the size and type of sites and the distance between them. A city develops in a region where only towns, villages, and hamlets existed a few centuries earlier. The number of settlement levels (city, town, village, hamlet) in a society is a measure of social complexity. Buildings offer clues about political and religious features. Temples and pyramids suggest that an ancient society had an authority structure capable of marshaling the labor needed to build such monuments. The presence or absence of certain structures, like the pyramids of ancient Egypt and Mexico, reveals differences in function between settlements. For example, some towns were places where people went to attend ceremonies. Others were burial sites; still others were farming communities.

Archaeologists also reconstruct behavior patterns and lifestyles of the past by excavating. This involves digging through a succession of levels at a particular site. In a given area, through time, settlements may change in form and purpose, as may the connections between settlements. Excavation can document changes in economic, social, and political activities.

Although archaeologists are best known for studying prehistory, that is, the period before the invention of writing, they also study the cultures of historical and even living peoples (see Sabloff 2008). Studying sunken ships off the Florida coast, underwater archaeologists have been able to verify the living conditions on the vessels that brought ancestral African Americans to the New World as enslaved people. In a research project begun in 1973 in Tucson, Arizona, archaeologist William Rathje has learned about contemporary life by studying modern garbage. The value of "garbology," as Rathje calls it, is that it provides "evidence of what people did, not what they think they did, what they think they should have done, or what the interviewer thinks they should have done" (Harrison, Rathje, and Hughes 1994, p. 108). What people report may contrast strongly with their real behavior as revealed by garbology. For example, the garbologists discovered that the three Tucson neighborhoods that reported the lowest beer consumption actually had the highest number of discarded beer cans per household (Podolefsky and Brown 1992, p. 100)! Rathje's garbology also has exposed misconceptions about how much of different kinds of trash are in landfills: While most people thought that fast-food containers and disposable diapers were major waste problems, in fact they were relatively insignificant compared with paper (Rathje and Murphy 2001).

Biological, or Physical, Anthropology

The subject matter of **biological,** or **physical, anthropology** is human biological diversity in time and space. The focus on biological variation unites five special interests within biological anthropology:

1. Human evolution as revealed by the fossil record (paleoanthropology).
2. Human genetics.
3. Human growth and development.
4. Human biological plasticity (the body's ability to change as it copes with stresses, such as heat, cold, and altitude).
5. The biology, evolution, behavior, and social life of monkeys, apes, and other non-human primates.

   These interests link physical anthropology to other fields: biology, zoology, geology, anatomy, physiology, medicine, and public health. Osteology—the study of bones—helps paleoanthropologists, who examine skulls, teeth, and bones, to identify human ancestors and to chart changes in anatomy over time. A paleontologist is a scientist who studies fossils. A paleoanthropologist is one sort of paleontologist, one who studies the fossil record of human evolution (see Wood 2011). Paleoanthropologists often collaborate with archaeologists, who study artifacts, in reconstructing biological and cultural aspects of human evolution. Fossils and tools often are found together. Different types of tools provide information about the lifestyles of the ancestral humans who used them.

   More than a century ago, Charles Darwin noticed that the variety that exists within any population permits some individuals (those with the favored characteristics) to do better than others at surviving and reproducing. Genetics, which developed later, enlightens us about the causes and transmission of this variety. However, it isn't just genes that cause variety. During any individual's lifetime, the environment works along with heredity to determine biological features. For example, people with a genetic tendency to be tall will be shorter if they are poorly nourished during childhood. Thus, biological anthropology also investigates the influence of environment on the body as it grows and matures. Among the environmental factors that influence the body as it develops are nutrition, altitude, temperature, and disease, as well as cultural factors, such as standards of attractiveness.

   Biological anthropology (along with zoology) also includes primatology. The primates include our closest relatives—apes and monkeys. Primatologists study their biology, evolution, behavior, and social life, often in their natural environments (see Campbell 2011). Primatology assists paleoanthropology, because primate behavior may shed light on early human behavior and human nature.

Linguistic Anthropology

We don't know (and probably never will) when our ancestors acquired the ability to speak, although biological anthropologists have looked to the anatomy of the face and the skull to speculate about the origin of language. And primatologists have described the communication systems of monkeys and apes. We do know that grammatically complex languages have existed for thousands of years. Linguistic anthropology offers further illustration of anthropology's interest in comparison, variation, and change. **Linguistic anthropology** studies language in its social and cultural context, across space and over time. Some linguistic anthropologists make inferences about universal features of language, linked perhaps to uniformities in the human brain. Others reconstruct ancient languages by comparing their contemporary descendants and in so doing make discoveries about history. Still others study linguistic differences to discover varied perceptions and patterns of thought in different cultures (see Bonvillain 2012).

Historical linguistics considers variation in time, such as the changes in sounds, grammar, and vocabulary between Middle English (spoken from approximately C.E. [formerly A.D.] 1050 to 1550) and modern English. **Sociolinguistics** investigates relationships between social and linguistic variation. No language is a homogeneous system in which everyone speaks just like everyone else. How do different speakers use a given language? How do linguistic features correlate with social factors, including class and gender differences (Tannen 1990)? One reason for variation is geography, as in regional dialects and accents. Linguistic variation also is expressed in the bilingualism of ethnic groups. Linguistic and cultural anthropologists collaborate in studying links between language and many other aspects of culture, such as how people reckon kinship and how they perceive and classify colors.

Anthropology and Other Academic Fields

As mentioned previously, one of the main differences between anthropology and the other fields that study people is holism, anthropology's unique blend of biological, social, cultural, linguistic, historical, and contemporary perspectives. Paradoxically, while distinguishing anthropology, this breadth is what also links it to many other disciplines. Techniques used to date fossils and artifacts have come to anthropology from physics, chemistry, and geology. Because plant and animal remains often are found with human bones and artifacts, anthropologists collaborate with botanists, zoologists, and paleontologists.

As a discipline that is both scientific and humanistic, anthropology has links with many other academic fields. Anthropology is a **science**—a "systematic field of study or body of knowledge that aims, through experiment, observation, and deduction, to produce reliable explanations of phenomena, with references to the material and physical world" (*Webster's New World Encyclopedia* 1993, p. 937). The chapters that follow present anthropology as a humanistic science devoted to discovering, describing, understanding, and explaining similarities and differences in time and space among humans and our ancestors. Clyde Kluckhohn (1944) described anthropology as "the science of human similarities and differences" (p. 9). His statement of the need for such a field still stands: "Anthropology provides a scientific basis for dealing with the crucial dilemma of the world today: how can peoples of different appearance, mutually unintelligible languages, and dissimilar ways of life get along peaceably together?" (p. 9). Anthropology has compiled an impressive body of knowledge that this textbook attempts to encapsulate.

Besides its links to the natural sciences (e.g., geology, zoology) and social sciences (e.g., sociology, psychology), anthropology also has strong links to the humanities. The humanities include English, comparative literature, classics, folklore, philosophy, and the arts. These fields study languages, texts, philosophies, arts, music, performances, and other forms of creative expression. Ethnomusicology, which studies forms of musical expression on a worldwide basis, is especially closely related to anthropology. Also linked is folklore, the systematic study of tales, myths, and legends from a variety of cultures. One might well argue that anthropology is among the most humanistic of all academic fields because of its fundamental respect for human diversity. Anthropologists listen to, record, and represent voices from a multitude of nations and cultures. Anthropology values local knowledge, diverse worldviews, and alternative philosophies. Cultural anthropology and linguistic anthropology in particular bring a comparative and nonelitist perspective to forms of creative expression, including language, art, narratives, music, and dance, viewed in their social and cultural context.

Applied Anthropology

Anthropology is not a science of the exotic carried on by quaint scholars in ivory towers. Rather, anthropology has a lot to tell the public. Anthropology's foremost professional organization, the American Anthropological Association (AAA), has formally acknowledged a public service role by recognizing that anthropology has two dimensions: (1) academic, or general, anthropology and (2) practicing, or **applied, anthropology.** The latter refers to the application of anthropological data, perspectives, theory, and methods to identify, assess, and solve contemporary social problems (see Bodley 2012). As Erve Chambers (1987, p. 309) states it, applied anthropology is the "field of inquiry concerned with the relationships between anthropological knowledge and the uses of that knowledge in the world beyond anthropology." More and more anthropologists from the four subfields now work in such "applied" areas as public health, family planning, business, economic development, and cultural resource management.

Applied anthropology encompasses any use of the knowledge and/or techniques of the four subfields to identify, assess, and solve practical problems. Because of anthropology's breadth, it has many applications. For example, applied medical anthropologists consider both the sociocultural and the biological contexts and implications of disease and illness. Perceptions of good and bad health, along with actual health threats and problems, differ among societies. Various ethnic groups recognize different illnesses, symptoms, and causes and have developed different health care systems and treatment strategies.

Anthropology Today   *His Mother, the Anthropologist*

It is widely known that President Barack Obama is the son of a Kenyan father and a White American mother from Kansas. Less recognized is the fact that the 44th president of the United States is the son of an anthropologist—Dr. Stanley Ann Dunham Soetoro (usually called simply Ann Dunham). The following account focuses on her life and her attraction to diversity, which led her to a career in anthropology. Dunham's work on socioeconomic issues affecting Indonesian women illustrates the application of anthropology to identify and solve contemporary problems. In other words, she was both a cultural and an applied anthropologist. A fuller account of Dunham's life appears in Janny Scott's recent book A Singular Woman: The Untold Story of Barack Obama's Mother *(2011).*

Anthropologists study humanity in varied times and places and in a rapidly changing world. By virtue of his parentage, his enculturation, and his experience abroad, Barack Obama provides an excellent symbol of the diversity and interconnections that characterize today's world. As well, his election and reelection constitute a tribute to an increasingly diverse United States of America.

In the capsule version of the Barack Obama story, his mother is simply the white woman from Kansas. . . . On the campaign trail, he has called her his "single mom." But neither description begins to capture the unconventional life of Stanley Ann Dunham Soetoro, the parent who most shaped Mr. Obama. . . .

In Hawaii, she married an African student at age 18. Then she married an Indonesian, moved to Jakarta, became an anthropologist, wrote an 800-page dissertation on peasant blacksmithing in Java, worked for the Ford Foundation, championed women's work and helped bring microcredit to the world's poor.

She had high expectations for her children. In Indonesia, she would wake her

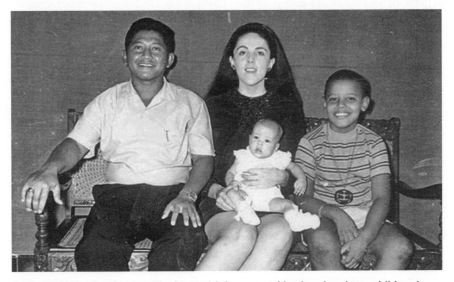

Anthropologist Stanley Ann Dunham with her second husband and two children in Indonesia.

continued

son at 4 a.m. for correspondence courses in English before school; she brought home recordings of Mahalia Jackson, speeches by the Rev. Dr. Martin Luther King Jr. And when Mr. Obama asked to stay in Hawaii for high school rather than return to Asia, she accepted living apart—a decision her daughter says was one of the hardest in Ms. Soetoro's life.

"She felt that somehow, wandering through uncharted territory, we might stumble upon something that will, in an instant, seem to represent who we are at the core," said Maya Soetoro-Ng, Mr. Obama's half-sister. "That was very much her philosophy of life—to not be limited by fear or narrow definitions, to not build walls around ourselves and to do our best to find kinship and beauty in unexpected places." . . .

Mr. Obama . . . barely saw his father after the age of 2. Though it is impossible to pinpoint the imprint of a parent on the life of a grown child, people who knew Ms. Soetoro well say they see her influence unmistakably in Mr. Obama. . . .

"She was a very, very big thinker," said Nancy Barry, a former president of Women's World Banking, an international network of microfinance providers, where Ms. Soetoro worked in New York City in the early 1990s. . . .

In a Russian class at the University of Hawaii, she met the college's first African student, Barack Obama. They married and had a son in August 1961, in an era when interracial marriage was rare in the United States. . . .

The marriage was brief. In 1963, Mr. Obama left for Harvard, leaving his wife and child. She then married Lolo Soetoro, an Indonesian student. When he was summoned home in 1966 after the turmoil surrounding the rise of Suharto, Ms. Soetoro and Barack followed. . . .

Her second marriage faded, too, in the 1970s. Ms. Soetoro wanted to work, one friend said, and Mr. Soetoro wanted more children. He became more American, she once said, as she became more Javanese. "There's a Javanese belief that if you're married to someone and it doesn't work, it will make you sick," said Alice G. Dewey, an anthropologist and friend. "It's just stupid to stay married.". . .

By 1974, Ms. Soetoro was back in Honolulu, a graduate student and raising Barack and Maya, nine years younger. . . . When Ms. Soetoro decided to return to Indonesia three years later for her field work, Barack chose not to go. . . .

Fluent in Indonesian, Ms. Soetoro moved with Maya first to Yogyakarta, the center of Javanese handicrafts. A weaver in college, she was fascinated with what Ms. Soetoro-Ng calls "life's gorgeous minutiae." That interest inspired her study of village industries, which became the basis of her 1992 doctoral dissertation.

"She loved living in Java," said Dr. Dewey, who recalled accompanying Ms. Soetoro to a metalworking village. "People said: 'Hi! How are you?' She said: 'How's your wife? Did your daughter have the baby?' They were friends. Then she'd whip out her notebook and she'd say: 'How many of you have electricity? Are you having trouble getting iron?'"

She became a consultant for the United States Agency for International Development on setting up a village credit program, then a Ford Foundation program officer in Jakarta specializing in women's work. Later, she was a consultant in Pakistan, then joined Indonesia's oldest bank to work on what is described as the world's largest sustainable microfinance program, creating services like credit and savings for the poor.

Visitors flowed constantly through her Ford Foundation office in downtown

Jakarta and through her house in a neighborhood to the south, where papaya and banana trees grew in the front yard and Javanese dishes . . . were served for dinner. Her guests were leaders in the Indonesian human rights movement, people from women's organizations, representatives of community groups doing grassroots development. . . .

Ms. Soetoro-Ng . . . remembers conversations with her mother about philosophy or politics, books, esoteric Indonesian woodworking motifs. . . .

"She gave us a very broad understanding of the world," her daughter said. "She hated bigotry. She was very determined to be remembered for a life of service and thought that service was really the true measure of a life." Many of her friends see her legacy in Mr. Obama—in his self-assurance and drive, his boundary bridging, even his apparent comfort with strong women. She died in November 1995, as Mr. Obama was starting his first campaign for public office. After a memorial service at the University of Hawaii, one friend said, a small group of friends drove to the South Shore in Oahu. With the wind whipping the waves onto the rocks, Mr. Obama and Ms. Soetoro-Ng placed their mother's ashes in the Pacific, sending them off in the direction of Indonesia.

Source: Janny Scott, "A Free-Spirited Wanderer Who Set Obama's Path." From *The New York Times,* March 14, 2008. © 2008 The New York Times. All rights reserved. Used by permission and protected by the Copyright Laws of the United States. The printing, copying, redistribution, or retransmission of this Content without express written permission is prohibited. www.nytimes.com.

TABLE 1.3   **The Four Subfields and Two Dimensions of Anthropology**

Anthropology's Subfields (General Anthropology)	Examples of Application (Applied Anthropology)
Cultural anthropology	Development anthropology
Archaeological anthropology	Cultural resource management (CRM)
Biological (physical) anthropology	Forensic anthropology
Linguistic anthropology	Study of linguistic diversity in classrooms

Applied archaeology, usually called *public archaeology,* includes such activities as cultural resource management, contract archaeology, public educational programs, and historic preservation. An important role for public archaeology has been created by legislation requiring evaluation of sites threatened by dams, highways, and other construction activities. To decide what needs saving, and to preserve significant information about the past when sites cannot be saved, is the work of **cultural resource management (CRM).** CRM involves not only preserving sites but also allowing their destruction if they are not significant. The "management" part of the term refers to the evaluation and decision-making process. Cultural resource managers work for federal, state, and county agencies and other clients. Applied cultural anthropologists sometimes work with the public archaeologists, assessing the human problems generated by the proposed change and determining how they can be reduced. Table 1.3 relates anthropology's four subfields to its two dimensions.

Summary

1. Anthropology is the holistic, biocultural, and comparative study of humanity. It is the systematic exploration of human biological and cultural diversity across time and space. Examining the origins of, and changes in, human biology and culture, anthropology provides explanations for similarities and differences among humans and their societies.

2. The four subfields of general anthropology are (socio)cultural, archaeological, biological, and linguistic. All consider variation in time and space. Each also examines adaptation—the process by which organisms cope with environmental stresses. Anthropology's biocultural perspective is a particularly effective way of approaching interrelations between biology and culture. Cultural forces mold human biology, including our body types and images.

3. Cultural anthropology explores the cultural diversity of the present and the recent past. Archaeology reconstructs cultural patterns, often of prehistoric populations. Biological anthropology documents diversity involving fossils, genetics, growth and development, bodily responses, and nonhuman primates. Linguistic anthropology considers diversity among languages. It also studies how speech changes in social situations and over time.

4. Concerns with biology, society, culture, and language link anthropology to many other fields—natural sciences, social sciences, and humanities.

5. Anthropology has two dimensions: general and applied. The latter uses anthropological perspectives, theory, methods, and data to identify, assess, and solve social problems. The fields in which applied anthropologists work include business, government, economic development, education, and social services, action, and outreach. Applied anthropologists come from all four subfields.

Key Terms

adaptation, *3*
anthropology, *2*
applied
  anthropology, *12*
archaeological
  anthropology, *7*
biocultural, *5*
biological
  (physical)
  anthropology, *10*

cultural
  anthropology, *7*
cultural resource
  management
  (CRM), *15*
culture, *2*
ethnography, *7*
ethnology, *7*
food
  production, *4*

general
  anthropology, *4*
holistic, *2*
linguistic
  anthropology, *11*
science, *11*
society, *2*
sociolinguistics, *11*

Chapter 2

Culture

In Chapter 1 we saw that humans share *society,* organized life in groups, with social animals, such as apes, monkeys, wolves, and ants. Although other animals, especially apes, have rudimentary cultural abilities, only humans have fully elaborated cultures—distinctive traditions and customs transmitted over the generations through learning and through language.

The concept of culture has long been basic to anthropology. Well over a century ago, in his book *Primitive Culture,* the British anthropologist Edward Tylor proposed that cultures, systems of human behavior and thought, obey natural laws and therefore can be studied scientifically. Tylor's definition of culture still offers an overview of the subject matter of anthropology and is widely quoted.

"Culture . . . is that complex whole which includes knowledge, belief, arts, morals, law, custom, and any other capabilities and habits acquired by man as a member of society" (Tylor 1871/1958, p. 1). The crucial phrase here is "acquired . . . as a member of society." Tylor's definition focuses on attributes that people acquire not through biological inheritance but by growing up in a particular society in which they are exposed to a specific cultural tradition. **Enculturation** is the process by which a child *learns* his or her culture.

What Is Culture?

Culture Is Learned

The ease with which children absorb any cultural tradition rests on the uniquely elaborated human capacity to learn. Other animals may learn from experience, so that, for example, they avoid fire after discovering that it hurts. Social animals also learn from other members of their group. Wolves, for instance, learn hunting strategies from other pack members. Such social learning is particularly important among monkeys and apes, our closest biological relatives. But our own *cultural learning* depends on the uniquely developed human capacity to use **symbols,** signs that have no necessary or natural connection to the things they stand for, or signify.

Through cultural learning, people create, remember, and deal with ideas. They understand and apply specific systems of symbolic meaning. Anthropologist Clifford Geertz described cultures as sets of "control mechanisms—plans, recipes, rules, instructions" and likens them to computer programs that govern human behavior (Geertz 1973, p. 44). During enculturation, people gradually absorb and internalize their particular culture—a previously established system of meanings and symbols that helps guide their behavior and perceptions throughout their lives.

Every person begins immediately, through a process of conscious and unconscious learning and interaction with others, to internalize, or incorporate, a cultural tradition through the process of enculturation. Sometimes culture is taught directly, as when parents tell their children to say "thank you" when someone gives them something or does them a favor.

Culture also is transmitted through observation. Children pay attention to the things that go on around them. They modify their behavior not just because other people tell them to do so but as a result of their own observations and growing awareness of what their culture considers right and wrong. Culture also is absorbed unconsciously. North Americans acquire their culture's notions about how far apart people should stand when they talk, not by being told directly to maintain a certain distance but through a gradual process of observation, experience, and conscious and unconscious behavior modification. No one tells Latins to stand closer together than North Americans do; they learn to do so as part of their cultural tradition. (See this chapter's "Anthropology Today.")

Culture Is Symbolic

Symbolic thought is unique and crucial to humans and to cultural learning. A symbol is something verbal or nonverbal, within a particular language or culture, that comes to stand for something else. Anthropologist Leslie White defined culture as

> dependent upon symbolling. . . . Culture consists of tools, implements, utensils, clothing, ornaments, customs, institutions, beliefs, rituals, games, works of art, language, etc. (White 1959, p. 3)

According to White, culture originated when our ancestors acquired the ability to use symbols, that is, to originate and bestow meaning on a thing or an event and, correspondingly, to grasp and appreciate such meanings (White 1959).

There need be no obvious, natural, or necessary connection between a symbol and what it symbolizes. The familiar pet that barks is no more naturally a *dog* than it is a *chien, Hund,* or *mbwa,* the words for "dog" in French, German, and Swahili, respectively. Language is one of the distinctive possessions of *Homo sapiens.* No other animal has developed anything approaching the complexity of language, with its multitude of symbols.

Symbols often are linguistic. There also are myriad nonverbal symbols, such as flags, which stand for various countries, and the golden arches that symbolize a particular hamburger chain. Holy water is a potent symbol in Roman Catholicism. As is true of all symbols, the association between a symbol (water) and what is symbolized (holiness) is arbitrary and conventional. Water probably is not intrinsically holier than milk, blood, or other natural liquids. Nor is holy water chemically different from ordinary water. Holy water is a symbol within Roman Catholicism, which is part of an international cultural system. A natural thing has been associated arbitrarily with a particular meaning for Catholics, who share common beliefs and experiences that are based on learning and that are transmitted across the generations.

All humans possess the abilities on which culture rests—the abilities to learn, to think symbolically, to manipulate language, and to use tools and other cultural products in organizing their lives and coping with their environments. Every contemporary human population has the ability to use symbols and thus to create and maintain culture. Our nearest relatives—chimpanzees and gorillas—have rudimentary cultural abilities. However, no other animal has elaborated cultural abilities to the extent that *Homo* has.

Culture Is Shared

Culture is an attribute not of individuals per se but of individuals as members of *groups.* Culture is transmitted socially—in society. That is, we learn our culture by observing, listening, talking, and interacting with many other people. Shared beliefs, values, memories, and expectations link people who grow up in the same culture. Enculturation unifies people by providing us with common experiences.

People in the United States sometimes have trouble understanding the power of culture because of the value that American culture places on the idea of the individual. Americans are fond of saying that everyone is unique and special in some way. However, in American culture individualism itself is a distinctive shared value. Individualism is transmitted through hundreds of statements and settings in our daily lives. From media personalities to parents, grandparents, and teachers, our enculturative agents insist that we are all "someone special."

People become agents in the enculturation of their children, just as their parents were for them. Although a culture constantly changes, certain fundamental beliefs, values, worldviews, addages, and child-rearing practices endure. Consider a simple American example of enduring shared enculturation. As children, when we didn't finish a meal, our parents may have reminded us of starving children in some foreign country, just as our grandparents might have done a generation earlier. The specific country changes (China, India, Bangladesh, Ethiopia, Somalia, Rwanda—what was it in your home?). Still, American culture goes on transmitting the idea that by eating all our brussels sprouts or broccoli we can justify our own good fortune, compared to a hungry child in an impoverished or war-ravaged country.

Culture and Nature

Culture takes the natural biological urges we share with other animals and teaches us how to express them in particular ways. People have to eat, but culture teaches us what, when, and how. In many cultures people have their main meal at noon, but most North Americans prefer a large dinner. English people eat fish (e.g., kippers—kippered herring) for breakfast, but North Americans prefer hot cakes and cold cereals. Brazilians put hot milk into strong coffee, whereas many North Americans pour cold milk into a weaker brew. Midwesterners dine at 5 or 6, Spaniards at 10.

Cultural habits, perceptions, and inventions mold "human nature" into many forms. People have to eliminate wastes from their bodies. But some cultures teach people to defecate standing, while others tell them to do it sitting down. Peasant women in the Andean highlands squat in the streets and urinate, getting all the privacy they need from their massive skirts. All these habits are parts of cultural traditions that have converted natural acts into cultural customs.

Culture affects how we perceive nature, human nature, and "the natural," and cultural advances have overcome many "natural" limitations. We prevent and cure diseases, such as polio and smallpox, that felled our ancestors. Viagra and Cialis are used to enhance or restore sexual potency. Through cloning, scientists have challenged the way we think about biological identity and the meaning of life itself. Culture, of course, does not always protect us from natural threats. Hurricanes, floods, earthquakes, and other natural forces regularly overthrow our wishes to modify the environment through building, development, and expansion. What are some of the other ways in which nature strikes back at culture?

Culture Is All-Encompassing

For anthropologists, culture includes much more than refinement, good taste, sophistication, education, and appreciation of the fine arts. Not only college graduates but all people are "cultured." The most interesting and significant cultural forces are those that affect people every day of their lives, particularly those that influence children during enculturation.

Culture, as defined anthropologically, encompasses features that are sometimes regarded as trivial or unworthy of serious study, such as those of "popular" culture. To understand contemporary North American culture, we must consider mass media, the Internet, fast-food restaurants, sports, and games. As a cultural manifestation, a rock star may be as interesting as a symphony conductor (or vice versa); a comic book may be as significant as a book-award winner.

Culture Is Integrated

Cultures are not haphazard collections of customs and beliefs. Cultures are integrated, patterned systems. If one part of the system (the overall economy, for instance) changes, other parts change as well. For example, during the 1950s most American women planned domestic careers as homemakers and mothers. Most of today's college women, by contrast, hope to get paying jobs when they graduate.

What are some of the social repercussions of this particular economic change? Attitudes and behavior regarding marriage, family, and children have changed. Late marriage, "living together," and divorce have become more common. Work competes with marriage and family responsibilities and reduces the time available to invest in child care.

Cultures are integrated not simply by their dominant economic activities and related social patterns but also by sets of values, ideas, symbols, and judgments. Cultures train their individual members to share certain personality traits. A set of characteristic **core values** (key, basic, central values) integrates each culture and helps distinguish it from others. For instance, the work ethic and individualism are core values that have integrated American culture for generations. Different sets of dominant values influence the patterns of other cultures.

Culture Is Instrumental, Adaptive, and Maladaptive

Culture is the main reason for human adaptability and success. Other animals rely on biological means of adaptation (such as fur or blubber, which are adaptations to cold). Humans also adapt biologically—for example, by shivering when we get cold or sweating when we get hot. But in addition to biological responses, people also have cultural ways of adapting. To cope with environmental stresses we habitually use technology, or tools. We hunt cold-adapted animals and use their fur coats as our own. We turn the thermostat up in the winter and down in the summer. Or we plan action to increase our comfort. We have a cold drink, jump in a pool, or travel to someplace cooler in the summer or warmer in the winter. People use culture *instrumentally,* that is, to fulfill their basic biological needs for food, drink, shelter, comfort, and reproduction.

People also use culture to fulfill psychological and emotional needs, such as friendship, companionship, approval, and sexual desirability. People seek *informal support*—help from people who care about them—as well as *formal support* from associations and institutions. To these ends, individuals cultivate ties with others on the basis of common experiences, political interests, aesthetic sensibilities, or personal attraction.

On one level, cultural traits (e.g., air conditioning) may be called *adaptive* if they help individuals cope with environmental stresses. But, on a different level, such traits can also be *maladaptive.* That is, they may threaten a group's continued existence. Thus, chlorofluorocarbons (e.g., as found in old air conditioners) have been banned in the United States because they deplete the ozone layer and, by doing so, can harm humans and other life. Many modern cultural patterns may be maladaptive in the long run. Some examples of maladaptive aspects of culture are policies that encourage overpopulation, poor food-distribution systems, overconsumption, and industrial pollution of the environment.

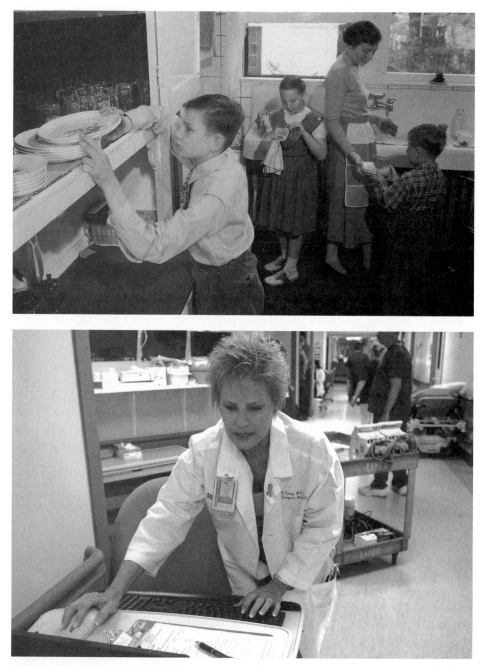

Cultures are integrated systems. When one behavior pattern changes, others also change. During the 1950s, most American women expected to have careers as wives, mothers, and domestic managers. As more and more women have entered the workforce, attitudes toward work and family have changed. On the top, mom and kids do the dishes in 1952. On the bottom, in this 2010 photo, an emergency room physician in Tampa, Florida, types patient information into a computer. What do you imagine she does when she gets home?

Culture's Evolutionary Basis

The human capacity for culture has an evolutionary basis that extends back at least 2.6 million years to early toolmakers. Evidence for these toolmakers exists in the archaeological record. However, based on observation of tool use and manufacture by apes, scientists believe the evolutionary basis for culture may extend even further back.

Similarities between humans and apes, our closest relatives, are evident in anatomy, brain structure, genetics, and biochemistry. Most closely related to us are the African great apes: chimpanzees and gorillas. *Hominidae* is the zoological family that includes fossil and living humans, as well as chimps and gorillas. We refer to members of this family as **hominids.** The term **hominins** is used for the group that leads to humans but not to chimps and gorillas and that encompasses all the human species that ever have existed.

Many human traits reflect the fact that our primate ancestors lived in the trees. These traits include grasping ability and manual dexterity (especially opposable thumbs), depth and color vision, learning ability based on a large brain, substantial parental investment in a limited number of offspring, and tendencies toward sociality and cooperation. Like other primates, humans have flexible, five-fingered hands and *opposable thumbs:* Each thumb can touch all the other fingers on the same hand. Like monkeys and apes, humans also have excellent depth and color vision. Our eyes are placed forward in the skull and look directly ahead, so that their fields of vision overlap. Depth perception, impossible without overlapping visual fields, proved adaptive—e.g., for judging distance—in the trees. Having color and depth vision also facilitates the identification of various food sources, as well as mutual grooming among primates— picking out burrs, insects, and other small objects from hair. Such grooming is one way of forming and maintaining social bonds.

The combination of manual dexterity and depth perception allows monkeys, apes, and humans to pick up small objects, hold them in front of their eyes, and appraise them. Our ability to thread a needle reflects an intricate interplay of hands and eyes that took millions of years of primate evolution to achieve. Such dexterity, including the opposable thumb, confers a tremendous advantage in manipulating objects and is essential to a major human adaptive capacity: tool making. In primates, and especially in humans, the ratio of brain size to body size exceeds that of most mammals. Even more important, the brain's outer layer— concerned with memory, association, and integration—is relatively larger. Monkeys, apes, and humans store an array of images in their memories, which permits them to learn more. Such a capacity for learning is another tremendous adaptive advantage. Like most other primates, humans usually give birth to a single offspring rather than a litter. Receiving more parental attention, that one infant has enhanced learning opportunities. The need for longer and more attentive care of offspring places a selective value on support by a social group. Humans have developed considerably the primate tendency to be social animals, living and interacting regularly with other members of their species.

What We Share with Other Primates

There is a substantial gap between primate *society* (organized life in groups) and fully developed human *culture,* which is based on symbolic thought. Nevertheless, studies of nonhuman primates reveal many similarities with humans, such as the ability to learn from experience and change behavior as a result. Monkeys, and especially apes, learn throughout their lives (see Choi 2011). In one group of Japanese macaques (land-dwelling monkeys), for example, a 3-year-old female started washing sweet potatoes before she ate them. First her mother, then her age peers, and finally the entire troop began washing sweet potatoes as well. The ability to benefit from experience confers a tremendous adaptive advantage, permitting the avoidance of fatal mistakes. Faced with environmental change, humans and other primates don't have to wait for a genetic or physiological response. They can modify learned behavior and social patterns instead.

Although humans employ tools much more than any other animal does, tool use also turns up among several nonhuman species, including birds, beavers, sea otters, and especially apes (see Campbell 2011; Mayell 2003). Humans are not the only animals that make tools with a specific purpose in mind. Chimpanzees living in the Tai forest of Ivory Coast make and use stone tools to break open hard, golfball-sized nuts (Mercader, Panger, and Boesch 2002; Wilford 2007*b*). At specific sites, the chimps gather nuts, place them on stumps or flat rocks, which they use as anvils, and pound the nuts with heavy stones. The chimps must select hammer stones suited to smashing the nuts and carry them to where the nut trees grow. Nut cracking is a learned skill, with mothers showing their young how to do it.

In 1960, Jane Goodall (1996) began observing wild chimps—including their tool use and hunting behavior—at Gombe Stream National Park in Tanzania, East Africa. The most studied form of ape tool making involves "termiting," in which chimps make tools to probe termite hills. They choose twigs, which they modify by removing leaves and peeling off bark to expose the sticky surface beneath. They carry the twigs to termite hills, dig holes with their fingers, and insert the twigs. Finally, they pull out the twigs and dine on termites that were attracted to the sticky surface. Given what is known about ape tool use and manufacture, it is almost certain that early hominins shared this ability, although the first evidence for hominin stone tool making dates back only 2.6 million years. In addition, bipedalism (moving around upright on two legs) would have permitted the carrying and use of tools and weapons against predators and competitors in an open grassland habitat.

The apes have other abilities essential to culture. Wild chimps and orangs aim and throw objects. Gorillas build nests, and they throw branches, grass, vines, and other objects. Hominins have elaborated the capacity to aim and throw, without which we never would have developed projectile technology and weaponry—or baseball.

Like tool making, hunting once was cited as a distinctive human activity not shared with the apes. Again, however, primate research shows that other primates, especially chimpanzees, are habitual hunters. For example, in Uganda's Kibale National Park chimps form large hunting parties, including an average of 26 individuals (almost always adult and adolescent males). Most hunts (78 percent) result in at least one prey item being caught—a much higher success rate than that among lions (26 percent), hyenas (34 percent), or cheetahs (30 percent). Chimps' favored prey there is the red colobus monkey (Mitani and Watts 1999).

Tool use by chimps. These chimps in Liberia are using stone tools to crack palm nuts, as described in the text.

Archaeological evidence suggests that humans hunted by at least 2.6 million years ago, based on stone tools found in Ethiopia and, later, at Olduvai Gorge in Tanzania. Given our current understanding of chimp hunting and tool making, we can infer that hominids may have been hunting much earlier than the first archaeological evidence attests. However, because chimps typically devour the monkeys they kill, leaving few remains, we may never find archaeological evidence for the first hominin hunt, especially if it was done without stone tools.

How We Differ from Other Primates

Although chimps often share meat from a hunt, apes and monkeys (except for nursing infants) tend to feed themselves individually. Cooperation and sharing are much more developed among humans. Until fairly recently (12,000 to 10,000 years ago), all humans were hunter-gatherers who lived in small social groups called bands. In some world areas, the hunter-gatherer way of life persisted into recent times, permitting study by ethnographers. In such societies, men and women take resources back to the camp and share them. Everyone shares the meat from a large animal. Nourished and protected by younger band members, elders live past reproductive age and are respected for their knowledge and experience. Humans are among the most cooperative of the primates—in the food quest and other social activities. As well, the amount of information stored in a human band is far greater than that in any other primate group.

TABLE 2.1 **Cultural Features of Chimpanzees (Rudimentary) and Humans (Fully Developed)**

	Chimpanzees	Humans
Cultural learning	Rudimentary	Fully developed
Tool use	Occasional	Habitual
Tool manufacture	Occasional: hammer stones, termiting	Habitual and sophisticated
Aimed throwing	Occasional objects, not tools	Projectile technology
Hunting	Significant, but no tools	Basic hominin subsistence strategy, with tools
Food sharing	Meat sharing after hunt	Basic to human life
Cooperation	Occasional in hunting	Basic to human life
Mating and marriage	Female estrus cycle, limited pair bonds	Year-round mating, marriage, and exogamy
Kin ties	Limited by dispersal at adolescence	Maintained through sons and daughters

Another difference between humans and other primates involves mating. Among baboons and chimps, most mating occurs when females enter **estrus,** during which they ovulate. In estrus, the vaginal area swells and reddens, and receptive females form temporary bonds with, and mate with, males. Human females, by contrast, lack a visible estrus cycle, and their ovulation is concealed. Not knowing when ovulation is occurring, humans maximize their reproductive success by mating throughout the year. Human pair bonds for mating are more exclusive and more durable than are those of chimps. Related to our more constant sexuality, all human societies have some form of marriage. Marriage gives mating a reliable basis and grants to each spouse special, though not always exclusive, sexual rights in the other.

Marriage creates another major contrast between humans and other primates: exogamy and kinship systems. Most cultures have rules of exogamy requiring marriage outside one's kin or local group. Exogamy confers adaptive advantages because it creates ties between the spouses' different kin groups. Their children have relatives, and therefore allies, in two kin groups rather than just one. Such ties of affection and mutual support between members of different local groups tend to be absent among primates other than *Homo.* Other primates tend to disperse at adolescence. Among chimps and gorillas, females tend to migrate, seeking mates in other groups. Humans also choose mates from outside the natal group, and usually at least one spouse moves. However, *humans maintain lifelong ties with sons and daughters.* The systems of kinship and marriage that preserve these links provide a major contrast between humans and other primates (see Chapais 2008; Hill, Walker, et al. 2011). Table 2.1 lists differences in the cultural abilities of humans and chimpanzees, our nearest relatives.

Universality, Generality, and Particularity

Anthropologists agree that cultural learning is uniquely elaborated among humans and that all humans have culture. Anthropologists also accept a doctrine termed in the 19th century, the "psychic unity" (biopsychological equality) of humankind. This means that although *individuals* differ in their emotional and intellectual tendencies and capacities, all human *populations* have equivalent capacities for culture. Regardless of their genes or their physical appearance, people can learn *any* cultural tradition.

To understand this point, consider that contemporary Americans and Canadians are the genetically mixed descendants of people from all over the world. Our ancestors were biologically varied, lived in different countries and continents, and participated in hundreds of cultural traditions. However, early colonists, later immigrants, and their descendants all have become active participants in American and Canadian life. All now share a common national culture.

To recognize biopsychological equality is not to deny differences among populations. In studying human diversity in time and space, anthropologists distinguish among the universal, the generalized, and the particular. Certain biological, psychological, social, and cultural features are **universal,** found in every culture. Others are merely **generalities,** common to several but not all human groups. Still other traits are **particularities,** unique to certain cultural traditions.

Universals and Generalities

Biologically based universals include a long period of infant dependency, year-round (rather than seasonal) sexuality, and a complex brain that enables us to use symbols, languages, and tools. Among the social universals is life in groups and in some kind of family (see Brown 1991). Generalities occur in certain times and places but not in all cultures. They may be widespread, but they are not universal. One cultural generality that is present in many but not all societies is the *nuclear family,* a kinship group consisting of parents and children. Although many middle-class Americans ethnocentrically view the nuclear family as a proper and "natural" group, it is not universal. It was absent, for example, among the Nayars, an ethnic group located on the Malabar Coast of India. Traditionally, the Nayars lived in female-headed households, and husbands and wives did not live together. In many other societies, the nuclear family is submerged in larger kin groups, such as extended families, lineages, and clans.

Societies can share the same beliefs and customs because of borrowing or through (cultural) inheritance from a common cultural ancestor. Speaking English is a generality shared by North Americans and Australians because both countries had English settlers. Another reason for generalities is domination, as in colonial rule, when customs and procedures are imposed on one culture by another one that is more powerful. In many countries, use of the English language reflects colonial history. More recently, English has spread through *diffusion* (cultural borrowing) to many other countries, as it has become the world's foremost language for business and travel.

Particularity: Patterns of Culture

A cultural particularity is a trait or feature of culture that is not generalized or widespread; rather, it is confined to a single place, culture, or society. Yet because of cultural borrowing, which has accelerated through modern transportation and communication systems, traits that once were limited in their distribution have become more widespread. Traits that are useful, that have the capacity to please large audiences, and that don't clash with the cultural values of potential adopters are more likely to be borrowed than others are. Still, certain cultural particularities persist. One example would be a particular food dish (e.g., pork barbeque with a mustard-based sauce available only in South Carolina, or the pasty—beef stew baked in pie dough characteristic, for example, of Michigan's upper peninsula). Besides diffusion, which, for example, has spread McDonald's food outlets, once confined to San Bernadino, California, across the globe, there are other reasons that cultural particularities are increasingly rare. Many cultural traits are shared as cultural universals and as a result of independent invention. Facing similar problems, people in different places have come up with similar solutions. Again and again, similar cultural causes have produced similar cultural results.

At the level of the individual cultural trait or element (e.g., bow and arrow, hot dog, MTV), particularities may be getting rarer. But at a higher level, particularity is more obvious. Different cultures emphasize different things. *Cultures are integrated and patterned differently and display tremendous variation and diversity.* When cultural traits are borrowed, they are modified to fit the culture that adopts them. They are *reintegrated*—patterned anew—to fit their new setting. MTV in Germany or Brazil isn't at all the same thing as MTV in the United States. As was stated in the earlier section "Culture Is Integrated," patterned beliefs, customs, and practices lend distinctiveness to particular cultural traditions.

Consider universal life-cycle events, such as birth, puberty, marriage, parenthood, and death, that many cultures observe and celebrate. The occasions (e.g., marriage, death) may be the same and universal, but the patterns of ceremonial observance may be dramatically different. Cultures vary in just which events merit special celebration. Americans, for example, regard expensive weddings as more socially appropriate than lavish funerals. The Betsileo of Madagascar take the opposite view. The marriage ceremony is a minor event that brings together just the couple and a few close relatives. However, a funeral is a measure of the deceased person's social position and lifetime achievement, and it may attract a thousand people. Why use money on a house, the Betsileo say, when one can use it on the tomb where one will spend eternity in the company of dead relatives? How unlike contemporary Americans' dreams of home ownership and preference for quick and inexpensive funerals (see Sack 2011). Cremation, an increasingly common option in the United States, would horrify the Betsileo, for whom ancestral bones and relics are important ritual objects.

Cultures vary tremendously in their beliefs, practices, integration, and patterning. By focusing on and trying to explain alternative customs, anthropology forces us to reappraise our familiar ways of thinking. In a world full of cultural diversity, contemporary American culture is just one cultural variant, more powerful perhaps, but no more natural, than the others.

Culture and the Individual: Agency and Practice

Generations of anthropologists have theorized about the relationship between the "system," on one hand and the "person" or "individual" on the other. The "system" can refer to various concepts, including culture, society, social relations, or social structure.

Individual human beings always make up, or constitute, the system. But living within that system, humans also are constrained (to some extent, at least) by its rules and by the actions of other individuals. Cultural rules provide guidance about what to do and how to do it, but people don't always do what the rules say should be done. People use their culture actively and creatively, rather than blindly following its dictates (see Handwerker 2009). Humans aren't passive beings doomed to follow their cultural traditions like programmed robots. Cultures are dynamic and constantly changing. People learn, interpret, and manipulate the same rule in different ways—or they emphasize different rules that better suit their interests. Culture is *contested:* Different groups in society struggle with one another over whose ideas, values, goals, and beliefs will prevail. Even common symbols may have radically different *meanings* to different individuals and groups in the same culture. Golden arches may cause one person to salivate, while another plots a vegetarian protest. The same flag may be waved to support or oppose a given war.

Even when they agree about what should be done, people don't always do as their culture directs or as other people expect. Many rules are violated, some very often (for example, automobile speed limits). Some anthropologists find it useful to distinguish between ideal and real culture. The *ideal culture* consists of what people say they should do and what they say they do. *Real culture* refers to their actual behavior as observed by the anthropologist.

Culture is both public and individual, both in the world and in people's minds. Anthropologists are interested not only in public and collective behavior but also in how *individuals* think, feel, and act. The individual and culture are linked because human social life is a process in which individuals internalize the meanings of *public* (i.e., cultural) messages. Then, alone and in groups, people influence culture by converting their private (and often divergent) understandings into public expressions (D'Andrade 1984).

Conventionally, culture has been seen as social glue transmitted across the generations, binding people through their common past, rather than as something being continually created and reworked in the present. The tendency to view culture as an entity rather than as a process is changing. Contemporary anthropologists now emphasize how day-to-day action, practice, or resistance can make and remake culture (Gupta and Ferguson, eds. 1997*b*). *Agency* refers to the actions that individuals take, both alone and in groups, in forming and transforming cultural identities.

The approach to culture known as *practice theory* (Ortner 1984) recognizes that individuals within a society or culture have diverse motives and intentions and different degrees of power and influence. Such contrasts may be associated with gender, age, ethnicity, class, and other social variables. Practice theory focuses on how such varied individuals—through their ordinary and extraordinary actions and practices—manage to influence, create, and transform the world they live in. Practice theory appropriately recognizes a reciprocal relation between culture (the system—see above) and the individual. The system shapes how individuals experience and respond to external events, but individuals also play an active role in how society functions and changes. Practice theory recognizes both constraints on individuals and the flexibility and changeability of cultures and social systems.

Popular, Civic, and Public Culture

In the contemporary world, the *systems* in which we participate as individuals are not merely local or regional; they have national and international scope. The next section distinguishes between systems that are larger and smaller than nations. Here we focus on domains of national culture, which include popular, civic, and public culture. Any contemporary nation, such as the United States, Canada, Italy, Brazil, India, or Japan, has its national cultural traditions; its own media and popular culture; its own civic culture consisting of laws, institutions, and associations; and its own ways of doing things in public. To be sure, there are international spillovers. For example, the civic cultures of the United States, Canada, and India have been influenced by British law. The spillover is even greater in popular culture: American movies are watched worldwide; Simon Cowell is a powerful media figure both in England and the United States; you can take yoga or Bollywood classes in Los Angeles; Godzilla has visited New York. Despite its international spread, popular culture still varies and is patterned differently from country to country.

Today's consumption patterns both reflect and fuel *popular culture,* supplying widely shared images, information, narratives, products, events, and celebrations that have meaning for many or most people within the same national culture. American examples include Thanksgiving, Halloween, homecoming dances, reality shows, dinner-and-a-movie dates, and retirement parties. Although popular culture is available to us all, we use it selectively, and its meaning varies from one person to the next. The media scholar John Fiske (1989, 2011) argues that each individual's use of popular culture is a creative act. For example, the World Cup, the Super Bowl, Taylor Swift, *The Hunger Games,* and *The Simpsons* mean something different to each of their fans. As Fiske puts it, "the meanings I make . . . [from popular culture] are pleasurable when I feel that they are *my* meanings and that they relate to *my* everyday life in a practical, direct way" (1989, p. 57). All of us creatively consume and interpret print media, music, television, films, theme parks, celebrities, politicians, and other popular culture products.

A nation's *civic culture* includes its citizens' compliance with the legal system, participation in formal elections, and membership in voluntary and faith-based associations. Fellow countrymen and -women also share a *public culture:* generally accepted social behaviors, dress codes, speech, and other forms of expression that citizens enact in public spaces, including bars, parks, malls, and even grieving sites, such as Ground Zero (see Morrill, Snow, and White 2005; Shaffer 2008; and this chapter's "Anthropology Today").

Levels of Culture

Anthropologists also recognize cultural systems—levels of culture—that are larger and smaller than nation-states. **National culture,** examined in the previous section, embodies those beliefs, learned behavior patterns, values, and institutions that are shared by citizens of the same nation. **International culture** extends beyond and across national boundaries. Because culture is transmitted through learning rather than genetics, cultural traits can spread through borrowing or diffusion from one group to another.

Because of diffusion, migration, colonialism, and globalization, many cultural traits and patterns have acquired international scope. The contemporary United States, Canada, Great Britain, and Australia share cultural traits they have inherited from their common linguistic and cultural ancestors in Great Britain. Roman Catholics in many different countries share beliefs, symbols, experiences, and values transmitted by their church. The World Cup has become an international cultural event, as people in many countries know the rules of, play, and follow soccer.

Cultures also can be smaller than nations (see Jenks 2005). Although people who live in the same country share a national cultural tradition, all cultures also contain diversity. Individuals, families, communities, regions, classes, and other groups within a culture have different learning experiences as well as shared ones. **Subcultures** are different symbol-based patterns and traditions associated with particular groups in the same complex society. In large or diverse nations such as the United States or Canada, a variety of subcultures originate in region, ethnicity, language, class, and religion. The religious backgrounds of Jews, Baptists, and Roman Catholics create subcultural differences between them. While sharing a common national culture, U.S. northerners and southerners also differ in their beliefs, values, and customary behavior as a result of national and regional history. French-speaking Canadians sometimes pointedly contrast with English-speaking people in the same country. Italian Americans have ethnic traditions different from those of Irish, Polish, and African Americans.

Nowadays, many anthropologists are reluctant to use the term *subculture*. They feel that the prefix *sub-* is offensive because it means "below." Subcultures thus may be perceived as "less than" or somehow inferior to a dominant, elite, or national culture. In this discussion of levels of culture, I intend no such implication. My point is simply that nations may contain many different culturally defined groups. As mentioned earlier, culture is contested. Various groups may strive to promote the correctness and value of their own practices, values, and beliefs in comparison with those of other groups or the nation as a whole.

Ethnocentrism, Cultural Relativism, and Human Rights

Ethnocentrism is the tendency to view one's own culture as superior and to apply one's own cultural values in judging the behavior and beliefs of people raised in other cultures. We hear ethnocentric statements all the time. Ethnocentrism contributes to social solidarity, a sense of value and community, among people who share a cultural tradition. People everywhere think that the familiar explanations, opinions, and customs are true, right, proper, and moral. They regard different behavior as strange, immoral, or savage. Often other societies are not considered fully human. Their members may be castigated as cannibals, thieves, or people who do not bury their dead.

Among several tribes in the Trans-Fly region of Papua New Guinea, sexual activity between males was valued over sex acts involving males and females (see the chapter "Gender"). Men who grew up in the Etoro tribe (Kelly 1976) favored oral sex between males, while their neighbors, the Marind-anim, encouraged men to engage in anal sex. (In both groups heterosexual intercourse was stigmatized and allowed only for reproduction.) Etoro men considered Marind-anim anal sex to be disgusting, seeing nothing abnormal about their own oral practices.

Opposing ethnocentrism is **cultural relativism,** the viewpoint that behavior in one culture should not be judged by the standards of another culture. This position also can present problems. At its most extreme, cultural relativism argues that there is no superior, international, or universal morality, that the moral and ethical rules of all cultures deserve equal respect. In the extreme relativist view, Nazi Germany would be evaluated as nonjudgmentally as Athenian Greece.

In today's world, human rights advocates challenge many of the tenets of cultural relativism. For example, several societies in Africa and the Middle East have traditions of female genital modification (FGM). *Clitoridectomy* is the removal of a girl's clitoris. *Infibulation* involves sewing the lips (labia) of the vagina, to constrict the vaginal opening. Both procedures reduce female sexual pleasure and, it is believed in some cultures, the likelihood of adultery. Such practices have been opposed by human rights advocates, especially women's rights groups. The idea is that the tradition infringes on a basic human right—disposition over one's body and one's sexuality. Some African countries have banned or otherwise discouraged the procedures, as have Western nations that receive immigration from such cultures. Similar issues arise with circumcision and other male genital operations. Is it proper to require adolescent boys to undergo collective circumcision to fulfill cultural tradition, as has been done in parts of Africa and Australia? Is it right for a baby boy to be circumcised without his permission, as has been done routinely in the United States and as is customary among Jews and Muslims? (A 2011 initiative aimed at banning circumcision in San Francisco, California, failed to make it to the ballot.)

Some would argue that the problems with relativism can be solved by distinguishing between methodological and moral relativism (see Kellenberger 2008). In anthropology, cultural relativism is not a moral position, but a methodological one. It states: To understand another culture fully, you must try to see how the people in that culture see things. What motivates them—what are they thinking—when they do those things? Such an approach does not preclude making moral judgments or taking action. When faced with Nazi atrocities, a methodological relativist would have a moral obligation to stop doing anthropology and take action to intervene. In the FGM example, one only can understand the *motivations* for the practice by looking at the situation from the point of view of those who engage in it. Having done this, one then faces the moral question of whether to intervene to stop it. We should recognize as well that different people and groups living in the same society—for example, women and men, old and young, the more and less powerful—can have widely different views about what is proper, necessary, and moral (see Hunt 2007).

The idea of **human rights** invokes a realm of justice and morality beyond and superior to the laws and customs of particular countries, cultures, and religions (see R. Wilson, ed. 1996). Human rights include the right to speak freely, to hold religious beliefs without persecution, and not to be murdered, injured, or enslaved or imprisoned without charge. Such rights are seen as *inalienable* (nations cannot abridge or terminate them) and international (larger than and superior to individual nations and cultures). Four United Nations documents describe nearly all the human rights that have been internationally recognized. Those documents are the U.N. Charter; the Universal Declaration

The notion of indigenous intellectual property rights (IPR) has arisen in an attempt to conserve each society's cultural base, including its medicinal plants, which may have commercial value. Shown here is the hoodia plant, a cactus that grows in the Kalahari Desert of southern Africa. Hoodia, which traditionally is used by the San people to stave off hunger, is used now in diet pills marketed on the Internet.

of Human Rights; the Covenant on Economic, Social and Cultural Rights; and the Covenant on Civil and Political Rights.

Alongside the human rights movement has arisen an awareness of the need to preserve cultural rights. Unlike human rights, **cultural rights** are vested not in individuals but in *groups,* such as religious and ethnic minorities and indigenous societies. Cultural rights include a group's ability to preserve its culture, to raise its children in the ways of its forebears, to continue its language, and not to be deprived of its economic base by the nation in which it is located (Greaves 1995). The related notion of indigenous **intellectual property rights (IPR)** has arisen in an attempt to conserve each society's cultural base— its core beliefs, knowledge, and practices (see Merry 2006). Much traditional cultural knowledge has commercial value. Examples include ethnomedicine (traditional medical knowledge and techniques), cosmetics, cultivated plants, foods, folklore, arts, crafts, songs, dances, costumes, and rituals (see Nazarea 2006). According to the IPR concept, a particular group may determine how indigenous knowledge and its products may be used and distributed and the level of compensation required.

The notion of cultural rights is related to the idea of cultural relativism, and the problem discussed previously arises again. What does one do about cultural rights that interfere with human rights? I believe that anthropology's main job is to present accurate accounts and explanations of cultural phenomena. The anthropologist doesn't have to approve infanticide, cannibalism, or torture to record their existence and determine their causes and the motivations behind them. However, each anthropologist has a choice about where he or she will do fieldwork. Some anthropologists choose not to study a particular culture because they discover in advance or early in fieldwork that behavior they consider morally repugnant is practiced there. Anthropologists respect human diversity. Most ethnographers try to be objective, accurate, and sensitive in their accounts of other cultures. However, objectivity, sensitivity, and a cross-cultural perspective don't mean that anthropologists have to ignore international standards of justice and morality. What do you think?

Mechanisms of Cultural Change

Why and how do cultures change? One way is **diffusion,** or borrowing, of traits between cultures. Such exchange of information and products has gone on throughout human history because cultures never have been truly isolated. Contact between neighboring groups has always existed and has extended over vast areas (Boas 1940/1966). Diffusion is *direct* when two cultures trade with, intermarry among, or wage war on one another. Diffusion is *forced* when one culture subjugates another and imposes its customs on the dominated group. Diffusion is *indirect* when items or traits move from group A to group C via group B without any firsthand contact between A and C. In this case, group B might consist of traders or merchants who take products from a variety of places to new markets. Or group B might be geographically situated between A and C, so that what it gets from A eventually winds up in C, and vice versa. In today's world, much international diffusion is indirect—culture spread by the mass media and advanced information technology.

Acculturation, a second mechanism of cultural change, is the ongoing exchange of cultural features that results when groups have continuous firsthand contact. The cultures of either or both groups may be changed by this contact (Redfield, Linton, and Herskovits 1936). With acculturation, parts of the cultures change, but each group remains distinct. One example of acculturation is a *pidgin,* a mixed language that develops to ease communication between members of different cultures in contact. This usually happens in situations of trade or colonialism. Pidgin English, for example, is a simplified form of English. It blends English grammar with the grammar of a native language. Pidgin English was first used for commerce in Chinese ports. Similar pidgins developed later in Papua New Guinea and West Africa. In situations of continuous contact, cultures also have exchanged and blended foods, recipes, music, dances, clothing, tools, and technologies.

Independent invention—the process by which humans innovate, creatively finding solutions to problems—is a third mechanism of cultural change. Faced with comparable problems and challenges, people in different societies have innovated and changed in similar ways, which is one reason cultural generalities exist. One example is the independent invention of agriculture in the Middle East and Mexico. Over the course of human history, major innovations have spread at the expense of earlier ones. Often a major invention, such as agriculture, triggers a series of subsequent interrelated changes. These economic revolutions have social and cultural repercussions. Thus, in both Mexico and the Middle East, agriculture led to many social, political, and legal changes, including notions of property and distinctions in wealth, class, and power (see Naylor 1996).

Globalization

The term **globalization** encompasses a series of processes that work transnationally to promote change in a world in which nations and people are increasingly interlinked and mutually dependent. Promoting globalization are economic and political forces, along with modern systems of transportation and communication. The forces of globalization include international commerce and finance, travel and tourism, transnational migration, and the media—including the Internet and other high-tech information flows (see Appadurai 2001; Friedman and Friedman 2008; Haugerud, Stone, and Little 2011; Kjaerulff 2010). New economic unions (which have met considerable resistance in their member nations) have been created through the World Trade Organization (WTO), the International Monetary Fund (IMF), and the European Union (EU).

The media, including the Internet, play a key role in globalization. Long-distance communication is faster and easier than ever and now covers most of the globe. I can now e-mail or call families in Arembepe, Brazil, which lacked phones and even postal service when I first began to study the community. Information about Arembepe is now

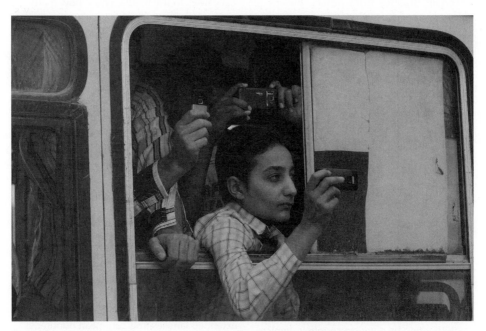

Contemporary media play a key role in globalization. Here we see Syrian youths using their cell phones to film (and potentially transmit globally) a protest against the regime of Syrian President Bashar al-Assad in the northern city of Aleppo on October 12, 2012.

Anthropology Today   *Experiencing Culture: Personal Space and Displays of Affection*

A few years ago I created and taught a course called Experiencing Culture to American college students in Italy. Students wrote biweekly journals reflecting on the cultural differences they observed between Europeans and Americans. One thing that really struck them was the greater frequency and intensity of PDAs—public displays of affection—between romantic couples in Italy, compared with the United States.

The world's nations and cultures have strikingly different notions about displays of affection and personal space. Cocktail parties in international meeting places such as the United Nations can resemble an elaborate insect mating ritual as diplomats from different countries advance, withdraw, and sidestep. When Americans talk, walk, and dance, they maintain a certain distance from others. Italians or

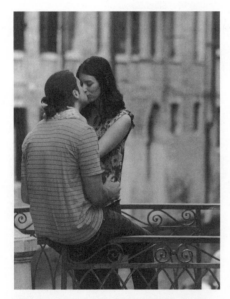

What do you think of this public display of affection by a young couple in Venice, Italy? How would such behavior be viewed in your hometown?

Brazilians, who need less personal space, may interpret such "standoffishness" as a sign of coldness. In conversational pairs, the Italian or Brazilian typically moves in, while the American "instinctively" retreats from a "close talker." Such bodily movements illustrate not instinct, but culture—behavior programmed by years of exposure to a particular cultural tradition.

To what extent are you a product of your particular culture? How much does, and should, your cultural background influence your actions and decisions? Americans may not fully appreciate the power of culture because of the value their culture places on the individual. We have seen that individualism is a distinctive *shared* value, a feature of American culture, transmitted constantly in our daily lives. In the media, count how many stories focus on individuals versus groups. That we are individuals first and members of groups second is the opposite of this chapter's lesson about culture. Certainly we have distinctive features because we are individuals, but we have other distinct attributes because we belong to cultural groups.

To return to the cultural contrast that so impressed my American students in Italy, there are striking contrasts between a national culture (American) that tends to be reserved about displays of physical affection and national cultures in which the opposite is true. Brazilians approach, touch, and kiss one another much more frequently than North Americans do. Middle-class Brazilians teach their kids—both boys and girls—to kiss (on the cheek, two or three times, coming and going) every adult relative they ever see. Given the size of Brazilian extended families, this can mean hundreds of people. Women continue kissing all those people throughout their lives. Until they are adolescents, boys kiss all adult relatives. Men typically continue to kiss female relatives and friends, as well as their fathers and uncles throughout their lives.

Do you kiss your father? Your uncle? Your grandfather? How about your mother, aunt, or grandmother? The answer to these questions may differ between men and women, and for male and female relatives. Culture can help us to make sense of these differences. In America, a cultural homophobia (fear of homosexuality) may prevent American men from engaging in displays of affection with other men. Similarly, American girls typically are encouraged to show affection; this is less true for boys.

However, culture is not static. Sarah Kershaw (2009) describes a recent surge of teenage hugging behavior in American schools. Concerned about potential sexual harassment issues, parents and school officials remain suspicious of such PDAs, even if the younger generation is more tolerant. Even American boys appear to be more likely nowadays to share nonromantic hugs, as such expressions as "bromance" and "man crush" enter our vocabulary. Hugging also has migrated online, where Facebook applications allowing friends to send hugs have tens of thousands of fans.

It's important to note that cultural traits exist because they are learned, not because they are natural or inherently right. Ethnocentrism is the error of viewing one's own culture as superior and applying one's own cultural values in judging people from other cultures. How easy is it for you to see beyond the ethnocentric blinders of your own experience? Do you have an ethnocentric position regarding displays of affection?

available to anyone, including potential tourists, on hundreds of websites. Anything can be Googled. The media help propel a transnational culture of consumption, as they spread information about products, services, rights, institutions, lifestyles, and the perceived costs and benefits of globalization. Emigrants transmit information and resources transnationally, as they maintain their ties with home (phoning, Skyping, texting, e-mailing, visiting, sending money). In a sense, such people live multilocally—in different places and cultures at once. They learn to play various social roles and to change behavior and identity depending on the situation (see Cresswell 2006).

Local people must cope increasingly with forces generated by progressively larger systems—region, nation, and world. An army of outsiders and potential change agents now intrudes on people everywhere. Tourism has become the world's number one industry (see Holden 2005). Economic development agents and the media promote the idea that work should be for cash rather than mainly for subsistence. The effects of globalization aren't always welcome. Indigenous peoples and traditional societies have devised various strategies to deal with threats to their autonomy, identity, and livelihood (Maybury-Lewis 2002; Maybury-Lewis, Macdonald, and Maybury-Lewis, 2009). New forms of cultural expression and political mobilization, including the rights movements discussed previously, are emerging from the interplay of local, regional, national, and international cultural forces (see Ong and Collier, eds. 2005).

Illustrating political mobilization against globalization are regular protests at meetings of the principal agencies concerned with international trade. Protesters continue to show their disapproval of policies of the WTO, the IMF, and the World Bank. Anti-globalization activists fault those organizations for policies that, they say, promote corporate wealth at the expense of farmers, workers, and others at or near the bottom of the economy. Protesters also include environmentalists seeking tougher environmental regulations and trade unionists advocating global labor standards. Related to these protests was the 2011 Occupy movement, which quickly spread from Wall Street to other American (and Canadian) cities. That movement protested growing North American inequality—between the top 1 percent and everyone else. Do you consider such protests valid and effective? What's your opinion of globalization?

Summary

1. *Culture,* which is distinctive to humanity, refers to customary behavior and beliefs that are passed on through enculturation. Culture rests on the human capacity for cultural learning. Culture encompasses rules for conduct internalized in human beings, which lead them to think and act in characteristic ways.

2. Although other animals learn, only humans have cultural learning, dependent on symbols. Humans think symbolically—arbitrarily bestowing meaning on things and events. By convention, a symbol stands for something with which it has no necessary or natural relation. Symbols have special meaning for people who share memories, values, and beliefs because of common enculturation.

3. Cultural traditions mold biologically based desires and needs in particular directions. Everyone is cultured, not just people with elite educations. Cultures may be integrated and patterned through economic and social forces, key symbols, and core values. Cultural rules don't rigidly dictate our behavior. There is room for creativity, flexibility, diversity, and disagreement within societies. Cultural means of adaptation have been crucial in human evolution. Aspects of culture also can be maladaptive.

4. The human capacity for culture has an evolutionary basis that extends back at least 2.6 million years—to early toolmakers whose products survive in the archaeological record (and most probably even further back—based on observation of tool use and manufacture by apes). Humans share with monkeys and apes such traits as manual dexterity (especially opposable thumbs), depth and color vision, learning ability based on a large brain, substantial parental investment in a limited number of offspring, and tendencies toward sociality and cooperation.

5. Many hominin traits are foreshadowed in other primates, particularly in the African apes, which, like us, belong to the hominid family. The ability to learn, basic to culture, is an adaptive advantage available to monkeys and apes. Chimpanzees make tools for several purposes. They also hunt and share meat. Sharing and cooperation are more developed among humans than among the apes, and only humans have systems of kinship and marriage that permit us to maintain lifelong ties with relatives in different local groups.

6. Using a comparative perspective, anthropology examines biological, psychological, social, and cultural universals and generalities. There also are unique and distinctive aspects of the human condition (cultural particularities). North American cultural traditions are no more natural than any others. Levels of culture can be larger or smaller than a nation. Cultural traits may be shared across national boundaries. Nations also include cultural differences associated with ethnicity, region, and social class.

7. Ethnocentrism describes judging other cultures by using one's own cultural standards. Cultural relativism, which anthropologists may use as a methodological position rather than a moral stance, is the idea of avoiding the use of outside standards to judge behavior in a given society. Human rights are those based on justice and morality beyond and superior to particular countries, cultures, and religions. Cultural rights are vested in religious and ethnic minorities and indigenous societies, and IPR, or intellectual property rights, apply to an indigenous group's collective knowledge and its applications.

8. Diffusion, migration, and colonialism have carried cultural traits and patterns to different world areas. Mechanisms of cultural change include diffusion, acculturation, and independent invention. Globalization comprises a series of processes that promote change in a world in which nations and people are interlinked and mutually dependent.

Key Terms

acculturation, *34*
core values, *21*
cultural relativism, *32*
cultural rights, *33*
diffusion, *34*
enculturation, *18*
estrus, *26*
ethnocentrism, *31*
generality, *27*
globalization, *34*
hominids, *23*
hominins, *23*
human rights, *32*
independent invention, *34*
intellectual property rights (IPR), *33*
international culture, *30*
national culture, *30*
particularity, *27*
subcultures, *31*
symbol, *18*
universal, *27*

Chapter 3

Doing Anthropology

"Been on any digs lately?" Ask your professor how many times she or he has been asked this question. Then ask how often he or she actually has been on a dig. Remember that anthropology has four subfields, only two of which (archaeology and biological anthropology) require much digging—in the ground, at least. To be sure, cultural anthropologists "dig out" information about varied lifestyles, as linguistic anthropologists do about the features of language. Traditionally, cultural anthropologists have done a variant on the *Star Trek* theme of seeking out, if not new, at least different "life" and "civilizations," sometimes boldly going where no scientist has gone before.

Despite globalization, the cultural diversity under anthropological scrutiny right now may be as great as ever before, because the anthropological universe has expanded to modern nations. Today's cultural anthropologists are as likely to be studying artists in Miami or bankers in Beirut as Polynesians in outrigger canoes. Still, we can't forget that anthropology did originate in non-Western, nonindustrial societies. Its research techniques, especially those subsumed under the label "ethnography," were developed to deal with small populations. Even when working in modern nations, anthropologists

World famous anthropologist Margaret Mead in the field in Bali, Indonesia, in 1957.

still consider ethnography with small groups to be an excellent way of learning about how people live their lives and make decisions.

Before this course, did you know the names of any anthropologists? If so, which ones—real or fictional? For the general public, biological anthropologists and archaeologists tend to be better known than cultural anthropologists because of what they study and discover—making them attractive subjects for the Discovery Channel. You're more likely to have watched the TV series *Bones,* seen film of Jane Goodall with chimps, or seen a paleoanthropologist holding a skull than to have seen a linguistic or cultural anthropologist at work. One cultural anthropologist was an important public and media figure for much of the 20th century. Margaret Mead, famed for her work on teen sexuality in Samoa and gender roles in New Guinea, may well be the most famous anthropologist who ever lived. Mead, one of my own professors at Columbia University, appeared regularly on NBC's *Tonight Show.* In all her venues, including teaching, museum work, TV, anthropological films, popular books, and magazines, Mead helped Americans appreciate the relevance of anthropology to understanding their daily lives. That's a worthy goal that more contemporary anthropologists should emulate.

This chapter is about what cultural anthropologists do. Linguistic methods are discussed in Chapter 4; applied anthropology, in Chapter 11.

Research Methods in Cultural Anthropology

Cultural anthropology and sociology share an interest in social relations, organization, and behavior. Early students of society, such as the French scholar Émile Durkheim, were among the founders of both sociology and anthropology. Durkheim studied the religions of Native Australians (Durkheim 1912/2001), as well as mass phenomena, such as suicide rates, in modern nations (Durkheim 1897/1951). Key differences between anthropology and sociology eventually emerged from the kinds of societies each studied. Sociologists focused on the industrial West; anthropologists, on nonindustrial societies. Different methods of data collection and analysis were developed to deal with those different kinds of societies. To study large-scale, complex nations, sociologists came to rely on questionnaires and other means of gathering masses of quantifiable data. For many years sampling and statistical techniques have been basic to sociology, whereas statistical training has been less common in anthropology (although this is changing somewhat as anthropologists increasingly work in modern nations).

Traditional ethnographers studied small, nonliterate (without writing) populations and relied on ethnographic methods appropriate to that context. "Ethnography is a research process in which the anthropologist closely observes, records, and engages in the daily life of another culture—an experience labeled as the fieldwork method—and then writes accounts of this culture, emphasizing descriptive detail" (Marcus and Fischer 1986, p. 18). One key method described in this quote is **participant observation**—taking part in the events one is observing, describing, and analyzing.

Ethnography: Anthropology's Distinctive Strategy

Anthropology became a separate field as its early scholars focused on Native Americans or traveled to distant lands to study small groups of foragers (hunters and gatherers) and cultivators. Traditionally, the process of becoming a cultural anthropologist has required a field experience in another society. Early ethnographers studied small-scale, relatively isolated societies with simple technologies and economies.

Ethnography thus emerged as a research strategy in societies with less social differentiation than is found in large, modern nations. Traditionally, ethnographers have tried to understand the whole of a particular culture (or, more realistically, as much as they can, given limitations of time and perception). To pursue this goal, ethnographers adopt a free-ranging strategy for gathering information. The ethnographer moves from setting to setting, person to person, and place to place to discover the totality and interconnectedness of social life. By expanding our knowledge of the range of human diversity, ethnography provides a foundation for generalizations about human behavior and social life. Ethnographers draw on varied techniques to piece together a picture of otherwise alien lifestyles. Anthropologists usually employ several (but rarely all) of the techniques discussed below (see also Bernard 2011; Wolcott 2010).

Ethnographic Techniques

The characteristic field techniques of the ethnographer include the following:

1. Direct, firsthand observation of behavior, including participant observation.
2. Conversation with varying degrees of formality, from the daily chitchat that helps maintain rapport and provides knowledge about what is going on to prolonged interviews, which can be unstructured or structured.
3. The genealogical method.
4. Detailed work with key consultants, or informants, about particular areas of community life.
5. In-depth interviewing, often leading to the collection of life histories of particular people (narrators).
6. Discovery of local (native) beliefs and perceptions, which may be compared with the ethnographer's own observations and conclusions.
7. Problem-oriented research of many sorts.
8. Longitudinal research—the continuous, long-term study of an area or a site.
9. Team research—coordinated research by multiple ethnographers.
10. Multisited research that studies the various sites and systems in which people participate.

Observation and Participant Observation

Ethnographers must pay attention to hundreds of details of daily life, seasonal events, and unusual happenings. They should record what they see as they see it. Things never will seem quite as strange as they do during the first few weeks in the field. The ethnographer eventually gets used to, and accepts as normal, cultural patterns that initially were alien. Staying a bit more than a year in the field allows the ethnographer to repeat the season of his or her arrival, when certain events and processes may have been missed because of initial unfamiliarity and culture shock.

Many ethnographers record their impressions in a personal diary, which is kept separate from more formal field notes. Later, this record of early impressions will help point out some of the most basic aspects of cultural diversity. Such aspects include distinctive smells, noises people make, how they cover their mouths when they eat, and how they gaze at others. These patterns, which are so basic as to seem almost trivial, are part of what Bronislaw Malinowski called "the *imponderabilia* of native life and of typical behavior" (Malinowski 1922/1961, p. 20). These features of culture are so fundamental that natives take them for granted. They are too basic even to talk about, but the unaccustomed eye of the fledgling ethnographer picks them up. Thereafter, becoming familiar, they fade to the edge of consciousness. Initial impressions are valuable and should be recorded. First and foremost, ethnographers should try to be accurate observers, recorders, and reporters of what they see in the field.

Ethnographers strive to establish *rapport,* a good, friendly working relationship based on personal contact, with their hosts. One of ethnography's most characteristic procedures is participant observation, which means that we take part in community life

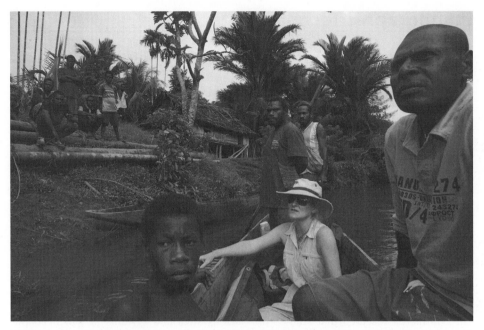

Sebastian Haraha (right), a researcher from Papua New Guinea's Office of Tourism, Arts and Culture, accompanies anthropologist Nancy Sullivan (seated) as they travel with local people up the Arafundi River on a 2009 visit to the Meakambut ethnic group.

as we study it. As human beings living among others, we cannot be totally impartial and detached observers. We take part in many events and processes we are observing and trying to comprehend. By participating, we may learn why people find such events meaningful, as we see how they are organized and conducted.

In Arembepe, Brazil, I learned about fishing by sailing on the Atlantic with local fishers. I gave Jeep rides to malnourished babies and their parents, to pregnant mothers, and once to a teenage girl possessed by a spirit. All those people needed to consult specialists outside the village. I danced on Arembepe's festive occasions, drank libations commemorating new births, and became a godfather to a village girl. Most anthropologists have similar field experiences. The common humanity of the student and the studied, the ethnographer and the research community, makes participant observation inevitable.

Conversation, Interviewing, and Interview Schedules

Participating in local life means that ethnographers constantly talk to people and ask questions. As their knowledge of the local language and culture increases, they understand more. There are several stages in learning a field language. First is the naming phase—asking name after name of the objects around us. Later we are able to pose more complex questions and understand the replies. We begin to understand simple conversations between two villagers. If our language expertise proceeds far enough, we eventually become able to comprehend rapid-fire public discussions and group conversations.

One data-gathering technique I have used in both Arembepe and Madagascar involves an ethnographic survey that includes an interview schedule. Soon after I began research in Arembepe, my fellow field workers and I attempted to complete an interview schedule in each of Arembepe's (then) 160 households. We entered almost every household (fewer than 5 percent refused to participate) to ask a set of questions on a printed form. Our results provided us with a census and basic information about the village. We wrote down the name, age, and gender of each household member. We gathered data on family type, religion, present and previous jobs, income, expenditures, diet, possessions, and many other items on our eight-page form.

Although we were doing a survey, our approach differed from the survey research design routinely used by sociologists and other social scientists working in large, industrial nations. That survey research, discussed later in the chapter, involves sampling (choosing a **sample**—a small, manageable study group from a larger population). We did not select a partial sample from the total population. Instead, we tried to interview in all households in the community (that is, to have a total sample). We used an interview schedule rather than a questionnaire. With the **interview schedule,** the ethnographer talks face to face with people, asks the questions, and writes down the answers. Questionnaire procedures tend to be more impersonal; often the respondent fills in the form.

Our goal of getting a total sample allowed us to meet almost everyone in the village and helped us establish rapport. Decades later, Arembepeiros still talk warmly about how we were interested enough in them to visit their homes and ask them questions. We stood in sharp contrast to the other outsiders the villagers had known, who considered them too poor and backward to be taken seriously.

Like other survey research, however, our interview schedule did gather comparable quantifiable information. It gave us a basis for assessing patterns and exceptions in village life. Our schedules included a core set of questions that were posed to everyone. However, some interesting side issues often came up during the interview, which we would pursue then or later.

We followed such leads into many dimensions of village life. One woman, for instance, a midwife, became the key cultural consultant we sought out later when we wanted detailed information about local childbirth. Another woman had done an internship in an Afro-Brazilian cult (*candomblé*) in the city. She still went there regularly to study, dance, and get possessed. She became our *candomblé* expert.

Thus, our interview schedule provided a structure that directed but did not confine us as researchers. It enabled our ethnography to be both quantitative and qualitative. The quantitative part consisted of the basic information we gathered and later analyzed statistically. The qualitative dimension came from our follow-up questions, open-ended discussions, pauses for gossip, and work with key consultants.

The Genealogical Method

Many of us learn about our own ancestry and relatives by tracing our genealogies. Websites like ancestry.com allow us to trace our "family trees" and degrees of relationship. The **genealogical method** is a well-established ethnographic technique. Early ethnographers developed notation and symbols to deal with kinship, descent, and marriage. Genealogy is a prominent building block in the social organization of nonindustrial societies, where people live and work each day with their close kin. Anthropologists need to collect genealogical data to understand current social relations and to reconstruct history. Indeed, another term for such cultures is "kin-based societies," because everyone is related and spends most of his or her time with relatives. Rules of behavior attached to particular kin relations are basic to everyday life (see Carsten 2004). Marriage also is crucial in organizing nonindustrial societies because strategic marriages between villages, tribes, and clans create political alliances.

Key Cultural Consultants

Every community has people who by accident, experience, talent, or training can provide the most complete or useful information about particular aspects of life. These people are **key cultural consultants,** also called *key informants.* In Ivato, the Betsileo village in Madagascar where I spent most of my time, a man named Rakoto was particularly knowledgeable about village history. However, when I asked him to work with me on a genealogy of the 50 to 60 people buried in the village tomb, he called in his cousin Tuesdaysfather, who knew more about that subject. Tuesdaysfather had survived an epidemic of influenza that ravaged Madagascar, along with much of the world, around 1919. Immune to the disease himself, Tuesdaysfather had the grim job of burying his kin as they died. He kept track of everyone buried in the tomb. Tuesdaysfather helped me with the tomb genealogy. Rakoto joined him in telling me personal details about the deceased villagers.

Life Histories

In nonindustrial societies as in our own, individual personalities, interests, and abilities vary. Some villagers prove to be more interested in the ethnographer's work and are more helpful, interesting, and pleasant than others are. Anthropologists develop likes and dislikes in the field, as we do at home. Often, when we find someone unusually interesting, we collect his or her **life history.** This recollection of a lifetime of experiences provides a more intimate and personal cultural portrait than would be possible otherwise. Life histories, which may be recorded or videoed for later review and analysis, reveal how specific people perceive, react to, and contribute to changes that affect their lives. Many ethnographers include the collection of life histories as an important part of their research strategy.

Local Beliefs and Perceptions, and the Ethnographer's

One goal of ethnography is to discover local (native) views, beliefs, and perceptions, which may be compared with the ethnographer's own observations and conclusions. In the field, ethnographers typically combine two research strategies, the emic (local-oriented) and the etic (scientist-oriented). These terms, derived from linguistics, have been applied to ethnography by various anthropologists. Marvin Harris (1968/2001) popularized the following meanings of the terms: An **emic** approach investigates how local people think. How do they perceive and categorize the world? What are their rules for behavior? What has meaning for them? How do they imagine and explain things? Operating emically, the ethnographer relies on local people to explain things and to say whether something is significant or not. The term **cultural consultant,** or informant, refers to individuals the ethnographer gets to know in the field, the people who teach him or her about their culture, who provide the emic perspective.

The **etic** (scientist-oriented) approach shifts the focus from local observations, categories, explanations, and interpretations to those of the anthropologist. The etic approach realizes that members of a culture often are too involved in what they are doing to interpret their cultures impartially. Operating etically, the ethnographer emphasizes what he or she (the observer) notices and considers important. As a trained scientist, the ethnographer should try to bring an objective and comprehensive viewpoint to the study of other cultures. Of course, the ethnographer, like any other scientist, is also a human being with cultural blinders that prevent complete objectivity. As in other sciences, proper training can reduce, but not totally eliminate, the observer's bias. But anthropologists do have special training to compare behavior between different societies.

What are some examples of emic versus etic perspectives? Consider our holidays. For North Americans, Thanksgiving Day has special significance. In our view (emically) it is a unique cultural celebration that commemorates particular historical themes. But a wider, etic, perspective sees Thanksgiving as just one more example of the postharvest festivals held in many societies. Another example: Local people give folk explanations for illnesses caused by germs and other pathogens. Emic agents that cause illness include angry or envious spirits, ancestors, witches, and sorcerers. *Illness* refers to a culture's (emic) perception and explanation of bad health, whereas *disease* refers to the scientific (etic) explanation of poor health, involving known pathogens (see this chapter's "Anthropology Today").

Ethnographers typically combine emic and etic strategies in their fieldwork. The statements, perceptions, categories, and opinions of local people help ethnographers understand how cultures work. Local beliefs are also interesting and valuable in themselves. However, people often fail to admit, or even recognize, certain causes and consequences of their behavior. This is as true of North Americans as it is of people in other societies.

The Evolution of Ethnography

Bronislaw Malinowski (1884–1942), a Polish anthropologist who spent most of his professional life in England, is generally considered the founder of ethnography. Like most anthropologists of his time, Malinowski did *salvage ethnography*, in the belief that the ethnographer's job is to study and record cultural diversity threatened by Westernization. Early ethnographic accounts (*ethnographies*), such as Malinowski's classic *Argonauts of the Western Pacific* (1922/1961), were similar to earlier traveler and explorer accounts in describing the writer's discovery of unknown people and places. However, the *scientific* aims of ethnographies set them apart from books by explorers and amateurs.

The style that dominated "classic" ethnographies was *ethnographic realism*. The writer's goal was to present an accurate, objective, scientific account of a different way of life, written by someone who knew it firsthand. This knowledge came from an "ethnographic adventure" involving immersion in an alien language and culture. Ethnographers derived their authority—both as scientists and as voices of "the native" or "the other"—from this personal research experience.

Malinowski's ethnographies were guided by the assumption that aspects of culture are linked and intertwined. Beginning by describing a Trobriand sailing expedition, the ethnographer then follows the links between that entry point and other areas of the culture, such as magic, religion, myths, kinship, and trade. Today's ethnographies tend to be less inclusive and holistic, focusing on particular topics, such as kinship or religion.

According to Malinowski, a primary task of the ethnographer is "to grasp the native's point of view, *his* relation to life, to realize his vision of *his* world" (1922/1961, p. 25—Malinowski's italics). This is a good statement of the need for the emic perspective, as

Bronislaw Malinowski (1884–1942), who was born in Poland but spent most of his professional life in England, did fieldwork in the Trobriand Islands from 1914 to 1918. Malinowski is generally considered to be the father of ethnography. Does this photo suggest anything about his relationship with Trobriand villagers?

was discussed in the previous section. Since the 1970s, *interpretive anthropology* has considered the task of describing and interpreting that which is meaningful to natives. Interpretivists such as Clifford Geertz (1973) view cultures as meaningful texts that natives constantly "read" and ethnographers must decipher. According to Geertz, anthropologists may choose anything in a culture that interests them, fill in details, and elaborate to inform their readers about meanings in that culture. Meanings are carried by public symbolic forms, including words, rituals, and customs.

A recent trend in ethnographic writing has been to question traditional goals, methods, and styles, including ethnographic realism and salvage ethnography (Brettell 1996; Clifford 1982, 1988; Marcus and Cushman 1982; Waterston and Vesperi 2009). Marcus and Fischer argue that experimentation in ethnographic writing is necessary because all peoples and cultures have already been "discovered" and must now be "*re*discovered . . . in changing historical circumstances" (1986, p. 24).

Some contemporary cultural anthropologists see ethnographic writing as an art as much as a science. Such a view might regard an ethnographic account as a literary creation in which the ethnographer, as mediator, communicates information from the "natives" to readers. Some experimental ethnographies are *dialogic,* presenting ethnography as a dialogue between the anthropologist and one or more informants (e.g., Behar 1993; Dwyer 1982). These works draw attention to ways in which ethnographers, and by extension their readers, communicate with other cultures. However, some such ethnographies have been criticized for spending too much time talking about the anthropologist and too little time describing the local people and their culture.

The dialogic ethnography is one genre within a larger experimental category—*reflexive ethnography*. Here the ethnographer puts his or her personal feelings and reactions to the field situation right in the text. Experimental writing strategies are prominent in reflexive accounts. The ethnographer may adopt some of the conventions of the novel, including first-person narration, conversations, dialogues, and humor. Experimental ethnographies, using new ways of showing what it means to be a Samoan or a Brazilian, may convey to the reader a richer and more complex understanding of human experience.

Linked to Malinowski's salvage ethnography was the idea of the *ethnographic present*—the period before Westernization, when the "true" native culture flourished. This notion often gives classic ethnographies an unrealistic timeless quality. Providing the only jarring note in this idealized picture are occasional comments by the author about traders or missionaries, suggesting that in actuality the natives were already part of the world system. Anthropologists now recognize that the ethnographic present is a rather unrealistic construct. Cultures have been in contact—and have been changing—throughout history. Most native cultures had at least one major foreign encounter before any anthropologist ever came their way. Most of them already had been incorporated in some fashion into nation-states or colonial systems.

Contemporary ethnographies usually recognize that cultures constantly change and that an ethnographic account applies to a particular moment. A current trend in ethnography is to focus on the ways in which cultural ideas serve political and economic interests (see Brettell 1996; Wolf 1992). Another approach is to describe how various particular "natives" participate in broader historical, political, and economic processes (Shostak 1981).

Problem-Oriented Ethnography

Although anthropologists are interested in the whole context of human behavior, it's impossible to study everything. Most ethnographers now enter the field with a specific problem in mind, and they collect data relevant to that problem (see Kutsche 1998; Sunstein and Chiseri-Strater 2012). Local people's answers to questions aren't the only data source. Anthropologists also gather information on factors such as population density, environmental quality, climate, physical geography, diet, and land use. Sometimes this involves direct measurement—of rainfall, temperature, fields, yields, dietary quantities, or time allocation (Bailey 1990; Johnson 1978). Often it means that we consult government records or archives.

The information of interest to ethnographers isn't limited to what local people can and do tell us. In an increasingly interconnected and complicated world, local people lack knowledge about many factors that affect their lives. Our local consultants may be as mystified as we are by the exercise of power from regional, national, and international centers.

Longitudinal Studies, Team Research, and Multisited Ethnography

Geography limits anthropologists much less now than in the past, when it could take months to reach a field site, and return visits were rare. Modern systems of transportation allow anthropologists to widen the scope of their research and to return repeatedly. Ethnographic reports now routinely include data from two or more field stays. We can even follow the people we study as they move from village to city, cross the border, or travel internationally. **Longitudinal research** is the long-term study of an area or a population, usually based on repeated visits.

One example is the ongoing study of Gwembe District, Zambia. This study, planned in 1956 as a longitudinal project by Elizabeth Colson and Thayer Scudder, continues with Colson, Scudder, and their associates and successors of various nationalities. As is often the case with longitudinal research, the Gwembe study also illustrates *team research*— coordinated research by multiple ethnographers (Colson and Scudder 1975; Scudder and Colson 1980). Four villages in different areas have been followed for more than half a century. Periodic censuses provide basic data on population, economy, kinship, and religious behavior. Censused people who have moved are traced and interviewed to see how their lives compare with those of people who have stayed behind. The initial focus of study was the impact of a large hydroelectric dam, which subjected the Gwembe people to forced resettlement. Thereafter, Scudder and Colson (1980) examined how education provided access to new opportunities as it also widened a social gap between people with different educational levels. They next focused on a change in brewing and drinking patterns, including a rise in alcoholism, in relation to changing markets, transportation, and exposure to town values (Colson and Scudder 1988). Retired from the University of California at Berkeley, where she holds the title of Professor Emerita, Colson, now in her nineties, currently resides in Gwembe district, where the project continues.

As mentioned, longitudinal research often is team research. My own field site of Arembepe, Brazil, first entered the world of anthropology as a field-team village in the 1960s. It was one of four sites for the now defunct Columbia-Cornell-Harvard-Illinois Summer Field Studies Program in Anthropology. For at least three years, that program sent a total of about 20 undergraduates annually, the author included, to do summer research abroad. The teams were stationed in rural communities in four countries: Brazil, Ecuador, Mexico, and Peru. Since my wife, Isabel Wagley Kottak, and I began studying it in 1962, Arembepe has become a longitudinal field site. Generations of researchers have monitored various aspects of change and development. The community has changed from a village into a town and illustrates the process of globalization at the local level. Its economy, religion, and social life have been transformed (see Kottak 2006).

Brazilian and American researchers worked with us on team research projects during the 1980s (on television's impact) and the 1990s (on ecological awareness and environmental risk perception). Students from various universities have drawn on our baseline information from the 1960s in their recent studies in Arembepe. Their topics have included standards of physical attractiveness, family planning and changing female reproductive strategies, conversion to Protestantism, and changing food habits in relation to globalization. Arembepe is thus a site where various field workers have worked as members of a longitudinal, multigenerational team. The more recent researchers have built on prior contacts and findings to increase knowledge about how local people meet and manage new circumstances. As of this writing (2013), new researchers are at work in Arembepe and other Brazilian communities, updating our study of media, which began during the 1980s.

Traditional ethnographic research focused on a single community or "culture," treated as more or less isolated and unique in time and space. In recent years ethnography has shifted toward studies of change and of contemporary flows of people, technology, images, and information. Reflecting today's world, fieldwork must be more flexible and on

Janet Dunn, one of many anthropologists who have worked in Arembepe. Where is Arembepe, and what kinds of research have been done there?

a larger scale. Ethnography increasingly is *multitimed* and *multisited*. That is, it studies people through time and in multiple places. Malinowski could focus on Trobriand culture and spend most of his field time in a particular community. Nowadays we cannot afford to ignore, as Malinowski did, the outside forces that increasingly impinge on the places we study. Integral to our analyses now are the external entities (e.g., governments, corporations, nongovernmental organizations, new social movements) now laying claim to land, people, and resources throughout the world. Also important in contemporary ethnography is increased recognition of power differentials and how they affect cultures, and of the importance of diversity within cultures and societies.

Anthropologists increasingly study people in motion. Examples include people living on or near national borders, nomads, seasonal migrants, homeless and displaced people, immigrants, and refugees (see Lugo 1997). As fieldwork changes, with less and less of a spatially set field, what can we take from traditional ethnography? Gupta and Ferguson correctly cite the "characteristically anthropological emphasis on daily routine and lived experience" (1997*a*, p. 5). The treatment of communities as discrete entities may be a thing of the past. However, "anthropology's traditional attention to the close observation of particular lives in particular places" has an enduring importance (Gupta and Ferguson 1997*b*, p. 25). The method of close observation helps distinguish cultural anthropology from sociology and survey research, to which we now turn.

Survey Research

Working increasingly in large-scale societies, anthropologists have developed innovative ways of blending ethnography and survey research (Fricke 1994). Before examining such mixed field methods, let's consider the main differences between survey research and ethnography. Sociologists have developed and refined the **survey research** design, which involves sampling, impersonal data collection, and statistical analysis. Survey research draws a sample (a manageable study group) from a much larger population. A properly selected and representative sample permits accurate inferences about the larger population.

In small communities, ethnographers can get to know almost everyone. Given the greater size and complexity of nations, survey research can't help being more impersonal. Survey researchers call the people they study *respondents*—those who respond to questions during a survey. Sometimes survey researchers interview their sample of respondents personally or by phone. Sometimes they ask them to fill out a questionnaire, often online.

Probably the most familiar example of survey research and sampling is the polling that is done to predict political races. An ever increasing number of organizations now gather information designed to estimate outcomes and to determine what kinds of people voted for which candidates. During sampling, researchers gather information about age, gender, religion, occupation, income, and political party preference. These characteristics (**variables**—attributes that vary among members of a sample or population) are known to influence political decisions.

Many more variables affect social identities, experiences, and activities in a modern nation than in the small communities where ethnography grew up. In contemporary North America, hundreds of factors influence our behavior and attitudes. These *social predictors* include our religion; the region of the country we grew up in; whether we come from a town, suburb, or city; and our parents' professions, ethnic origins, and income levels. In any large nation, many predictor variables (social indicators) influence behavior and opinions. Because we must be able to detect, measure, and compare the influence of social indicators, many contemporary anthropological studies have a statistical foundation. Even in rural fieldwork, more anthropologists now draw samples, gather quantitative data, and use statistics to interpret them (see Bernard 2011; Bernard, ed. 1998). Quantifiable information may permit a more precise assessment of similarities and differences among communities. Statistical analysis can support and round out an ethnographic account of local social life.

In the best studies, however, the hallmark of ethnography remains: Anthropologists enter the community and get to know the people. They participate in local activities, networks, and associations. They observe and experience social conditions and problems. They watch the effects of national policies and globalization on local life. The ethnographic method and the emphasis on personal relationships in social research are valuable gifts that cultural anthropology brings to the study of any society.

Doing Anthropology Right and Wrong: Ethical Issues

Science exists in society and in the context of law and ethics. Anthropologists can't study things simply because they happen to be interesting or of value to science. Ethical issues also must be considered. Anthropologists typically have worked abroad, outside their own society. In the context of international contacts and cultural diversity, different ethical codes and value systems will meet, and sometimes challenge, one another.

Anthropologists must be sensitive to cultural differences and aware of procedures and standards in the host country (the place where the research takes place). The researcher must inform officials and colleagues in the host country about the purpose, funding, and likely results, products, and impacts of their research. **Informed consent** (agreement to take part in the research—after having been informed about its nature, procedures, and possible impacts) should be obtained from anyone who provides information or who might be affected by the research.

It is appropriate for North American anthropologists working in another country to (1) include host country colleagues in their research planning and requests for funding; (2) establish truly collaborative relationships with those colleagues and their institutions before, during, and after fieldwork; (3) include host country colleagues in dissemination, including publication, of the research results; and (4) ensure that something is "given back" to host country colleagues. For example, research equipment and technology are allowed to remain in the host country. Or funding is provided for host country colleagues to do research, attend international meetings, or visit foreign institutions—especially those where their international collaborators work.

The Code of Ethics

To guide its members in making decisions involving ethics and values, the American Anthropological Association (AAA) offers a Code of Ethics. The most recent code, approved in 2012, points out that anthropologists have obligations to their scholarly field, to the wider society and culture, and to the human species, other species, and the environment. Like physicians who take the Hippocratic oath, the anthropologist's first concern should be to *do no harm* to the people, animals, or artifacts being studied. The stated aim of the AAA code is to offer guidelines and to promote discussion and education, rather than to investigate possible misconduct. The code addresses several contexts in which anthropologists work. Some of its main points are highlighted here.

Anthropologists should be open and honest about their research projects with all parties affected by the research. These parties should be informed about the nature, procedures, purpose(s), potential impacts, and source(s) of support for the research. Researchers should pay attention to proper relations between themselves as guests and the host nations and communities where they work. The AAA does not advise anthropologists to avoid taking stands on issues. Indeed, seeking to shape actions and policies may be as ethically justifiable as inaction. The full Code of Ethics is available at the AAA website http://aaanet.org/coe/Code_of_Ethics.pdf.

Anthropologists and Terrorism

Anthropologists often complain that government officials ignore anthropological findings that are relevant to making informed policies. The AAA has deemed it of "paramount importance" that anthropologists study the roots of terrorism and violence. How should such studies be conducted? What ethical issues might arise?

Consider a Pentagon program, Project Minerva, initiated late in the George W. Bush administration, designed to draw on social science expertise to combat national security threats. Project Minerva sought scholars to translate original documents captured in Iraq, study China's shift to a more open political system, and explain the resurgence of the Taliban in Afghanistan (Cohen 2008). Project Minerva raised concerns that governments might use anthropological research in ethically problematic ways. Government policies and military operations have the potential to harm the people anthropologists study.

Anthropology Today *Studying Health in the Bolivian Amazon*

This account describes ongoing interdisciplinary research initiated by anthropologists among Bolivia's indigenous Tsimane people. This study provides an excellent example of the biocultural field of medical anthropology, which includes both cultural and biological anthropologists. (See the chapter "Applying Anthropology" for more on medical anthropology). Also illustrated here is a proper concern with ethical issues in research. Informed consent is obtained prior to participation. The researchers repeatedly explain what they are doing, including showing patients a video about where their blood goes for testing.

SANTA MARÍA, Bolivia—There seems to be little that distinguishes the indigenous Tsimane of northern Bolivia from dozens of other native Amazonian peoples. They still live in small communities, fishing daily, hunting and relying on subsistence farming. They remain relatively isolated from the outside world. They still have large families and fall victim to parasites, worms and infectious diseases. And until a decade ago, few had contact with doctors.

Yet since 2002, when the Tsimane Health and Life History Project was founded, the Tsimane (pronounced chee-MAH-nay) have become arguably the most intensely studied indigenous people in the Western Hemisphere, and perhaps the world.

More than 50 Bolivian and American researchers, doctors and students have participated in the health project, generating an array of landmark studies. The population of 13,000, which stretches along the Maniqui River, has become the scientific community's 21st-century "traditional man."

Research on the Tsimane led to the finding in 2009 that cardiovascular disease is probably an ill of modern societies. Studies of the group also provided the most conclusive data supporting the idea that high levels of physical activity drastically reduce the risk of diabetes, obesity and hypertension. . . .

There have been 42 studies with results published, and at least 33 more are under way. "This is the most productive research site in anthropology today," Ray Hames, an anthropologist at the University of Nebraska–Lincoln, said. . . .

Michael Gurven, an anthropologist at University of California, Santa Barbara, who is a founder and a director of the project, said the primary focus of the Tsimane studies was aging. "We look at what's different and what's similar between the Tsimane and Western populations," he said. The Tsimane were chosen because of their numbers; of all Amazonian indigenous groups still living relatively traditionally, the Tsimane are one of the most numerous. . . .

The Tsimane also have the advantage of variety within that population, said Hillard Kaplan, an anthropologist at the University of New Mexico and the project's other founder and director. A small number of the Tsimane live in or around San Borja, the area's only town; they own motorcycles and use cellphones. The farther up the Maniqui River from San Borja you go, the more traditional the way of life.

In Puerto Yucumo, a village of thatched huts in plantain groves, women sit in groups at midday, their legs outstretched, attending to babies (the average family has nine children), cooking or weaving. They chatter in their native tongue; few speak Spanish and fewer have finished primary school. . . . The infiltration of doctors and anthropologists has had some effect on the culture, the researchers acknowledge, but not as much as might be expected.

"The world is changing around the Tsimane, and they are changing with it, regardless of our presence," said Dr. Kaplan.

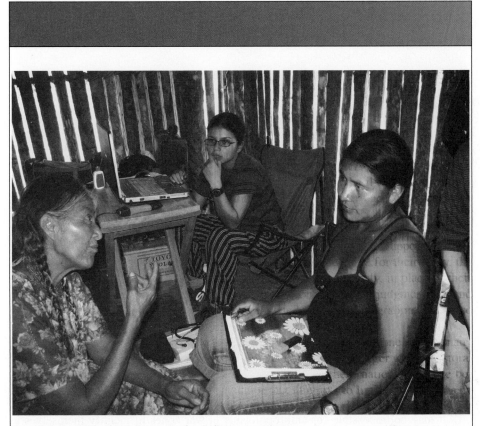

Researchers study the Tsimane in the Bolivian Amazon.

He said the Tsimane lifestyle was altered much more by government stipends for the children and the elderly, altering the subsistence economy. Nevertheless, the researchers had a threshold moment as they began the study. Could they, in good conscience, send doctors into the villages to study the population without also providing the Tsimane with basic medical care?

They decided they could not. "The depth of our science and the depth of our helping are two sides of the same coin," Dr. Kaplan said. His field team offers basic medical exams for anyone who shows up, provides free medicine for common ailments like stomach parasites, and does on-the-spot analysis of blood, urine and fecal samples.

"It would be unethical not to do this," Jane Lancaster, editor of the journal Human Nature, said. "If you are performing research and bothering these people, the least you can do is provide medical care."

Still, officials at one of the project's supporters, the National Science Foundation, wondered: How can you study health conditions while simultaneously altering them? Dr. Kaplan and Dr. Gurven said they convinced the foundation and others that the kind of medical care they administer—sporadic treatment for parasites, ibuprofen for headaches, stitches for machete wounds—does not taint data on chronic, long-term disease. . . .

continued

Anthropology Today   *continued*

About 4 to 6 percent of the Tsimane die before age 1, according to the project's unpublished estimates. (That's down from 12 percent in 2002, when Dr. Kaplan and Dr. Gurven began their work; reductions in child and maternal mortality have been the team's most notable public health contribution.) About 15 percent die before age 5. . . .

Dr. Gurven said the researchers repeatedly explain what they are doing. Every patient must give oral consent, and all are shown a video about where their blood goes for testing. . . .

More recently, anthropologists have been especially critical of the Pentagon's Human Terrain System (HTS) program. Launched in February 2007, HTS has embedded anthropologists and other social scientists in military teams in Iraq and Afghanistan. On October 31, 2007, the AAA Executive Board issued a statement of disapproval of HTS—outlining how HTS violates the AAA Code of Ethics (see http://www.aaanet.org/about/Policies/statements/Human-Terrain-System-Statement.cfm). The Board noted that HTS places anthropologists, as contractors with the U.S. military, in war zones, where they are charged with collecting cultural and social data for use by the military. The ethical concerns raised by these activities include the following:

1. It may be impossible for anthropologists in war zones to identify themselves as anthropologists, as distinct from military personnel. This constrains their ethical responsibility as anthropologists to disclose who they are and what they are doing.

2. HTS anthropologists are asked to negotiate relations among several groups, including local populations and the military units in which they are embedded. Their responsibilities to their units may conflict with their obligations to the local people they study or consult. This may interfere with the obligation, stipulated in the AAA Code of Ethics, to do no harm.

3. In an active war zone, it is difficult for local people to give "informed consent" without feeling coerced to provide information. As a result, "voluntary informed consent" (as stipulated by the AAA Code of Ethics) is compromised.

4. Information supplied by HTS anthropologists to military field commanders could help target specific groups for military action. Such use of fieldwork-derived information would violate the AAA Code of Ethics stipulation that those studied not be harmed.

5. The identification of anthropology and anthropologists with the U.S. military may indirectly (through suspicion of "guilt by association") endanger the research, and even the personal safety, of other anthropologists and their consultants throughout the world.

How should anthropologists study terrorism? What do you think about anthropologists' role in war?

Summary

1. Ethnographic methods include firsthand and participant observation, rapport building, interviews, genealogies, work with key consultants or informants, collection of life histories, discovery of local beliefs and perceptions, problem-oriented and longitudinal research, and team research. Ethnographers work in communities and form personal relationships with local people as they study their lives.

2. An interview schedule is a form an ethnographer completes as he or she visits a series of households. Key consultants, or informants, teach us about particular areas of local life. Life histories document personal experiences with culture and culture change. Genealogical information is particularly useful in societies in which principles of kinship and marriage organize social and political life. Emic approaches focus on native perceptions and explanations. Etic approaches give priority to the ethnographer's own observations and conclusions. Longitudinal research is the systematic study of an area or a population over time. Longitudinal, team, and multisited ethnographic research are increasingly common.

3. Traditionally, anthropologists worked in small-scale societies; sociologists, in modern nations. Different techniques developed to study these different kinds of societies. Anthropologists do their fieldwork in communities and study the totality of social life. Sociologists use surveys and study samples to make inferences about a larger population. Anthropologists may employ ethnographic procedures to study cities, towns, or rural areas.

4. Because science exists in society, and in the context of law and ethics, anthropologists can't study things simply because they happen to be interesting or of scientific value. Anthropologists have obligations to their scholarly field, to the wider society and culture (including that of the host country), and to the human species, other species, and the environment. The AAA Code of Ethics offers ethical guidelines for anthropologists. Ethical problems often arise when anthropologists work for governments, especially the military.

Key Terms

cultural
  consultant, *46*
emic, *46*
etic, *46*
genealogical
  method, *45*
informed
  consent, *53*

interview
  schedule, *45*
key cultural
  consultants, *46*
life history, *46*
longitudinal
  research, *50*

participant
  observation, *42*
sample, *45*
survey
  research, *51*
variables, *52*

Chapter 4

Language and Communication

North Americans have certain stereotypes about how people in other regions talk. Some stereotypes, spread by the mass media, are more generalized than others are (see this chapter's "Anthropology Today" for stereotypes and the reality of California speech patterns). Most Americans think they can imitate a "Southern accent." We also stereotype speech in New York City (the pronunciation of *coffee,* for example), Boston ("I pahked the kah in Hahvahd Yahd"), and Canada ("oot" for "out").

It's sometimes thought that midwesterners don't have accents. This belief stems from the fact that midwestern dialects don't have many stigmatized linguistic variants—speech patterns that people in other regions recognize and look down on, such as *r*lessness and *dem, dese,* and *dere* (instead of *them, these,* and *there*).

Far from having no accents, midwesterners, even in the same high school, exhibit linguistic diversity (see Eckert 1989, 2000). One of the best examples of variable midwestern speech, involving vowels, is pronunciation of the *e* sound (called the /e/ phoneme), in such words as *ten, rent, section, lecture, effect, best,* and *test.* In southeastern

Michigan, there are four different ways of pronouncing this *e* sound. Speakers of Black English and immigrants from Appalachia often pronounce *ten* as "tin," just as Southerners habitually do. Some Michiganders say "ten," the correct pronunciation in Standard English. However, two other pronunciations also are common. Instead of "ten," many Michiganders say "tan," or "tun" (as though they were using the word *ton,* a unit of weight).

My students often astound me with their pronunciation. One day I met one of my Michigan-raised teaching assistants in the hall. She was deliriously happy. When I asked why, she replied, "I've just had the best suction."

"What?" I said.

She finally spoke more precisely. "I've just had the best saction." She considered this a clearer pronunciation of the word *section.*

Another TA complimented me, "You luctured to great effuct today." After an exam a student lamented that she had not done her "bust on the tust" (i.e., "best on the test").

The truth is, regional patterns affect the way we all speak.

Language

Linguistic anthropology illustrates anthropology's characteristic interests in diversity, comparison, and change—but here the focus is on language (see Duranti 2009; Salzmann 2012). Language, spoken (*speech*) and written (*writing*—which has existed for less than 6,000 years), is our primary means of communication. Like culture in general, of which language is a part, language is transmitted through learning. Language is based on arbitrary, learned associations between words and the things they stand for. Unlike the communication systems of other animals, language allows us to discuss the past and future, share our experiences with others, and benefit from their experiences.

Anthropologists study language in its social and cultural context (see Bonvillain 2012; Salzmann, Stanlaw, and Adachi 2012). Some linguistic anthropologists reconstruct ancient languages by comparing their contemporary descendants and in doing so make discoveries about history. Others study linguistic differences to discover the varied worldviews and patterns of thought in a multitude of cultures. Sociolinguists examine dialects and styles in a single language to show how speech reflects social differences, as in the above discussion of regional speech contrasts. Linguistic anthropologists also explore the role of language in colonization and globalization (Blommaert 2010; Geis 1987; Trudgill 2010).

Nonhuman Primate Communication

Call Systems

Only humans speak. No other animal has anything approaching the complexity of language. The natural communication systems of other primates (monkeys and apes) are **call systems.** These vocal systems consist of a limited number of sounds—*calls*—that are produced only when particular environmental stimuli are encountered. Such calls may be varied in intensity and duration, but they are much less flexible than language because they are automatic and can't be combined. When primates encounter food and danger simultaneously, they can make only one call. They can't combine the calls for food and danger into a single utterance, indicating that both are present. At some point in human evolution, however, our ancestors began to combine calls and to understand the combinations. The number of calls also expanded, eventually becoming too great to be transmitted even partly through the genes. Communication came to rely almost totally on learning.

Although wild primates use call systems, the vocal tract of apes is not suitable for speech. Until the 1960s, attempts to teach spoken language to apes suggested that they lack linguistic abilities. In the 1950s, a couple raised a chimpanzee, Viki, as a member of their family and systematically tried to teach her to speak. However, Viki learned only four words ("mama," "papa," "up," and "cup").

Sign Language

More recent experiments have shown that apes can learn to use, if not speak, true language (Fouts 1997; Miles 1983). Several apes have learned to converse with people through means other than speech. One such communication system is American Sign Language, or ASL, which is widely used by hearing-impaired Americans. ASL employs

Apes, such as these Congo chimpanzees, use call systems to communicate in the wild. Their vocal systems consist of a limited number of sounds—calls—that are produced only when particular environmental stimuli are encountered.

a limited number of basic gesture units that are analogous to sounds in spoken language. These units combine to form words and larger units of meaning.

The first chimpanzee to learn ASL was Washoe, a female, who died in 2007 at the age of 42. Captured in West Africa, Washoe was acquired by R. Allen Gardner and Beatrice Gardner, scientists at the University of Nevada in Reno, in 1966, when she was a year old. Four years later, she moved to Norman, Oklahoma, to a converted farm that had become the Institute for Primate Studies. Washoe revolutionized the discussion of the language-learning abilities of apes (Carey 2007). At first she lived in a trailer and heard no spoken language. The researchers always used ASL to communicate with each other in her presence. The chimp gradually acquired a vocabulary of more than 100 signs representing English words (Gardner, Gardner, and Van Cantfort, eds. 1989). At the age of 2, Washoe began to combine as many as five signs into rudimentary sentences such as "you, me, go out, hurry."

The second chimp to learn ASL was Lucy, Washoe's junior by one year. Lucy died, or was murdered by poachers, in 1986, after having been introduced to "the wild" in Africa in 1979 (Carter 1988). From her second day of life until her move to Africa, Lucy lived with a family in Norman, Oklahoma. Roger Fouts, a researcher from the nearby Institute for Primate Studies, came two days a week to test and improve Lucy's knowledge of ASL. During the rest of the week, Lucy used ASL to converse with her foster parents. After acquiring language, Washoe and Lucy exhibited several human traits: swearing, joking, telling lies, and trying to teach language to others (Fouts 1997).

When irritated, Washoe called her monkey neighbors at the institute "dirty monkeys." Lucy insulted her "dirty cat." On arrival at Lucy's place, Fouts once found a pile of excrement on the floor. When he asked the chimp what it was, she replied, "dirty, dirty," her expression for feces. Asked whose "dirty, dirty" it was, Lucy named Fouts's coworker, Sue. When Fouts refused to believe her about Sue, the chimp blamed the excrement on Fouts himself.

Cultural transmission of a communication system through learning is a fundamental attribute of language. Washoe, Lucy, and other chimps have tried to teach ASL to other animals, including their own offspring. Washoe taught gestures to other institute chimps, including her son Sequoia, who died in infancy (Fouts, Fouts, and Van Cantfort 1989).

Because of their size and strength as adults, gorillas are less likely subjects than chimps for such experiments. Lean adult male gorillas in the wild weigh 400 pounds (180 kilograms), and full-grown females can easily reach 250 pounds (110 kilograms). Because of this, psychologist Penny Patterson's work with gorillas at Stanford University seems more daring than the chimp experiments. Patterson raised the now full-grown female gorilla Koko in a trailer next to a Stanford museum. Koko's vocabulary surpasses that of any chimp. She regularly employs 400 ASL signs and has used about 700 at least once.

Koko and the chimps also show that apes share still another linguistic ability with humans: **productivity.** Speakers routinely use the rules of their language to produce entirely new expressions that are comprehensible to other native speakers. I can, for example, create "baboonlet" to refer to a baboon infant. I do this by analogy with English words in which the suffix -*let* designates the young of a species. Anyone who speaks English immediately understands the meaning of my new word. Koko, Washoe, Lucy, and others have shown that apes also are able to use language productively. Lucy used gestures she already knew to create "drinkfruit" for "watermelon." Washoe, seeing a swan for the first time, coined "waterbird." Koko, who knew the gestures for "finger" and "bracelet," formed "finger bracelet" when she was given a ring.

Chimps and gorillas have a rudimentary capacity for language. They may never have invented a meaningful gesture system in the wild. However, given such a system, they show many humanlike abilities in learning and using it. Of course, language use by apes is a product of human intervention and teaching. The experiments mentioned here do not suggest that apes can invent language (nor are human children ever faced with that task). However, young apes have managed to learn the basics of gestural language. They can employ it productively and creatively, although not with the sophistication of human ASL users.

Apes also have demonstrated linguistic **displacement.** Absent in call systems, this is a key ingredient in language. Normally, each call is tied to an environmental stimulus such as food. Calls are uttered only when that stimulus is present. Displacement means that humans can talk about things that are not present. We don't have to see the objects before we say the words. Human conversations are not limited by place. We can discuss the past and future, share our experiences with others, and benefit from theirs.

Patterson (1978) has described several examples of Koko's capacity for displacement. The gorilla once expressed sorrow about having bitten Penny three days earlier. Koko has used the sign "later" to postpone doing things she doesn't want to do. Table 4.1 summarizes the contrasts between language, whether sign or spoken, and call systems.

Certain scholars doubt the linguistic abilities of chimps and gorillas (Sebeok and Umiker-Sebeok, eds. 1980; Terrace 1979). These people contend that Koko and the chimps are comparable to trained circus animals and don't really have linguistic ability. However, in defense of Patterson and the other researchers (Hill 1978; Van Cantfort and Rimpau 1982), only one of their critics has worked with an ape. This was Herbert Terrace, whose experience teaching a chimp sign language lacked the continuity and personal involvement that have contributed so much to Patterson's success with Koko. (For more on Terrace and his ill-fated chimp, Nim Chimpsky, see Hess [2008] and the acclaimed 2011 documentary film *Project Nim*.)

No one denies the huge difference between human language and gorilla signs. There is a major gap between the ability to write a book or say a prayer and the few hundred

TABLE 4.1   Language Contrasted with Call Systems

Human Language	Primate Call Systems
Has the capacity to speak of things and events that are not present (displacement)	Are stimuli dependent; the food call will be made only in the presence of food; it cannot be faked
Has the capacity to generate new expressions by combining other expressions (productivity)	Consist of a limited number of calls that cannot be combined to produce new calls
Is group specific in that all humans have the capacity for language, but each linguistic community has its own language, which is culturally transmitted	Tend to be species specific, with little variation among communities of the same species for each call

gestures employed by a well-trained chimp. Apes aren't people, but they aren't just animals, either. Let Koko express it: When asked by a reporter whether she was a person or an animal, Koko signed "fine animal gorilla" (Patterson 1978). For the latest on Koko, see http://www.koko.org.

The Origin of Language

Although the capacity to remember and combine linguistic symbols may be latent in the apes, human evolution was needed for this seed to flower into language. A mutated gene known as FOXP2 helps explain why humans speak and chimps don't (Paulson 2005). The key role of FOXP2 in speech came to light in a study of a British family, identified only as KE, half of whose members had an inherited, severe deficit in speech (Trivedi 2001). The same variant form of FOXP2 that is found in chimpanzees causes this disorder. Those who have the nonspeech version of the gene cannot make the fine tongue and lip movements that are necessary for clear speech, and their speech is unintelligible—even to other members of the KE family (Trivedi 2001). Chimps have the same (genetic) sequence as the KE family members with the speech deficit. Comparing chimp and human genomes, it appears that the speech-friendly form of FOXP2 took hold in humans around 150,000 years ago. This mutation conferred selective advantages (linguistic and cultural abilities) that allowed those who had it to spread at the expense of those who did not (Paulson 2005).

Language offered a tremendous adaptive advantage to *Homo sapiens*. Language permits the information stored by a human society to exceed by far that of any nonhuman group. Language is a uniquely effective vehicle for learning. Because we can speak of things we have never experienced, we can anticipate responses before we encounter the stimuli. Adaptation can occur more rapidly in *Homo* than in the other primates because our adaptive means are much more flexible.

Nonverbal Communication

Language is our principal means of communicating, but it isn't the only one we use. We *communicate* when we transmit information about ourselves to others and receive such information from them. Our expressions, stances, gestures, and movements, even if unconscious, convey information and are part of our communication styles. Deborah Tannen (1990) discusses differences in the communication styles of American men and women, and her comments go beyond language. She notes that American girls and women tend to look directly at each other when they talk, whereas American boys and men do not. Males are more likely to look straight ahead rather than turn and make eye contact with someone, especially another man, seated beside them. Also, in conversational groups, American men tend to relax and sprawl out. American women may adopt a similar relaxed posture in all-female groups, but when they are with men, they tend to draw in their limbs and adopt a tighter stance.

Kinesics is the study of communication through body movements, stances, gestures, and expressions. Linguists pay attention not only to what is said but also to how it is said and to the features besides language itself that convey meaning. A speaker's enthusiasm is conveyed not only through words but also through facial expressions, gestures, and other signs of animation. We use gestures, such as a jab of the hand, for emphasis. We vary our intonation and the pitch or loudness of our voices. We communicate through strategic pauses, and even by being silent. An effective communication strategy may be to alter pitch, voice level, and grammatical forms, such as declaratives ("I am . . ."), imperatives ("Go forth . . ."), and questions ("Are you . . . ?"). Culture teaches us that certain manners and styles should accompany certain kinds of speech. Our demeanor, verbal and nonverbal, when our favorite team is winning would be out of place at a funeral, or when a somber subject is being discussed.

Much of what we communicate is nonverbal and reflects our emotional states and intentions. This can create problems when we use contemporary means of communication such as texting and online messaging. People can use emoticons (☺,☹, :~/ [confused], :~0 ["hah!" no way!]) and abbreviations (lol—laugh out loud; lmao—laugh my a** off; wtf—what the f**; omg—oh my god) to fill in what would otherwise be communicated by tone of voice, laughter, and facial expression (see Baron 2009; Tannen and Trester 2012).

Culture always plays a role in shaping the "natural." Cross-culturally, nodding does not always mean affirmative, nor does head shaking from side to side always mean negative. Brazilians wag a finger to mean no. Americans say "uh huh" to affirm, whereas in Madagascar a similar sound is made to deny. Americans point with their fingers; the people of Madagascar point with their lips.

Body movements communicate social differences. In Japan, bowing is a regular part of social interaction, but different bows are used depending on the social status of the people who are interacting. In Madagascar and Polynesia, people of lower status should not hold their heads above those of people of higher status. When one approaches someone older or of higher status, one bends one's knees and lowers one's head as a sign of respect. In Madagascar, one always does this, for politeness, when passing between two people. Although our gestures, facial expressions, and body stances have roots in our primate heritage, and can be seen in the monkeys and the apes, they have not escaped cultural shaping. Language, which is so highly dependent on the use of symbols, is the domain of communication in which culture plays the strongest role.

The Structure of Language

The scientific study of a spoken language (**descriptive linguistics**) involves several interrelated areas of analysis: phonology, morphology, lexicon, and syntax. **Phonology,** the study of speech sounds, considers which sounds are present and meaningful in a given language. **Morphology** studies how sounds combine to form *morphemes*—words and their meaningful parts. Thus, the word *cats* would be analyzed as containing two morphemes—*cat,* the name for a kind of animal, and *-s,* a morpheme indicating plurality. A language's **lexicon** is a dictionary containing all its morphemes and their meanings. **Syntax** refers to the arrangement and order of words in phrases and sentences. For example, do nouns usually come before or after verbs? Do adjectives normally precede or follow the nouns they modify?

Syntax refers to the arrangement and order of words in phrases and sentences. A photo of Yoda from *Star Wars* (*Revenge of the Sith*) this is. What's odd about Yoda's syntax?

Speech Sounds

From the movies and TV, and from meeting foreigners, we know something about foreign accents and mispronunciations. We know that someone with a marked French accent doesn't pronounce *r* as an American does. But at least someone from France can distinguish between "craw" and "claw," which someone from Japan may not be able to do. The difference between *r* and *l* makes a difference in English and in French, but it doesn't in Japanese. In linguistics we say that the difference between *r* and *l* is *phonemic* in English and French but not in Japanese. In English and French *r* and *l* are phonemes but not in Japanese. A **phoneme** is a sound contrast that makes a difference, that differentiates meaning.

We find the phonemes in a given language by comparing *minimal pairs,* words that resemble each other in all but one sound. The words have different meanings, but they differ in just one sound. The contrasting sounds therefore are phonemes in that language. An example in English is the minimal pair *pit/bit*. These two words are distinguished by a single sound contrast between /p/ and /b/ (we enclose phonemes in slashes). Thus, /p/ and /b/ are phonemes in English. Another example is the different vowel sound of *bit* and *beat* (Figure 4.1). This contrast distinguishes these two words and the two vowel phonemes written /I/ and /i/ in English.

Standard (American) English (SE), the "region-free" dialect of TV network newscasters, has about 35 phonemes—at least 11 vowels and 24 consonants. The number of phonemes varies from language to language—from 15 to 60, averaging between 30 and 40. The number of phonemes also varies between dialects of a given language. In North American English, for example, vowel phonemes vary noticeably from dialect to dialect. Readers should pronounce the words in Figure 4.1, paying attention to (or asking

FIGURE 4.1   Vowel Phonemes in Standard American English

They are shown according to height of tongue and tongue position at front, center, or back of mouth. Phonetic symbols are identified by English words that include them; note that most are minimal pairs.

Source: Dwight Bolinger, *Aspects of Language,* 3rd ed., fig. 2.1. Copyright © 1981 Heinle/Arts & Sciences, a part of Cengage Learning, Inc. Reproduced by permission. www.cengage.com/permissions.

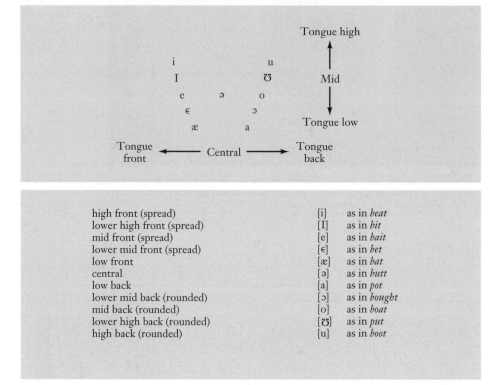

high front (spread)	[i]	as in *beat*
lower high front (spread)	[I]	as in *bit*
mid front (spread)	[e]	as in *bait*
lower mid front (spread)	[ε]	as in *bet*
low front	[æ]	as in *bat*
central	[ə]	as in *butt*
low back	[a]	as in *pot*
lower mid back (rounded)	[ɔ]	as in *bought*
mid back (rounded)	[o]	as in *boat*
lower high back (rounded)	[ʊ]	as in *put*
high back (rounded)	[u]	as in *boot*

someone else) whether they distinguish each of the vowel sounds. Most North Americans don't pronounce them all.

Phonetics is the study of speech sounds in general, what people actually say in various languages, like the differences in vowel pronunciation described in the discussion of midwestern speech at the beginning of the chapter (for California vowels, see this chapter's "Anthropology Today"). **Phonemics** studies only the *significant* sound contrasts (phonemes) of a given language. In English, like /r/ and /l/ (remember *craw* and *claw*), /b/ and /v/ also are phonemes, occurring in minimal pairs like *bat* and *vat*. In Spanish, however, the contrast between [b] and [v] doesn't distinguish meaning, and they therefore are not phonemes (we enclose sounds that are not phonemic in brackets). Spanish speakers normally use the [b] sound to pronounce words spelled with either *b* or *v*.

In any language a given phoneme extends over a phonetic range. In English the phoneme /p/ ignores the phonetic contrast between the [pʰ] in *pin* and the [p] in *spin*. Most English speakers don't even notice that there is a phonetic difference. The [pʰ] is aspirated, so that a puff of air follows the [p]. The [p] in *spin* is not. (To see the difference, light a match, hold it in front of your mouth, and watch the flame as you pronounce the two words.) The contrast between [pʰ] and [p] *is* phonemic in some languages, such as Hindi (spoken in India). That is, there are words whose meaning is distinguished only by the contrast between an aspirated and an unaspirated [p].

Native speakers vary in their pronunciation of certain phonemes, such as the /e/ phoneme in the midwestern United States. This variation is important in the evolution of language. Without shifts in pronunciation, there could be no linguistic change. The section on sociolinguistics later in this chapter considers phonetic variation and its relationship to social divisions and the evolution of language.

Language, Thought, and Culture

The well-known linguist Noam Chomsky (1957) has argued that the human brain contains a limited set of rules for organizing language, so that all languages have a common structural basis. (Chomsky calls this set of rules *universal grammar.*) That people can learn foreign languages and that words and ideas translate from one language to another supports Chomsky's position that all humans have similar linguistic abilities and thought processes. Another line of support comes from creole languages. Such languages develop from *pidgins,* languages that form in situations of acculturation, when different societies come into contact and must devise a system of communication. Pidgins based on English and native languages developed through trade and colonialism in many world areas, including China, Papua New Guinea, and West Africa (see Gu 2012). Eventually, after generations of being spoken, pidgins may develop into *creole* languages. These are more mature languages, with developed grammatical rules and native speakers (people who learn the language as their primary one during enculturation).

Creoles are spoken in several Caribbean societies. Gullah, which is spoken by African Americans on coastal islands in South Carolina and Georgia, is a creole language. Supporting the idea that creoles are based on universal grammar is the fact that such languages all share certain features. Syntactically, all use particles (e.g., will, was) to form future and past tenses and multiple negation to deny or negate (e.g., he don't got none). Also, all form questions by changing inflection rather than by changing word order. For example, "You're going home for the holidays?" (with a rising tone at the end) rather than "Are you going home for the holidays?"

The Sapir-Whorf Hypothesis

Other linguists and anthropologists take a different approach to the relation between language and thought. Rather than seeking universal linguistic structures and processes, they believe that different languages produce different ways of thinking. This position sometimes is known as the **Sapir-Whorf hypothesis** after Edward Sapir (1931) and his student Benjamin Lee Whorf (1956), its prominent early advocates. Sapir and Whorf argued that the grammatical categories of particular languages lead their speakers to think about things in different ways. For example, English divides time into past, present, and future. Hopi, a language of the Pueblo region of the Native American Southwest, does not. Rather, Hopi distinguishes between events that exist or have existed (what we use present and past to discuss) and those that don't or don't yet (our future events, along with imaginary and hypothetical events). Whorf argued that this difference leads Hopi speakers to think about time and reality in different ways than English speakers do.

A similar example comes from Portuguese, which employs a future subjunctive verb form, introducing a degree of uncertainty into discussions of the future. In English we routinely use the future tense to talk about something we think will happen. We don't feel the need to qualify "The sun'll come out tomorrow" by adding "if it doesn't go supernova." We don't hesitate to proclaim "I'll see you next year," even when we can't be absolutely sure we will. The Portuguese future subjunctive qualifies the future event, recognizing that the future can't be certain. Our way of expressing the future as certain is so ingrained that we don't even think about it, just as the Hopi don't see the need to distinguish between present and past, both of which are real, while the future remains hypothetical. It seems, however, that language does not tightly restrict thought, because cultural changes can produce changes in thought and in language, as we'll see in the next section (see also Gumperz and Levinson, eds. 1996).

Focal Vocabulary

A lexicon (vocabulary) is a language's dictionary, its set of names for things, events, and ideas. Lexicon influences perception. Thus, Eskimos (Inuit) have several distinct words for different types of snow that in English are all called *snow*. Most English speakers never notice the differences between these types of snow and might have trouble seeing

Shown here (in 1995) is Leigh Jenkins, who was or is director of Cultural Preservation for the Hopi tribal council. The Hopi language would not distinguish between *was* and *is* in the previous sentence. For the Hopi, present and past are real and are expressed grammatically in the same way, while the future remains hypothetical and has a different grammatical expression.

them even if someone pointed them out. Eskimos recognize and think about differences in snow that English speakers don't see because our language gives us just one word.

Similarly, the Nuer of South Sudan have an elaborate vocabulary to describe cattle. Eskimos have several words for snow and Nuer have dozens for cattle because of their particular histories, economies, and environments (Robson 2013). When the need arises, English speakers can also elaborate their snow and cattle vocabularies. For example, skiers name varieties of snow with words that are missing from the lexicons of Florida retirees. Similarly, the cattle vocabulary of a Texas rancher is much more ample than that of a salesperson in a New York City department store. Such specialized sets of terms and distinctions that are particularly important to certain groups (those with particular *foci* of experience or activity) are known as **focal vocabulary.**

Vocabulary is the area of language that changes most readily. New words and distinctions, when needed, appear and spread. For example, who would have "texted" someone a generation ago? Names for items get simpler as they become common and important. A television has become a *TV,* an automobile a *car,* and an application for a smartphone an *app.*

Language, culture, and thought are interrelated. Opposing the Sapir-Whorf hypothesis, however, it might be more accurate to say that changes in culture produce changes in language and thought than to say the reverse. Consider differences between female and male Americans regarding the color terms they use (Lakoff 2004). Distinctions implied by such terms as *salmon, rust, peach, beige, teal, mauve, cranberry,* and *dusky orange* aren't in the vocabularies of most American men. However, many of them weren't even in American women's lexicons 60–70 years ago. These changes reflect changes in American economy, society, and culture. Color terms and distinctions have increased

Action from game three of the 2012 NHL Stanley Cup finals between the New Jersey Devils and the Los Angeles Kings. The Kings won this game and went on to take the series 4-2. How might an avid soccer fan describe what's happening in this photo?

TABLE 4.2
Focal Vocabulary for Hockey
Insiders have special terms for the major elements of the game.

Elements of Hockey	Insiders' Term
puck	biscuit
goal/net	pipes
penalty box	sin bin
hockey stick	twig
helmet	bucket
space between a goalie's leg pads	five hole

with the growth of the fashion and cosmetic industries. A similar contrast (and growth) in Americans' lexicons shows up in football, basketball, and hockey vocabularies. Sports fans, more often males than females, use more terms concerning, and make more elaborate distinctions between, the games they watch, such as hockey (see Table 4.2). Thus, cultural contrasts and changes affect lexical distinctions (for instance, *peach* versus *salmon*) within semantic domains (for instance, color terminology). **Semantics** refers to a language's meaning system.

The ways in which people divide the world—the lexical contrasts they perceive as meaningful or significant—reflect their experiences (see Bicker, Sillitoe, and Pottier, eds. 2004). Anthropologists have discovered that certain sets of vocabulary items evolve in a determined order. For example, after studying more than 100 languages, Berlin and Kay (1969/1992) discovered 10 basic color terms: *white, black, red, yellow, blue, green, brown, pink, orange,* and *purple* (they evolved in more or less that order). The number of terms varied with cultural complexity. Representing one extreme were Papua New Guinea cultivators and Australian hunters and gatherers, who used only 2 basic terms, which translate as *black* and *white* or *dark* and *light*. At the other end of the continuum were European and Asian languages with all the color terms. Color terminology was most developed in areas with a history of using dyes and artificial coloring.

Sociolinguistics

Social and Linguistic Variation

Do you think there's anything distinctive or unusual about the way you talk? If you're from Canada, Virginia, or Savannah, you may say "oot" instead of "out." A southerner might request a "soft drink" rather than a New Yorker's "soda" or someone else's "pop." Can you imitate how a "Valley Girl" or "surfer dude" might talk? Usually when we pay attention to how we talk, it's because someone comments on our speech. It may be only when students move from one state or region to another that they realize how much of a regional accent they have. I moved as a teenager from Atlanta to New York City. Previously I hadn't realized I had a southern accent, but some guardians of linguistic correctness in my new high school did. They put me in a speech class, pointing out linguistic flaws I never knew I had. One was my "dull *s,*" particularly in terminal consonant clusters, as in the words *tusks* and *breakfasts*. Apparently I didn't pronounce all three consonants at the ends of those words. Later it occurred to me that these weren't words I used very often. As far as I know, I've never had a conversation about tusks or proclaimed, "I ate seven breakfasts last week."

Unlike grammarians, linguists and anthropologists are interested in what people do say, rather than what they should say. Speech differences are associated with, and tell us a lot about, social variation, such as region, education, ethnic background, and gender. Men and women talk differently. I'm sure you can think of examples based on your own experience, although you probably never realized that women tend to peripheralize their vowels (think of the sounds in *weasel* and *whee*), whereas men tend to centralize them (think of *rough* and *ugh*). Men are more likely to speak "ungrammatically" than women are. As mentioned previously, men and women also show differences in their sports and color terminologies. Men typically know more sports terms, make more distinctions among them (e.g., *runs* versus *points*), and try to use the terms more precisely than women do. Correspondingly, women use more color terms and attempt to use them more specifically than men do. To make this point when I lecture, I bring an off-purple shirt to class. Holding it up, I first ask women to say aloud what color the shirt is. The women rarely answer with a uniform voice, as they try to distinguish the actual shade (mauve, lilac, lavender, wisteria, or some other purplish hue). I then ask the men, who consistently answer as one, "PURPLE." Rare is the man who on the spur of the moment can imagine the difference between fuchsia and magenta or grape and aubergine.

No language is a uniform system in which everyone talks just like everyone else. The field of **sociolinguistics** investigates relationships between social and linguistic variation (Romaine 2000; Spencer 2010; Trudgill 2000). How do different speakers use a given language? How do linguistic features correlate with social diversity and stratification, including class, ethnic, and gender differences (McConnell-Ginet 2010; Tannen 1990; Tannen, ed. 1993)? How is language used to express, reinforce, or resist power (Geis 1987; G. Lakoff 2008; Mooney 2011; Trudgill 2010)?

Sociolinguists focus on features that vary systematically with social position and situation. To study variation, sociolinguists must observe, define, and measure variable use of language in real-world situations. To show that linguistic features correlate with social, economic, and political differences, the social attributes of speakers also must be measured and related to speech (Fasold and Connor-Linton 2006; Labov 1972*a*, 2006).

Variation within a language at a given time is historical change in progress. The same forces that, working gradually, have produced large-scale linguistic change over the centuries are still at work today. Linguistic change doesn't occur in a vacuum but in society. When new ways of speaking are associated with social factors, they are imitated, and they spread (see Blommaert 2010). In this way, a language changes.

Linguistic Diversity within Nations

As an illustration of the linguistic variation encountered in all nations, consider the contemporary United States. Ethnic diversity is revealed by the fact that millions of Americans learn first languages other than English. Spanish is the most common. Most of those people eventually become bilinguals, adding English as a second language. In many multilingual (including colonized) nations, people use two languages on different occasions—one in the home, for example, and the other on the job or in public.

Ethnic and linguistic
diversity characterize
many nations, especially
in big cities, as
illustrated by this
California sign written
in seven languages:
Chinese, Korean,
Spanish, Vietnamese,
Japanese, Tagalog, and
English.

Whether bilingual or not, we all vary our speech in different contexts; we engage in **style shifts.** In certain parts of Europe, people regularly switch dialects. This phenomenon, known as **diglossia,** applies to "high" and "low" variants of the same language, for example, in German and Flemish (spoken in Belgium). People employ the high variant at universities and in writing, professions, and the mass media. They use the low variant for ordinary conversation with family members and friends. (See Tannen [2005] and Tannen, Kendall, and Gordon [2007] for analysis of communication among American families and friends.)

Just as social situations influence our speech, so do geographical, cultural, and socioeconomic differences. Many dialects coexist in the United States with Standard (American) English (SE). SE itself is a dialect that differs, say, from "BBC English," which is the preferred dialect in Great Britain. Different dialects are equally effective as systems of communication, which is language's main job. Our tendency to think of particular dialects as cruder or more sophisticated than others is a social rather than a linguistic judgment. We rank certain speech patterns as better or worse because we recognize that they are used by groups that we also rank. People who say *dese, dem,* and *dere* instead of *these, them,* and *there* communicate perfectly well with anyone who recognizes that the *d* sound systematically replaces the *th* sound in their speech. However, this form of speech has become an indicator of low social rank. We call it, like the use of *ain't,* "uneducated speech." The use of *dem, dese,* and *dere* is one of many phonological differences that Americans recognize and look down on (see Labov 2012).

Gender Speech Contrasts

Comparing men and women, there are differences in phonology, grammar, and vocabulary and in the body stances and movements that accompany speech (Eckert and McConnell-Ginet 2013; R. Lakoff 2004; Tannen 1990). In public contexts, Japanese women tend to adopt an artificially high voice, for the sake of politeness, according to their traditional culture. Women tend to be more careful about uneducated speech. This trend shows up in both the United States and England. Men may adopt working-class speech because they associate it with masculinity. Perhaps women pay more attention to the media, in which standard dialects are employed.

According to Robin Lakoff (2004), the use of certain types of words and expressions has been associated with women's traditional lesser power in American society (see also Romaine 1999; Tannen 1990; Tannen, ed. 1993). For example, *Oh dear, Oh fudge,* and *Goodness!* are less forceful than *Hell* and *Damn.* Watch the lips of a disgruntled athlete in a televised competition, such as a football game. What's the likelihood he's saying "Phooey on you"? Women are more likely to use such adjectives as *adorable, charming, sweet, cute, lovely,* and *divine* than men are.

Differences in the linguistic strategies and behavior of men and women are examined in several books by the well-known sociolinguist Deborah Tannen (1990; ed. 1993). Tannen uses the terms *rapport* and *report* to contrast women's and men's overall linguistic styles. Women, says Tannen, typically use language and the body movements that accompany it to build rapport, social connections with others. Men, on the other hand, tend to make reports, reciting information to establish a place for themselves in a hierarchy, as they also attempt to determine the relative ranks of their conversation mates.

Stratification and Symbolic Domination

We use and evaluate speech in the context of *extralinguistic* forces—social, political, and economic. Mainstream Americans evaluate the speech of low-status groups negatively, calling it "uneducated." This is not because these ways of speaking are bad in themselves but because they have come to symbolize low status. Consider variation in the pronunciation of *r.* In some parts of the United States, *r* is regularly pronounced, and in other (*r*less) areas it is not. Originally, American *r*less speech was modeled on the fashionable speech of England. Because of its prestige, *r*lessness was adopted in many areas and continues as the norm around Boston and in the South.

New Yorkers sought prestige by dropping their *r*'s in the 19th century, after having pronounced them in the 18th. However, contemporary New Yorkers are going back to the 18th-century pattern of pronouncing *r*'s. What matters, and what governs linguistic change, is not the reverberation of a strong midwestern *r* but *social* evaluation, whether *r*'s happen to be "in" or "out."

Studies of *r* pronunciation in New York City have clarified the mechanisms of phonological change. William Labov (1972*b*) focused on whether *r* was pronounced after vowels in such words as *car, floor, card,* and *fourth.* To get data on how this linguistic variation correlated with social class, he used a series of rapid encounters with employees in three New York City department stores, each of whose prices and locations attracted a different socioeconomic group. Saks Fifth Avenue (68 encounters) catered to the upper middle class, Macy's (125) attracted middle-class shoppers, and S. Klein's (71) had predominantly lower-middle-class and working-class customers. The class origins of store personnel reflected those of their customers.

Having already determined that a certain department was on the fourth floor, Labov approached ground-floor salespeople and asked where that department was. After the salesperson had answered, "Fourth floor," Labov repeated his "Where?" in order to get a second response. The second reply was more formal and emphatic, the salesperson presumably thinking that Labov hadn't heard or understood the first answer. For each salesperson, therefore, Labov had two samples of /r/ pronunciation in two words.

Labov calculated the percentages of workers who pronounced /r/ at least once during the interview. These were 62 percent at Saks, 51 percent at Macy's, but only 20 percent at S. Klein's. He also found that personnel on upper floors, where he asked, "What floor is this?" (and where more expensive items were sold), pronounced *r* more often than ground-floor salespeople did (see also Labov 2006).

In Labov's study, *r* pronunciation was clearly associated with prestige. Certainly the job interviewers who had hired the salespeople never counted *r*'s before offering employment. However, they did use speech evaluations to make judgments about how effective certain people would be in selling particular kinds of merchandise. In other words, they practiced sociolinguistic discrimination, using linguistic features in deciding who got certain jobs.

Our speech habits help determine our access to employment and other material resources. Because of this, "proper language" itself becomes a strategic resource—and a path to wealth, prestige, and power (Gal 1989; Thomas and Wareing, eds. 2004). Illustrating this, many ethnographers have described the importance of verbal skill and oratory in politics (Beeman 1986; Brenneis 1988; Geis 1987; G. Lakoff 2008). Ronald Reagan, known as a "great communicator," dominated American society in the 1980s as a two-term president. Another twice-elected president, Bill Clinton, despite his southern accent, was known for his verbal skills in certain contexts (e.g., televised debates and town-hall meetings). Communications flaws may have helped doom the presidencies of Gerald Ford, Jimmy Carter, and George Bush the elder. Does his use of language affect your perception of the current president of the United States?

The French anthropologist Pierre Bourdieu views linguistic practices as *symbolic capital* that properly trained people may convert into economic and social capital. The value of a dialect—its standing in a "linguistic market"—depends on the extent to which it provides access to desired positions in the labor market. In turn, this reflects its legitimation by formal institutions—educational institutions, state, church, and prestige media. Even people who don't use the prestige dialect accept its authority and correctness, its "symbolic domination" (Bourdieu 1982, 1984; Labov 2012). Thus, linguistic forms, which lack power in themselves, take on the power of the groups they symbolize. The education system, however (defending its own worth), denies linguistic relativity. It misrepresents prestige speech as being inherently better. The linguistic insecurity often felt by lower-class and minority speakers is a result of this symbolic domination.

*My dream was to became a shool teacher.
Mrs Stone is rich.
I have talents but not opportunity.
I ~~have~~ am used to standing behind
Mrs Stone.
I have been a servant for 40 years.
Vickie Figueroa.*

Proper language is a strategic resource, correlated with wealth, prestige, and power. How is linguistic (and social) stratification illustrated in this photo, including the handwritten comments below it?

Black English Vernacular (BEV)

The sociolinguist William Labov and several associates, both White and Black, have conducted detailed studies of what they call **Black English Vernacular (BEV).** (*Vernacular* means ordinary, casual speech.) BEV is the "relatively uniform dialect spoken by the majority of black youth in most parts of the United States today, especially in the inner city areas of New York, Boston, Detroit, Philadelphia, Washington, Cleveland, . . . and other urban centers. It is also spoken in most rural areas and used in the casual, intimate speech of many adults" (Labov 1972a, p. xiii). This does not imply that all, or even most, African Americans speak BEV.

BEV is a complex linguistic system with its own rules, which linguists have described. Consider some of the phonological and grammatical differences between BEV and SE. One phonological difference is that BEV speakers are less likely to pronounce *r* than SE speakers are. Actually, many SE speakers don't pronounce *r*'s that come right before a consonant (ca*r*d) or at the end of a word (ca*r*). But SE speakers usually do pronounce an *r* that comes right before a vowel, either at the end of a word (fou*r* o'clock)

U.S. Vice President Biden looks on as President Obama speaks on March 28, 2013. Surrounded by families of victims of the Newtown, Connecticut school shooting, Obama pressed the Senate to pass legislation to curb gun violence. How would you evaluate the way President Obama speaks from a sociolinguistic perspective?

or within a word (Ca*r*ol). BEV speakers, by contrast, are much more likely to omit such intervocalic (between vowels) *r*'s. The result is that speakers of the two dialects have different *homonyms* (words that sound the same but have different meanings). BEV speakers who don't pronounce intervocalic *r*'s have the following homonyms: Carol/Cal; Paris/pass.

Observing different phonological rules, BEV speakers pronounce certain words differently than SE speakers do. Particularly in the elementary school context, the homonyms of BEV-speaking students typically differ from those of their SE-speaking teachers. To evaluate reading accuracy, teachers should determine whether students are recognizing the different meanings of such BEV homonyms as *passed, past,* and *pass.* Teachers need to make sure students understand what they are reading, which is probably more important than whether they are pronouncing words correctly according to the SE norm.

Phonological rules may lead BEV speakers to omit *-ed* as a past-tense marker and *-s* as a marker of plurality. However, other speech contexts demonstrate that BEV speakers do understand the difference between past and present verbs, and between singular and plural nouns. Confirming this are irregular verbs (e.g., *tell, told*) and irregular plurals (e.g., *child, children*), in which BEV works the same as SE.

SE is not superior to BEV as a linguistic system, but it does happen to be the prestige dialect—the one used in the mass media, in writing, and in most public and professional contexts. SE is the dialect that has the most "symbolic capital." In areas of Germany where there is diglossia, speakers of Plattdeusch (Low German) learn the High German dialect to communicate appropriately in the national context. Similarly, upwardly mobile BEV-speaking students learn SE.

Historical Linguistics

Sociolinguists study contemporary variation in speech, which is language change in progress. **Historical linguistics** deals with longer-term change. Historical linguists can reconstruct many features of past languages by studying contemporary **daughter languages.** These are languages that descend from the same parent language and that have been changing separately for hundreds or even thousands of years. We call the original language from which they diverge the **protolanguage.** Romance languages such as French and Spanish, for example, are daughter languages of Latin, their common protolanguage. German, English, Dutch, and the Scandinavian languages are daughter languages of proto-Germanic. The Romance languages and the Germanic languages all belong to the Indo-European language family. Their common protolanguage is called Proto-Indo-European, PIE. Historical linguists classify languages according to their degree of relationship (see Figure 4.2).

Language changes over time. It evolves—varies, spreads, and divides into **subgroups** (languages within a taxonomy of related languages that are most closely related). Dialects of a single parent language become distinct daughter languages, especially if they are isolated from one another. Some of them split, and new "granddaughter" languages develop. If people remain in the ancestral homeland, their speech patterns also change. The evolving speech in the ancestral homeland should be considered a daughter language like the others.

A close relationship between languages doesn't necessarily mean that their speakers are closely related biologically or culturally, because people can adopt new languages. In the equatorial forests of Africa, "pygmy" hunters have discarded their ancestral languages and now speak those of the cultivators who have migrated to the area. Immigrants to the United States spoke many different languages on arrival, but their descendants now speak fluent English.

Knowledge of linguistic relationships often is valuable to anthropologists interested in history, particularly events during the past 5,000 years. Cultural features may (or may not) correlate with the distribution of language families. Groups that speak related languages may (or may not) be more culturally similar to each other than they are to groups whose speech derives from different linguistic ancestors. Of course, cultural similarities aren't limited to speakers of related languages. Even groups whose members speak unrelated languages have contact through trade, intermarriage, and warfare. Ideas and inventions diffuse widely among human groups. Many items of vocabulary in contemporary English, particularly food items such as "beef" and "pork," come from French. Even without written documentation of France's influence after the Norman Conquest of England in 1066, linguistic evidence in contemporary English would reveal a long period of important firsthand contact with France. Similarly, linguistic evidence may

FIGURE 4.2   PIE Family Tree

Main languages and subgroups of the Indo-European language stock, showing approximate time to their divergence.

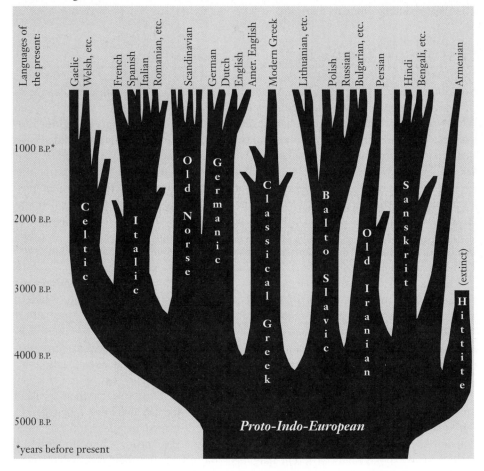

confirm cultural contact and borrowing when written history is lacking. By considering which words have been borrowed, we also can make inferences about the nature of the contact.

Language Loss

One aspect of linguistic history is language loss. When languages disappear, cultural diversity is reduced as well. According to linguist K. David Harrison, "When we lose a language, we lose centuries of thinking about time, seasons, sea creatures, reindeer, edible flowers, mathematics, landscapes, myths, music, the unknown and the everyday" (quoted in Maugh 2007). Harrison's book *When Languages Die* (2007) notes that an indigenous language goes extinct every two weeks, as its last speakers die. The world's linguistic diversity has been cut in half (measured by number of distinct languages) in

In India's remote Arunachal Pradesh, linguist Gregory Anderson, director of the Living Tongues Institute for Endangered Languages, makes one of the first ever recordings of Koro language, whose existence was announced in 2010.

the past 500 years, and half of the remaining languages are predicted to disappear during this century. Colonial languages (e.g., English, Spanish, Portuguese, French, Dutch, Russian) have expanded at the expense of indigenous ones. Of approximately 7,000 remaining languages, about 20 percent are endangered, compared with 18 percent of mammals, 8 percent of plants, and 5 percent of birds (Harrison 2010; Maugh 2007).

Harrison, who teaches at Swarthmore College, is director of research for the Living Tongues Institute for Endangered Languages (http://www.livingtongues.org), which works to maintain, preserve, and revitalize endangered languages through multimedia documentation projects. Researchers from the institute use digital audio and video equipment to record the last speakers of the most endangered languages. *National Geographic*'s Enduring Voices Project (http://travel.nationalgeographic.com/travel/enduring-voices/) strives to preserve endangered languages by identifying the geographic areas with unique, poorly understood, or threatened languages and by documenting those languages and cultures.

The website shows various language hot spots where the endangerment rate ranges from low to severe. The rate is high in an area encompassing Oklahoma, Texas, and New Mexico, where 40 Native American languages are at risk. The top hot spot is northern Australia, where 153 Aboriginal languages are endangered (Maugh 2007). Other hot spots are in central South America, the Pacific Northwest of North America, and eastern Siberia. In all these areas indigenous tongues have yielded, either voluntarily or through coercion, to a colonial language.

Anthropology Today   *I Wish They All Could Be California Vowels*

Is there a "California accent"? Popular stereotypes of how Californians talk reflect exposure to media images of White, blonde, valley girls and White, blond surfers, who say things like "dude," "gnarly," "Like, totally!" and "Gag me with a spoon!" Such stereotypes have some accuracy, as we'll see. Just as striking, however, is the linguistic diversity that also marks contemporary California.

To document this diversity, Professor Penelope Eckert, a sociolinguist at Stanford University, and her graduate students are engaged in an ongoing, multiyear research project called Voices of California (see http://www.stanford.edu/dept/linguistics/VoCal/). Eckert's team of 10–15 researchers visits a new site each fall, spending about 10 days interviewing residents who grew up in the area. Recently, their focus has been on inland California, which has been less studied than have the main coastal cities. In previous years, the group visited Merced and Redding; in 2012, they focused on Bakersfield. The researchers always test certain words that elicit specific pronunciations. These words include *wash*, sometimes pronounced "warsh," *greasy* ("greezy"), and *pin* and *pen*, which some people pronounce the same. Interviews in Merced and Shasta Counties have revealed ways that Depression-era migrants from Oklahoma's Dust Bowl left their mark on California speech, such as their pronunciation of *wash* and *greasy* (see King 2012).

We see, then, that one factor in determining how people speak is where their ancestors came from. Another factor is their own attitudes and feelings about the people around them and about the outside world. For example, in California's Central Valley, which is economically depressed, young people must choose whether to stay put or to move elsewhere, seeking work. When people are, and want to stay, involved in their home community, they tend to talk like locals. A desire not to be perceived as being from a particular place also affects how people talk (King 2012).

I know this feeling well, having abandoned my original southern accent when I was an adolescent. In fact, my own speech shift wasn't totally voluntary: as mentioned in the text, I was placed in a speech class when I moved from Atlanta to New York City at the age of 13. The same thing happened to my college roommate, from Baton Rouge, Louisiana, when he enrolled at Columbia University in New York City. By then, my own speech had become sufficiently accent free to avoid further speech indoctrination.

In addition to regional diversity, the speech of Californians also reflects ethnic contrasts. Non-Hispanic Whites now represent under 40 percent of the state's total population, while Latinos (Hispanics) constitute 38 percent. California also has a large and diverse Asian American population and a sizeable group of African Americans.

Representing California's largest minority, as well as its earliest nonindigenous settlers, Chicanos (Mexican Americans) display interesting speech patterns. California's Mexican-derived populations can claim the longest continuous (nonindigenous) linguistic history in the state, including Spanish/English bilingualism and the source of most important place names. So strong is the Spanish heritage that Spanish-like vowels even influence the way English is spoken by Hispanics who learn English as their first or native language. For example, among Chicano speakers in northern California the vowel in the second syllable of *nothing* has come to resemble the Spanish "ee" sound. Not all innovations in Chicano English come from Spanish. One widespread speech innovation in Los Angeles has been the lowering of the vowel in the first syllable of *elevator, so that it rhymes with the first syllable of alligator.* That shift owes nothing to Spanish (see Eckert and Mendoza-Denton 2002).

Despite the well-documented diversity in California speech, linguists have detected trends toward uniformity as well, particularly among coastal Whites. Since the 1940s, a distinctive "California accent" has been developing, and some of its features were indeed highlighted in Moon Unit Zappa's 1982 recording of "Valley Girl."

The accent is most evident in vowels, as we see in the following examples. First, the vowels in *hock* and *hawk,* or *cot* and *caught,* are pronounced the same, so that *awesome* rhymes with *possum.* Second, the vowel sound in *boot* and *dude* has shifted and now is pronounced as in *pure*

or *cute* (thus, *boot* becomes "beaut," and *dude* becomes "dewed," rather than "dood"). Third, the vowel sound in *but* and *cut* is shifting, so that those words sound more like *bet* and *ket.* Finally, *black* is being pronounced more like *block*; and *bet*, like *bat* (see Eckert and Mendoza-Denton 2002).

Such coordinated phonological changes are known as chain shifts. The most extreme versions of these chain-shifted vowel sounds are found in the speech of young White Californians. Young people tend to be leaders in speech innovations, which is why linguists spend a lot of time studying them. California's communities bring together adolescents from varied backgrounds. Their linguistic styles, like their clothing and behavioral styles, influence one another. Hostility may cause people to differentiate and diversify their styles, while curiosity or admiration may cause people to copy, or adopt elements from, other styles. Whose styles, linguistic or otherwise, might you have copied—or avoided?

Summary

1. Wild primates use call systems to communicate. Environmental stimuli trigger calls, which cannot be combined when multiple stimuli are present. Contrasts between language and call systems include displacement, productivity, and cultural transmission. Over time, our ancestral call systems grew too complex for genetic transmission, and hominin communication began to rely on learning. Humans still use nonverbal communication, such as facial expressions, gestures, and body stances and movements. But language is the main system humans use to communicate. Chimps and gorillas can understand and manipulate nonverbal symbols based on language.

2. No language uses all the sounds the human vocal tract can make. Phonology—the study of speech sounds—focuses on sound contrasts (phonemes) that distinguish meaning. The grammars and lexicons of particular languages can lead their speakers to perceive and think in certain ways.

3. Linguistic anthropologists share anthropology's general interest in diversity in time and space. Sociolinguistics investigates relationships between social and linguistic variation by focusing on the actual use of language. Only when features of speech acquire social meaning are they imitated. If they are valued, they will spread. People vary their speech, shifting styles, dialects, and languages.

4. As linguistic systems, all languages and dialects are equally complex, rule-governed, and effective for communication. However, speech is used, is evaluated, and changes in the context of political, economic, and social forces. Often the linguistic traits of a low-status group are negatively evaluated. This devaluation is not because of linguistic features per se. Rather, it reflects the association of such features with low social status. One dialect, supported by the dominant institutions of the state, exercises symbolic domination over the others.

5. Historical linguistics is useful for anthropologists interested in historical relationships among populations. Cultural similarities and differences often correlate with linguistic ones. Linguistic clues can suggest past contacts between cultures. Related languages—members of the same language family—descend from an original protolanguage. Relationships between languages don't necessarily mean there are biological ties between their speakers, because people can learn new languages.

6. One aspect of linguistic history is language loss. The world's linguistic diversity has been cut in half in the past 500 years, and half of the remaining 7,000 languages are predicted to disappear during this century.

Key Terms

Black English
  Vernacular
  (BEV), *75*
call systems, *59*
cultural
  transmission, *61*
daughter
  languages, *77*
descriptive
  linguistics, *64*
diglossia, *72*

displacement, *62*
focal
  vocabulary, *69*
historical
  linguistics, *77*
kinesics, *63*
lexicon, *64*
morphology, *64*
phoneme, *65*
phonemics, *66*
phonetics, *66*

phonology, *64*
productivity, *61*
protolanguage, *77*
Sapir-Whorf
  hypothesis, *67*
semantics, *70*
sociolinguistics,
  71
style shifts, *72*
subgroups, *77*
syntax, *64*

Chapter 5

Making a Living

In today's globalizing world, communities and societies are being incorporated, at an accelerating rate, into larger systems. The first major acceleration in the growth of human social systems can be traced back to around 12,000–10,000 years ago, when humans started intervening in the reproductive cycles of plants and animals. **Food production** refers to human control over the reproduction of plants and animals, and it contrasts with the foraging economies that preceded it and that still persist in some parts of the world. To make their living, foragers hunt, gather, and collect what nature has to offer. Foragers may harvest, but they don't plant. They may hunt animals, but (except for the dog) they don't domesticate them. Only food producers systematically select and breed for desirable traits in plants and animals. With the advent of food production, which includes plant cultivation and animal domestication, people, rather than nature, become selective agents. Human selection replaces natural selection as food collectors become food producers.

The origin and spread of food production accelerated human population growth and led to the formation of larger and more powerful social and political systems. The pace of cultural transformation increased enormously. This chapter provides a framework for understanding a variety of human adaptive strategies and economic systems.

Adaptive Strategies

The anthropologist Yehudi Cohen (1974) used the term *adaptive strategy* to describe a society's main system of economic production. Cohen argued that the most important reason for similarities between two (or more) unrelated societies is their possession of a similar adaptive strategy. In other words, similar economic causes have similar socio-cultural effects. For example, there are clear similarities among societies that have a foraging (hunting and gathering) strategy. Cohen developed a typology of societies based on correlations between their economies and their social features. His typology includes these five adaptive strategies: foraging, horticulture, agriculture, pastoralism, and industrialism. Industrialism is the focus of the last two chapters of this book. The present chapter focuses on the first four adaptive strategies, which are characteristic of nonindustrial societies.

Foraging

Until about 12,000 years ago all humans were foragers (see Barnard 2004). However, environmental differences did create substantial contrasts among the world's foragers. Some, like the people who lived in Europe during the Ice Ages, were big-game hunters. Today, hunters in the Arctic still focus on large animals; they have much less vegetation and variety in their diets than do tropical foragers. Moving from colder to hotter areas, the number of species increases. The tropics contain tremendous biodiversity, and tropical foragers typically hunt and gather a wide range of plant and animal species. The same may be true in temperate areas. For example, on the North Pacific Coast of North America, foragers could draw on varied sea, river, and land species, such as salmon and other fish, sea mammals, berries, and mountain goats. Despite differences caused by such environmental variation, all foraging economies have shared one essential feature: People rely on nature to make their living. They don't grow crops or breed and tend animals.

Animal domestication (initially of sheep and goats) and plant cultivation (of wheat and barley) began 12,000 to 10,000 years ago in the Middle East. Cultivation based on different crops, such as corn (maize), manioc (cassava), and potatoes, arose independently in the Americas. In both hemispheres most societies eventually turned from foraging to food production. Today most foragers have at least some dependence on food production or on food producers (Kent 1992, 2002).

The foraging way of life survived into modern times in certain forests, deserts, islands, and very cold areas—places where cultivation was not practicable with simple technology (see Lee and Daly 1999). In many areas, foragers knew about food production but never adopted it because their own economies provided a perfectly satisfactory lifestyle and an adequate and nutritious diet. In some places, people reverted to foraging after trying food production and abandoning it.

All contemporary foragers live in nation-states and are influenced by national policies. Typically, they are in contact with food-producing neighbors as well as with missionaries and other outsiders. We should not view contemporary foragers as isolated or pristine survivors of the Stone Age. Modern foragers are influenced by national and international policies and political and economic events in the world system.

Geographic Distribution of Foragers

In Africa we can identify two broad belts of contemporary or recent foraging. One is the Kalahari Desert of southern Africa. This is the home of the San ("Bushmen"), who include the Ju/'hoansi (see Kent 1996; Lee 2003). The other main African foraging area is the equatorial forest of central and eastern Africa, home of the Mbuti, Efe, and other "pygmies" (Bailey et al. 1989; Turnbull 1965).

People still do, or until recently did, subsistence foraging in certain remote forests in Madagascar, in South and Southeast Asia, in Malaysia, in the Philippines, and on certain islands off the Indian coast. Some of the best-known recent foragers are the aborigines of Australia. Those Native Australians lived on their island continent for perhaps 50,000 years without developing food production.

The Western Hemisphere also had recent foragers. The Eskimos, or Inuit, of Alaska and Canada are well-known hunters. These (and other) northern foragers now use modern technology, including rifles and snowmobiles, in their subsistence activities (Pelto 1973). The native populations of California, Oregon, Washington, and British Columbia all were foragers, as were those of inland subarctic Canada and the Great Lakes. For many Native Americans, fishing, hunting, and gathering remain important subsistence (and sometimes commercial) activities.

Coastal foragers also lived near the southern tip of South America, in Patagonia. On the grassy plains of Argentina, southern Brazil, Uruguay, and Paraguay, there were other hunter-gatherers. The contemporary Aché of Paraguay usually are called "hunter-gatherers," although they now get just a third of their livelihood from foraging. The Aché also grow crops, have domesticated animals, and live in or near mission posts, where they receive food from missionaries (Hawkes, O'Connell, and Hill 1982; Hill et al. 1987).

Jana Fortier (2009) summarizes key attributes of foragers in South Asia, which today is home to more full- and part-time hunter-gatherers than any other world area. In India, Nepal, and Sri Lanka, about 40 societies and an estimated 150,000 people continue to derive their subsistence from full- or part-time foraging. Hill Kharias and Yanadis are the largest contemporary South Asian (SA) foraging populations, with about 20,000 members each. Several other ethnic groups are highly endangered, with fewer than 350 members still doing subsistence foraging.

Surviving SA foraging societies are those whose members, despite having lost many of their natural resources to deforestation and spreading farming populations, have been unwilling to adopt food cultivation and its cultural correlates. These hunter-gatherers share features with other foragers worldwide: small social groups, mobile settlement patterns, sharing of resources, immediate food consumption, egalitarianism, and decision making by mutual consent (Fortier 2009).

As is true elsewhere, specific foraging techniques reflect variations in environment and resource distribution. Hill and mountain SA foragers favor focused hunting of medium-sized prey (langur monkey, macaque, porcupine). Other groups pursue several small species or practice broad-spectrum foraging of bats, porcupines, and deer. Larger groups use communal hunting techniques, such as spreading nets over large fig trees to entangle sleeping bats. Some South Indian foragers focus on such wild plant resources as yams, palms, and taro, in addition to 100+ locally available plants. Harvesting honey and beeswax has been prominent in many SA foraging societies (Fortier 2009).

Their members cherish their identities as people who forage for a living in biologically rich and diverse environments. They stress their need for continued access to rich forest resources to continue their lifestyles, yet many have been evicted from their traditional habitats. Their best chances for cultural survival depend on national governments that maintain healthy forests, allow foragers access to their traditional resources, and foster cultural survival rather than assimilation (Fortier 2009).

Throughout the world, foraging survived in environments that posed major obstacles to food production. The difficulties of cultivating at the North Pole are obvious. In southern Africa the Dobe Ju/'hoansi San area studied by Richard Lee and others is surrounded by a waterless belt 43 to 124 miles (70 to 200 kilometers) in breadth (Solway and Lee 1990).

Environmental obstacles to food production aren't the only reason foragers survived. Their niches had one thing in common—their marginality. Their environments were not of immediate interest to farmers, herders, or colonialists. See Figure 5.1 for a partial distribution of recent hunter-gatherers.

As the modern world system spreads, the number of foragers continues to decline. Each year more and more foragers come under the control of nation-states and are influenced by forces of globalization. As described by Motseta (2006), for example, between 1997 and 2002, the government of Botswana in southern Africa relocated about 3,000 Basarwa San Bushmen outside their ancestral territory, which was converted into a reserve for wildlife protection. Botswana's High Court eventually ruled that the Basarwa

FIGURE 5.1 Locations of Some Recent Hunter-Gatherers

Source: Robert L. Kelly, *The Foraging Spectrum: Diversity in Hunter-Gatherer Lifeways*, fig. 1.1. Copyright © 2007 by Eliot Werner Publications, Inc. Reprinted by permission of the publisher.

had been wrongly evicted from the "Central Kalahari Game Reserve" and issued a court order allowing them to return, but under conditions likely to prevent most of them from doing so. Only the 189 people who actually filed the lawsuit were granted automatic right of return with their children, compared with some 2,000 Basarwa wishing to go back. The others would have to apply for special permits. Returning Basarwa would be allowed to build only temporary structures and to use enough water for subsistence needs. Water would be a major obstacle, since the government shut the main well in 2002. Furthermore, anyone wishing to hunt would have to apply for a permit. So goes the foraging way of life in today's world.

Correlates of Foraging

Typologies, such as Cohen's adaptive strategies, are useful because they suggest **correlations**—that is, associations or covariations between two or more variables. (Correlated variables are factors that are linked and interrelated, such as food intake and body weight, such that when one increases or decreases, the other changes as well.) Ethnographic studies in hundreds of societies have revealed many correlations between the economy and social life. Associated (correlated) with each adaptive strategy is a bundle of particular sociocultural features. Correlations, however, rarely are perfect. Some foragers lack cultural features usually associated with foraging, and some of those features are found in groups with other adaptive strategies.

What, then, are some correlates of foraging? People who subsisted by hunting and gathering often, but not always, lived in band-organized societies. Their basic social unit, the **band,** was a small group of fewer than a hundred people, all related by kinship or marriage. Among some foragers, band size stayed about the same year-round. In others, the band split up for part of the year. Families left to gather resources that were better exploited by just a few people. Later, they regrouped for cooperative work and ceremonies.

Typical characteristics of the foraging life are flexibility and mobility. In many San groups, as among the Mbuti of Congo, people shifted band membership several times in a lifetime. One might be born, for example, in a band in which one's mother had kin. Later, one's family might move to a band in which the father had relatives. Because bands were exogamous (people married outside their own band), one's parents came from two different bands, and one's grandparents might have come from four. People could join any band to which they had kin or marital links. A couple could live in, or shift between, the husband's and the wife's band.

Many foraging societies make distinctions based on age. Old people may receive respect as guardians of myths, legends, stories, and traditions. Younger people may value the elders' special knowledge of ritual and practical matters. In general, foraging societies tend to be *egalitarian*, with only minor contrasts in prestige and no significant contrasts in wealth and power.

When considering issues of "human nature," we should remember that the egalitarian society associated with the foraging strategy of adaptation was a basic form of human social life for most of our history. Food production has existed less than 1 percent of the time *Homo* has spent on Earth. However, it has produced huge social differences. We now consider the main economic features of food-producing strategies.

Adaptive Strategies Based on Food Production

In Cohen's typology, the three adaptive strategies based on food production in nonindustrial societies are horticulture, agriculture, and pastoralism. With horticulture and agriculture, plant cultivation is the mainstay of the economy, while with pastoralism, herding is key. All three strategies originated in nonindustrial societies, although they may persist as ways of making a living even after some degree of industrialization reaches the nation-states that include them. In fully industrial societies, such as the United States and Canada, most cultivation has become large-scale, commercial, mechanized, agrochemical-dependent farming. Rather than simple pastoralism, industrial societies use technologically sophisticated systems of ranch and livestock management. These industrial societies, and their global context, will be the focus of the last two chapters of this book. This chapter's focus is on nonindustrial strategies of adaptation.

Just as they do in the United States and Canada, people in nonindustrial societies carry out a variety of economic activities. In Cohen's typology, each adaptive strategy refers to the main economic activity. Pastoralists (herders), for example, consume milk, butter, blood, and meat from their animals as mainstays of their diet. However, they also add grain to their diet by doing some cultivating or by trading with neighbors.

Horticulture

The two types of plant cultivation found in nonindustrial societies are **horticulture** (nonintensive, shifting cultivation) and **agriculture** (intensive, continuous cultivation). Both differ from the commercially oriented farming systems of industrial nations, which use large land areas and rely on machinery and petrochemicals.

Horticulturalists use simple tools such as hoes and digging sticks to grow their crops. Horticulturalists preserve their ecosystems by allowing their fields to lie fallow for varying lengths of time. Often horticulturalists employ *slash-and-burn* techniques; they clear land by cutting down (slashing) and burning forest or bush or by setting fire to the grass covering the plot. The vegetation is broken down, pests are killed, and the ashes remain to fertilize the soil. Crops then are sown, tended, and harvested. Use of the plot is not continuous. Often it is cultivated only for a year or two.

When horticulturalists abandon a plot, they clear another piece of land, and the original plot reverts to forest. After several years of fallowing, the cultivator returns to farm the original plot again. Because the relationship between people and their plots is not permanent, horticulture also is called *shifting cultivation*. Shifting cultivation does not mean that whole villages must move when plots are abandoned. Among the Kuikuru of the South American tropical forest, one village of 150 people remained in the same place for 90 years (Carneiro 1956). Kuikuru houses were large and well made. Because the work involved in building their houses was substantial, the Kuikuru preferred to walk farther to their fields than to construct a new village. They shifted their plots rather than their settlements. On the other hand, horticulturalists in the montaña (Andean foothills) of Peru lived in small villages of about 30 people (Carneiro 1961/1968). Their houses were small and simple. After a few years in one place, these people built new

In slash-and-burn cultivation, the land is cleared by cutting down (slashing) and burning trees and bush. Here, a worker uses the slash-and-burn method to clear sugarcane in Rio Formosa, Pernambuco State, Brazil.

villages near virgin land. Because their houses were so simple, they preferred rebuilding to walking even a half mile to their fields.

Agriculture

The greater labor demands associated with agriculture, as compared with horticulture, reflect its use of domesticated animals, irrigation, or terracing.

Domesticated Animals

Many agriculturists use animals as means of production—for transport, as cultivating machines, and for their manure. Asian farmers typically incorporate cattle and/or water buffalo into their agricultural economies. Those rice farmers may use cattle to trample pre-tilled flooded fields, thus mixing soil and water, before transplanting. Many agriculturists attach animals to plows and harrows for field preparation before planting or transplanting. Also, agriculturists typically collect manure from their animals, using it to fertilize their plots, thus increasing yields. Animals are attached to carts for transport and to implements of cultivation.

Irrigation

While horticulturalists must await the rainy season, agriculturists can schedule their planting in advance because they control water. Like other irrigation experts in the Philippines, the Ifugao water their fields with canals from rivers, streams, springs, and ponds. Irrigation makes it possible to cultivate a plot year after year. Irrigation enriches the soil because the irrigated field is a unique ecosystem with several species of plants and animals, many of them minute organisms, whose wastes fertilize the land.

Agriculture requires longer work hours than horticulture does and uses land intensively and continuously. Labor demands associated with agriculture reflect its use of domesticated animals, irrigation, and terracing. Shown here, rice farmers in Saramsa, Sikkim, India, work in flooded terraces.

An irrigated field is a capital investment that usually increases in value. It takes time for a field to start yielding; it reaches full productivity only after several years of cultivation. The Ifugao, like other irrigators, have farmed the same fields for generations. In some agricultural areas, including the Middle East, however, salts carried in the irrigation water can make fields unusable after 50 or 60 years.

Terracing

Terracing is another agricultural technique the Ifugao have mastered. Their homeland has small valleys separated by steep hillsides. Because the population is dense, people need to farm the hills. However, if they simply planted on the steep hillsides, fertile soil and crops would be washed away during the rainy season. To prevent this, the Ifugao cut into the hillside and build stage after stage of terraced fields rising above the valley floor. Springs located above the terraces supply their irrigation water. The labor necessary to build and maintain a system of terraces is great. Terrace walls crumble each year and must be partially rebuilt. The canals that bring water down through the terraces also demand attention.

Costs and Benefits of Agriculture

Agriculture requires human labor to build and maintain irrigation systems, terraces, and other works. People must feed, water, and care for their animals. But agricultural land can yield one or two crops annually for years, or even generations. An agricultural field does not necessarily produce a higher single-year yield than does a horticultural plot.

The first crop grown by horticulturalists on long-idle land may be larger than that from an agricultural plot of the same size. Furthermore, because agriculturists have to work more hours than horticulturalists do, agriculture's yield relative to the labor time invested also is lower. Agriculture's main advantage is that the long-term yield per area is far greater and more dependable. Because a single field sustains its owners year after year, there is no need to maintain a reserve of uncultivated land as horticulturalists do. This is why agricultural societies tend to be more densely populated than horticultural ones.

The Cultivation Continuum

Because some nonindustrial economies have features of both horticulture and agriculture, it is useful to discuss cultivators as being arranged along a cultivation continuum. Horticultural systems stand at one end—the "low-labor, shifting-plot" end. Agriculturalists are at the other—the "labor-intensive, permanent-plot" end.

We speak of a continuum because there are intermediate economies, combining horticultural and agricultural features—more intensive than annually shifting horticulture but less intensive than agriculture. Unlike horticulturalists who farm a plot just once before fallowing it, the South American Kuikuru grow two or three crops of manioc, or cassava—an edible tuber—before abandoning their plots. Cultivation is even more intense in certain densely populated areas of Papua New Guinea, where plots are planted for two or three years, allowed to rest for three to five, and then recultivated. After several of these cycles, the plots are abandoned for a longer fallow period. Such a pattern is called *sectorial fallowing* (Wolf 1966). Besides Papua New Guinea, such systems occur in places as distant as West Africa and highland Mexico. Sectorial fallowing is associated with denser populations than is simple horticulture.

The key difference between horticulture and agriculture is that horticulture always has a fallow period, whereas agriculture does not. The earliest cultivators in the Middle East and in Mexico were rainfall-dependent horticulturalists. Until recently, horticulture was the main form of cultivation in several areas, including parts of Africa, Southeast Asia, the Pacific islands, Mexico, Central America, and the South American tropical forest.

Agricultural Intensification: People and the Environment

The range of environments available for cultivation has widened as people have increased their control over nature. Agriculturists have been able to colonize many areas that are too arid for nonirrigators or too hilly for nonterracers. Agriculture's increased labor intensity and permanent land use have major demographic, social, political, and environmental consequences.

Thus, because of their permanent fields, agriculturists tend to be sedentary. People live in larger and more permanent communities located closer to other settlements. Growth in population size and density increases contact between individuals and groups. There is more need to regulate interpersonal relations, including conflicts of interest. Economies that support more people usually require more coordination in the use of land, labor, and other resources (see the next chapter).

Intensive agriculture has significant environmental effects. Irrigation ditches and paddies (fields with irrigated rice) become repositories for organic wastes, chemicals (such as salts), and disease microorganisms. Intensive agriculture typically spreads at the expense of trees and forests, which are cut down to be replaced by fields. Accompanying such deforestation is loss of environmental diversity (see Dove and Carpenter 2008; Srivastava, Smith, and Forno 1999). Compared with horticulture, agricultural economies are specialized. They focus on one or a few caloric staples, such as rice, and on the animals that aid the agricultural economy. Because tropical horticultural-ists typically cultivate dozens of plant species simultaneously, a horticultural plot mirrors the botanical diversity that is found in a tropical forest. Agricultural plots, by contrast, reduce ecological diversity by cutting down trees and concentrating on just a few staple foods. Such crop specialization is true of agriculturists both in the tropics (e.g., Indonesian paddy farmers) and outside the tropics (e.g., Middle Eastern irriga-tion farmers).

Agriculturists attempt to reduce risk in production by favoring stability in the form of a reliable annual harvest and long-term production. Tropical foragers and horticultur-alists, by contrast, attempt to reduce risk by relying on multiple species and benefiting from ecological diversity. The agricultural strategy is to put all one's eggs in one big and very dependable basket. The strategy of tropical foragers and horticulturalists is to have several smaller baskets, a few of which may fail without endangering subsistence. The agricultural strategy makes sense when there are lots of children to raise and adults to be fed. Foraging and horticulture, of course, are associated with smaller, sparser, and more mobile populations.

Agricultural economies also pose a series of regulatory problems. How is water to be managed? How are disputes about access to and distribution of water to be resolved? With more people living closer together on more valuable land, agriculturists have more opportunities for interpersonal contact and conflict than foragers and horticulturalists do. The social and political implications of food production and intensification are ex-amined more fully in the next chapter, "Political Systems."

Anthropologists know that many indigenous groups—especially foragers and nonin-tensive cultivators—have done a reasonable job of managing their resources and pre-serving their ecosystems (see also Menzies 2006). Such societies had traditional ways of categorizing resources and regulating their use. Increasingly, however, these tradi-tional management systems have been challenged by national and international incen-tives to exploit and degrade the environment (see Dove, Sajise, and Doolittle 2011). These challenges are the focus of the last two chapters of this book.

Pastoralism

Herders, or **pastoralists,** are people whose activities focus on such domesticated animals as cattle, sheep, goats, camels, yak, and reindeer. They live in North and sub-Saharan Africa, the Middle East, Europe, and Asia. East African pastoralists, like many others, live in symbiosis with their herds. (*Symbiosis* is an obligatory interaction between groups—here humans and animals—that is beneficial to each.) Herders attempt to pro-tect their animals and to ensure their reproduction in return for food (dairy products and meat) and other products, such as leather.

People use livestock in various ways. Natives of North America's Great Plains, for example, didn't eat, but only rode, their horses. (They got those horses after Europeans reintroduced them to the Western Hemisphere; the native American horse had gone extinct thousands of years earlier.) For Plains Indians, horses served as "tools of the trade," means of production used to *hunt* buffalo, the main target of their economies. So the Plains Indians were not true pastoralists but hunters who used horses—as many agriculturists use animals—as means of production.

Pastoralists, by contrast, typically use their herds for food. They consume their meat, blood, and milk, from which they make yogurt, butter, and cheese. Although some pastoralists rely on their herds more completely than others do, it is impossible to base subsistence solely on animals. Most pastoralists therefore supplement their diet by hunting, gathering, fishing, cultivating, or trading.

The Samis (also known as Lapps or Laplanders) of Norway, Sweden, and Finland domesticated the reindeer, which their ancestors once hunted, in the 16th century. Like other herders, they follow their animals as they make an annual trek, in this case from coast to interior. Today's Samis use modern technology, such as snowmobiles and four-wheel-drive vehicles, to accompany their herds on their annual nomadic trek. Some of them probably use reindeer management software on their laptops and PDAs. Although their environment is harsher, the Samis, like other herders, live in nation-states and must deal with outsiders, including government officials, as they follow their herds and make their living through animal husbandry, trade, and sales (Hoge 2001; Paine 2009).

Unlike foraging and cultivation, which existed throughout the world before the Industrial Revolution, pastoralism was confined almost totally to the Old World. Before European conquest, the only herders in the Americas lived in the Andean region of South America. They used their llamas and alpacas for food and wool and in agriculture and transport. Much more recently, Navajo of the southwestern United States developed a pastoral economy based on sheep, which were brought to North America by Europeans. The populous Navajo became the major pastoral population in the Western Hemisphere.

Two patterns of movement occur with pastoralism: *nomadism* and *transhumance*. Both are based on the fact that herds must move to use pasture available in particular places in different seasons. In **pastoral nomadism,** the entire group—women, men, and children—moves with the animals throughout the year. The Middle East and North Africa provide numerous examples of pastoral nomads (see Salzman 2008). In Iran, for example, the Basseri and the Qashqai ethnic groups traditionally followed a nomadic route more than 300 miles (480 kilometers) long (see Salzman 2004).

With **transhumance,** part of the group moves with the herds, but most people stay in the home village. There are examples from Europe and Africa. In Europe's Alps it is just the shepherds and goatherds—not the whole hamlet, village, or town—who accompany the flocks to highland meadows in summer. Among the Turkana of Uganda, men and boys take the herds to distant pastures, while much of the village stays put and does some horticultural farming. During their annual trek, pastoral nomads trade for crops and other products with more sedentary people. Transhumants don't have to trade for crops. Because only part of the population accompanies the herds, transhumants can maintain year-round villages and grow their own crops.

Economic Systems

An **economy** is a system of production, distribution, and consumption of resources; *economics* is the study of such systems. Economists tend to focus on modern nations and capitalist systems. Anthropologists have broadened understanding of economic principles by gathering data on nonindustrial economies. Economic anthropology brings a comparative perspective to the study of economics (see Chibnik 2011; Gudeman, ed. 1999; Hann and Hart 2011; Sahlins 2004; Wilk and Cliggett 2007).

A **mode of production** is a way of organizing production—"a set of social relations through which labor is deployed to wrest energy from nature by means of tools, skills, organization, and knowledge" (Wolf 1982, p. 75). In the capitalist mode of production, money buys labor power, and there is a social gap between the people (bosses and workers) involved in the production process. By contrast, in nonindustrial societies, labor usually is not bought but is given as a social obligation. In such a *kin-based* mode of production, mutual aid in production is one among many expressions of a larger web of social relations (see Marshall 2011).

Societies representing each of the adaptive strategies just discussed (e.g., foraging) tend to have roughly similar modes of production. Differences in the mode of production within a given strategy may reflect differences in environments, target resources, or cultural traditions (Kelly 1995). Thus, a foraging mode of production may be based on individual hunters or teams, depending on whether the game is solitary, or a herd or flocking animal. Gathering usually is more individualistic than hunting, although collecting teams may assemble when abundant resources ripen and must be harvested quickly. Fishing may be done alone (as in ice or spear fishing) or in crews (as with open-sea fishing and hunting of sea mammals).

Production in Nonindustrial Societies

Although some kind of division of economic labor related to age and gender is a cultural universal, the specific tasks assigned to each sex and to people of different ages vary (see the chapter "Gender"). Many horticultural societies assign a major productive role to women, but some make men's work primary. Similarly, among pastoralists men generally tend large animals, but in some societies women do the milking. Jobs accomplished through teamwork in some cultivating societies are done in other societies by smaller groups or by individuals working over a longer period.

The Betsileo of Madagascar have two stages of teamwork in rice cultivation: transplanting and harvesting. Both feature a traditional division of labor by age and gender that is well known and repeated across the generations. The first job in transplanting is the trampling of a flooded, previously tilled field by young men driving cattle, in order to mix earth and water. They take cattle to the fields just before transplanting. The young men yell at and beat the cattle, striving to drive them into a frenzy, so that they will trample the fields properly. Trampling breaks up clumps of earth and mixes irrigation water with soil to form a smooth mud, into which women transplant seedlings. Once the tramplers leave the field, older men arrive. With their spades they break up the clumps the cattle missed. Meanwhile, the owner and other adults uproot rice seedlings and take them to the field. Women plant the seedlings.

At harvest time, four or five months later, young men cut the rice off the stalks. Young women carry it to the clearing above the field. Older women arrange and stack it. The oldest men and women then stand on the stack, stomping and compacting it. Three days later, young men thresh the rice, beating the stalks against a rock to remove the grain. Older men then beat the stalks with sticks to make sure all the grains have fallen off.

Means of Production

In nonindustrial societies the relationship between the worker and the means of production is more intimate than it is in industrial nations. **Means, or factors, of production** include land (territory), labor, and technology.

Land as a Means of Production

Among foragers, ties between people and land were less permanent than among food producers. Although many bands had territories, the boundaries usually were not marked, and there was no way they could be enforced. The hunter's stake in an animal was more important than where the animal finally died. A person acquired the rights to use a band's territory by being born in the band or by joining it through a tie of kinship, marriage, or fictive kinship. In Botswana in southern Africa, Ju/'hoansi San women habitually used specific tracts of berry-bearing trees. When a woman changed bands, she immediately acquired a new gathering area.

Among food producers, rights to the means of production also come through kinship and marriage. Descent groups (groups whose members claim common ancestry) are common among nonindustrial food producers. Those who descend from the founder share the group's territory and resources. If the adaptive strategy is horticulture, the estate includes gardens and fallow land for shifting cultivation. As members of a descent group, pastoralists have access to animals to start their own herds, to grazing land, to garden land, and to other means of production.

Labor, Tools, and Specialization

Like land, labor is a means of production. In nonindustrial societies, access to both land and labor comes through social links such as kinship, marriage, and descent. Mutual aid in production is merely one aspect of ongoing social relations that are expressed on many other occasions.

Nonindustrial societies contrast with industrial nations regarding another means of production—technology. Manufacturing often is linked to age and gender. Women may weave and men may make pottery, or vice versa. Most people of a particular age and gender share the technical knowledge associated with that age and gender. If married women customarily make baskets, most married women know how to make baskets. Neither technology nor technical knowledge is very specialized.

Some tribal societies, however, do promote specialization. Among the Yanomami of Venezuela and Brazil, for instance, certain villages manufacture clay pots and others make hammocks. They don't specialize, as one might suppose, because certain raw materials happen to be available near particular villages. Clay suitable for pots is widely available. Everyone knows how to make pots, but not everybody does so. Craft specialization reflects the social and political environment rather than the natural environment. Such specialization promotes trade, which is the first step in creating an alliance with enemy villages (Chagnon 1997).

Alienation in Industrial Economies

There are significant contrasts between nonindustrial economies and industrial ones. In the former, economic relations are just one part of a larger, multidimensional social matrix. People don't just work for and with others; they live with those same people; they pray with, feast with, and care about them. One works for and with people with whom one has long-term personal and social bonds (e.g., kin and in-laws).

In industrial societies, by contrast, workers sell their labor to bosses who can fire them. Work and the workplace are separated—*alienated*—from one's social essence. Rather than expressing an ongoing, mutual social relationship, labor becomes a thing (commodity) to be paid for, bought, and sold—and from which the boss can generate an individual profit. Furthermore, industrial workers usually don't work with their relatives and neighbors. If coworkers are friends, the personal relationship often develops out of their common employment rather than a previous social tie.

In nonindustrial societies, an individual who makes something can use or dispose of it as he or she sees fit. The maker may feel pride in such a personal product and, if it is given away, a renewed commitment to the social relationship that is reinforced by the gift. On the other hand, when factory workers produce for their employer's profit, their products as well as their labor are alienated. Their bosses have use or disposal rights. Human labor and its products belong to someone other than the individual producer. Unlike

Female factory workers make toy lions in Qingdao City, Shandong province, East China. How might factory work create alienation?

assembly-line workers, producers in nonindustrial societies typically see their work through from start to finish and feel a sense of accomplishment.

Thus, industrial workers have impersonal relations with their employers, coworkers, and products. People sell their labor for cash in a market economy, and work stands apart from family life. In nonindustrial societies, by contrast, the relations of production, distribution, and consumption are social relations with economic aspects. Economy is not a separate entity but is *embedded* in the society.

A Case of Industrial Alienation

For decades, the government of Malaysia has promoted export-oriented industry, allowing transnational companies to install manufacturing operations in rural Malaysia. In search of cheaper labor, corporations headquartered in Japan, Western Europe, and the United States have moved labor-intensive factories to developing countries. Malaysia has hundreds of Japanese and American subsidiaries, which produce garments, foodstuffs, and electronics components. Thousands of young Malaysian women from rural families now assemble microchips and microcomponents for transistors and capacitors. Aihwa Ong (1987, 2010) did a study of electronics assembly workers in an area where 85 percent of the workers were young, unmarried females from nearby villages.

Ong found that, unlike village women, female factory workers had to cope with a rigid work routine and constant supervision by men. The discipline that factories value was being taught in local schools, where uniforms helped prepare girls for the factory dress code. Village women wear loose, flowing tunics, sarongs, and sandals, but factory workers had to don tight overalls and heavy rubber gloves, in which they felt constrained. Assembling electronics components requires precise, concentrated labor. Labor in these factories illustrates the separation of intellectual and manual activity—the alienation that Karl Marx considered the defining feature of industrial work. One woman said about her bosses, "They exhaust us very much, as if they do not think that we too are human beings" (Ong 1987, p. 202). Nor does factory work bring women a substantial financial reward, given low wages, job uncertainty, and family claims on wages. Although young women typically work just a few years, production quotas, three daily shifts, overtime, and surveillance take their toll in mental and physical exhaustion.

One response to factory relations of production has been spirit possession (factory women are possessed by spirits). Ong interprets this phenomenon as the women's unconscious protest against labor discipline and male control of the industrial setting. Sometimes possession takes the form of mass hysteria. Spirits have simultaneously invaded as many as 120 factory workers. Weretigers (the Malay equivalent of the werewolf) arrive to avenge the construction of a factory on aboriginal burial grounds. Disturbed earth and grave spirits swarm on the shop floor. First the women see the spirits; then their bodies are invaded. The weretigers send the women into sobbing, laughing, and shrieking fits. To deal with possession, factories employ local medicine men, who sacrifice chickens and goats to fend off the spirits. This solution works only some of the time; possession still goes on. Ong argues that spirit possession expresses anguish at, and resistance to, capitalist relations of production. By engaging in this form of rebellion, however, factory women avoid a direct confrontation with the source of their distress. Ong concludes that spirit possession, while expressing repressed resentment, doesn't do much to modify factory conditions. (Other tactics, such as unionization, would do more.) Spirit possession may even help maintain the current system by operating as a safety valve for accumulated tensions.

Economizing and Maximization

Economic anthropologists have been concerned with two main questions:

1. How are production, distribution, and consumption organized in different societies? This question focuses on *systems* of human behavior and their organization.
2. What motivates people in different societies to produce, distribute or exchange, and consume? Here the focus is not on systems of behavior but on the *individuals* who participate in those systems.

Anthropologists view economic systems and motivations in a cross-cultural perspective. Motivation is a concern of psychologists, but it also has been a concern of economists and anthropologists. American economists assume that people make decisions rationally, guided by the *profit motive*. Although anthropologists know that the profit motive is not universal, the assumption that individuals try to maximize profits is basic to capitalism and to Western economic theory. In fact, the subject matter of economics often is defined as economizing, or the rational allocation of scarce means (or resources) to alternative ends (or uses) (see Chibnik 2011).

What does that mean? Classical economic theory assumes that our wants are infinite, while our means are limited. People must make choices about how to use their scarce resources—their time, labor, money, and capital. (The "Anthropology Today" at the end of this chapter disputes the idea that people always make economic choices based on scarcity.) Western economists assume that when confronted with choices and decisions, people tend to make the one that maximizes profit. This is assumed to be the most rational choice.

The idea that individuals choose to maximize profits was a basic assumption of the classical economists of the 19th century and one held by many contemporary economists. However, certain economists now recognize that individuals may be motivated by many other goals. Depending on the society and the situation, people may try to maximize profit, wealth, prestige, pleasure, comfort, or social harmony. Individuals may want to realize their personal or family ambitions or those of another group to which they belong (see Chibnik 2011; Sahlins 2004).

Alternative Ends

To what uses do people put their scarce resources? Throughout the world, people devote some of their time and energy to building up a *subsistence fund* (Wolf 1966). In other words, they have to work to eat, to replace the calories they use in daily activity. People also must invest in a *replacement fund*. They must maintain their technology and other items essential to production. If a hoe or plow breaks, they must repair or replace it.

They also must obtain and replace items that are essential not to production but to everyday life, such as clothing and shelter.

People everywhere also have to invest in a *social fund*. They must help their friends, relatives, in-laws, and neighbors. It is useful to distinguish between a social fund and a *ceremonial fund*. The latter term refers to expenditures on ceremonies or rituals. To prepare a festival honoring one's ancestors, for example, requires time and the outlay of wealth.

Citizens of nation-states also must allocate scarce resources to a *rent fund*. We think of rent as payment for the use of property. Rent fund, however, has a wider meaning. It refers to resources that people must render to an individual or agency that is superior politically or economically. Tenant farmers and sharecroppers, for example, either pay rent or give some of their produce to their landlords, as peasants did under feudalism.

Peasants are small-scale agriculturists who live in nonindustrial states and have rent fund obligations (see Kearney 1996). They produce to feed themselves, to sell their produce, and to pay rent. All peasants have two things in common:

1. They live in state-organized societies.
2. They produce food without the elaborate technology—chemical fertilizers, tractors, airplanes to spray crops, and so on—of modern farming or agribusiness.

Besides paying rent to landlords, peasants must satisfy government obligations, paying taxes in the form of money, produce, or labor. The rent fund is not simply an *additional* obligation for peasants. Often it becomes their foremost and unavoidable duty. Sometimes their own diets suffer as a result. The demands of social superiors may divert resources from subsistence, replacement, social, and ceremonial funds.

Motivations vary from society to society, and people often lack freedom of choice in allocating their resources. Because of obligations to pay rent, peasants may allocate their scarce means toward ends that are not their own but those of government officials. Thus, even in societies in which there is a profit motive, people often are prevented from rationally maximizing self-interest by factors beyond their control.

Distribution, Exchange

The economist Karl Polanyi (1968) stimulated the comparative study of exchange, and several anthropologists followed his lead. Polanyi defined three principles that guide exchanges: the market principle, redistribution, and reciprocity. These principles all can be present in the same society, but in that case they govern different kinds of transactions. In any society, one of them usually dominates. The principle of exchange that dominates in a given society is the one that allocates the means of production (see Chibnik 2011; Hann and Hart 2011).

The Market Principle

In today's world capitalist economy, the **market principle** dominates. It governs the distribution of the means of production—land, labor, natural resources, technology, knowledge, and capital. With market exchange, items are bought and sold, using money, with an eye to maximizing profit, and value is determined by the *law of supply and* *demand* (things cost more the scarcer they are and the more people want them). Bargaining is characteristic of market-principle exchanges. The buyer and seller strive to maximize—to get their "money's worth." Bargaining doesn't require that the buyer and seller meet. Consumers bargain whenever they shop around or use advertisements or the Internet in their decision making (see Hann and Hart 2009; Madra 2004).

Redistribution

Redistribution operates when goods, services, or their equivalent move from the local level to a center. The center may be a capital, a regional collection point, or a storehouse near a chief's residence. Products often move through a hierarchy of officials for storage at the center. Along the way officials and their dependents may consume some of them, but the exchange principle here is *re*distribution. The flow of goods eventually reverses direction— out from the center, down through the hierarchy, and back to the common people.

One example of a redistributive system comes from the Cherokee, the original owners of the Tennessee Valley. The Cherokee were productive cultivators of maize, beans, and squash, which they supplemented by hunting and fishing. They also had chiefs. Each of their main villages had a central plaza, where meetings of the chief's council took place and where redistributive feasts were held. According to Cherokee custom, each family farm had an area where the family could set aside part of its annual harvest for the chief. This supply of corn was used to feed the needy, as well as travelers and warriors journeying through friendly territory. This store of food was available to all who needed it, with the understanding that it "belonged" to the chief and was available through his generosity. The chief also hosted the redistributive feasts held in the main settlements (Harris 1978).

Reciprocity

Reciprocity is exchange between social equals, who normally are related by kinship, marriage, or another close personal tie. Because it occurs between social equals, it is dominant in the more egalitarian societies—among foragers, cultivators, and pastoralists. There are three degrees of reciprocity: *generalized, balanced,* and *negative* (Sahlins 1968, 2004; Service 1966). These may be imagined as areas of a continuum defined by these questions:

1. How closely related are the parties to the exchange?
2. How quickly and unselfishly are gifts reciprocated?

Generalized reciprocity, the purest form of reciprocity, is characteristic of exchanges between closely related people. In balanced reciprocity, social distance increases, as does the need to reciprocate. In negative reciprocity, social distance is greatest and reciprocation is most calculated. This range, from generalized to negative, is called the **reciprocity continuum.**

With **generalized reciprocity,** someone gives to another person and expects nothing immediate in return. Such exchanges are not primarily economic transactions but expressions of personal relationships. Most parents don't keep accounts of every penny they spend on their children. They merely hope their children will respect their culture's customs involving obligations to parents.

Among foragers, generalized reciprocity usually has governed exchanges. People routinely have shared with other band members (Bird-David 1992; Kent 1992). So strong is the ethic of sharing that most foragers have lacked an expression for "thank you." To offer thanks would be impolite because it would imply that a particular act of sharing, which is the keystone of egalitarian society, was unusual. Among the Semai, foragers of central Malaysia (Dentan 1979, 2008), to express gratitude would suggest surprise at the hunter's success (Harris 1974).

Balanced reciprocity applies to exchanges between people who are more distantly related than are members of the same band or household. In a horticultural society, for example, a man presents a gift to a distant cousin, a trading partner, or a brother's fictive kinsman. The giver expects something in return. This may not come immediately, but the social relationship will be strained if there is no reciprocation.

Exchanges in nonindustrial societies also may illustrate **negative reciprocity,** mainly in dealing with people beyond their social systems. To people who live in a world of close personal relations, exchanges with outsiders are full of ambiguity and distrust. Exchange is one way of establishing friendly relations, but when trade begins, the relationship is still tentative. Initially, people seek to get something back immediately. Just as in market economies, but without using money, they try to get the best possible immediate return for their investment (see Clark 2010; Hann and Hart 2009).

Generalized reciprocity and balanced reciprocity are based on trust and a social tie. With negative reciprocity, the goal is to get something for as little as possible, even if it means being cagey or deceitful or cheating. Among the most extreme and "negative" examples was 19th-century horse thievery by North American Plains Indians. Men would sneak into camps of neighboring tribes to steal horses. Such thefts were likely to be reciprocated. A similar pattern of livestock (cattle) raiding continues today in East Africa, among tribes such as the Kuria (Fleisher 2000). In these cases, the party that starts the raiding can expect reciprocity—a raid on their own village—or worse. The Kuria hunt down cattle thieves and kill them. It's still reciprocity, governed by "Do unto others as they have done unto you."

One way of reducing the tension in situations of potential negative reciprocity is to engage in "silent trade." One example was the silent trade of the Mbuti pygmy foragers of the African equatorial forest and their neighboring horticultural villagers. There was no personal contact during their exchanges. A Mbuti hunter left game, honey, or another forest product at a customary site. Villagers collected it and left crops in exchange. Often the parties bargained silently. If one felt the return was insufficient, he or she simply left it at the trading site. If the other party wanted to continue trade, it was increased.

Coexistence of Exchange Principles

In today's North America, the market principle governs most exchanges, from the sale of the means of production to the sale of consumer goods. We also have redistribution. Some of our tax money goes to support the government, but some of it also comes back to us in the form of social services, education, health care, and road building. We also have reciprocal exchanges. Generalized reciprocity characterizes the relationship between parents and children. However, even here the dominant market mentality surfaces in comments about the high cost of raising children and in the stereotypical statement of the disappointed parent: "We gave you everything money could buy."

Exchanges of gifts, cards, and invitations exemplify reciprocity, usually balanced. Everyone has heard remarks like "They invited us to their daughter's wedding, so when ours gets married, we'll have to invite them" and "They've been here for dinner three times and haven't invited us yet. I don't think we should ask them back until they do." Such precise balancing of reciprocity would be out of place in a foraging band, where resources are communal (common to all) and daily sharing based on generalized reciprocity is an essential ingredient of social life and survival.

Potlatching

One of the most famous cultural practices studied by ethnographers is the **potlatch.** This is a festive event within a regional exchange system among tribes of the North Pacific Coast of North America, including the Salish and Kwakiutl of Washington and British Columbia. Some tribes still practice the potlatch, sometimes as a memorial to the dead (Kan 1986, 1989). At each such event, assisted by members of their communities, potlatch sponsors traditionally gave away food, blankets, pieces of copper, or other items. In return for this, they got prestige. To give a potlatch enhanced one's reputation. Prestige increased with the lavishness of the potlatch, the value of the goods given away in it.

The potlatching tribes were foragers, but atypical ones for relatively recent times. They were sedentary and had chiefs. They had access to a wide variety of land and sea

The historic photo shows the amassing of blankets to be given away at a Kwakiutl potlatch. The man in the foreground is making a speech praising the generosity of the potlatch host.

resources. Among their most important foods were salmon, herring, candlefish, berries, mountain goats, seals, and porpoises (Piddocke 1969).

According to classical economic theory, the profit motive is universal, with the goal of maximizing material benefits. How, then, does one explain the potlatch, in which substantial wealth is given away (and even destroyed)? Christian missionaries considered potlatching to be wasteful and antithetical to the Protestant work ethic. By 1885, under pressure from Indian agents, missionaries, and Indian converts to Christianity, both Canada and the United States had outlawed potlatching. Between 1885 and 1951 the custom went underground. By 1951, however, both countries had discreetly dropped the antipotlatching laws from the books.

Some scholars seized on this view of the potlatch as a classic case of economically wasteful behavior. The economist and social commentator Thorstein Veblen cited potlatching as an example of conspicuous consumption in his influential book *Theory of the Leisure Class* (1934), claiming that potlatching was based on an economically irrational drive for prestige. This interpretation stressed the lavishness and supposed wastefulness, especially of the Kwakiutl displays, to support the contention that in some societies people strive to maximize prestige at the expense of their material well-being. This interpretation has been challenged.

Ecological anthropology, also known as *cultural ecology,* is a theoretical school that attempts to interpret cultural practices, such as the potlatch, in terms of their long-term role in helping humans adapt to their environments. Wayne Suttles (1960) and Andrew Vayda (1961/1968) saw potlatching not in terms of its immediate wastefulness but in terms of its long-term role as a cultural adaptive mechanism. This view also helps us understand similar patterns of lavish feasting throughout the world. Here is the ecological interpretation: *Customs such as the potlatch are cultural adaptations to alternating periods of local abundance and shortage.*

How does this work? Although the natural environment of the North Pacific Coast is favorable, resources do fluctuate from year to year and place to place. Salmon and herring aren't equally abundant every year in a given locality. One village can have a good year while another is experiencing a bad one. Later their fortunes reverse. In this context, the potlatch cycle had adaptive value; the potlatch was not a competitive display that brought no material benefit.

A village enjoying an especially good year had a surplus of subsistence items, which it could trade for more durable wealth items, such as blankets, canoes, or pieces of copper. Wealth, in turn, by being distributed, could be converted into prestige. Members of several villages were invited to any potlatch and got to take home the resources that were given away. In this way, potlatching linked villages together in a regional economy—an exchange system that distributed food and wealth from wealthy to needy communities. In return, the potlatch sponsors and their villages got prestige. The decision to potlatch was determined by the health of the local economy. If there had been subsistence surpluses, and thus a buildup of wealth over several good years, a village could afford a potlatch to convert its surplus food and wealth into prestige.

The long-term adaptive value of intercommunity feasting becomes clear when a formerly prosperous village had a run of bad luck. Its people started accepting invitations to potlatches in villages that were doing better. The tables were turned as the temporarily

Anthropology Today   *Scarcity and the Betsileo*

In the realm of cultural diversity, perceptions and motivations can change substantially over time. Consider some changes I've observed among the Betsileo of Madagascar during the decades I've been studying them. Initially, compared with modern consumers, the Betsileo had little perception of scarcity. Now, with population increase and the spread of a cash-oriented economy, perceived wants and needs have increased relative to means. Motivations have changed, too, as people increasingly seek profits, even if it means stealing from their neighbors or destroying ancestral farms.

In the late 1960s my wife and I first lived among the Betsileo, studying their economy and social life (Kottak 1980). Soon after our arrival we met two well-educated schoolteachers (first cousins) who were interested in our research. The woman's father was a congressional representative who became a cabinet minister during our stay. Their family came from a historically important and typical Betsileo village called Ivato, which they invited us to visit with them.

We had visited many other Betsileo villages, where often, as we drove up, children would run away screaming. Women would hurry inside, and men would retreat to doorways. This behavior expressed their fear of the *mpakafo*. Believed to cut out and devour his victim's heart and liver, the mpakafo is the Malagasy vampire. These cannibals are said to have fair skin and to be very tall. Because I have light skin and stand over 6 feet tall, I was a natural suspect. The fact that such creatures were not known to travel with their wives helped convince the Betsileo that I wasn't really a mpakafo.

When we visited Ivato, however, its people were friendly and hospitable. Our very first day there we did a brief census and found out who lived in which households. We learned people's names and their relationships to our schoolteacher friends and to each other. We met an excellent informant who knew all about the local history. In a few afternoons I learned much more than I had in the other villages in several sessions.

Ivatans were so willing to talk because we had powerful sponsors, villagers who had made it in the outside world, people the Ivatans knew would protect them. The schoolteachers vouched for us, but even more significant was the cabinet minister, who was like a grandfather and benefactor to everyone in town. The Ivatans had no reason to fear us because their more influential native son had asked them to answer our questions.

Once we moved to Ivato, the elders established a pattern of visiting us every evening. They came to talk, attracted by the inquisitive foreigners but also by the wine, tobacco, and food we offered. I asked question after question about their customs and beliefs.

As our stay neared its end, our Ivatan friends lamented, saying, "We'll miss you. When you leave, there won't be any more cigarettes, any more wine, or any more questions." They wondered what it would be like for us back in the United States. They knew we had an automobile and that we regularly purchased things, including the items we shared with them. We could afford to buy products they never would have. They commented, "When you go back to your country, you'll need a lot of money for things like cars, clothes, and food. We don't need to buy those things. We make almost everything we use. We don't need as much money as you, because we produce for ourselves."

The Betsileo weren't unusual for nonindustrial people. Strange as it may seem to an American consumer, those rice farmers actually believed *they had all they needed*. The lesson from the Betsileo of the 1960s is that scarcity, which economists view as universal, is variable. Although shortages do arise in nonindustrial societies, the concept of scarcity (insufficient means) is much less developed in stable subsistence-oriented economies than in industrial societies that rely on a host of consumer goods.

But, with globalization over the past few decades, significant changes have affected the Betsileo—and most nonindustrial peoples. On my last visit to Ivato, in 2006, the effects of cash and of population increase were evident there—and throughout Madagascar—where the population growth rate has been about 3 percent annually. Madagascar's population doubled between 1966 and 1991—from 6 to 12 million people. Today it approaches 20 million. One result of population pressure has been agricultural intensification. In Ivato, farmers who formerly grew only rice in their fields now use the same land for commercial crops, such as carrots, after the annual rice harvest. More tragically, Ivato has witnessed a breakdown of social and political order, fueled by increasing demand for cash.

Cattle rustling has become a growing threat. Cattle thieves (sometimes from neighboring villages) have terrorized peasants who previously felt secure in their villages. Some of the rustled cattle are driven to the coasts for commercial export. Prominent among the rustlers are relatively well-educated young men who have studied long enough to be comfortable negotiating with outsiders, but who have been unable to find formal work, and who are unwilling to work the rice fields as their peasant ancestors did. The formal education system has familiarized them with external institutions and norms, including the need for cash. The concepts of scarcity,

Women hull rice in a Betsileo village. In the village of Ivato, farmers who traditionally grew only rice in their fields now use the same land for commercial crops, such as carrots, after the annual rice harvest. *continued*

Anthropology Today   *continued*

commerce, and negative reciprocity now thrive among the Betsileo.

I've witnessed other striking evidence of the new addiction to cash during my most recent visits to Betsileo country. Near Ivato's county seat, people now sell precious stones—tourmalines, which were found by chance in local rice fields. We saw an amazing sight: dozens of villagers destroying an ancestral resource, digging up a large rice field, seeking tourmalines—clear evidence of the encroachment of cash on the local subsistence economy.

Throughout the Betsileo homeland, population growth and density are pro-pelling emigration. Locally, land, jobs, and money are all scarce. One woman with ancestors from Ivato, herself now a resident of the national capital (Antananarivo), remarked that half the children of Ivato now lived in that city. Although she was exaggerating, a census of all the descendants of Ivato reveals a substantial emigrant and urban population.

Ivato's recent history is one of increasing participation in a cash economy. That history, combined with the pressure of a growing population on local resources, has made scarcity not just a concept but a reality for Ivatans and their neighbors.

rich became temporarily poor and vice versa. The newly needy accepted food and wealth items. They were willing to receive rather than bestow gifts and thus to relinquish some of their stored-up prestige. They hoped their luck would eventually improve so that resources could be recouped and prestige regained.

The potlatch linked local groups along the North Pacific Coast into a regional alliance and exchange network. Potlatching and intervillage exchange had adaptive functions, regardless of the motivations of the individual participants. The anthropologists who stressed rivalry for prestige were not wrong. They were merely emphasizing *motivations* at the expense of an analysis of economic and ecological *systems*.

The use of feasts to enhance individual and community reputations and to redistribute wealth is not peculiar to populations of the North Pacific Coast. Competitive feasting is widely characteristic of nonindustrial food producers. But among most surviving foragers, who live in marginal areas, resources are too meager to support feasting on such a level. In such societies, sharing rather than competition prevails.

Summary

1. Cohen's adaptive strategies include foraging (hunting and gathering), horticulture, agriculture, pastoralism, and industrialism. Foraging was the only human adaptive strategy until the advent of food production (farming and herding) 10,000 years ago. Food production eventually replaced foraging in most places. Almost all modern foragers have some dependence on food production or food producers.

2. Horticulture doesn't use land or labor intensively. Horticulturalists cultivate a plot for one or two years (sometimes longer) and then abandon it. There is always a fallow period. Agriculturists farm the same plot of land continuously and use labor

intensively. They use one or more of the following: irrigation, terracing, domesticated animals as means of production, and manuring.

3. The pastoral strategy is mixed. Nomadic pastoralists trade with cultivators. Part of a transhumant pastoral population cultivates while another part takes the herds to pasture. Except for some Peruvians and the Navajo, who are recent herders, the New World lacks native pastoralists.

4. Economic anthropology is the cross-cultural study of systems of production, distribution, and consumption. In nonindustrial societies, a kin-based mode of production prevails. One acquires rights to resources and labor through membership in social groups, not impersonally through purchase and sale. Work is just one aspect of social relations expressed in varied contexts.

5. Economics has been defined as the science of allocating scarce means to alternative ends. Western economists assume the notion of scarcity is universal—which it isn't—and that in making choices, people strive to maximize personal profit. In nonindustrial societies, indeed as in our own, people often maximize values other than individual profit.

6. In nonindustrial societies, people invest in subsistence, replacement, social, and ceremonial funds. States add a rent fund: People must share their output with their social superiors. In states, the obligation to pay rent often becomes primary.

7. Besides studying production, economic anthropologists study and compare exchange systems. The three principles of exchange are the market principle, redistribution, and reciprocity, which may coexist in a given society. The primary exchange mode is the one that allocates the means of production.

8. Patterns of feasting and exchanges of wealth among villages are common among nonindustrial food producers, as among the potlatching societies of North America's North Pacific Coast. Such systems help even out the availability of resources over time.

Key Terms

agriculture, *88*

balanced reciprocity, *101*

band, *87*

correlation, *87*

economy, *94*

food production, *83*

generalized reciprocity, *100*

horticulture, *88*

market principle, *99*

means (or factors) of production, *95*

mode of production, *94*

negative reciprocity, *101*

pastoral nomadism, *93*

pastoralists, *92*

peasants, *99*

potlatch, *102*

reciprocity, *100*

reciprocity continuum, *100*

redistribution, *100*

transhumance, *93*

Chapter 6

Political Systems

Anthropologists share an interest in political systems, power, and politics with political scientists. Here again, however, the anthropological approach is global and comparative and includes nonstates, while political scientists tend to focus on contemporary and recent nation-states. Anthropological studies have revealed substantial variation in power, authority, and legal systems in different societies. (**Power** is the ability to exercise one's will over others; **authority** is the formal, socially approved use of power—e.g., by government officials.) (See Kurtz 2001; Lewellen 2003; Nugent and Vincent 2004; Schwartz, Turner, and Tuden 2006; Wolf with Silverman 2001.)

What Is "The Political"?

Morton Fried offered the following definition of political organization:

> Political organization comprises those portions of social organization that specifically relate to the individuals or groups that manage the affairs of public policy or seek to control the appointment or activities of those individuals or groups. (Fried 1967, pp. 20–21)

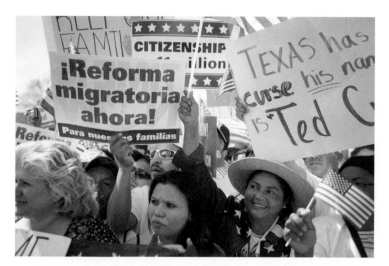

Seeking to influence public policy, tens of thousands of immigration rights supporters joined in the "Time is Now" Rally for Citizenship at the U.S. Capitol on Wednesday, April 10, 2013. What's the current status of legislation concerning immigrants in the United States?

This definition certainly fits contemporary North America. Under "individuals or groups that manage the affairs of public policy" come various agencies and levels of government. Those who seek to influence public policy include political parties, unions, corporations, consumers, lobbyists, activists, political action committees (including superpacs), religious groups, and nongovernmental organizations (NGOs).

Fried's definition is less applicable to nonstates, where it's often difficult to detect any "public policy." For this reason, I prefer to speak of *socio*political organization in discussing the exercise of power and the regulation of relations among groups and their representatives. *Political regulation* includes such processes as decision making, dispute management, and conflict resolution. The study of political regulation draws our attention to those who make decisions and resolve conflicts (are there formal leaders?).

Types and Trends

Ethnographic and archaeological studies in hundreds of places have revealed many correlations between the economy and social and political organization. Decades ago, the anthropologist Elman Service (1962) listed four types, or levels, of political organization: band, tribe, chiefdom, and state. Today, none of the first three types can be studied as a self-contained form of political organization, because all now exist within the context of nation-states and are subject to state control (see Ferguson 2002). There is archaeological evidence for early bands, tribes, and chiefdoms that existed before the first states appeared. However, because anthropology came into being long after the origin of the state, anthropologists never have been able to observe "in the flesh" a band, tribe, or chiefdom outside the influence of some state. There still may be local political leaders (e.g., village heads) and regional figures (e.g., chiefs) of the sort discussed in this chapter, but all now exist and function within the context of state organization.

A band is a small, kin-based group (all its members are related by kinship or marriage) found among foragers. **Tribes** typically have economies based on horticulture and pastoralism. Living in villages and organized into kin groups based on common descent (clans and lineages—see the next chapter), tribes have no formal government and no reliable means of enforcing political decisions. **Chiefdom** refers to a form of sociopolitical organization intermediate between the tribe and the state. In chiefdoms, social relations were based mainly on kinship, marriage, descent, age, generation, and gender—just as in bands and tribes. However, although chiefdoms were kin-based, they featured **differential access** to resources (some people had more wealth, prestige, and power than others did) and a permanent political structure. The **state** is a form of sociopolitical organization based on a formal government structure and socioeconomic stratification.

The four labels in Service's typology are much too simple to account for the full range of political diversity and complexity known to archaeology and ethnography. We'll see, for instance, that tribes have varied widely in their political systems and institutions. Nevertheless, Service's typology does highlight some significant contrasts in political organization, especially those between states and nonstates. For example, in bands and tribes—unlike states, which have clearly visible governments—political organization did not stand out as separate and distinct from the total social order. In bands and tribes, it was difficult to characterize an act or event as political rather than merely social.

Service's labels "band," "tribe," "chiefdom," and "state" are categories or types within a **sociopolitical typology.** These types are correlated with the adaptive strategies (an *economic typology*) discussed in the previous chapter. Thus, foragers (an economic type) tended to have band organization (a sociopolitical type). Similarly, many horticulturalists and pastoralists lived in tribes. Although most chiefdoms had farming economies, herding was important in some Middle Eastern chiefdoms. Nonindustrial states usually had an agricultural base.

Food production led to larger, denser populations and more complex economies than was the case among foragers. Many sociopolitical trends reflect the increased regulatory demands associated with cultivation and herding. Archaeologists have studied these trends through time, and cultural anthropologists have observed them among more recent, including contemporary, groups (see Shore, Wright, and Peró 2011).

Bands and Tribes

This chapter discusses a series of societies, as case studies, with different political systems. A common set of questions will be addressed for each one. What kinds of social groups does the society have? How do those groups represent themselves to each other? How are their internal and external relations regulated? To answer these questions, we begin with bands and tribes and then consider chiefdoms and states.

Foraging Bands

Modern hunter-gatherers are today's remnants of foraging band societies. The strong ties they now maintain with sociopolitical groups outside the band make them markedly different from Stone Age hunter-gatherers. Modern foragers live in nation-states and an interlinked world. The pygmies of Congo, for example, have for generations shared a social world and economic exchanges with their neighbors who are cultivators. All foragers now trade with food producers. In addition, most contemporary hunter-gatherers rely on governments and on missionaries for at least part of what they consume.

The San

In the previous chapter, we saw how the Basarwa San have been affected by policies of the government of Botswana, which relocated them after converting their ancestral lands into a wildlife reserve (Motseta 2006). More generally, San speakers ("Bushmen") of southern Africa have been influenced by Bantu speakers (farmers and herders) for 2,000 years and by Europeans for centuries. Edwin Wilmsen (1989) argues that many San descend from herders who were pushed into the desert by poverty or oppression. He sees the San today as a rural underclass in a larger political and economic system dominated by Europeans and Bantu food producers. Within this system, many San now tend cattle for wealthier Bantu rather than foraging independently. San also have their own domesticated animals, further illustrating their movement away from a foraging lifestyle.

Susan Kent (1992, 1996, 2002) noted a tendency to stereotype foragers, to treat them all as alike. They used to be stereotyped as isolated, primitive survivors of the Stone Age. A new, and more accurate, view of contemporary foragers sees them as groups forced into marginal environments by states, colonialism, and world events.

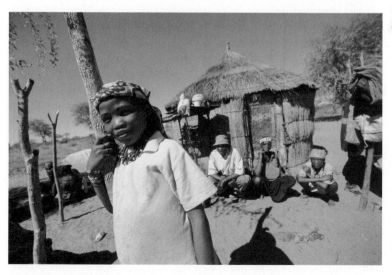

Among tropical foragers, women make an important economic contribution through gathering, as is true among the San shown here in Namibia. What evidence do you see in this photo that contemporary foragers participate in the modern world system?

Susan Kent (1996, 2002) focused on variation among foragers, describing considerable diversity in time and space among the San. The nature of San life has changed considerably since the 1950s and 1960s, when a series of anthropologists from Harvard University, including Richard B. Lee, embarked on a systematic study of their lives. Studying the San over time, Lee and others have documented many changes (see Lee 1979, 1984, 2003, 2012; Silberbauer 1981; Tanaka 1980). Such longitudinal research monitors variation in time, while fieldwork in many San areas has revealed variation in space. One of the most important contrasts is between settled (sedentary) and nomadic groups (Kent and Vierich 1989). Although sedentism has increased substantially in recent years, some San groups (along rivers) have been sedentary for generations. Others, including the Dobe Ju/'hoansi San studied by Lee (1984, 2003, 2012) and the Kutse San whom Kent studied, have retained more of the hunter-gatherer lifestyle.

To the extent that foraging continues to be their subsistence base, groups like the San can illustrate links between a foraging economy and other aspects of life in bands. For example, San groups that still are mobile, or that were so until recently, emphasize social, political, and gender equality, which are traditional band characteristics. A social system based on kinship, reciprocity, and sharing is appropriate for an economy with few people and limited resources. People have to share meat when they get it; otherwise, it rots. The nomadic pursuit of wild plants and animals tends to discourage permanent settlement, wealth accumulation, and status distinctions.

In the past, foraging bands—small, nomadic or seminomadic social units—formed seasonally when component nuclear families got together. The particular families might vary from year to year. Marriage and kinship created ties between members of different bands. Trade and visiting also linked them. Band leaders were leaders in name only. In such an *egalitarian society,* they were first among equals. Sometimes they gave advice or made decisions, but they had no way to enforce those decisions. Because of the spread of states and globalization, it is increasingly difficult for ethnographers to find and observe such patterns of band organization.

The Inuit

The aboriginal Inuit (Hoebel 1954, 1954/1968), another group of foragers, provide a classic example of methods of settling disputes—**conflict resolution**—in stateless societies. All societies have ways of settling disputes (of variable effectiveness) along with cultural rules or norms about proper and improper behavior. **Norms** are cultural standards or guidelines that enable individuals to distinguish between appropriate and inappropriate behavior in a given society (N. Kottak 2002). While rules and norms are cultural universals, only state societies, those with established governments, have formal laws that are formulated, proclaimed, and enforced.

Foragers lacked formal **law** in the sense of a legal code with trial and enforcement, but they did have methods of social control and dispute settlement. The absence of law did not mean total anarchy. As described by E. A. Hoebel (1954) in a classic ethnographic study of conflict resolution, a sparse population of some 20,000 Inuit spanned 6,000 miles (9,500 kilometers) of the Arctic region. The most significant social groups were the nuclear family and the band. Personal relationships linked the families and bands. Some bands had headmen. There also were shamans (part-time religious specialists). However, these positions conferred little power on those who occupied them.

Hunting and fishing by men were the primary Inuit subsistence activities. The diverse and abundant plant foods available in warmer areas, where female labor in gathering is important, were absent in the Arctic. Traveling on land and sea in a bitter environment, Inuit men faced more dangers than women did. The traditional male role took its toll in lives, so that adult women outnumbered men. This permitted some men to have two or three wives. The ability to support more than one wife conferred a certain amount of prestige, but it also encouraged envy. (Prestige is social esteem, respect, or approval.) If a man seemed to be taking additional wives just to enhance his reputation, a rival was likely to steal one of them. Most Inuit disputes were between men and originated over women, caused by wife stealing or adultery.

A jilted husband had several options. He could try to kill the wife stealer. However, if he succeeded, one of his rival's kinsmen surely would try to kill him in retaliation. One dispute might escalate into several deaths as relatives avenged a succession of murders. No government existed to intervene and stop such a *blood feud* (a murderous feud between families). However, one also could challenge a rival to a song battle. In a public setting, contestants made up insulting songs about each other. At the end of the match, the audience proclaimed the winner. However, if the winner was the man whose wife had been stolen, there was no guarantee she would return. Often she stayed with her abductor.

Thefts are common in societies with marked property differentials, like our own, but thefts are uncommon among foragers. Each Inuit had access to the resources he or she needed to sustain life. Every man could hunt, fish, and make the tools necessary for subsistence. Every woman could obtain the materials needed to make clothing, prepare food, and do domestic work. Inuit men could even hunt and fish in the territories of other local groups. There was no notion of private ownership of territory or animals.

Tribal Cultivators

As is true of foraging bands, there are no totally autonomous tribes in today's world. Still, there are societies, for example, in Papua New Guinea and in South America's tropical forests, in which tribal principles continue to operate. Tribes typically have a horticultural or pastoral economy and are organized into villages and/or *descent groups* (kin groups whose members trace descent from a common ancestor). Tribes lack socioeconomic stratification (i.e., a class structure) and a formal government of their own. A few tribes still conduct small-scale warfare, in the form of intervillage raiding. Tribes have more effective regulatory mechanisms than foragers do, but tribal societies have no sure means of enforcing political decisions. The main regulatory officials are village heads, "big men," descent-group leaders, village councils, and leaders of pantribal associations (see later in the chapter). All these figures and groups have limited authority.

Like foragers, horticulturalists tend to be egalitarian, although some have marked *gender stratification:* an unequal distribution of resources, power, prestige, and personal freedom between men and women (see the chapter "Gender"). Horticultural villages usually are small, with low population density and open access to strategic resources. Age, gender, and personal traits determine how much respect people receive and how much support they get from others. Egalitarianism diminishes, however, as village size and population density increase. Horticultural villages usually have headmen—rarely, if ever, headwomen.

The Village Head

The Yanomami (Chagnon 1997; Ferguson 1995; Ramos 1995) are Native Americans who live in southern Venezuela and the adjacent part of Brazil. When anthropologists first studied them, they numbered about 26,000 people living in 200 to 250 widely scattered villages, each with a population between 40 and 250. The Yanomami are horticulturalists who also hunt and gather. Their staple crops are bananas and plantains (a bananalike crop). There are more significant social groups among the Yanomami than exist in a foraging society. The Yanomami have families, villages, and descent groups. Their descent groups, which span more than one village, are *patrilineal* (ancestry is traced back through males only) and *exogamous* (people must marry outside their own descent group). However, branches of two different descent groups may live in the same village and intermarry.

Traditionally among the Yanomami the only leadership position has been that of **village head** (always a man). His authority, like that of a foraging band's leader, is severely limited. If a headman wants something done, he must lead by example and persuasion. The headman lacks the right to issue orders. He can only persuade, harangue, and try to influence public opinion. For example, if he wants people to clean up the central plaza in preparation for a feast, he must start sweeping it himself, hoping his covillagers will take the hint and relieve him.

When conflict erupts within the village, the headman may be called on as a mediator who listens to both sides. He will give an opinion and advice. If a disputant is unsatisfied, the headman has no power to back his decisions and no way to impose punishments. Like the band leader, he is first among equals.

A Yanomami village headman also must lead in generosity. Expected to be more generous than any other villager, he cultivates more land. His garden provides much of the food consumed when his village hosts a feast for another village. The headman represents the village in its dealings with outsiders, including Venezuelan and Brazilian government agents.

The way someone acts as headman depends on his personal traits and the number of supporters he can muster. Napoleon Chagnon (1983/1992) describes how one village headman, Kaobawa, guaranteed safety to a delegation from a village with which a covillager of his wanted to start a war. Kaobawa was a particularly effective headman. He had demonstrated his fierceness in battle, but he also knew how to use diplomacy to avoid offending other villagers. No one in his village had a better personality for the headmanship. Nor (because Kaobawa had many brothers) did anyone have more supporters. Among the Yanomami, when a village is dissatisfied with its headman, its members can leave and found a new village. This happens from time to time and is called *village fissioning*.

With its many villages and descent groups, Yanomami sociopolitical organization is more complicated than that of a band-organized society. The Yanomami face more problems in regulating relations between groups and individuals. Although a headman sometimes can prevent a specific violent act, intervillage raiding has been a feature of some areas of Yanomami territory, particularly those studied by Chagnon (1997).

It's important to recognize as well that the Yanomami are not isolated from outside events. They live in two nation-states, Venezuela and Brazil, and attacks by outsiders, especially Brazilian ranchers and miners, have plagued them (Chagnon 1997; *Cultural Survival Quarterly* 1989; Ferguson 1995). During a Brazilian gold rush between 1987 and 1991, one Yanomami died each day, on average, from such attacks. By 1991, there were some 40,000 miners in the Brazilian Yanomami homeland. Some Yanomami were killed outright. The miners introduced new diseases, and the swollen population ensured that old diseases became epidemic. In 1991, the American Anthropological Association reported on the plight of the Yanomami (*Anthropology Newsletter,* September 1991). Brazilian Yanomami were dying at a rate of 10 percent annually, and their fertility rate had dropped to zero. Since then, one Brazilian president declared a huge Yanomami territory off-limits to outsiders. Unfortunately, local politicians, miners, and ranchers have managed to evade the ban. The future of the Yanomami remains uncertain (see Romero 2008).

The "Big Man"

Many societies of the South Pacific, particularly on the Melanesian Islands and in Papua New Guinea, had a kind of political leader that we call the big man. The **big man** (almost always a male) was an elaborate version of the village head, but with one significant difference. Unlike the village head, whose leadership is limited to one village, the big man had supporters in several villages. The big man thus was a regulator of *regional* political organization.

Consider the Kapauku Papuans, inhabitants of Irian Jaya, Indonesia (located on the island of New Guinea). Anthropologist Leopold Pospisil (1963) studied the Kapauku (then 45,000 people), who grew crops (with the sweet potato as their staple) and raised pigs. Their cultivation system was too labor-intensive to be described as simple horticulture. It required mutual aid in turning the soil before planting. The digging of long drainage ditches, which a big man often helped organize, was even more complex. Kapauku cultivation supported a larger and denser population than does the simpler horticulture of the Yanomami. The Kapauku economy required collective cultivation and political regulation of the more complex tasks.

The key political figure among the Kapauku was the big man. Known as a *tonowi,* he achieved his status through hard work, amassing wealth in the form of pigs and other native riches. Consider the term *status,* which often is used as a synonym for *prestige.* Thus, "she's got a lot of status" means she's got a lot of prestige; people look up to her. Among social scientists, however, that's not the primary meaning of *status.* Social scientists use **status** more neutrally—for any social position, no matter what its prestige. In this sense, status encompasses all the positions that people occupy in society, such as spouse, parent, trading partner, teacher, student, salesperson, big man, and many others. People always occupy multiple statuses (e.g., son, brother, father, big man). Among the statuses we occupy, particular ones dominate in particular settings, such as son or daughter at home and student in the classroom.

Some statuses are **ascribed:** People have little or no choice about occupying them. Age is an ascribed status; we can't choose not to age. One's status as a member of the nobility, or as a male or a female, usually is ascribed; people are born members of a

The big man persuades people to organize feasts, which distribute pork and wealth. Shown here is such a regional event, drawing on several villages, in Papua New Guinea. Big men owe their status to their individual personalities rather than to inherited wealth or position. Does our society have equivalents of big men?

certain social category and remain so all their lives. **Achieved statuses,** by contrast, aren't automatic; they are based on choices, actions, efforts, or circumstances and may be positive or negative. Examples of achieved statuses include big man, healer, senator, convicted felon, terrorist, salesperson, union member, father, and college student.

The achieved status of the big man rested on certain characteristics that distinguished the big man from his fellows. Key attributes included wealth, generosity, eloquence, physical fitness, bravery, supernatural powers, and the ability to gain the support and loyalty of others. Men became big men because they had certain personalities; they did not inherit their status but created it through hard work and good judgment. Wealth resulted from successful pig breeding and trading. As a man's pig herd and prestige grew, he attracted supporters. He sponsored pig feasts in which pork (provided by the big man and his supporters) was distributed to guests, bringing him more prestige and widening his network of support.

The big man's supporters, recognizing his past favors and anticipating future rewards, recognized him as a leader and accepted his decisions as binding. The tonowi was an important regulator of regional events in Kapauku life. He helped determine the dates for feasts and markets. He initiated economic projects requiring the cooperation of a regional community.

The Kapauku big man again exemplifies a generalization about leadership in tribal societies: If someone achieves wealth and widespread respect and support, he or she must be generous. The big man worked hard not to hoard wealth but to be able to give away the fruits of his labor, to convert wealth into prestige and gratitude. A stingy big man would lose his support. Selfish and greedy big men sometimes were murdered by their fellows (Zimmer-Tamakoshi 1997).

How similar are contemporary politicians to the big man? Big men get their loyalists to produce and deliver pigs, just as modern politicians persuade their supporters to make campaign contributions. And, like big men, successful American politicians try to be generous with their supporters. Payback may take the form of a night in the Lincoln bedroom, a strategic dinner invitation, an ambassadorship, or largesse to a place that was particularly supportive. Big men amass wealth, then distribute pigs and their meat.

Successful American politicians also give away "pork." As with the big man, elo-quence and communication skills contribute to political success (e.g., Ronald Reagan, Bill Clinton, Barack Obama), although lack of such skills isn't necessarily fatal (e.g., either President Bush). What about physical fitness? Hair, height, and health are still political advantages. Bravery, in the form of military service, also helps politi-cal careers (e.g., Wesley Clark and John McCain), but it certainly isn't required, nor does it guarantee success. Supernatural powers? Candidates who proclaim themselves atheists are even rarer than self-identified witches (or not witches). Almost all political candidates claim to belong to a mainstream religion. Some even present their candida-cies as promoting God's will.

On the other hand, contemporary politics isn't just about personality, as it is in big man systems. We live in a state-organized, stratified society with inherited wealth, power, and privilege, all of which have political implications. As is typical of states, inheritance and kin connections play a role in political success. Just think of Kennedys, Bushes, Gores, Clintons, and Gandhis.

Pantribal Sodalities

Big men could forge regional political organization, albeit temporarily, by mobilizing supporters from several villages. Other principles in tribal societies—such as a belief in common ancestry, kinship, or descent—could be used to link local groups within a re-gion. The same descent group, for example, might span several villages, and its dis-persed members might recognize the same leader.

Principles other than kinship also can link local groups, especially in modern societ-ies. People who live in different parts of the same nation may belong to the same labor union, sorority or fraternity, political party, or religious denomination. In tribes, nonkin groups called *associations* or *sodalities* may serve a similar linking function. Often, sodalities are based on common age or gender, with all-male sodalities more common than all-female ones.

Pantribal sodalities are groups that extend across the whole tribe, spanning several villages. Such sodalities were especially likely to develop in situations of warfare with a neighboring tribe. Mobilizing their members from multiple villages within the same tribe, pantribal sodalities could assemble a force to attack or retaliate against another tribe.

The best examples of pantribal sodalities come from the Central Plains of North America and from tropical Africa. During the 18th and 19th centuries, Native American populations of the Great Plains of the United States and Canada experienced a rapid growth of pantribal sodalities. This development reflected an economic change that fol-lowed the spread of horses, which had been reintroduced to the Americas by the Spanish, to the area between the Rocky Mountains and the Mississippi River. Many Plains Indian societies changed their adaptive strategies because of the horse. At first they had been foragers who hunted bison (buffalo) on foot. Later they adopted a mixed economy based on hunting, gathering, and horticulture. Finally they changed to a much more special-ized economy based on horseback hunting of bison (eventually with rifles).

As the Plains tribes were undergoing these changes, other Indians also adopted horseback hunting and moved into the Plains. Attempting to occupy the same area, groups came into conflict. A pattern of warfare developed in which the members of one tribe raided another, usually for horses. The economy demanded that people follow the movement of the bison herds. During the winter, when the bison dispersed, a tribe fragmented into small bands and families. In the summer, when huge herds assembled on the Plains, the tribe reunited. They camped together for social, political, and religious activities, but mainly for communal bison hunting.

Two activities demanded strong leadership: organizing and carrying out raids on enemy camps (to capture horses) and managing the summer bison hunt. All the Plains societies developed pantribal sodalities, and leadership roles within them, to police the summer hunt. Leaders coordinated hunting efforts, making sure that people did not cause a stampede with an early shot or an ill-advised action. Leaders imposed severe penalties, including seizure of a culprit's wealth, for disobedience.

Many tribes that adopted this Plains strategy of adaptation had once been foragers for whom hunting and gathering had been individual or small-group affairs. They never had come together previously as a single social unit. Age and gender were available as social principles that could quickly and efficiently forge unrelated people into pantribal sodalities.

Raiding of one tribe by another, this time for cattle rather than horses, also was common in eastern and southeastern Africa, where pantribal sodalities also developed. Among the pastoral Masai of Kenya, men born during the same four-year period were circumcised together and belonged to the same named group, an age set, throughout their lives. The sets moved through *age grades,* the most important of which was the warrior grade. Members of a set felt a strong allegiance to one another. Masai women lacked comparable set organization, but they also passed through culturally recognized age grades: the initiate, the married woman, and the female elder.

In certain parts of western and central Africa, pantribal sodalities are secret societies, made up exclusively of men or women. Like our college fraternities and sororities, these associations have secret initiation ceremonies. Among the Mende of Sierra Leone, men's and women's secret societies were very influential. The men's group, the Poro, trained boys in social conduct, ethics, and religion and supervised political and economic activities. Leadership roles in the Poro often overshadowed village headship and played an important part in social control, dispute management, and tribal political regulation. Age, gender, and ritual can link members of different local groups into a single social collectivity in a tribe and thus create a sense of ethnic identity, of belonging to the same cultural tradition.

Nomadic Politics

Herders have varied political systems. Unlike the Masai (just discussed) and other tribal herders, some pastoralists have chiefs and live in nation-states. The scope of political authority among pastoralists expands considerably as regulatory problems increase in densely populated regions (see Salzman 2008). Consider two Iranian pastoral nomadic tribes—the Basseri and the Qashqai (Salzman 1974). Starting each year from a plateau near the coast, these groups took their animals to grazing land 17,000 feet (5,400 meters) above sea level. The Basseri and the Qashqai shared this route with one another and with several other ethnic groups.

Use of the same pasture land at different times of year was carefully scheduled. Ethnic-group movements were tightly coordinated. Expressing this schedule is *il-rah,* a concept common to all Iranian nomads. A group's il-rah is its customary path in time and space. It is the schedule, different for each group, of when specific areas can be used in the annual trek.

Each tribe had its own leader, known as the *khan* or *il-khan*. The Basseri khan, because he dealt with a smaller population, faced fewer problems in coordinating its movements than did the leaders of the Qashqai. Correspondingly, his rights, privileges, duties, and authority were weaker. Nevertheless, his authority exceeded that of any political figure discussed so far. The khan's authority still came from his personal traits rather than from his office. That is, the Basseri followed a particular khan not because of a political position he happened to fill but because of their personal allegiance and loyalty to him as a man. The khan relied on the support of the heads of the descent groups into which Basseri society was divided.

Among the Qashqai, however, allegiance shifted from the person to the office. The Qashqai had multiple levels of authority and more powerful chiefs or khans. Managing 400,000 people required a complex hierarchy. Heading it was the il-khan, helped by a deputy, under whom were the heads of constituent tribes, under each of whom were descent-group heads.

A case illustrates just how developed the Qashqai authority structure was. A hailstorm prevented some nomads from joining the annual migration at the appointed time. Although all the nomads recognized that they were not responsible for their delay, the il-khan assigned them less favorable grazing land, for that year only, in place of their usual pasture. The tardy herders and other Qashqai considered the judgment fair and didn't question it. Thus, Qashqai authorities regulated the annual migration. They also adjudicated disputes between people, tribes, and descent groups.

These Iranian cases illustrate the fact that pastoralism often is just one among many specialized economic activities within a nation-state. As part of a larger whole, pastoral tribes are constantly pitted against other ethnic groups. In these nations, the state becomes a final authority, a higher-level regulator that attempts to limit conflict between ethnic groups. State organization arose not just to manage agricultural economies but also to regulate the activities of ethnic groups within expanding social and economic systems (see Das and Poole, eds. 2004).

Chiefdoms

The first states emerged in the Old World around 5,500 years ago. The first chiefdoms developed perhaps a thousand years earlier, but few survive today. In many parts of the world, the chiefdom was a transitional form of organization that emerged during the evolution of tribes into states. State formation began in Mesopotamia (currently Iran and Iraq). It next occurred in Egypt, the Indus Valley of Pakistan and India, and northern China. A few thousand years later states arose in two parts of the Western Hemisphere—Mesoamerica (Mexico, Guatemala, Belize) and the central Andes (Peru and Bolivia). Early states are known as *archaic,* or *nonindustrial,* states, in contrast to modern industrial nation-states. Robert Carneiro defines the state as "an autonomous political unit encompassing many communities within its territory, having a centralized government with the power to collect taxes, draft men for work or war, and decree and enforce laws" (1970, p. 733).

The chiefdom and the state, like many categories used by social scientists, are *ideal types*. That is, they are labels that make social contrasts seem sharper than they really are. In reality there is a continuum from tribe to chiefdom to state. Some societies had many attributes of chiefdoms but retained tribal features. Some advanced chiefdoms had many attributes of archaic states and thus are difficult to assign to either category. Recognizing this "continuous change" (Johnson and Earle 2000), some anthropologists speak of "complex chiefdoms" (Earle 1987, 1997), which are almost states.

Political and Economic Systems

Geographic areas where chiefdoms existed included the circum-Caribbean (e.g., Caribbean islands, Panama, Colombia), lowland Amazonia, what is now the southeastern United States, and Polynesia. Chiefdoms created the megalithic cultures of Europe, including the one that built Stonehenge. Bear in mind that chiefdoms and states can fall (disintegrate) as well as rise. Before Rome's expansion, much of Europe was organized at the chiefdom level, to which it reverted for centuries after the fall of Rome in the 5th century C.E.

Stonehenge, England, and an educational display designed for tourists and visitors. Chiefdoms created the megalithic cultures of Europe, such as the one that built Stonehenge over 5,000 years ago. Between the emergence and spread of food production and the expansion of the Roman empire, much of Europe was organized at the chiefdom level, to which it reverted after the fall of Rome.

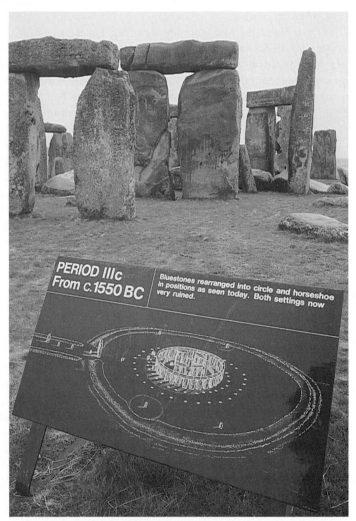

Much of our ethnographic knowledge about chiefdoms comes from Polynesia, where they were common at the time of European exploration. In chiefdoms, social relations are based mainly on kinship, marriage, descent, age, generation, and gender—just as in bands and tribes. This is a fundamental difference between chiefdoms and states. States bring nonrelatives together and oblige them all to pledge allegiance to a government.

Unlike bands and tribes, however, chiefdoms administer a clear-cut and permanent regional political system. Chiefdoms may include thousands of people living in many villages or hamlets. Regulation is carried out by the chief and his or her assistants, who occupy political offices. An **office** is a permanent position, which must be refilled when it is vacated by death or retirement. Because official vacancies are filled systematically, the political system that is the chiefdom endures across the generations, thus ensuring permanent political regulation.

Polynesian chiefs were full-time specialists whose duties included managing the economy. They regulated production by commanding or prohibiting (using religious taboos) the cultivation of certain lands and crops. Chiefs also regulated distribution and consumption. At certain seasons—often on a ritual occasion such as a first-fruit ceremony—people would offer part of their harvest to the chief through his or her representatives. Products moved up the hierarchy, eventually reaching the chief. Conversely, illustrating obligatory sharing with kin, chiefs sponsored feasts at which they gave back some of what they had received. Unlike big men, chiefs were exempt from ordinary work and had rights and privileges unavailable to the masses. Like big men, however, they still returned a portion of the wealth they took in.

Such a flow of resources to and then from a central place is known as *chiefly redistribution,* which offers economic advantages. If different parts of the chiefdom specialized in particular products, chiefly redistribution made those products available to the entire society. Chiefly redistribution also helped stimulate production beyond the basic subsistence level and provided a central storehouse for goods that might become scarce in times of famine (Earle 1987, 1997).

Status Systems

Social status in chiefdoms was based on seniority of descent. Polynesian chiefs kept extremely long genealogies. Some chiefs (without writing) managed to trace their ancestry back 50 generations. All the people in the chiefdom were thought to be related to each other. Presumably, all were descended from a group of founding ancestors.

The status of chief was ascribed, based on seniority of descent. The chief would be the oldest child (usually son) of the oldest child of the oldest child, and so on. Degrees of seniority were calculated so intricately on some islands that there were as many ranks as people. For example, the third son would rank below the second, who in turn would rank below the first. The children of an eldest brother, however, would all rank above the children of the next brother, whose children in turn would outrank those of younger brothers. However, even the lowest-ranking man or woman in a chiefdom was still the chief's relative. In such a kin-based context, everyone, even a chief, had to share with his or her relatives. Because everyone had a slightly different status, it was difficult to draw a line between elites and common people. Other chiefdoms calculated seniority differently and had shorter genealogies than did those in Polynesia.

Still, the concern for seniority and the lack of sharp gaps between elites and commoners are features of all chiefdoms.

The status systems of chiefdoms, as of states, were associated with differential access to resources. Some men and women had privileged access to power, prestige, and wealth. They controlled strategic resources such as land and water. Earle characterizes chiefs as "an incipient aristocracy with advantages in wealth and lifestyle" (1987, p. 290).

Compared with chiefdoms, archaic states drew a much firmer line between elites and masses, distinguishing at least between nobles and commoners. Kinship ties did not extend from the nobles to the commoners because of *stratum endogamy*—marriage within one's own group. Commoners married commoners; elites married elites.

The Emergence of Stratification

The status system of a chiefdom differed from that of a state because of the chiefdom's kinship basis. In the context of differential wealth and power, the chiefly type of status system didn't last very long. Chiefs would start acting like kings and try to erode the kinship basis of the chiefdom. In Madagascar they would do this by demoting their more distant relatives to commoner status and banning marriage between nobles and commoners (Kottak 1980). Such moves, if accepted by the society, created separate *social strata*—unrelated groups that differ in their access to wealth, prestige, and power. (A *stratum* is one of two or more groups that contrast in social status and access to strategic resources. Each stratum includes people of both sexes and all ages.) The creation of separate social strata is called *stratification,* and its emergence signified the transition from chiefdom to state. The presence of stratification is one of the key distinguishing features of a state.

The influential sociologist Max Weber (1922/1968) defined three related dimensions of social stratification: (1) Economic status, or **wealth,** encompasses all a person's material assets, including income, land, and other types of property. (2) Power, the ability to exercise one's will over others—to get what one wants—is the basis of political status. (3) **Prestige**—the basis of social status—refers to esteem, respect, or approval for acts, deeds, or qualities considered exemplary. Prestige, or "cultural capital" (Bourdieu 1984), gives people a sense of worth and respect, which they may often convert into economic advantage (Table 6.1).

Winning a lottery confers wealth, but not necessarily prestige or power. Shown here, on November 1, 2012 in San Bernardino, California, Julie Cervera, surrounded by family members, holds a $23 million lottery prize banner. Cervera almost missed out on her prize: The winning ticket lay undiscovered in her car's glove compartment for months and almost expired.

wealth	economic status
power	political status
prestige	social status

TABLE 6.1
**Max Weber's Three
Dimensions of
Stratification**

In archaic states—for the first time in human evolution—there were contrasts in wealth, power, and prestige between entire groups (social strata) of men and women. Each stratum included people of both genders and all ages. The **superordinate** (the higher, or elite) stratum had privileged access to valued resources. Access to those resources by members of the **subordinate** (lower, or underprivileged) stratum was limited by the privileged group.

State Systems

Table 6.2 summarizes the information presented so far on bands, tribes, chiefdoms, and states. States, remember, are autonomous political units with social strata and a formal government. States tend to be large and populous, and certain statuses, systems, and subsystems with specialized functions are found in all states (see Sharma and Gupta, eds. 2006). They include the following:

- Population control: fixing of boundaries, establishment of citizenship categories, and censusing.
- Judiciary: laws, legal procedure, and judges.
- Enforcement: permanent military and police forces.
- Fiscal support: taxation.

In archaic states, these subsystems were integrated by a ruling system or government composed of civil, military, and religious officials (Fried 1960). Let's look at the four subsystems one by one.

Population Control
To keep track of whom they govern, states conduct censuses. States demarcate boundaries to separate that state from other societies. Customs agents, immigration officers,

TABLE 6.2   **Economic Basis of and Political Regulation in Bands, Tribes, Chiefdoms, and States**

Sociopolitical Type	Economic Type	Examples	Type of Regulation
Band	Foraging	Inuit, San	Local
Tribe	Horticulture, pastoralism	Yanomami, Masai, Kapauku	Local, temporary, regional
Chiefdom	Intensive horti-culture, pastoral nomadism, agriculture	Qashqai, Polynesia, Cherokee	Permanent, regional
State	Agriculture, industrialism	Ancient Mesopotamia, contemporary U.S., Canada	Permanent, regional

navies, and coast guards patrol frontiers. States also regulate population through administrative subdivision: provinces, districts, "states," counties, subcounties, and parishes. Lower-level officials manage the populations and territories of the subdivisions.

States often promote geographic mobility and resettlement, severing longstanding ties among people, land, and kin (Smith 2003). Population displacements have increased with globalization and as war, famine, and job seeking churn up migratory currents. People in states come to identify themselves by new statuses, both ascribed and achieved—including residence, ethnicity, occupation, political party, religion, and team or club affiliation—rather than only as members of a descent group or extended family.

States also manage their populations by granting different rights and obligations to citizens and noncitizens. Status distinctions among citizens also are common. Archaic states granted different rights to nobles, commoners, and slaves. In American history before the Emancipation Proclamation, there were different laws for enslaved and free people. In European colonies, separate courts judged cases involving only natives and cases involving Europeans. In contemporary America, a military judiciary coexists alongside the civil system.

Judiciary

All states have laws based on precedent and legislative proclamations. Without writing, laws may be preserved in oral tradition. *Crimes* are violations of the legal code ("breaking the law"), with specified types of punishment. To handle crimes and disputes, all states have courts and judges.

A striking contrast between states and nonstates is intervention in family affairs. Governments step in to halt blood feuds and regulate previously private disputes. States attempt to curb *internal* conflict, but they aren't always successful. About 85 percent of the world's armed conflicts since 1945 have begun within states—in efforts to overthrow a ruling regime or as disputes over ethnic, religious, or human rights issues (see Barnaby, ed. 1984; Chatterjee 2004; Nordstrom 2004; Tishkov 2004).

Enforcement

All states have agents to enforce judicial decisions, for example, to impose punishments and collect fines. Confinement requires jailers. If there is a death penalty, executioners are needed. Government officials have the power to collect fines and confiscate property. The government attempts to suppress internal disorder (with police) and to guard against external threats (with the military and border officials).

Armies help states subdue and conquer neighboring nonstates, but this isn't the only reason state organization has spread. Although states impose hardships, they also offer advantages. They have formal mechanisms designed to protect against external threats and to preserve internal order. When they are successful in promoting internal peace, states enhance production. Their economies can support massive, dense populations, which supply armies and colonists to promote expansion.

Fiscal Support

States need financial, or **fiscal,** mechanisms (e.g., taxation) to support government officials and numerous other specialists. As in the chiefdom, the state intervenes in production, distribution, and consumption. The state may require a certain area to produce specific things or ban certain activities in particular places. Although, like chiefdoms, states have redistribution ("spreading the wealth around"), less of what comes in from the people actually goes back to the people.

In nonstates, people customarily share with their relatives, but citizens also have to turn over a substantial portion of what they produce to the state. Markets and trade usually are under at least some state oversight, with officials overseeing distribution and exchange, standardizing weights and measures, and collecting taxes on goods passing into or through the state. Of the revenues the state collects, it reallocates part for the general good and keeps another part (often larger) for itself—its agents and agencies. State organization doesn't bring more freedom or leisure to the common people, who may be conscripted to build monumental public works. Some projects, such as dams and irrigation systems, may be economically necessary, but residents of archaic states also had to build temples, palaces, and tombs for the elites. Those elites reveled in the consumption of sumptuary goods—jewelry, exotic food and drink, and stylish clothing reserved for, or affordable only by, the rich. Peasants' diets suffered as they struggled to meet government demands. Commoners perished in territorial wars that had little relevance to their own needs. Are any of these observations true of contemporary states?

Social Control

In studying political systems, anthropologists pay attention not only to the formal institutions but to other forms of social control as well. The concept of social control is broader than "the political." **Social control** refers to "those fields of the social system (beliefs, practices, and institutions) that are most actively involved in the maintenance of any norms and the regulation of any conflict" (N. Kottak 2002, p. 290). *Norms,* as defined earlier in this chapter, are cultural standards or guidelines that enable individuals to distinguish between appropriate and inappropriate behavior.

Previous sections of this chapter have focused more on formal political organization than on sociopolitical process. We've seen how the scale and strength of political systems have expanded in relation to economic changes. We've examined means of conflict resolution, or their absence, in various types of society. We've looked at political decision making, including leaders and their limits. We've also recognized that all contemporary humans have been affected by states, colonialism, and the spread of the world system (see Shore, Wright, and Peró [2011] and this chapter's "Anthropology Today").

Sociopolitical was introduced as a key concept at the beginning of this chapter. So far, we've focused mainly on the *political* part of sociopolitical; now we focus on the *social* part. In this section we'll see that political systems have their informal, social, and subtle aspects along with their formal, governmental, and public dimensions.

Hegemony and Resistance

Antonio Gramsci (1971) developed the concept of **hegemony** for a stratified social order in which subordinates comply with domination by internalizing their rulers' values and accepting the "naturalness" of domination (this is the way things were meant to be). According to Pierre Bourdieu (1977, p. 164), every social order tries to make its own arbitrariness (including its mechanisms of control and domination) seem natural and in everyone's interest. Often promises are made (things will get better if you're patient).

Both Bourdieu (1977) and Michel Foucault (1979) argue that it is easier and more effective to dominate people in their minds than to try to control their bodies. Nonphysical forms of social control include various techniques of persuading and managing people and of monitoring and recording their beliefs, activities, and contacts.

Hegemony, the internalization of a dominant ideology, is one way in which elites curb resistance and maintain power. Another way is to make subordinates believe they eventually will gain power—as young people usually foresee when they let their elders dominate them. Another way of curbing resistance is to separate or isolate people while supervising them closely, as is done in prisons (Foucault 1979).

Popular resistance is most likely to be expressed openly when people are allowed to assemble. The oppressed may draw courage from their common sentiments and the anonymity of the crowd. Sensing danger, the elites often discourage public gatherings. They try to limit and control holidays, funerals, dances, festivals, and other occasions that might unite the oppressed. For example, in the American South before the Civil War, gatherings of five or more slaves were prohibited unless a White person was present.

Factors that interfere with community formation—such as geographic, linguistic, and ethnic separation—also work to curb resistance. Consequently, Southern U.S. plantation owners sought slaves with diverse cultural and linguistic backgrounds. Despite the measures used to divide them, the slaves resisted, developing their own popular culture, linguistic codes, and religious vision. The masters stressed portions of the Bible that emphasized compliance, such as the book of Job. The slaves, however, preferred the story of Moses and deliverance. The cornerstone of slave religion became the idea of a reversal in the conditions of Whites and Blacks. Slaves also resisted directly, through sabotage and flight. In many New World areas, slaves managed to establish free communities in the hills and other isolated areas (Price, ed. 1973).

Weapons of the Weak

The study of sociopolitical systems also should consider the sentiments and activity that may lurk beneath the surface of evident, public behavior. In public, the oppressed may seem to accept their own domination, even as they question it in private. James Scott (1990) uses the phrase "public transcript" to describe the open, public interactions between superordinates and subordinates—the outer shell of power relations. He uses "hidden transcript" to describe the critique of power that proceeds out of sight of the power holders. In public, the elites and the oppressed may observe the etiquette of power relations. The dominants act like masters while their subordinates show humility and defer.

Often, situations that seem to be hegemonic do have active resistance, but it is individual and disguised rather than collective and defiant. James Scott (1985) uses Malay peasants, among whom he did fieldwork, to illustrate small-scale acts of resistance—which he calls "weapons of the weak." The Malay peasants used an indirect strategy to resist an Islamic tithe (religious tax). Peasants were expected to pay the tithe, usually in the form of rice, which was sent to the provincial capital. In theory, the tithe would come back as charity, but it never did. Peasants didn't resist the tithe by rioting, demonstrating, or protesting. Instead they used a "nibbling" strategy, based on small acts of resistance. For example, they failed to declare their land or lied about the amount they farmed. They underpaid, or they delivered rice contaminated with water, rocks, or mud, to add weight. Because of this resistance, only 15 percent of what was due actually was paid (Scott 1990, p. 89).

Hidden transcripts tend to be expressed publicly at certain times (festivals and Carnavals) and in certain places (such as markets). Because of its costumed anonymity, Carnaval (Mardi Gras in New Orleans) is an excellent arena for expressing normally suppressed feelings. Carnavals celebrate freedom through immodesty, dancing, gluttony, and sexuality (DaMatta 1991). Carnaval may begin as a playful outlet for frustrations built up during the year. Over time, it may evolve into a powerful annual critique of stratification and domination and thus a threat to the established order (Gilmore 1987). (Recognizing that ceremonial license could turn into political defiance, the Spanish dictator Francisco Franco outlawed Carnaval.)

Shame and Gossip

Many anthropologists have cited the importance of "informal" processes of social control, such as stigma, shame, and gossip, especially in small-scale societies (see Freilich, Raybeck, and Savishinsky 1991). Gossip, which can lead to shame, sometimes is used when a direct or formal sanction is risky or impossible (Herskovits 1937). Margaret Mead (1937) and Ruth Benedict (1946) distinguished between *shame* as an external sanction (i.e., forces set in motion by others) and *guilt* as an internal sanction, psychologically generated by the individual. They regarded shame as a more prominent form of social control in non-Western societies and guilt as a more dominant emotional sanction in Western societies. Of course, to be effective as a sanction, the prospect of being shamed or of shaming oneself must be internalized by the individual. In small-scale societies, in a social environment where everyone knows everyone else, most people try to avoid behavior that might spoil their reputations and alienate them from their social network (N. Kottak 2002).

Bronislaw Malinowski (1927) described how Trobriand Islanders might climb to the top of a palm tree and dive to their deaths because they couldn't tolerate the shame associated with public knowledge of some stigmatizing action. Nicholas Kottak (2002) heard Makua villagers in northern Mozambique tell the story of a man rumored to have fathered a child with his stepdaughter. The political authorities imposed no formal sanctions (e.g., a fine or jail time) on this man, but gossip about the affair circulated widely. The gossip crystallized in the lyrics of a song that groups of young women would perform. After the man heard his name and behavior mentioned in that song, he hanged himself by the neck from a tree. (Previously we saw the role of song in the social control system of the Inuit. We'll see it again in the case of the Igbo women's war, discussed in the next section.)

Although it isn't part of any formal or official authority structure, shame can be a powerful social sanction. People aren't just citizens of governments; they are members of society, and social sanctions exist alongside governmental ones. Such sanctions exemplify other "weapons of the weak," because they often are wielded most effectively by people, such as women or young people, who have limited access to the formal authority structure.

The Igbo Women's War

Shame and ridicule—used by women against men—played a key role in a decisive protest movement that took place in southeastern Nigeria in late 1929. This is remembered as the "Aba Women's Riots of 1929" in British colonial history and as the "Women's War" in Igbo history (see Dorward, ed. 1983; Martin 1988; Mba 1982; Oriji 2000; Van Allen 1971). During this two-month "war," at least 25,000 Igbo women joined protests against British officials, their agents, and their colonial policies. This massive revolt touched off the most serious challenge to British rule in the history of what was then the British colony of Nigeria.

In 1914, the British had implemented a policy of indirect rule by appointing local Nigerian men as their agents—known as "warrant chiefs." These chiefs became increasingly oppressive, seizing property, imposing arbitrary regulations, and imprisoning people who criticized them. Colonial administrators further stoked local outrage when they announced plans to impose taxes on Igbo market women. These women were key suppliers of food for Nigeria's growing urban population; they feared being forced out of business by the new tax. Market women were key organizers of the protests.

After hearing about the tax in November 1929, thousands of Igbo women assembled in various towns to protest both the warrant chiefs and the taxes on market women. They used a traditional practice of censoring and shaming men through all-night song and dance ridicule (often called "sitting on a man"). This process entailed constant singing and dancing around the houses and offices of the warrant chiefs. The women also followed the chiefs' every move, forcing the men to pay attention by invading their space.

Funmilayo Ransome Kuti (1900–1978), a prominent Nigerian leader, who fought for Nigerian women's right to vote. Kuti, mother of Fela Kuti, an internationally known musician, was the first woman in Nigeria to drive a car and to ride a bike.

Anthropology Today *Politics and Power in a Globalizing Countryside*

The news story that follows discusses local-level politics (and evidence of globalization) in rural Thailand, which has experienced a dramatic social, economic, and political transformation. Soon after this story was written, Thailand's newly empowered rural electorate was key to the election of Yingluck Shinawatra as that country's first female prime minister. In July 2011 her party won a landslide victory over a coalition backed by the nation's military and traditional elites. Prime Minister Shinawatra, at age 44, received 296 votes in Thailand's 500-seat Parliament. One of her early actions was to approve a development fund providing low- or no-interest loans to women.

BAAN NONG TUN, Thailand—Smiling farmers knee deep in emerald rice paddies and shirtless children riding on the backs of mud-caked water buffalo. These are the romantic images of the Thai countryside. There is one problem with it, says Udom Thapsuri, a farmer here. . . . It does not exist anymore. . . .

As campaigning for the national election . . . entered its final days, there was broad consensus that rural votes would be crucial in deciding the outcome. But no one is quite sure what rural means anymore.

Villagers here complain of slow Internet download speeds. . . . Residents tell of work stints in Taiwan, Singapore, Israel and Saudi Arabia. . . .

Villagers are now better educated, more mobile, less deferential and ultimately more politically demanding. . . .

The old social contract, whereby power flowed from Bangkok and the political establishment could count on quiet acquiescence in the Thai countryside, has broken down.

Charles Keyes, . . . who first studied village life here nearly five decades ago,

describes a transformation from "peasants to cosmopolitan villagers."

"There is a sense in Thai society that the social contract is being renegotiated," said Mr. Keyes, a professor emeritus of anthropology at the University of Washington.

The convulsive changes to village life and the breakdown of a national political consensus are not just relevant to Thailand, but are a cautionary tale for other countries in Asia that are developing so rapidly, Mr. Keyes says. . . . .

In the 1990s, as part of an effort to decentralize power, the government introduced a system of local councils, known as township administrative organizations.

Kayun Thapthani, who won a seat on the first council in Baan Nong Tun, remembers a timid gathering of farmers in a meeting hall next to the Buddhist temple. Villagers listened quietly and politely to proposals for road building and support for the elderly. But as time wore on, and when budgets rose and meetings dealt with controversial projects, the deference dissipated. . . .

The councils gave villagers a sense that they could control their own political destiny, said Mr. Udom. . . . The system has come with its disappointments—council budgets are strained and have shrunk in recent years—but the system has brought a greater sense of political intimacy than elections for the national Parliament in Bangkok. . . . "We have a lot more expectations," Mr. Udom said.

Those expectations were partly answered after the election a decade ago of the populist prime minister, Thaksin Shinawatra, whose power base was in rural areas. . . . Mr. Thaksin, a billionaire tycoon and thus a seemingly unlikely champion of the peasant class, managed

continued

Anthropology Today *continued*

to cement his popularity by introducing universal health care and funneling government funds into villages, where local officials decided how to distribute it.

When Mr. Thaksin's party was re-elected in 2005 by a wide margin, Mr. Keyes . . . remembers a villager's elation. "It used to be that the elite decided who was in power," Mr. Keyes remembers the villager saying. "Today we decide." But Mr. Thaksin's concentration of power—his critics would say his abuse of power—alienated many voters, especially the elite.

Mr. Thaksin faced large-scale street demonstrations in Bangkok against his rule and was overthrown in a military coup in 2006, polarizing the country. . . .

Mr. Thaksin's allies are trying once again to win power in the election Sunday

Two heads of state: President Barack Obama and Thai Prime Minister Yingluck Shinawatra listen to national anthems during a welcome ceremony for the American president at the government house in Bangkok, Thailand in November, 2012.

with the tycoon's sister, Yingluck Shinawatra, as the candidate for prime minister. Ms. Yingluck, who is leading in the polls, is up against the party of Abhisit Vejjajiva, the current prime minister, who is allied with the military leadership and the Bangkok establishment. . . .

More than two-thirds of Thailand's population lives in rural areas. . . . But migrations in recent decades have blurred the distinction between countryside and city.

Every family has someone who has gone to work in Bangkok or abroad. . . . Technology has brought great changes to many parts of the world in recent decades, but the pace of change has been particularly breathless in the Thai countryside.

Five decades ago, Mr. Keyes . . . witnessed isolated, self-sufficient villages where farmers grew their own food and rarely used money because they counted on their neighbors to help with farm work or build stilt houses out of local timber. There was no electricity, piped water or telephone service. . . .

Today, Baan Nong Tun is plugged into the rest of Thailand by television, radio and the Internet. Traveling to other provinces is routine, and every family has a motorcycle or pickup truck. . . .

The generation gap—from peasant to cosmopolitan villager—is evident in villagers' hands. Mr. Udom's calloused fingers are swollen by years of farm work. Younger people have the soft, thin fingers of city dwellers. . . .

Source: Thomas Fuller, "Rural Thais Find an Unaccustomed Power." From *The New York Times,* June 30, 2011. © 2011 The New York Times. All rights reserved. Used by permission and protected by the Copyright Laws of the United States. The printing, copying, redistribution, or retransmission of this Content without express written permission is prohibited. www.nytimes.com.

Disturbed by the whole process, wives of the warrant chiefs also pressured their husbands to listen to the protesters' demands.

The protests were remarkably effective. The tax was abandoned, and many of the warrant chiefs resigned, some to be replaced by women. Other women were appointed to the Native courts as judges. The position of women improved in Nigeria, where market women especially remain a powerful political force to this day. Many Nigerian political events in the 1930s, 1940s, and 1950s were inspired by the Women's War, including additional tax protests. This Women's War inspired many other protests in regions all over Africa. The Igbo uprising is seen as the first major challenge to British authority in Nigeria and West Africa during the colonial period.

At the beginning of this chapter, *power* was defined as the ability to exercise one's will over others. It was contrasted with *authority*—the formal, socially approved use of power by government officials and others. The case of the Igbo Women's War shows how women effectively used their social power (through song, dance, noise, and "in-your-face" behavior) to subvert the formal authority structure and, in so doing, gained greater influence within that structure. Can you think of other, perhaps recent examples?

Summary

1. Although no ethnographer has been able to observe a polity uninfluenced by some state, many anthropologists use a sociopolitical typology that classifies societies as bands, tribes, chiefdoms, or states. Foragers tended to live in egalitarian, band-organized societies. Personal networks linked individuals, families, and bands. Band leaders were first among equals, with no sure way to enforce decisions. Disputes rarely arose over strategic resources, which were open to all.

2. Political authority increased with growth in population size and density and in the scale of regulatory problems. More people mean more relations among individuals and groups to regulate. Increasingly complex economies pose further regulatory problems.

3. Heads of horticultural villages are local leaders with limited authority. They lead by example and persuasion. Big men have support and authority beyond a single village. They are regional regulators, but temporary ones. In organizing a feast, they mobilize labor from several villages. Sponsoring such events leaves them with little wealth but with prestige and a reputation for generosity.

4. Age and gender also can be used for regional political integration. Among North America's Plains Indians, men's associations (pantribal sodalities) organized raiding and buffalo hunting. Such sodalities provide offense and defense when there is intertribal raiding for animals. Among pastoralists, the degree of authority and political organization reflects population size and density, interethnic relations, and pressure on resources.

5. The state is an autonomous political unit that encompasses many communities. Its government collects taxes, drafts people for work and war, and decrees and enforces laws. The state is a form of sociopolitical organization based on central government and social stratification. Early states are known as archaic, or nonindustrial, states, in contrast to modern industrial nation-states.

6. Unlike tribes, but like states, chiefdoms had permanent regional regulation and differential access to resources. But chiefdoms lacked stratification. Unlike states, but like bands and tribes, chiefdoms were organized by kinship, descent, and marriage. Chiefdoms emerged in several areas, including the circum-Caribbean, lowland Amazonia, the southeastern United States, and Polynesia.

7. Weber's three dimensions of stratification are wealth, power, and prestige. In early states—for the first time in human history—contrasts in wealth, power, and prestige between entire groups of men and women came into being. A socioeconomic stratum includes people of both sexes and all ages. The superordinate—higher, or elite—stratum enjoys privileged access to resources.

8. Certain systems are found in all states: population control, judiciary, enforcement, and fiscal support. These are integrated by a ruling system or government composed of civil, military, and religious officials. States conduct censuses and demarcate boundaries. Laws are based on precedent and legislative proclamations. Courts and judges handle disputes and crimes. A police force maintains internal order, as a military defends against external threats. A financial or fiscal system supports rulers, officials, judges, and other specialists and government agencies.

9. *Hegemony* describes a stratified social order in which subordinates comply with domination by internalizing its values and accepting its "naturalness." Situations that appear hegemonic may have resistance that is individual and disguised rather than collective and defiant. "Public transcript" refers to the open, public interactions between the dominators and the oppressed. "Hidden transcript" describes the critique of power that goes on where the power holders can't see it. Discontent also may be expressed in public rituals such as Carnaval.

10. Broader than the political is the concept of social control—those fields of the social system most actively involved in the maintenance of norms and the regulation of conflict. Sanctions are social as well as governmental. Shame and gossip can be effective social sanctions. In the Igbo Women's War, women effectively used their social power (through song, dance, noise, and "in-your-face" behavior) to subvert the formal authority structure and, in so doing, gained greater influence within that structure.

Key Terms

achieved status, *116*
ascribed status, *115*
authority, *108*
big man, *115*
chiefdom, *110*
conflict
  resolution, *112*
differential
  access, *110*
fiscal, *124*

hegemony, *125*
law, *112*
norms, *112*
office, *121*
pantribal
  sodality, *117*
power, *108*
prestige, *122*
social
  control, *125*

sociopolitical
  typology, *110*
state, *110*
status, *115*
subordinate, *123*
superordinate, *123*
tribe, *110*
village head, *114*
wealth, *122*

Chapter 7

Families, Kinship, and Marriage

Although it still is something of an ideal in our culture, the nuclear family (parents and their children) now accounts for fewer than one-fourth of all American households. Such phrases as "marriage and the family" and "mom and pop" no longer apply to a majority of American households. What kind of family raised you? Perhaps it was a nuclear family. Or maybe you were raised by a single parent, with or without the help of extended kin. Perhaps your extended kin acted as your parents. Or maybe you had a stepparent and/or step or half siblings in a blended family. Maybe you had two moms or two dads. Given the diversity of families in contemporary North America, your family may not have fit any of these descriptions, or perhaps it varied over time.

Although contemporary American family types are diverse, other cultures offer family alternatives that Americans might have trouble understanding. Imagine a society in which someone doesn't know for sure, and doesn't care much about, who his actual mother was. Consider Joseph Rabe, a Betsileo man who was my field assistant in Madagascar. Rabe, who had been raised by his aunt—his father's sister—told me about two sisters, one of whom was his mother and the other his mother's sister. He knew their names, but he didn't know which was which. Illustrating an adoptive pattern common among the Betsileo, Rabe was given as a toddler to his childless aunt. His mother and her sister lived far away and died in his childhood (as did his father), and so he didn't really know them. But he was very close to his father's sister, for whom he used the term for mother. Indeed, he had to call her that, because the Betsileo have only one kin term, *reny,* for mother, mother's sister, and father's sister. (They also use a single term, *ray,* for father and all uncles.) The difference between "real" (biologically based) and socially constructed kinship didn't matter to Rabe.

Contrast this Betsileo case with Americans' attitudes about kinship and adoption. On family-oriented radio talk shows, I've heard hosts distinguish between "birth mothers" and adoptive mothers, and between "sperm daddies" and "daddies of the heart." The latter may be adoptive fathers, or stepfathers who have "been like fathers" to someone. American culture tends to promote the idea that kinship is, and should be, biological. It's increasingly common for adopted children to seek out their birth mothers or sperm donors (which used to be discouraged as disruptive), even after a perfectly satisfactory upbringing in an adoptive family. The American emphasis on biology for kinship is seen also in the recent proliferation of DNA testing. Viewing our beliefs through the lens of cross-cultural comparison helps us appreciate that kinship and biology don't always converge, nor do they need to.

The societies anthropologists traditionally have studied have stimulated a strong interest in families, along with larger systems of kinship and marriage. The wide web of kinship—as vital in daily life in nonindustrial societies as work outside the home is in our own—has become an essential part of anthropology because of its importance to the people we study. We are ready to take a closer look at the systems of kinship and marriage that have organized human life for much of our history.

Ethnographers quickly recognize social divisions, or groups, within any society they study. They learn about significant groups by observing their activities and membership. Often people live in the same village or neighborhood, or work, socialize, or celebrate together because they are related in some way. A significant kin group might consist of descendants of the same grandfather. These people live in neighboring houses, farm adjoining fields, and help each other in daily tasks. Groups based on other kin links get together less often in that society (see Strathern and Stewart 2010).

The nuclear family is one kind of kin group that is widespread in human societies. Other kin groups include extended families (families consisting of three or more generations) and descent groups—lineages and clans. Much of kinship is *culturally constructed,* that is, based on learning and variable from culture to culture (McKinnon 2005; Schneider 1967). Different societies have different kinds of families, households, kin groups, marriage customs, and living arrangements.

Families

Consider the term *family,* which is basic, familiar (so much so it even shares its root with *familiar*), and difficult to define in a way that applies to all cultures. A **family** is a group of people (e.g., parents, children, siblings, grandparents, grandchildren, uncles, aunts, nephews, nieces, cousins, spouses, siblings-in-law, parents-in-law, children-in-law) who are considered to be related in some way, for example, by "blood" (common ancestry or descent) or marriage. Some families, such as the nuclear family, are residentially based; its members live together. Others are not; they live apart but come together for family reunions of various sorts from time to time.

Consider a striking contrast between the United States and Brazil, the two most populous countries of the Western Hemisphere, in the meaning of family. American adults usually define their family as consisting of their spouse and children. However, when Brazilians talk about their family (*família*), they mean their parents, siblings, aunts, uncles, grandparents, and cousins. Later they add their children, but rarely their spouse, who has his or her own family. The children are shared by the two families. Because middle-class Americans typically lack an extended family support system, marriage assumes more importance. The husband–wife relationship is supposed to take precedence over either spouse's relationship with his or her own parents. This places a significant strain on American marriages (see this chapter's "Anthropology Today" for a study of American family life in the 21st century).

Living in a less mobile society, Brazilians stay in closer face-to-face contact with their relatives, including members of the extended family, than North Americans do. Residents of Rio de Janeiro and São Paulo, two of South America's largest cities, are reluctant to leave those urban centers to live away from family and friends. Brazilians find it hard to imagine, and unpleasant to live in, social worlds without relatives. Contrast this with a characteristic American theme: learning to live with strangers.

Nuclear and Extended Families

A nuclear family is *impermanent;* it lasts only as long as the parents and children remain together. Most people belong to at least two nuclear families at different times in their lives. They are born into a family consisting of their parents and siblings. When they reach adulthood, they may marry and establish a nuclear family that includes the spouse and eventually children. Since most societies permit divorce, some people establish more than one family through marriage.

Anthropologists distinguish between the **family of orientation** (the family in which one is born and grows up) and the **family of procreation** (formed when one marries and has children). From the individual's point of view, the critical relationships are with parents and siblings in the family of orientation and with spouse and children in the family of procreation. In Brazil, as we just saw, the family of orientation predominates, whereas in the United States it is the family of procreation.

In most societies, relations with nuclear family members (parents, siblings, and children) take precedence over relations with other kin. Nuclear family organization is very widespread but not universal, and its significance in society differs greatly from one place to another. In a few societies, such as the classic Nayar case described below, nuclear families are rare or nonexistent. In others, the nuclear family plays no special role in social life. Other social units—most notably descent groups and extended families—can assume many of the functions otherwise associated with the nuclear family.

Consider an example from the former Yugoslavia. Traditionally, among the Muslims of western Bosnia (Lockwood 1975), nuclear families lacked autonomy. Several such families lived in an extended family household called a *zadruga*. The zadruga was headed by a male household head and his wife, the senior woman. It included married sons and their wives and children, as well as unmarried sons and daughters. Each nuclear family had a sleeping room, decorated and partly furnished from the bride's trousseau. However, possessions—even clothing and trousseau items—were shared by zadruga members. Such a residential unit is known as a *patrilocal* extended family because each couple resides in the husband's father's household after marriage.

The zadruga took precedence over its component units. There were three successive meal settings—for men, women, and children, respectively. Traditionally, all children over the age of 12 slept together in boys' or girls' rooms. When a woman wished to visit another village, she sought the permission of the male zadruga head. Although men usually felt closer to their own children than to those of their brothers, they were obliged to treat them equally. Children were disciplined by any adult in the household. When a nuclear family broke up, children under age 7 went with the mother. Older children could choose between their parents. Children were considered part of the household where they were born, even if their mother left. One widow who remarried had to leave her five children, all over the age of 7, in their father's zadruga, now headed by his brother.

Another example of an alternative to the nuclear family is provided by the Nayars (or Nair), a large and powerful caste on the Malabar Coast of southern India (Gough 1959; Shivaram 1996). Their traditional kinship system was matrilineal (descent traced only through females). Nayar lived in matrilineal extended family compounds called

Unable to survive economically as nuclear family units, relatives may band together in an expanded family household and pool their resources. This photo, taken in 2002 in Munich, Germany, shows German Roma, or Gypsies. Together with her children and grandchildren, this grandmother resides in an expanded family household.

tarawads. The tarawad was a residential complex with several buildings, its own temple, granary, water well, orchards, gardens, and land holdings. Headed by a senior woman, assisted by her brother, the tarawad housed her siblings, sisters' children, and other matrikin—matrilineal relatives.

Traditional Nayar marriage seems to have been hardly more than a formality: a kind of coming-of-age ritual. A young woman would go through a marriage ceremony with a man, after which they might spend a few days together at her tarawad. Then the man would return to his own tarawad, where he lived with his sisters, aunts, and other matrikin. Nayar men belonged to a warrior class, who left home regularly for military expeditions, returning permanently to their tarawad on retirement. Nayar women could have multiple sexual partners. Children became members of the mother's tarawad; they were not considered to be relatives of their biological father. Indeed, many Nayar children didn't even know who their biological father (genitor) was. Child care was the responsibility of the tarawad. Nayar society therefore reproduced itself biologically without the nuclear family.

Industrialism and Family Organization

For many Americans and Canadians, the nuclear family is the only well-defined kin group. Family isolation arises from geographic mobility, which is associated with industrialism, so that a nuclear family focus is characteristic of many modern nations. Born into a family of orientation, North Americans leave home for college or work, and the break with parents is underway. Selling our labor on the market, we often move to

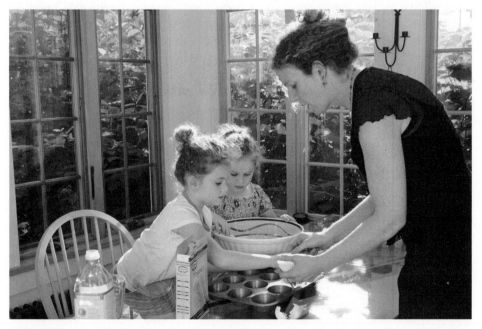

One among many kinds of American family: A single mother (by choice) bakes cupcakes with her twin daughters at their home in Brooklyn, New York.

places where jobs are available. Eventually most North Americans marry and start a family of procreation.

Many married couples live hundreds of miles from their parents. Their jobs have determined where they live. Such a postmarital residence pattern is **neolocality:** Married couples are expected to establish a new place of residence—a "home of their own." Among middle-class North Americans, neolocal residence is both a cultural preference and a statistical norm. Most middle-class Americans eventually establish households and nuclear families of their own.

There are significant differences between middle-class and poorer North Americans. For example, in the lower class the incidence of *expanded family households* (those that include nonnuclear relatives) is greater than it is in the middle class. When an expanded family household includes three or more generations, it is an **extended family household,** such as the zadruga. Another type of expanded family is the *collateral household,* which includes siblings and their spouses and children.

The higher proportion of expanded family households among poorer Americans has been explained as an adaptation to poverty (Stack 1975). Unable to survive economically as nuclear family units, relatives band together in an expanded household and pool their resources. Adaptation to poverty causes kinship values and attitudes to diverge from middle-class norms. Thus, when North Americans raised in poverty achieve financial success, they often feel obligated to provide financial help to a wide circle of less fortunate relatives (see Willie 2003).

Changes in North American Kinship

Although the nuclear family remains a cultural ideal for many Americans, Table 7.1 and Figure 7.1 show that nuclear families accounted for just 21 percent of American households in 2010. Other domestic arrangements now outnumber the "traditional"

TABLE 7.1   Changes in Family and Household Organization in the United States, 1970 versus 2010

Sources: From U.S. Census data in J. M. Fields, "America's Families and Living Arrangements: 2003," *Current Population Reports,* P20-553, November 2004, http://www.census.gov/prod/2004pubs/p20-553.pdf, p. 4; U.S. Census Bureau, *Statistical Abstract of the United States* 2012, Tables 59, 62, http://www.census.gov/prod/2011pubs/12statab/pop.pdf.compendia/statab/2009edition.html.

	1970	2010
Numbers:		
Total number of households	63 million	118 million
Number of people per household	3.1	2.6
Percentages:		
Married couples living with children	40%	21%
Family households	81%	67%
Households with five or more people	21%	10%
People living alone	17%	27%
Percentage of single-mother families	5%	11%
Percentage of single-father families	0%	3%
Households with own children under 18	45%	30%

FIGURE 7.1   **Households by Type: Selected Years, 1970 to 2010 (percent distribution).**

Sources: J. M. Fields, "America's Families and Living Arrangements: 2003," *Current Population Reports*, P20-553, November 2004, http://www.census.gov/prod/2004pubs/p20-553.pdf, p. 4; *Statistical Abstract of the United States* 2012, Tables 59, 62 http://www.census.gov/prod/2011pubs/12statab/pop.pdf.

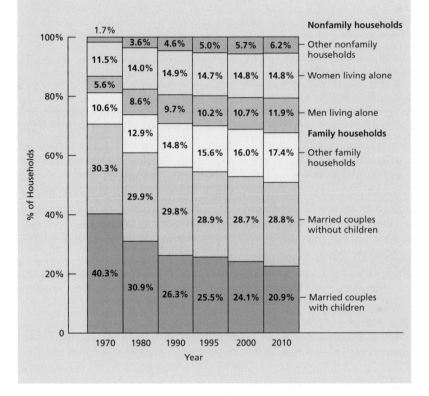

American household almost five to one. There are several reasons for this changing household composition. Women increasingly are joining men in the cash workforce. This often removes them from their family of orientation while making it economically feasible to delay marriage. Furthermore, job demands compete with romantic attachments. The median age at first marriage for American women rose from 21 years in 1970 to 26.5 in 2011. For men the comparable ages were 23 and 28.7 (U.S. Census Bureau 2012).

Also, the U.S. divorce rate has risen, making divorced Americans much more common today than they were in 1970. Between 1970 and 2010 the number of divorced Americans more than quintupled, from 4.3 million to 23.7 million. (Note, however, that each divorce creates two divorced people.) Table 7.2 shows the ratio of divorces to marriages in the United States for selected years between 1950 and 2010. A major jump in the divorce rate took place between 1960 and 1980. During that period the ratio of divorces to marriages doubled. Between 1980 and 2000, the ratio hovered around 50 percent. That is, each year there were about half as many

TABLE 7.2   Ratio of Divorces to Marriages per 1,000 U.S. Population, Selected Years, 1950–2010

Sources: *Statistical Abstract of the United States* 2009, Table 77, p. 63; *Statistical Abstract of the United States* 2012, Table 132, http://www.census.gov/prod/2011pubs/12statab/pop.pdf.

1950	1960	1970	1980	1990	2000	2010
3%	26%	35%	49%	48%	49%	55%

new divorces as there were new marriages. Since 2000 the rate has drifted up, to 55 percent in 2010.

The rate of growth in single-parent households also has outstripped population growth, almost tripling, from fewer than 4 million in 1970 to 10.6 million in 2010. (The overall American population in 2010 was 1.5 times its size in 1970.) The percentage (23.1 percent) of children living in fatherless (mother-headed, no resident dad) households in 2010 was more than twice the 1970 rate, while the percentage (3.4 percent) in motherless (father-headed, no resident mom) homes increased fourfold. About 56 percent of American women and 59 percent of American men were currently married in 2009, versus 60 and 65 percent, respectively, in 1970 (Fields 2004; *Statistical Abstract of the United States* 2012). However, more American women now live without a husband than with one. By 2005, 51 percent of women said they were living without a spouse, compared with 35 percent in 1950 (Roberts et al. 2007). To be sure, contemporary Americans maintain social lives through work, friendship, sports, clubs, religion, and organized social activities. However, the growing isolation from kin that these figures suggest may well be unprecedented in human history.

Table 7.3 documents similar changes in family and household size in the United States and Canada between 1980 and 2010. Those figures confirm a general trend toward smaller families and living units in North America. This trend is also detectable in Western Europe and other industrial nations.

TABLE 7.3   Household and Family Size in the United States and Canada, 1980 versus 2010

Sources: J. M. Fields, "America's Families and Living Arrangements: 2003," *Current Population Reports,* P20-553, November 2004, http://www.census.gov/prod/2004pubs/p20-553.pdf, pp. 3–4; Statistics Canada, 2006 Census, http://www.12.statcan.ca/english/census06/data/topics/; *Statistical Abstract of the United States* 2012, Table 62, http://www.census.gov/prod/2011pubs/12statab/pop.pdf.

	1980	2010
Average family size:		
United States	3.3	3.1
Canada	3.4	3.0
Average household size:		
United States	2.9	2.6
Canada	2.9	2.6

Immigrants often are shocked by what they perceive as weak kinship bonds and lack of proper respect for family in contemporary North America. In fact, most of the people whom middle-class North Americans see every day are either nonrelatives or members of the nuclear family. On the other hand, Stack's (1975) study of welfare-dependent families in a small midwestern city shows that regular sharing with nonnuclear relatives is an important strategy that the urban poor use to adapt to poverty.

The Family among Foragers

Foraging societies are far removed from industrial nations in terms of social complexity, but they do feature geographic mobility, which is associated with nomadic or seminomadic hunting and gathering. Here again, the nuclear family often is the most significant kin group, although in no foraging society is it the only group based on kinship. The two basic social units of traditional foraging societies are the nuclear family and the band.

Unlike middle-class couples in industrial nations, foragers don't usually reside neolocally. Instead, they join a band in which either the husband or the wife has relatives. However, couples and families may move from one band to another several times. Although nuclear families are ultimately as impermanent among foragers as they are in any other society, they usually are more stable than bands are.

Many foraging societies lacked year-round band organization. The Native American Shoshone of Utah and Nevada provide an example. The resources available to the Shoshone were so meager that for most of the year families traveled alone through the countryside, hunting and gathering. In certain seasons families assembled to hunt cooperatively as a band, but after just a few months together they dispersed.

In neither industrial nor foraging economies are people permanently tied to the land. The mobility and the emphasis on small, economically self-sufficient family units promote the nuclear family as a basic kin group in both types of societies.

Descent

We've seen that the nuclear family is important in industrial nations and among foragers. The analogous group among nonindustrial cultivators and herders is the descent group. A **descent group** is a *permanent* social unit whose members claim common ancestry. Descent group members believe they all descend from those common ancestors. The group endures even though its membership changes, as members are born and die, move in and move out. Often, descent-group membership is determined at birth and is life-long. In this case, it is an ascribed status.

Descent Groups

Descent groups frequently are exogamous (members seek their mates from other descent groups). Two common rules admit certain people as descent-group members while excluding others. With a rule of **patrilineal descent,** people automatically have lifetime membership in their father's group. The children of the group's men join the group, but the children of the group's women are excluded. With **matrilineal descent,** people join

FIGURE 7.2   A Patrilineage Five Generations Deep
Lineages are based on demonstrated descent from an apical ancestor. With patrilineal
descent, children of the group's men (shaded) are included as descent-group members.
Children of the group's women are excluded; they belong to *their* father's patrilineage.

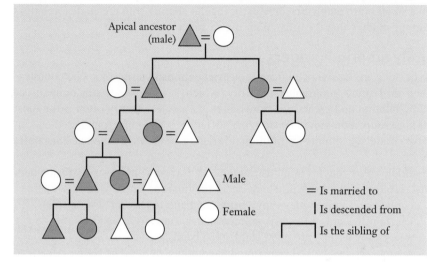

the mother's group automatically at birth and stay members throughout life. Matrilineal
descent groups therefore include only the children of the group's women. (In Figures 7.2
and 7.3, which show patrilineal and matrilineal descent groups, respectively, the
triangles stand for males and the circles for females.) Matrilineal and patrilineal descent
are types of **unilineal descent.** This means the descent rule uses one line only, either the
male or the female line. Patrilineal descent is much more common than matrilineal descent is. In a sample of 564 societies (Murdock 1957), about three times as many were
found to be patrilineal (247 to 84).

Descent groups may be **lineages** or **clans.** Common to both is the belief that members descend from the same *apical ancestor,* the person who stands at the apex, or top,
of the common genealogy. For example, Adam and Eve are the apical ancestors of the
biblical Jews and, according to the Bible, of all humanity. Since Eve is said to have
come from Adam's rib, Adam stands as the original apical ancestor for the patrilineal
genealogy laid out in the Bible.

How do lineages and clans differ? A lineage uses *demonstrated descent.* Members
recite the names of their forebears from the apical ancestor through the present. (This
doesn't mean their recitations are accurate, only that lineage members think they are.)
In the Bible the litany of men who "begat" other men is a demonstration of genealogical
descent for a large patrilineage that ultimately includes Jews and Arabs (who share
Abraham as their last common apical ancestor).

Unlike lineages, clans use *stipulated descent.* Clan members merely say they descend from the apical ancestor, without trying to trace the actual genealogical links.

FIGURE 7.3   A Matrilineage Five Generations Deep

Matrilineages are based on demonstrated descent from a female ancestor. Only the children of the group's women (shaded) belong to the matrilineage. The children of the group's men are excluded; they belong to *their* mother's matrilineage.

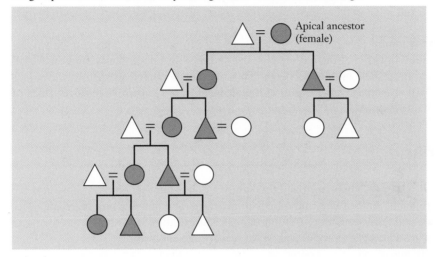

The Betsileo of Madagascar have both clans and lineages. Descent may be demonstrated for the most recent 8–10 generations, then stipulated for the more remote past—sometimes with mermaids and vaguely defined foreign royalty mentioned among the founders (Kottak 1980). Like the Betsileo, many societies have both lineages and clans. In such a case, clans have more members and cover a larger geographical area than lineages do. Sometimes a clan's apical ancestor is not a human at all but an animal or a plant (called a *totem*).

The economic types that usually have descent group organization are horticulture, pastoralism, and agriculture. Such societies tend to have several descent groups. Any one of them may be confined to a single village, but usually they span more than one village. Two or more local branches of different descent groups may live in the same village. Descent groups in the same village or different villages may establish alliances through frequent intermarriage.

Lineages, Clans, and Residence Rules

As we've seen, descent groups, unlike families, are permanent and enduring units, with new members added in every generation. Members have access to the lineage estate, where some of them must live, in order to benefit from and manage that estate across the generations. An easy way to keep members at home is to have a rule about who belongs to the descent group and where they should live after they get married. Patrilineal and matrilineal descent, and the postmarital residence rules that usually accompany them, ensure that about half the people born in each generation will spend their lives on the ancestral estate.

Patrilocality is the rule that when a couple marries, it moves to the husband's community, so that their children will grow up in their father's village. Patrilocality is associated with patrilineal descent. This makes sense. If the group's male members are expected to exercise their rights in the ancestral estate, it's a good idea to raise them on that estate and to keep them there after they marry. This can be done by having wives move to the husband's village, rather than vice versa.

A less common postmarital residence rule, often associated with matrilineal descent, is **matrilocality:** Married couples live in the wife's community, and their children grow up in their mother's village. This rule keeps related women together (see Stone 2010). Together, patrilocality and matrilocality are known as *unilocal* rules of postmarital residence.

Marriage

"Love and marriage," "marriage and the family": These familiar phrases show how we link the romantic love of two individuals to marriage, and how we link marriage to reproduction and family creation. But marriage is an institution with significant roles and functions in addition to reproduction. What is marriage, anyway?

No definition of marriage is broad enough to apply easily to all societies and situations. A commonly quoted definition comes from *Notes and Queries on Anthropology:*

> Marriage is a union between a man and a woman such that the children born to the
> woman are recognized as legitimate offspring of both partners. (Royal Anthropological
> Institute 1951, p. 111)

This definition isn't valid universally for several reasons. In many societies, marriages unite more than two spouses. Here we speak of *plural marriages,* as when a man weds two (or more) women, or a woman weds a group of brothers—an arrangement called *fraternal polyandry* that is characteristic of certain Himalayan cultures. In the Brazilian community of Arembepe, people can choose among various forms of marital union. Most people live in long-term "common-law" domestic partnerships that are not legally sanctioned. Some have civil marriages, which are licensed and legalized by a justice of the peace. Still others go through religious ceremonies, so they are united in "holy matrimony," although not legally. And some have both civil and religious ties. The different forms of union permit someone to have multiple spouses (e.g., one common-law, one civil, one religious) without ever getting divorced.

Some societies recognize various kinds of same-sex marriages. In Sudan, a Nuer woman could marry a woman if her father had only daughters but no male heirs, who are necessary if his patrilineage is to survive. He could ask his daughter to stand as a son in order to take a bride. This daughter would become the socially recognized husband of another woman (the wife). This was a symbolic and social relationship rather than a sexual one. The "wife" had sex with a man or men (whom her female "husband" had to approve) until she got pregnant. The children born to the wife were accepted as the offspring of both the female husband and the wife. Although the female husband was not the actual *genitor,* the biological father, of the children, she was their *pater,* or socially recognized father. What's important in this Nuer case is *social* rather than *biological paternity*. We see again how kinship is socially constructed. The bride's children were considered the legitimate offspring of her female husband, who was biologically a woman but socially a man, and the descent line continued.

Exogamy and Incest

In nonindustrial societies, a person's social world includes two main categories—friends and strangers. Strangers are potential or actual enemies. Marriage is one of the primary ways of converting strangers into friends, of creating and maintaining personal and political alliances. **Exogamy**—seeking a mate outside one's own group—links people into a wider social network that nurtures, helps, and protects them in times of need. Incest restrictions (prohibitions on sex with relatives) reinforce exogamy by pushing people to seek their mates outside the local group. Most societies discourage sexual contact involving close relatives, especially members of the same nuclear family.

Incest refers to sexual contact with a relative, but cultures define their kin, and thus incest, differently. In other words, incest, like kinship, is socially constructed. Marriage entails sex, so one can marry only someone with whom sex is permitted. Besides kinship, other factors that restrict sexual access include age and the range of sexual acts that are socially tolerated. In the United States the age of consent for sexual activity varies by state between 16 and 18. It is 16 in Canada and 14 in Italy. Cultures and governments routinely try to regulate sexual activity. Until 2003, when the Supreme Court struck down sodomy laws, several states used them mainly against gay men who engaged in nonreproductive sex. Most people probably don't know what is legal and what isn't in a given state or country and can get in trouble as a result (e.g., when an 18-year-old has sex with a 17-year-old).

Sex is contested. That is, people in the same culture can disagree and argue about the definition and propriety of particular sexual acts. President Bill Clinton famously asserted, "I did not have sexual relations with that woman." Should sexual practices other than heterosexual coitus (oral sex, for example) be considered "sexual relations"? With respect to incest restrictions, what, if any, kind of sexual contact is permissible between a teenager and his or her same-sex or opposite-sex cousin of comparable age? How about step siblings, half siblings, and siblings? Some U.S. states permit marriage, and therefore sex, with first cousins, while others ban it. The social construction of kinship, and of incest, is far from simple.

Let's turn from the United States to nonindustrial societies. When unilineal descent is very strongly developed, the parent who belongs to a different descent group than your own isn't considered a relative. Thus, with strict patrilineality, the mother is not a relative but a kind of in-law who has married a member of your own group—your father. With strict matrilineality, the father isn't a relative because he belongs to a different descent group.

The Lakher of Southeast Asia are strictly patrilineal (Leach 1961). Using the male ego (the reference point, the person in question) in Figure 7.4, let's suppose that ego's father and mother get divorced. Each remarries and has a daughter by a second marriage. A Lakher always belongs to his or her father's group, all of whose members (one's *agnates,* or patrikin) are considered relatives, because they belong to the same descent

FIGURE 7.4   **Patrilineal Descent-Group Identity and Incest among the Lakher**

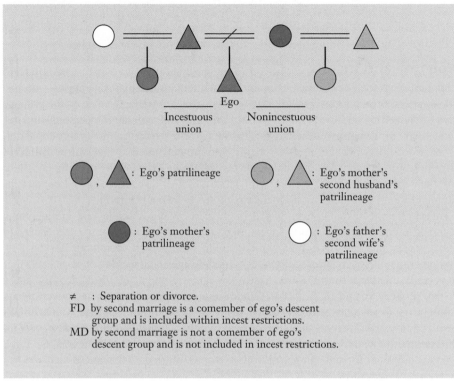

group. Ego can't have sex with or marry his father's daughter by the second marriage, just as in contemporary North America it's illegal for half siblings to have sex and marry. However, unlike our society, where all half siblings are restricted, sex between our Lakher ego and his maternal half sister would be nonincestuous. She isn't ego's relative because she belongs to her own father's descent group rather than ego's. The Lakher illustrate very well that definitions of relatives, and therefore of incest, vary from culture to culture.

Incest Happens

We know from primate research that adolescent males (among monkeys) or females (among apes) often move away from the group in which they were born (Rodseth et al. 1991). This emigration reduces the frequency of incestuous unions, but it doesn't eliminate them. DNA testing of wild chimps has confirmed incestuous unions between adult sons and their mothers, who reside in the same group. Human behavior with respect to mating with close relatives may express a generalized primate tendency, in which we see both urges and avoidance.

A cross-cultural study of 87 societies (Meigs and Barlow 2002) suggested that incest occurred in several of them. It's not clear, however, whether the authors of the study controlled for the social construction of incest. They report, for example, that incest occurs among the Yanomami, but they may be considering cross-cousin marriage to be incestuous, when it is not so considered by the Yanomami. Indeed it is the preferred form of marriage, not just for the Yanomami but in many tribal societies. Another society in their sample is the Ashanti, for whom the ethnographer Meyer Fortes reports "In the old days it [incest] was punished by death. Nowadays the culprits are heavily fined" (Fortes 1950, p. 257). This suggests that there really were violations of Ashanti incest restrictions and that such violations were, and still are, punished. More strikingly, among 24 Ojibwa individuals from whom he obtained information about incest, A. Irving Hallowell found 8 cases of parent–child incest and 10 cases of brother–sister incest (Hallowell 1955, pp. 294–95). Because reported cases of actual parent–child and sibling incest are rare in the ethnographic literature, questions about the possibility of social construction arise here, too. In many cultures, including the Ojibwa, people use the same terms for their mother and their aunt, their father and their uncle, and their cousins and siblings. Could the siblings in the Ojibwa case actually have been cousins, and the parents and children uncles and nieces?

In ancient Egypt, sibling marriage apparently was allowed both for royalty and for commoners, in some districts at least. Based on official census records from Roman Egypt (first to third centuries C.E.), 24 percent of all documented marriages in the Arsinoites district were between "brothers" and "sisters." The rates were 37 percent for the city of Arsinoe and 19 percent for the surrounding villages. These figures are much higher than any other documented levels of inbreeding among humans (Scheidel 1997). Again one wonders if the relatives involved were actually as close biologically as the kin terms would imply.

According to Anna Meigs and Kathleen Barlow (2002), for Western societies with nuclear family organization, "father–daughter incest" is much more common with stepfathers than with biological fathers. But is it really incest if they aren't biological relatives? American culture is unclear on this matter. Incest also happens with biological fathers, especially those who were absent or did little caretaking of their daughters in childhood (Williams and Finkelhor 1995). In a carefully designed study, Linda M. Williams and David Finkelhor (1995) found father–daughter incest to be least likely when there was substantial paternal parenting of daughters. This experience enhanced the father's parenting skills and his feelings of nurturance, protectiveness, and identification with his daughter, thus reducing the chance of incest.

A century ago, early anthropologists speculated that incest restrictions reflect an instinctive horror of mating with close relatives (Hobhouse 1915; Lowie 1920/1961). But why, one wonders, if humans really do have an instinctive aversion to incest, would formal restrictions be necessary? No one would want to have sexual contact with a relative. Yet, as social workers, judges, psychiatrists, and psychologists are well aware, incest is more common than we might suppose.

Endogamy

The practice of exogamy pushes social organization outward, establishing and preserving alliances among groups. In contrast, rules of **endogamy** dictate mating or marriage within a group to which one belongs. Endogamic rules are less common but are still familiar to anthropologists. Indeed, most cultures *are* endogamous units, although they usually do not need a formal rule requiring people to marry someone from their own society. In our own society, classes and ethnic groups are quasi-endogamous groups. Members of an ethnic or religious group often want their children to marry within that group, although many of them do not do so. The outmarriage rate varies among such groups, with some more committed to endogamy than others.

Caste

An extreme example of endogamy is India's **caste system,** which was formally abolished in 1949, although its structure and effects linger. Castes are stratified groups in which membership is ascribed at birth and is lifelong. Indian castes are grouped into five major categories, or *varna.* Each is ranked relative to the other four, and these categories extend throughout India. Each varna includes a large number of castes (*jati*), each of which includes people within a region who may intermarry. All the jati in a single varna in a given region are ranked, just as the varna themselves are ranked.

Occupational specialization often sets off one caste from another. A community may include castes of agricultural workers, merchants, artisans, priests, and sweepers. The untouchable varna, found throughout India, includes castes whose ancestry, ritual status, and occupations are considered so impure that higher-caste people consider even casual contact with untouchables to be defiling.

The belief that intercaste sexual unions lead to ritual impurity for the higher-caste partner has been important in maintaining endogamy. A man who has sex with a lower-caste woman can restore his purity with a bath and a prayer. However, a woman who has intercourse with a man of a lower caste has no such recourse. Her defilement cannot be undone. Because the women have the babies, these differences protect the purity of the caste line, ensuring the pure ancestry of high-caste children. Although Indian castes are endogamous groups, many of them are internally subdivided into exogamous lineages. Traditionally this meant that Indians had to marry a member of another descent group from the same caste. This shows that rules of exogamy and endogamy can coexist in the same society.

Marital Rights and Same-Sex Marriage

The British anthropologist Edmund Leach (1955) observed that, depending on the society, several kinds of rights are allocated by marriage. According to Leach, marriage can, but doesn't always, accomplish the following:

1. Establish the legal father of a woman's children and the legal mother of a man's.
2. Give either or both spouses a monopoly in the sexuality of the other.
3. Give either or both spouses rights to the labor of the other.
4. Give either or both spouses rights over the other's property.
5. Establish a joint fund of property—a partnership—for the benefit of the children.
6. Establish a socially significant "relationship of affinity" between spouses and their relatives.

The discussion of same-sex marriage that follows will illustrate the six rights just listed by seeing what happens in their absence (see also Stone 2004). What if same-sex marriages, which by and large remain illegal in the United States, were legal? Could a same-sex marriage establish legal parentage of children born to one or both partners after the partnership is formed? In the case of a different-sex marriage, children born to the wife after the marriage takes place usually are defined legally as her husband's regardless of whether he is the genitor.

Nowadays, of course, DNA testing makes it possible to establish paternity, just as modern reproductive technology makes it possible for a lesbian couple to have one or both partners artificially inseminated (see Levine 2008 and the 2010 movie *The Kids Are All Right*). When same-sex marriage is legal, the social construction of kinship easily can make both partners parents. If a Nuer woman married to a woman can be the pater of a child she did not father, why can't two lesbians be the *maters* (socially recognized mothers) of a child one of them did not give birth to? And if a married different-sex couple can adopt a child and have it be theirs through the social and legal construction of kinship, the same logic could be applied to a gay male or lesbian couple.

Continuing with Leach's list of the rights transmitted by marriage, same-sex marriage certainly could give each spouse rights to the sexuality of the other. Same-sex marriages, as forms of monogamous commitment, have been endorsed by representatives of many religions, including Unitarians, Quakers (the Society of Friends), and reform Jewish synagogues (Eskridge 1996). In June 2003 a court ruling established same-sex marriages as legal in the province of Ontario, Canada. On June 28, 2005, Canada's House of Commons voted to guarantee full marriage rights to same-sex couples throughout that nation. In the United States, the District of Columbia and twelve states—Connecticut, Delaware, Iowa, Maine, Maryland, Massachusetts, Minnesota, New Hampshire, New York, Rhode Island, Vermont, and Washington—allowed same-sex marriage as of this writing. Civil unions for same-sex couples are legal in New Jersey. In reaction to same-sex marriage, voters in at least 19 U.S. states have approved measures in their state constitutions defining marriage as an exclusively heterosexual union.

Legal same-sex marriages can easily give each spouse rights to the other spouse's labor and its products. Some societies do allow marriage between members of the same biological sex. Several Native American groups had figures known as *berdaches*. These were biological men who assumed many of the mannerisms, behavior patterns, and tasks of women. Sometimes berdaches married men, who shared the products of their labor from hunting and traditional male roles, as the berdache fulfilled the traditional wifely role. Also, in some Native American cultures, a marriage of a "manly-hearted woman" to another woman brought the traditional male–female division of labor to their household. The manly woman hunted and did other male tasks, while the wife played the traditional female role.

There's no logical reason that same-sex marriage cannot give spouses rights over the other's property. But in the United States, the same inheritance rights that apply to male–female couples usually don't apply to same-sex couples. For instance, even in the absence of a will, property can pass to a widow or a widower without going through probate. The wife or husband pays no inheritance tax. This benefit is not available to gay men and lesbians (Weston 1991).

As of 2013, same-sex couples can marry legally in twelve U.S. states and the District of Columbia. Shown here a Reform Jewish woman rabbi performs the same sex marriage of two men in Los Angeles.

What about Leach's fifth right—to establish a joint fund of property—to benefit the children? Here again, gay and lesbian couples are at a disadvantage. If there are children, property is separately, rather than jointly, transmitted. Some organizations do make staff benefits, such as health and dental insurance, available to same-sex domestic partners.

Finally, there is the matter of establishing a socially significant "relationship of affinity" between spouses and their relatives. In many societies, one of the main roles of marriage is to establish an alliance between groups, in addition to the individual bond. *Affinals* are relatives through marriage, such as a brother-in-law or mother-in-law. For same-sex couples in contemporary North America, affinal relations may be problematic. In an unofficial union, terms like "daughter-in-law" and "mother-in-law" may sound strange. Many parents are suspicious of their children's sexuality and lifestyle choices and may not recognize a relationship of affinity with a child's partner of the same sex.

This discussion of same-sex marriage has been intended to illustrate the different kinds of rights that typically accompany marriage, by seeing what may happen when there is a permanent pair bond without legal sanction. In just twelve of the United States are such unions fully legal. As we have seen, same-sex unions have been recognized in different historical and cultural settings. In certain African cultures, including the Igbo of Nigeria and the Lovedu of South Africa, women could marry other women. In situations in which women, such as prominent market women in West Africa, are able to amass property and other forms of wealth, they may take a wife. Such marriage allows the prominent woman to strengthen her social status and the economic importance of her household (Amadiume 1987).

Marriage across Cultures

Outside industrial societies, marriage often is more a relationship between groups than one between individuals. We think of marriage as an individual matter. Although the bride and groom usually seek their parents' approval, the final choice (to live together, to marry, to divorce) lies with the couple. The idea of romantic love symbolizes this individual relationship.

In nonindustrial societies, although there can be romantic love (Goleman 1992), marriage is a group concern. People don't just take a spouse; they assume obligations to a group of in-laws. When residence is patrilocal, for example, a woman must leave the community where she was born. She faces the prospect of spending the rest of her life in her husband's village, with his relatives.

Gifts at Marriage

In societies with descent groups, people often enter marriage with significant help from their descent group. Often it is customary for a substantial gift to be given before, at, or after the marriage by the husband and his kin to the wife and her kin. The BaThonga of Mozambique call such a gift *lobola*, and the custom of giving something like **lobola** is very widespread in patrilineal societies (Radcliffe-Brown 1924/1952). This gift compensates the bride's group for the loss of her companionship and labor. More important, it makes the children born to the woman full members of her husband's descent group. In matrilineal societies, children are members of the mother's group, and there is no reason for a lobolalike gift.

Another kind of marital gift, **dowry**, occurs when the bride's family or kin group provides substantial gifts when their daughter marries. For rural Greece, Ernestine Friedl (1962) has described a form of dowry in which the bride gets a wealth transfer from her mother, to serve as a kind of trust fund during her marriage. Usually, however, the dowry goes to the husband's family, and the custom is correlated with low female status. In this form of dowry, best known from India, women are perceived as burdens. When a man and his family take a wife, they expect to be compensated for the added responsibility.

Lobolalike gifts exist in many more cultures than dowry does, but the nature and quantity of transferred items differ. Among the BaThonga of Mozambique, whose name—lobola—I am using for this widespread custom, the gift consists of cattle. Use of livestock (usually cattle in Africa, pigs in Papua New Guinea) for lobola is common, but the number of animals given varies from society to society. We can generalize, however, that the larger the gift, the more stable the marriage. Lobola is insurance against divorce.

Imagine a patrilineal society in which a marriage requires the transfer of about 25 cattle from the groom's descent group to the bride's. Michael, a member of descent group A, marries Sarah from group B. His relatives help him assemble the lobola. He gets the most help from his close agnates—his older brother, father, father's brother, and closest patrilineal cousins.

The distribution of the cattle once they reach Sarah's group mirrors the manner in which they were assembled. Sarah's father, or her oldest brother if the father is dead, receives her lobola. He keeps most of the cattle to use as lobola for his sons' marriages. However, a share also goes to everyone who will be expected to help when Sarah's brothers marry.

When Sarah's brother David gets married, many of the cattle go to a third group—C, which is David's wife's group. Thereafter, they may serve as lobola to still other groups. Men constantly use their sisters' lobola cattle to acquire their own wives. In a decade, the cattle given when Michael married Sarah will have been exchanged widely.

In such societies, marriage entails an agreement between descent groups. If Sarah and Michael try to make their marriage succeed but fail to do so, both groups may conclude that the marriage can't last. Here it becomes especially obvious that marriages are relationships between groups as well as between individuals. If Sarah has a younger sister or niece (her older brother's daughter, for example), the concerned parties may agree to Sarah's replacement by a kinswoman.

However, incompatibility isn't the main problem that threatens marriage in societies with lobola customs. Infertility is a more important concern. If Sarah has no children, she and her group have not fulfilled their part of the marriage agreement. If the relationship is to endure, Sarah's group must furnish another woman, perhaps her younger sister, who can have children. If this happens, Sarah may choose to stay in her husband's village. Perhaps she will someday have a child. If she does stay on, her husband will have established a plural marriage.

Most nonindustrial food-producing societies, unlike most industrial nations, allow **plural marriages,** or **polygamy.** There are two varieties; one is common and the other is very rare. The more common variant is **polygyny,** in which a man has more than one wife. The rare variant is **polyandry,** in which a woman has more than one husband. If the infertile wife remains married to her husband after he has taken a substitute wife provided by her descent group, this is polygyny.

Durable Alliances

It is possible to exemplify the group-alliance nature of marriage by examining still another common practice—continuation of marital alliances when one spouse dies.

Sororate

What happens if Sarah dies young? Michael's group will ask Sarah's group for a substitute, often her sister. This custom is known as the **sororate** (Figure 7.5). If Sarah has no sister, or if all her sisters already are married, another woman from her group may be available. Michael marries her, there is no need to return the lobola, and the alliance continues.

The sororate exists in both matrilineal and patrilineal societies. In a matrilineal society with matrilocal postmarital residence, a widower may remain with his wife's group by marrying her sister or another female member of her matrilineage (Figure 7.5).

FIGURE 7.5
Sororate and
Levirate

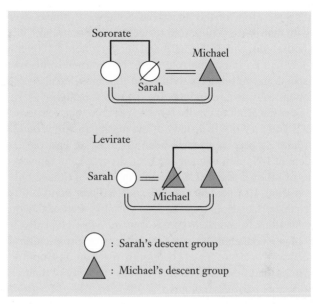

Levirate

What happens if the husband dies? In many societies, the widow may marry his brother. This custom is known as the **levirate** (Figure 7.5). Like the sororate, it is a continuation marriage that maintains the alliance between descent groups, in this case by replacing the husband with another member of his group. The implications of the levirate vary with age. One study found that in African societies the levirate, although widely permitted, rarely involves cohabitation of the widow and her new husband. Furthermore, widows don't automatically marry the husband's brother just because they are allowed to. Often they prefer to make other arrangements (Potash 1986).

Divorce

In some societies marriages may seem to go on forever, but in our own they are fairly brittle. Ease of divorce varies across cultures. What factors work for and against divorce? As we've seen, marriages that are political alliances between groups are more difficult to dissolve than are marriages that are more individual affairs, of concern mainly to the married couple and their children. We've seen that a substantial lobola gift may reduce the divorce rate for individuals; replacement marriages (levirate and sororate) also work to preserve group alliances. Divorce tends to be more common in matrilineal than in patrilineal societies. When residence is matrilocal (in the wife's home village), the wife may simply send off a man with whom she's incompatible.

Among the Hopi of the American Southwest, houses were owned by matrilineal clans, with matrilocal postmarital residence. The household head was the senior woman of that household, which also included her daughters and their husbands and children. A son-in-law had no important role there; he returned to his own mother's home for his clan's social and religious activities. In this matrilineal society, women were socially and economically secure and the divorce rate was high.

Consider the Hopi of Oraibi (Orayvi) pueblo, northeastern Arizona (Levy with Pepper 1992; Titiev 1992). In a study of the marital histories of 423 Oraibi women, Mischa Titiev found 35 percent to have been divorced at least once. Jerome Levy found that 31 percent of 147 adult women had been divorced and remarried at least once. For comparison, of all ever-married women in the United States, only 4 percent had been divorced in 1960, 10.7 percent in 1980, and 16.3 percent in 2009 (Kreider and Ellis 2011). Titiev characterizes Hopi marriages as unstable. Part of this brittleness was due to conflicting loyalties to matrikin versus spouse. Most Hopi divorces appear to have been matters of personal choice. Levy generalizes that, cross-culturally, high divorce rates are correlated with a secure female economic position. In Hopi society women were secure in their home and land ownership and in the custody of their children. In addition, there were no formal barriers to divorce.

Divorce is harder in a patrilineal society, especially when a substantial lobola gift would have to be reassembled and repaid if the marriage failed. A woman residing patrilocally (in her husband's household and community) might be reluctant to leave him. Unlike the Hopi, where the kids stay with the mother, in patrilineal, patrilocal societies the children of divorce would be expected to remain with their father, as members of his patrilineage. From the women's perspective this is a strong impediment to divorce.

In contemporary Western societies, we have the idea that romantic love is necessary for a good marriage (see Ingraham 2008). When romance fails, so may the marriage. Or it may not fail, if the other rights associated with marriage, as discussed previously in this chapter, are compelling. Economic ties and obligations to children, along with other factors, such as concern about public opinion, or simple inertia, may keep marriages intact after sex, romance, or companionship fades.

Plural Marriages

In contemporary North America, where divorce is fairly easy and common, polygamy (marriage to more than one spouse at the same time) is against the law. Marriage in industrial nations joins individuals, and relationships between individuals can be severed more easily than can those between groups. North Americans are allowed to practice *serial monogamy:* Individuals may have more than one spouse but never, legally, more than one at the same time. As stated earlier, the two forms of polygamy are polygyny and polyandry. Polyandry is practiced in only a few societies, notably among certain groups in Tibet, Nepal, and India. Polygyny is much more common.

Polygyny

We must distinguish between the social approval of plural marriage and its actual frequency in a particular society. Many cultures approve of a man's having more than one wife. However, even when polygyny is encouraged, most people are monogamous, and polygyny characterizes only a fraction of the marriages. Why?

One reason is equal sex ratios. In the United States, about 105 males are born for every 100 females. In adulthood the ratio of men to women equalizes, and eventually it reverses. The average North American woman outlives the average man. In many nonindustrial societies as well, the male-biased sex ratio among children reverses in adulthood.

The custom of men marrying later than women also promotes polygyny. Among Nigeria's Kanuri people (Cohen 1967), men got married between the ages of 18 and 30; women, between 12 and 14. The age difference between spouses meant there were more widows than widowers. Most of the widows remarried, some in polygynous unions. Among the Kanuri and in other polygynous societies, such as the Tiwi of northern Australia, widows made up a large number of the women involved in plural marriages (Hart, Pilling, and Goodale 1988).

In certain societies, the first wife requests a second wife to help with household chores. The second wife's status is lower than that of the first; they are senior and junior wives. The senior wife sometimes chooses the junior one from among her close kinswomen. Among the Betsileo of Madagascar, the different wives always lived in different villages. A man's first and senior wife, called "Big Wife," lived in the village where he cultivated his best rice field and spent most of his time. High-status men with several rice fields and multiple wives had households near each field. They spent most of their time with the senior wife but visited the others throughout the year.

Plural wives can play important political roles in nonindustrial states. The king of the Merina, a populous society in the highlands of Madagascar, had palaces for each of his 12 wives in different provinces. He stayed with them when he traveled through the

Modern day polygyny is illustrated by this photo (left) of South African President Jacob Zuma and his three wives. In the United States as in South Africa, powerful men often have multiple wives, but legally not at the same time. The three marriages of former Speaker of the House Newt Gingrich illustrate serial monogamy.

Anthropology Today   *American Family Life in the 21st Century*

Anthropologists today increasingly study daily life in the United States, including that of middle-class families. An excellent example is Life at Home in the Twenty-First Century: 32 Families Open Their Doors *(Arnold et al. 2012), a study of home life in 32 middle-class, dual-income families in Los Angeles, focusing on physical surroundings and material culture, the items owned and used in daily life. The book's authors are three UCLA anthropologists—Jeanne Arnold, Anthony Graesch, and Elinor Ochs—and Italian photographer Enzo Ragazzini. All did research through UCLA's Center on Everyday Lives of Families (CELF), which was founded in 2001 and is directed by Ochs.*

The families selected for, and agreeing to participate in, the study on which *Life at Home* was based were all middle-class and owned or were buying their homes. They varied in ethnicity, income level, and neighborhood. A few same-sex couples were included.

The authors took a systematic approach to their subjects. They videotaped the activities of family members, tracked their movements using positioning devices, measured their stress levels through saliva samples, and took almost 20,000 photographs (approximately 600 per family) of homes, yards, and activities. The researchers also asked family members to narrate tours of their homes and videotaped them as they did so. Over a four-year period the project generated 47 hours of family-narrated video home tours and 1,540 hours of videotaped family interactions and interviews (see Arnold, et al. 2012; Feuer 2012; Sullivan 2012).

A key finding of the study was the extent of clutter in those homes, a manifestation of a high degree of consumerism among dual-income American families. Never in human history, the researchers conclude, have families accumulated so many personal possessions. Hypothesizing that dealing with so much clutter would have psychological effects, the researchers collected saliva samples from the subjects in order to measure diurnal cortisol, an indicator of stress. Mothers' saliva, it turned out, contained more diurnal cortisol than did fathers'. The researchers also noticed that, in their video tours, mothers often used words like "mess" and "chaotic" to describe their homes, while fathers rarely mentioned messiness. Author Anthony Graesch reasons that clutter bothers moms so much because it challenges deeply ingrained notions that homes should be tidy and well managed (see Feuer 2012). The role of domestic manager, of course, is traditionally a female one. For dads and kids, more than for moms, possessions appeared to be a source of pleasure, pride, and contentment rather than stress (Arnold et al. 2012; Feuer 2012).

Another finding was that children rarely went outside, despite the overall mild weather in Los Angeles. They used their possessions indoors, resulting in more clutter, including whole walls devoted to displays of dolls and toys. More than half of the 32 households had special rooms designed for work or schoolwork, but even in home offices kids' stuff tended to crowd parental items. The researchers speculate that guilt motivates dual-income parents to buy so much stuff for their kids. The parents in the study managed to spend, on an average weekday, no more than four hours with their kids, perhaps leading them to overcompensate with toys, clothes, and other possessions (Graesch quoted in Feuer 2012).

The study found that the kitchen was the center of home life. In this space, family members met, interacted, exchanged information, and socialized their children. And in the kitchen, the refrigerator played a key role. Stuck on its doors and sides were such items as pictures, displays of children's achievements, reminders, addresses, and phone lists (including many outdated ones). The typical refrigerator front panel held 52 objects. The most crowded refrigerator had 166 stick-ons. The refrigerator served as a compact representation of that family's history and activities (Feuer 2012; Sullivan 2012).

Researchers found a correlation between the number of objects on the refrigerator and the overall clutter in a home. The refrigerator thus served not only as a chronicler of family life but also as a measure of its degree of consumerism—and perhaps of stress. We might hypothesize that a high number of refrigerator stick-ons indicates that someone in the household needs to take blood pressure medication.

kingdom. They were his local agents, overseeing and reporting on provincial matters. The king of Buganda, the major precolonial state of Uganda, took hundreds of wives, representing all the clans in his nation. Everyone in the kingdom became the king's in-law, and all the clans had a chance to provide the next ruler. This was a way of giving the common people a stake in the government.

These examples show there is no single explanation for polygyny. Its context and function vary from society to society and even within the same society. Some men are polygynous because they have inherited a widow from a brother. Others have plural wives because they seek prestige or want to increase household productivity. Men and women with political and economic ambitions cultivate marital alliances that serve their aims. In many societies, including the Betsileo of Madagascar and the Igbo of Nigeria, women arrange the marriages.

Polyandry

Polyandry is rare and is practiced under very specific conditions. Most of the world's polyandrous peoples live in South Asia—Tibet, Nepal, India, and Sri Lanka. In some of these areas, polyandry seems to be a cultural adaptation to mobility associated with customary male travel for trade, commerce, and military operations. Polyandry ensures there will be at least one man at home to accomplish male activities within a gender-based division of labor. Fraternal polyandry is also an effective strategy when resources are scarce. Brothers with limited resources (in land) pool their resources in expanded (polyandrous) households. They take just one wife. Polyandry restricts the number of wives and heirs. Less competition among heirs means that land can be transmitted with minimal fragmentation.

Summary

1. Kinship and marriage organize social and political life in nonindustrial societies. One widespread kin group is the nuclear family, consisting of a married couple and their children. Other groups, such as extended families and descent groups, may assume functions usually associated with the nuclear family. Nuclear families tend to be especially important in foraging and industrial societies.

2. In contemporary North America, the nuclear family is the characteristic kin group for the middle class. Expanded households and sharing with extended family kin occur more frequently among the poor, who may pool their resources in dealing with poverty. Today, however, even in the American middle class, nuclear family households are declining as single-person households and other domestic arrangements increase.

3. The descent group is a basic kin group among nonindustrial food producers (farmers and herders). Unlike families, descent groups have perpetuity, lasting for generations. Descent-group members share and manage an estate. Lineages are based on demonstrated descent; clans, on stipulated descent. Unilineal (patrilineal and matrilineal) descent is associated with unilocal (patrilocal and matrilocal, respectively) postmarital residence.

4. Most societies have incest restrictions. Because kinship is socially constructed, such restrictions apply to different relatives in different societies. Human behavior with respect to mating with close relatives may express a generalized primate tendency, illustrating both urges and avoidance. But types, risks, and avoidance of incest also reflect specific kinship structures. Exogamy extends social and political ties outward; endogamy does the reverse. Endogamic rules are common in stratified societies. One extreme example is India, where castes are the endogamous units.

5. The discussion of same-sex marriage, which, by and large, is illegal in the United States, illustrates the various rights that go along with marriage. Marriage establishes the legal parents of children. It gives spouses rights to the sexuality, labor, and property of the other. And it establishes a socially significant "relationship of affinity" between spouses and each other's relatives.

6. In societies with descent groups, marriages are relationships between groups as well as between spouses. With lobola, the groom and his relatives transfer wealth to the bride and her relatives. As the value of the lobola gift increases, the divorce rate declines. Lobola customs show that marriages among nonindustrial food producers create and maintain group alliances. So does the sororate, by which a man marries the sister of his deceased wife, and the levirate, by which a woman marries the brother of her deceased husband.

7. The ease and frequency of divorce vary across cultures. When marriage is a matter of intergroup alliance, as is typically true in societies with descent groups, divorce is less common. A large fund of joint property also complicates divorce.

8. Many societies permit plural marriages. The two kinds of polygamy are polygyny and polyandry. The former involves multiple wives; the latter, multiple husbands. Polygyny is much more common than polyandry.

Key Terms

caste system, *148*
clan, *142*
descent
  group, *141*
dowry, *151*
endogamy, *147*
exogamy, *145*
extended family
  household, *138*
family, *134*
family of
  orientation, *135*

family of
  procreation, *135*
incest, *145*
levirate, *153*
lineage, *142*
lobola, *151*
matrilineal
  descent, *141*
matrilocality, *144*
neolocality, *138*
patrilineal
  descent, *141*

patrilocality, *144*
plural
  marriages, *152*
polyandry, *152*
polygamy, *152*
polygyny, *152*
sororate, *152*
unilineal
  descent, *142*

Chapter

Gender

Because anthropologists study biology, society, and culture, they are in a unique position to comment on nature (biological predispositions) and nurture (environment) as determinants of human behavior. Human attitudes, values, and behavior are limited not only by our genetic predispositions—which often are difficult to identify—but also by our experiences during enculturation. Our attributes as adults are determined both by our genes and by our environment during growth and development.

Sex and Gender

Questions about nature and nurture emerge in the discussion of human sex–gender roles and sexuality. Men and women differ genetically. Women have two X chromosomes, and men have an X and a Y. The father determines a baby's sex because only he has the Y chromosome to transmit. The mother always provides an X chromosome.

The chromosomal difference is expressed in hormonal and physiological contrasts. Humans are sexually dimorphic, more so than some primates, such as gibbons (small, tree-living Asiatic apes) and less so than others, such as gorillas and orangutans. **Sexual dimorphism** refers to differences in male and female biology besides the contrasts in breasts and genitals. Women and men differ not just in primary (genitalia and reproductive organs) and secondary (breasts, voice, hair distribution) sexual characteristics, but in average weight, height, strength, and longevity. Women tend to live longer than men and have excellent endurance capabilities. In a given population, men tend to be taller and to weigh more than women do. Of course, there is a considerable overlap between the sexes in terms of height, weight, and physical strength, and there has been a pronounced reduction in sexual dimorphism during human biological evolution.

Just how far, however, do such genetically and physiologically determined differences go? What effects do they have on the way men and women act and are treated in different societies? Anthropologists have discovered both similarities and differences in the roles of men and women in different cultures. The predominant anthropological position on sex–gender roles and biology may be stated as follows:

> The biological nature of men and women [should be seen] not as a narrow enclosure limiting the human organism, but rather as a broad base upon which a variety of structures can be built. (Friedl 1975, p. 6)

Although in most societies men tend to be somewhat more aggressive than women are, many of the behavioral and attitudinal differences between the sexes emerge from culture rather than biology. Sex differences are biological, but gender encompasses all the traits that a culture assigns to and inculcates in males and females. *Gender,* in other words, refers to the cultural construction of whether one is female, male, or something else.

Given the "rich and various constructions of gender" within the realm of cultural diversity, Susan Bourque and Kay Warren (1987) note that the same images of masculinity and femininity do not always apply. Margaret Mead did an early ethnographic study of variation in gender roles. Her book *Sex and Temperament in Three Primitive Societies* (1935/1950) was based on field work in three societies in Papua New Guinea: the Arapesh, Mundugumor, and Tchambuli. The extent of personality variation in men and women in those three societies on the same island amazed Mead. She found that Arapesh men and women both acted as Americans have traditionally expected women to act: in a mild, parental, responsive way. Mundugumor men and women both, in contrast, acted as she believed we expect men to act: fiercely and aggressively. Finally, Tchambuli men were "catty," wore curls, and went shopping, but Tchambuli women were energetic and managerial and placed less emphasis on personal adornment than did the men. [Drawing on their case study of the Tchambuli, whom they call the Chambri, Errington and Gewertz (1987), while recognizing gender malleability, have disputed the specifics of Mead's account.]

There is a well-established field of feminist scholarship within anthropology (Di Leonardo 1991*a*; Rosaldo 1980*b*; Strathern 1988). Anthropologists have gathered systematic ethnographic data about similarities and differences involving gender in many cultural settings (Bonvillain 2007; Brettell and Sargent 2009; Kimmel 2007; Mascia-Lees 2010; Nanda 2000; Ward and Edelstein 2009). Before we examine the cross-cultural data, some definitions are in order.

Gender roles are the tasks and activities a culture assigns by gender. Related to gender roles are **gender stereotypes,** which are oversimplified but strongly held ideas about the characteristics of males and females. **Gender stratification** describes an unequal distribution of rewards (socially valued resources, power, prestige, human rights, and personal freedom) between men and women, reflecting their different positions in a social hierarchy. According to Ann Stoler (1977), the economic determinants of gender status include freedom or autonomy (in disposing of one's labor and its fruits) and social power (control over the lives, labor, and produce of others).

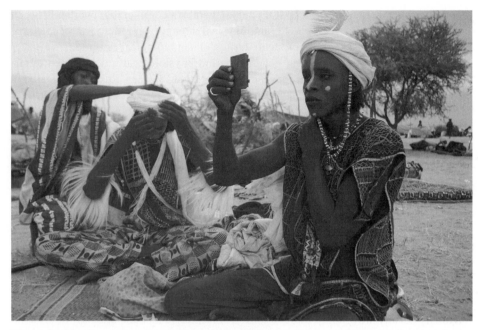

The realm of cultural diversity contains richly different social constructions and expressions of gender roles. In Niger, this Wodaabe man prepares for the Gerewol male beauty contest, an annual reunion.

In stateless societies, gender stratification often is more obvious in regard to prestige than it is in regard to wealth. In her study of the Ilongots of northern Luzon in the Philippines, Michelle Rosaldo (1980*a*) described gender differences related to the positive cultural value placed on adventure, travel, and knowledge of the external world. More often than women, Ilongot men, as headhunters, visited distant places. They acquired knowledge of the external world, amassed experiences there, and returned to express their knowledge, adventures, and feelings in public oratory. They received acclaim as a result. Ilongot women had inferior prestige because they lacked external experiences on which to base knowledge and dramatic expression. On the basis of Rosaldo's study and findings in other stateless societies, Ong (1989) argues that we must distinguish between prestige systems and actual power in a given society. High male prestige does not necessarily entail economic or political power held by men over their families. (For more on Rosaldo's contributions to gender studies, see Lugo and Maurer 2000.)

Recurrent Gender Patterns

You probably had chores when you were growing up. Was there any gender bias in what you were asked to do compared with your brother or sister? If you were raised by two parents, did any tension arise over your parental division of labor? Based on cross-cultural data from societies worldwide, Table 8.1 lists activities that are generally

TABLE 8.1   Generalities in the Division of Labor by Gender, Based on Data from 185 Societies

Source: Murdock and Provost 1973.

Generally Male Activities	Swing (Male or Female) Activities	Generally Female Activities
Hunting large aquatic animals (e.g., whales, walrus)	Making fire	Gathering fuel (e.g., firewood)
Smelting ores	Body mutilation	Making drinks
Metalworking	Preparing skins	Gathering wild vegetal foods
Lumbering	Gathering small land animals	Dairy production (e.g., churning)
Hunting large land animals	Planting crops	Spinning
Working wood	Making leather products	Doing the laundry
Hunting fowl	Harvesting	Fetching water
Making musical instruments	Tending crops	Cooking
Trapping	Milking	Preparing vegetal food (e.g., processing cereal grains)
Building boats	Making baskets	
Working stone	Carrying burdens	
Working bone, horn, and shell	Making mats	
Mining and quarrying	Caring for small animals	
Setting bones	Preserving meat and fish	
Butchering*	Loom weaving	
Collecting wild honey	Gathering small aquatic animals	
Clearing land	Manufacturing clothing	
Fishing	Making pottery	
Tending large herd animals		
Building houses		
Preparing the soil		
Making nets		
Making rope		

*All the activities above "butchering" are almost always done by men; those from "butchering" through "making rope" usually are done by men.

male, generally female, or swing (either male or female). Before you look at that table, see if you can assign the following to one gender or the other (M or F): hunting large animals ( ), gathering wild vegetable foods ( ), tending crops ( ), fishing ( ), cooking ( ), fetching water ( ), making baskets ( ), making drinks ( ). Now consult Table 8.1 and see how you did. Reflect on your results. Is what's true cross-culturally still true of the division of labor by gender in today's world, including the United States?

Even if we still think in terms of "men's work" and "women's work," ideas about gender are changing along with the employment patterns of men and women. But old beliefs, cultural expectations and challenges, and gender stereotypes linger. As of this writing, only 20 out of 100 United States senators are women. Only 4 women have ever served on the U.S. Supreme Court. Women, in general, remain less powerful than men (see this chapter's "Anthropology Today.")

The lingering American expectation that proper female behavior should be polite, restrained, or meek poses a challenge for women, because American culture also values decisiveness and "standing up for your beliefs." When American men and women display certain behavior—speaking up for their ideas, for example—they are judged differently. A man's assertive behavior may be admired and rewarded, but a woman's similar behavior may be labeled "aggressive"—or worse.

Both men and women are constrained by their cultural training, stereotypes, and expectations. For example, American men are told they should "be decisive"—make decisions and stick to them. In our stereotypes, changing one's mind is more associated with women than men and may be perceived as a sign of weakness. Politicians routinely criticize their opponents for being indecisive, for waffling or "flip-flopping" on issues. What a strange idea—that people shouldn't change their positions if they've discovered there's a better way. Males, females, and humanity may be equally victimized by aspects of cultural training.

Data relevant to the cross-cultural study of gender can be drawn from the domains of economics, politics, domestic activity, kinship, and marriage. Review Table 8.1 for cross-cultural data from 185 randomly selected societies on the division of labor by gender.

Remembering the discussion in Chapter 2 of universals, generalities, and particularities, the findings in Table 8.1 about the division of labor by gender illustrate generalities rather than universals. That is, among the societies known to ethnography, there is a very strong tendency for men to build boats, but there are exceptions. One was the Hidatsa, a Native American group in which the women made the boats used to cross the Missouri River. (Traditionally, the Hidatsa were village farmers and bison hunters on the North American Plains; they now live in North Dakota.) Another exception is that Pawnee women worked wood; this is the only Native American group that assigned this activity to women. (The Pawnee, also traditionally Plains farmers and bison hunters, originally lived in what is now central Nebraska and central Kansas; they now live on a reservation in north central Oklahoma.)

Exceptions to cross-cultural generalizations may involve societies or individuals. That is, a society like the Hidatsa can contradict the cross-cultural generalization that men build boats by assigning that task to women. Or, in a society where the cultural expectation is that only men build boats, a particular woman or women can contradict that expectation by doing the male activity. Table 8.1 shows that in a sample of 185 societies, certain activities ("swing activities") are assigned to either or both men and women. Among the most important of such activities are planting, tending, and harvesting crops. Some societies customarily assign more farming chores to women, whereas others make men the primary farmers. Among the tasks almost always assigned to men (Table 8.1), some (e.g., hunting large animals on land and sea) seem clearly related to the greater average size and strength of males. Others, such as working wood and making musical instruments, seem more culturally arbitrary. And women, of course, are not exempt from arduous and time-consuming physical labor, such as gathering firewood and fetching water. In Arembepe, Bahia, Brazil, women routinely transported water in 5-gallon tins, balanced on their heads, from wells and lagoons located long distances from their homes.

The original coding of the data in Table 8.1 probably illustrates a male bias in that extradomestic activities received much more prominence than domestic activities did. Think about how female domestic activities could have been specified in greater detail in Table 8.1. One wonders whether collecting wild honey (listed in Table 8.1) is more necessary or time-consuming than nursing a baby (absent from Table 8.1). Also, notice that Table 8.1 does not mention trade and market activity, in which either or both men and women are active.

Both women and men have to fit their activities into 24-hour days. Turn now to Table 8.2, which shows that the time and effort spent in subsistence activities by men and women tend to be about equal. If anything, men do slightly less subsistence work than women do. But in domestic activities and child care, female labor clearly predominates, as we see in Tables 8.3 and 8.4. Table 8.3 shows that in about half the societies studied, men did virtually no domestic work. Even in societies where men did domestic chores, the bulk of such work was done by women. Adding together their subsistence activities and their domestic work, women tend to work more hours than men do. Has this changed in the contemporary world?

What about child care? Women tend to be the main caregivers in most societies, but men often play a role. Table 8.4 uses cross-cultural data to answer the question

TABLE 8.2   **Time and Effort Expended on Subsistence Activities by Men and Women**[*]

Source: M. F. Whyte, "Cross-Cultural Codes Dealing with the Relative Status of Women," *Ethnology* 17(2):211–239.

More by men	16
Roughly equal	61
More by women	23

[*]Percentage of 88 randomly selected societies for which information was available on this variable.

TABLE 8.3   **Who Does the Domestic Work?**[*]

Source: M. F. Whyte, "Cross-Cultural Codes Dealing with the Relative Status of Women," *Ethnology* 17(2):211–239.

Males do virtually none	51
Males do some, but females do most	49

[*]Percentage of 92 randomly selected societies for which information was available on this variable.

TABLE 8.4   **Who Has Final Authority over the Care, Handling, and Discipline of Infant Children (under 4 Years Old)?**[*]

Source: M. F. Whyte, "Cross-Cultural Codes Dealing with the Relative Status of Women," *Ethnology* 17(2):211–239.

Males have more say	18
Roughly equal	16
Females have more say	66

[*]Percentage of 67 randomly selected societies for which information was available on this variable.

"Who—men or women—has final authority over the care, handling, and discipline of children younger than 4 years?" Women have primary authority over infants in two-thirds of the societies. Given the critical role of breast-feeding in ensuring infant survival, it makes sense, for infants especially, for the mother to be the primary caregiver.

There are differences in male and female reproductive strategies. Women work to ensure their progeny will survive by establishing a close bond with each baby. It's also advantageous for a woman to have a reliable mate to ease the child-rearing process and ensure the survival of her children. (Again, there are exceptions, for example, the matrilineal Nayars discussed in the previous chapter.) Women can have only so many babies during their reproductive years, which begin after menarche (the advent of first menstruation) and end with menopause (cessation of menstruation). Men, in contrast, have a longer reproductive period, which can last into the elder years. If they choose to do so, men can enhance their reproductive success by impregnating several women over a longer time period. Although men do not always have multiple mates, they do have a greater tendency to do so than women do (see Tables 8.5, 8.6, and 8.7). Among the societies known to ethnography, polygyny is much more common than polyandry (see Table 8.5).

TABLE 8.5   Does the Society Allow Multiple Spouses?[*]

Source: M. F. Whyte, "Cross-Cultural Codes Dealing with the Relative Status of Women," *Ethnology* 17(2):211–239.

Only for males	77
For both, but more commonly for males	4
For neither	16
For both, but more commonly for females	2

[*]Percentage of 92 randomly selected societies.

TABLE 8.6   Is There a Double Standard with Respect to Premarital Sex?[*]

Source: M. F. Whyte, "Cross-Cultural Codes Dealing with the Relative Status of Women," *Ethnology* 17(2):211–239.

Yes—females are more restricted	44
No—equal restrictions on males and females	56

[*]Percentage of 73 randomly selected societies for which information was available on this variable.

TABLE 8.7   Is There a Double Standard with Respect to Extramarital Sex?[*]

Source: M. F. Whyte, "Cross-Cultural Codes Dealing with the Relative Status of Women," Ethnology 17(2):211–239.

Yes—females are more restricted	43
Equal restrictions on males and females	55
Males punished more severely for transgression	3

[*]Percentage of 75 randomly selected societies for which information was available on this variable.

Men mate, within and outside marriage, more than women do. Table 8.6 shows cross-cultural data on premarital sex, and Table 8.7 summarizes the data on extramarital sex. In both cases men are less restricted than women are, although the restrictions are equal in about half the societies studied. Double standards that restrict women more than men are one illustration of gender stratification, which we now examine more systematically.

Gender Roles and Gender Stratification

Economic roles affect gender stratification. In one cross-cultural study, Sanday (1974) found that gender stratification decreased when men and women made roughly equal contributions to subsistence. She found that gender stratification was greatest when the women contributed either much more or much less than the men did.

In foraging societies, gender stratification was most marked when men contributed much *more* to the diet than women did. This was true among the Inuit and other northern hunters and fishers. Among tropical and semitropical foragers, by contrast, gathering usually supplies more food than hunting and fishing do. Gathering is generally women's work. Men usually hunt and fish, but women also do some fishing and may hunt small animals, as is true among the Agta of the Philippines (Griffin and Estioko-Griffin 1985). When gathering is prominent, gender status tends to be more equal than it is when hunting and fishing are the main subsistence activities.

Gender status also is more equal when the domestic and public spheres aren't sharply separated. (**Domestic** means within or pertaining to the home.) Strong differentiation between the home and the outside world is called the **domestic-public dichotomy,** or the *private-public contrast*. The outside world can include politics, trade, warfare, or work. Often when domestic and public spheres are clearly separated, public activities have greater prestige than domestic ones do. This can promote gender stratification, because men are more likely to be active in the public domain than women are. Cross-culturally, women's activities tend to be closer to home than men's are. Thus, another reason hunter-gatherers have less gender stratification than food producers do is that the domestic–public dichotomy is less developed among foragers.

We've seen that certain gender roles are more sex-linked than others. Men are the usual hunters and warriors. Given such tools and weapons as spears, knives, and bows, men make better hunters and fighters because they are bigger and stronger on the average than are women in the same population (Divale and Harris 1976). The male hunter–fighter role also reflects a tendency toward greater male mobility.

Reduced Gender Stratification—Matrilineal–Matrilocal Societies

Cross-cultural variation in gender status also is related to rules of descent and postmarital residence (Friedl 1975; Martin and Voorhies 1975). With matrilineal descent and *matrilocality* (residence after marriage with the wife's relatives), female status tends to be high. Matriliny and matrilocality disperse related males, rather than consolidating them. By contrast, patriliny and *patrilocality* (residence after marriage with the husband's kin) keep male relatives together. Matrilineal–matrilocal systems tend to occur in societies where population pressure on strategic resources is minimal and warfare is infrequent.

Women tend to have high status in matrilineal–matrilocal societies for several reasons. Descent-group membership, succession to political positions, allocation of land, and overall social identity all come through female links. Among the matrilineal Malays of Negeri Sembilan, Malaysia (Peletz 1988), matriliny gave women sole inheritance of ancestral rice fields. Matrilocality created solidary clusters of female kin. These Malay women had considerable influence beyond the household (Swift 1963). In such matrilineal contexts, women are the basis of the entire social structure. Although public authority nominally may be assigned to the men, much of the power and decision making actually may belong to the senior women.

Matriarchy

Cross-culturally, anthropologists have described tremendous variation in the roles of men and women, and the power differentials between them. If a patriarchy is a political system ruled by men, is a matriarchy necessarily a political system ruled by women? Or might we apply the term *matriarchy,* as anthropologist Peggy Sanday (2002) does, to a political system in which women play a much more prominent role than men do in social and political organization? One example would be the Minangkabau of West Sumatra, Indonesia,

A Minangkabau bride and groom in West Sumatra, Indonesia, where anthropologist Peggy Reeves Sanday has conducted several years of ethnographic fieldwork.

whom Sanday (2002) has studied for decades. Sanday considers the Minangkabau a matriarchy because women are the center, origin, and foundation of the social order. Senior women are associated with the central pillar of the traditional house, the oldest one in the village. The oldest village in a cluster is called the "mother village." In ceremonies, women are addressed by the term used for their mythical Queen Mother. Women control land inheritance, and couples reside matrilocally. In the wedding ceremony, the wife collects her husband from his household and, with her female kin, escorts him to hers. If there is a divorce, the husband simply takes his things and leaves. Yet despite the special position of women, the Minangkabau matriarchy is not the equivalent of female rule, given the Minangkabau belief that all decision making should be by consensus.

Increased Gender Stratification—Patrilineal–Patrilocal Societies

Martin and Voorhies (1975) link the decline of matriliny and the spread of the **patrilineal–patrilocal complex** (consisting of patrilineality, patrilocality, warfare, and male supremacy) to pressure on resources. Faced with scarce resources, patrilineal–patrilocal cultivators such as the Yanomami often wage warfare against other villages. This favors patrilocality and patriliny, customs that keep related men together in the same village, where they make strong allies in battle. Such societies tend to have a sharp domestic–public dichotomy, and men tend to dominate the prestige hierarchy. Men may use their public roles in warfare and trade and their greater prestige to symbolize and reinforce the devaluation or oppression of women.

The patrilineal–patrilocal complex characterizes many societies in highland Papua New Guinea. Women work hard growing and processing subsistence crops, raising and tending pigs (the main domesticated animal and a favorite food), and doing domestic cooking, but they are isolated from the public domain, which men control. Men grow and distribute prestige crops, prepare food for feasts, and arrange marriages. The men even get to trade the pigs and control their use in ritual.

In many parts of Papua New Guinea, special possessions, including ritual objects and the sculpture being created in this photo, are stored in separate men's houses. Shown here are members of the Abelam ethnic group, who live in the East Sepik province of Papua New Guinea. Are there places like this in your society?

In densely populated areas of the Papua New Guinea highlands, male–female avoidance is associated with strong pressure on resources (Lindenbaum 1972). Men fear all female contacts, including sexual acts. They think that sexual contact with women will weaken them. Indeed, men see everything female as dangerous and polluting. They segregate themselves in men's houses and hide their precious ritual objects from women. They delay marriage, and some never marry.

By contrast, the sparsely populated areas of Papua New Guinea, such as recently settled areas, lack taboos on male–female contacts. The image of woman as polluter fades, heterosexual intercourse is valued, men and women live together, and reproductive rates are high.

Patriarchy and Violence

Patriarchy describes a political system ruled by men in which women have inferior social and political status, including basic human rights. Barbara Miller (1997), in a study of systematic neglect of females, describes women in rural northern India as "the endangered sex." Societies that feature a full-fledged patrilineal–patrilocal complex, replete with warfare and intervillage raiding, also typify patriarchy. Such practices as dowry murders, female infanticide, and clitoridectomy exemplify patriarchy, which extends from tribal societies such as the Yanomami to state societies such as India and Pakistan.

Although more prevalent in certain social settings than in others, family violence and domestic abuse of women are worldwide problems. Domestic violence certainly occurs in nuclear family settings, such as Canada and the United States. Cities, with their impersonality and isolation from extended kin networks, are breeding grounds for domestic violence, as also may be rural areas where women lead isolated lives.

When a woman resides matrilocally, she has kin nearby to look after and protect her interests. Even in patrilocal polygynous settings, women often count on the support of their cowives and sons in disputes with potentially abusive husbands. Such settings, which tend to provide a safe haven for women, are retracting rather than expanding in today's world. Isolated families and patrilineal social forms have spread at the expense of matrilineality. Many nations have declared polygyny illegal. More and more women, and men, find themselves cut off from extended kin and families of orientation.

With the spread of the women's rights movement and the human rights movement, attention to domestic violence and abuse of women has increased. Laws have been passed and mediating institutions established. Brazil's female-run police stations for battered women provide an example, as do shelters for victims of domestic abuse in the United States and Canada. But patriarchal institutions do persist in what should be a more enlightened world.

Gender in Industrial Societies

The domestic–public dichotomy also influences gender stratification in industrial societies, including Canada and the United States, where gender roles have been changing rapidly. In early industrial Europe, men, women, and children flocked to factories as wage laborers. Enslaved Americans of both sexes toiled in cotton fields. After abolition, southern African American women continued working as field hands and domestics. Poor White women labored in the South's early cotton mills. In the 1890s more than one million American women held menial and repetitive unskilled factory positions.

In the early 20th century, a wave of European immigration provided a male labor force willing to work for wages lower than those of American-born men. Immigrant men were hired for factory jobs that previously would have gone to women. As

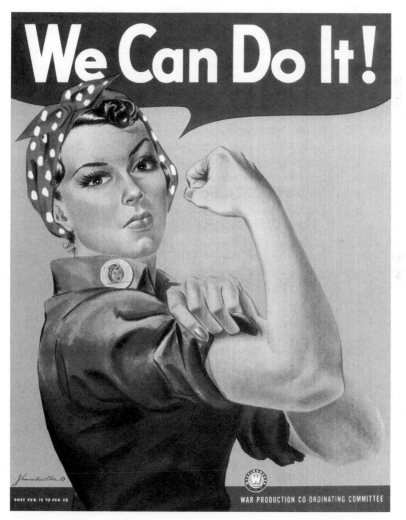

During the world wars the notion that women were biologically unfit for hard physical labor faded. Shown here is World War II's famous Rosie the Riveter. Is there a comparable poster woman today? What does her image say about modern gender roles?

machine tools and mass production further reduced the need for female labor, the notion gained ground that women were biologically unfit for factory work (Martin and Voorhies 1975).

Maxine Margolis (1984, 2000) has shown how gendered work, attitudes, and beliefs have varied in response to American economic needs. For example, wartime shortages of men have promoted the idea that work outside the home is women's patriotic duty. During the world wars the notion that women were unfit for hard physical labor faded. Inflation and the culture of consumption also have spurred female employment. When prices or demand rises, multiple paychecks help maintain family living standards.

The increase in female paid employment in the United States since World War II also reflects the baby boom and industrial expansion. American culture traditionally has defined clerical work, teaching, and nursing as female occupations. With rapid population growth and business expansion after World War II, the demand for women to fill such jobs grew steadily. Employers also found they could increase their profits by paying women lower wages than they would have to pay returning male war veterans.

Economic changes paved the way for the contemporary women's movement, which also was spurred by the publication of Betty Friedan's book *The Feminine Mystique* in 1963 and the founding of NOW, the National Organization for Women, in 1966. The movement in turn promoted expanded work opportunities for women, including the as yet unrealized goal of equal pay for equal work. Between 1970 and 2010, the female percentage of the American workforce rose from 38 to 47 percent. In other words, almost half of all Americans who work outside the home are women. Over 65 million women now have paid jobs, compared with 73 million men. Women fill more than half (52 percent) of all management/professional jobs (*Statistical Abstract of the United States* 2012, Table 616). And it's not mainly single women working, as once was the case. Table 8.8 presents figures on the ever-increasing

TABLE 8.8   Cash Employment of American Mothers, Wives, and Husbands, 1960–2010[*]

Source: *Statistical Abstract of the United States* 2012, Tables 597, 599. http://www.census.gov/prod/2011pubs/12statab/labor.pdf.

Year	Percentage of Married Women, Husband Present with Children under 6	Percentage of All Married Women[†]	Percentage of All Married Men[‡]
1960	19	32	89
1970	30	40	86
1980	45	50	81
1990	59	58	79
2010	62	61	76

[*]Civilian population 16 years of age and older.
[†]Husband present.
[‡]Wife present.

cash employment of American wives and mothers, including those with children under 6 years old.

Note in Table 8.8 that the cash employment of American married men has been falling, while that of American married women has been rising. There has been a dramatic change in behavior and attitudes since 1960, when 89 percent of all married men worked, compared with just 32 percent of married women. The comparable figures in 2010 were 76 percent and 61 percent. The ratio of female to male earnings rose from 68 percent in 1989 to 77 percent in 2006, then fell to 72 percent in 2010.

Ideas about the gender roles of males and females have changed. Compare your grandparents and your parents. Chances are you have a working mother, but your grandmother was more likely a stay-at-home mom. Your grandfather is more likely than your father to have worked in manufacturing and to have belonged to a union. Your father is more likely than your grandfather to have shared child care and domestic responsibilities. Age at marriage has been delayed for both men and women. College educations and professional degrees have increased. What other changes do you associate with the increase in female employment outside the home?

The Feminization of Poverty

Alongside the economic gains of many American women stands an opposite extreme: the feminization of poverty, or the increasing representation of women (and their children) among America's poorest people. Women head over half of U.S. households with incomes below the poverty line. The average income for married-couple families is more than twice that of families maintained by a single woman. The median one-earner family maintained by a single woman had an annual income of $32,597 in 2009, compared with $71,830 for a married-couple household.

The feminization of poverty isn't just a North American trend. The percentage of single-parent (usually female-headed) households has been increasing worldwide. The figure ranges from about 10 percent in Japan to below 20 percent in certain South Asian and Southeast Asian countries to almost 50 percent in certain African countries and the Caribbean (Buvinic 1995; *Statistical Abstract of the United States* 2012, Table 1337). The percentage of single-parent households rose in every nation listed in Table 8.9 between 1980–1981 and 2009. The United States maintains the largest percentage of single-parent households (29.5 percent), followed by the United Kingdom (25 percent),

TABLE 8.9 Percentage of Single-Parent Households, Selected Countries, 1980–1981 and 2009		
Country	**1980–1981**	**2009**
United States	19.5%	29.5%
United Kingdom	13.9	25.0
Canada	12.7	24.6
Ireland	7.2	22.6
Denmark	13.4	21.7
France	10.2	19.8
Japan	4.9	10.2

Canada (24.6 percent), Ireland (22.6 percent), and Denmark (21.7 percent). The rate of increase in single-parent households over the past 30 years has been highest in Ireland, where it has tripled, from 7.2 to 22.6 percent.

Globally, households headed by women tend to be poorer than those headed by men. In one study, the percentage of single-parent families considered poor was 18 percent in Britain, 20 percent in Italy, 25 percent in Switzerland, 40 percent in Ireland, 52 percent in Canada, and 63 percent in the United States.

It is widely believed that one way to improve the situation of poor women is to encourage them to organize. New women's groups can in some cases revive or replace traditional forms of social organization that have been disrupted. Membership in a group can help women to mobilize resources, to rationalize production, and to reduce the risks and costs associated with credit. Organization also allows women to develop self-confidence and to decrease dependence on others. Through such organization, poor women throughout the world are working to determine their own needs and priorities and to change things so as to improve their social and economic situation (Buvinic 1995).

Work and Happiness

Table 8.10 shows female labor force participation in various countries—condensed from 30 countries for which data were available—in 2008. The United States, with 69.3 percent of its women employed that year, ranked 13th, while Canada (74.4 percent) ranked 6th. Iceland topped the list, with 82.5 percent of its women in the workforce. Turkey was lowest; only 26.7 percent of its women were employed.

In 2010, Gallup conducted a survey of the world's 132 happiest countries, based on various measures, including the percentages of people in that country who were thriving—and suffering. Respondents also were asked to rate their own lives on a scale from 0 (worst possible) to 10 (best possible). Denmark was the world's happiest nation; Canada came in 6th; the United States, 12th.

Interestingly, we can detect a correlation between the two rankings—of happiness and of women's work outside the home. We see in Table 8.10 that of the 13 countries with greatest female labor force participation, 10 ranked among the world's happiest (see Levy 2010). Why, as more women work outside the home, might a country's population achieve a greater sense of well-being? Note that many of the countries listed as among the world's happiest not only have more employed women but also have a higher living standard and a more secure government safety net. What other factors might help explain this correlation?

Denmark, which has a high rate of workplace women, a rising birthrate, and readily available child care, is rated the world's happiest country. The genetics researcher shown here is the mother of a toddler.

TABLE 8.10
Female Labor Force Participation by Country, 2008

Source: *Statistical Abstract of the United States* 2010, Table 1330; Huffington Post, http://www.huffingtonpost.com/2010/07/03/worlds-happiest-countries_n_633814.

Country	Percentage of Women in Labor Force	Rank among World's 15 "Happiest Countries"
Iceland	82.5	*
Sweden	78.2	9
Norway	77.4	3
Denmark	77.3	1
Switzerland	76.6	7
Canada	74.4	6
Finland	74.0	2
New Zealand	72.0	8
Netherlands	72.6	4
United Kingdom	70.2	*
Australia	69.9	11
Germany	69.7	*
United States	69.3	12
Turkey (lowest in table)	26.7	*

*These countries were not among the 15 "happiest countries."

Beyond Male and Female

Gender is socially constructed, and societies may recognize more than two genders. The contemporary United States, for example, includes individuals who self-identify using such labels as "transgender," "intersex," "third gender," and "transsexual." Such persons contradict dominant male/female gender distinctions by being part male and female, or neither male nor female. Because people who self-identify as "transgender" are increasingly visible, we must be careful about seeing "masculine " and "feminine" as absolute and binary categories.

Sex, we have seen, is biological, whereas gender is socially constructed. Transgender is a social category that includes individuals who *may or may not* contrast biologically with ordinary males and females. Within the transgender category, intersex people (see below) usually contrast biologically with ordinary males and females, but *transgender also includes people whose gender identity has no apparent biological roots.*

The term **intersex** encompasses a group of conditions involving a discrepancy between the external genitals (penis, vagina, etc.) and the internal genitals (testes, ovaries, etc.). The older term for this condition, *hermaphroditism,* combined the names of a Greek god and goddess. Hermes was a god of male sexuality (among other things) and Aphrodite a goddess of female sexuality, love, and beauty.

The causes of intersex are varied and complex (Kaneshiro 2009): (1) An XX intersex person has the chromosomes of a woman (XX) and normal ovaries, uterus, and fallopian tubes, but the external genitals appear male. Usually this results from a female fetus having been exposed to an excess of male hormones before birth. (2) An XY intersex person has the chromosomes of a man (XY), but the external genitals are incompletely formed, ambiguous, or female. The testes may be normal, malformed, or absent. (3) A true gonadal intersex person has both ovarian and testicular tissue. The external genitals may be ambiguous or may appear to be female or male. (4) Intersex also can result from an unusual chromosome combination, such as X0 (only one X chromosome), XXY, XYY, and XXX. In the last three cases there is an extra sex chromosome, either an X or a Y. These chromosomal combinations don't typically produce a discrepancy between internal and external genitalia, but there may be problems with sex hormone levels and overall sexual development.

The XXY configuration, known as *Klinefelter syndrome,* is the most common of these combinations and the second most common condition (after Down syndrome) caused by the presence of extra chromosomes in humans. Effects of Klinefelter occur in about 1 of every 1,000 males. One in every 500 males has an extra X chromosome but lacks the main symptoms—small testicles and reduced fertility. With XXX, or *triple X syndrome,* there is an extra X chromosome in each cell of a human female. Triple X occurs in about 1 of every 1,000 female births. There usually is no physically distinguishable difference between triple X women and other women. The same is true of XYY compared with other males.

Turner syndrome encompasses several conditions, of which X0 (absence of one sex chromosome) is most common. In this case, all or part of one of the sex chromosomes is absent. Girls with Turner syndrome typically are sterile because of nonworking ovaries and amenorrhea (absence of a menstrual cycle). Biology isn't destiny; people construct their identities in society. Many individuals affected by one of the biological conditions just described see themselves simply as male or female, rather than transgender. Self-identified **transgender** people tend to be individuals whose gender identity contradicts their biological sex at birth and the gender identity that society assigned to them in infancy. Feeling that their previous gender assignment was incorrect, they assert or seek to achieve a new one. The transgender category is diverse. Some transgender individuals lean toward male; some, female; and some toward neither of the dominant genders.

The anthropological record attests that gender diversity beyond male and female exists in many societies and has taken many forms across societies and cultures. Consider, for example, the eunuch, or "perfect servant" (a castrated man who served as a safe attendant to harems in Byzantium [Tougher 2008]). Hijras, who live mainly in northern India, are culturally defined as "neither men nor women," or as men who become women by undergoing castration and adopting women's dress and behavior. Hijras identify with the Indian mother goddess and are believed to channel her power. They are known for their ritualized performances at births and marriages, where they dance and sing, conferring the mother goddess's blessing on the child or the married couple. Although culturally defined as celibate, some hijras now engage in prostitution, in which their role is as women with men (Nanda 1996, 1998). Hijra social movements have campaigned for recognition as a third gender, and in 2005, Indian passport application forms were updated with three gender options: M, F, and E (for male, female, and eunuch [i.e, hijra], respectively) (Telegraph 2005).

Neither man nor woman, hijras constitute India's third gender. Many hijras get their income from performing at ceremonies, begging, or prostitution. The beauty contest shown here was organized by an AIDS prevention and relief organization that works with the local hijra community.

Roscoe writes of the "Zuni man-woman," or berdache, in the 19th century. A berdache was a male who adopted social roles traditionally assigned to women and, through performance of a third gender, contributed to the social and spiritual well-being of the community (1991, 1998). Some Balkan societies included "sworn virgins," born females who assumed male gender roles and activities to meet societal needs when there was a shortage of men (Gremaux 1993).

Among the Gheg tribes of North Albania, "virginal transvestites" were biologically female, but locals consider them "honorary men" (Shryock 1988). Some Albanian adolescent girls have chosen to become men, remain celibate, and live among men, with the support of their families and villagers (Young 2000). And consider Polynesia. In Tonga the term *fakaleitis* describes males who behave as women do, thereby contrasting with mainstream Tongan men. Similar to Tonga's *fakaleitis*, Samoan *fa'afafine* and Hawaiian *mahu* are men who adopt feminine attributes, behaviors, and visual markers.

In the contemporary West, the category transgender encompasses varied individuals whose gender performance and identity enlarge an otherwise binary gender structure. The lesbian and gay rights movement has expanded to include bisexual and transgender individuals. This Lesbian, Gay, Bisexual, and Transgender (LGBT) community works to promote government policies and social practices that protect its members' civil and human rights. In recent years, the LGBT movement and its supporters have achieved many successes, including the legalization of same-sex marriage in several states and the repeal of the "Don't Ask Don't Tell" (DADT) policy of the U.S. armed services.

Sexual Orientation

Gender identity refers to whether a person feels, and is regarded as, male, female, or something else. One's gender identity does not dictate one's sexual orientation. Men who have no doubt about their masculinity can be sexually attracted to women or to other men. Ditto women with regard to female gender identity and variable sexual attraction. **Sexual orientation**, to which we now turn, refers to a person's sexual attraction to, and habitual sexual activities with, persons of the opposite sex (*heterosexuality*), the same sex (*homosexuality*), or both sexes (*bisexuality*). *Asexuality,* indifference toward or lack of attraction to either sex, also is a sexual orientation. All four of these forms are found throughout the world. But each type of desire and experience holds different meanings for individuals and groups. For example, male–male sexual activity may be a private affair in Mexico, rather than public, socially sanctioned, and encouraged as it is among the Etoro (see p. 179) of Papua New Guinea (see also Blackwood 2010; Boellstorff 2007; Herdt 2006; Kottak and Kozaitis 2012; Nanda 2000).

Recently in the United States there has been a tendency to see sexual orientation as fixed and biologically based. There is not enough information at this time to determine the extent to which sexual orientation is based on biology. What we can say is that all human activities and preferences, including erotic expression, are at least partially constructed and influenced by culture.

In any society, individuals will differ in the nature, range, and intensity of their sexual interests and urges. No one knows for sure why such individual sexual differences exist. Part of the answer probably is biological, reflecting genes or hormones (Wade 2005). Another part may have to do with experiences during growth and development. But whatever the reasons for individual variation, culture always plays a role in molding individual sexual urges toward a collective norm. And such sexual norms vary from culture to culture.

What do we know about variation in sexual norms from society to society and over time? A classic cross-cultural study of 76 societies (Ford and Beach 1951) found wide variation in attitudes about forms of sexual activity. In a single society, such as the United States, attitudes about sex differ over time and with socioeconomic status, region, and rural versus urban residence. However, even in the 1950s, prior to the "age of sexual permissiveness" (the pre-HIV period from the mid-1960s through the 1970s), research showed that almost all American men (92 percent) and more than half of American women (54 percent) admitted to masturbation. In the famous Kinsey report (Kinsey, Pomeroy, and Martin 1948), 37 percent of the men surveyed admitted having had at least one sexual experience leading to orgasm with another male. In a later study of 1,200 unmarried women, 26 percent reported same-sex sexual activities. (Because Kinsey's research relied on nonrandom samples, it should be considered merely illustrative, rather than a statistically accurate representation, of sexual behavior at the time.)

In almost two-thirds (63 percent) of the 76 societies in the Ford and Beach study, various forms of same-sex sexual activity were acceptable. Occasionally sexual relations between people of the same sex involved transvestism on the part of one of the partners (see Kulick 1998). Transvestism did not characterize male–male sex among the Sudanese Azande, who valued the warrior role (Evans-Pritchard 1970). Prospective warriors—young men aged 12 to 20—left their families and shared quarters with adult fighting men, who paid lobola for, and had sex with, them. During this apprenticeship, the young men did the domestic duties of women. Upon reaching warrior status, these young men took their own younger male brides. Later, retiring from the warrior role, Azande men married women. Flexible in their sexual expression, Azande males had no difficulty shifting from sex with older men (as male brides) to sex with younger men (as warriors) to sex with women (as husbands) (see Murray and Roscoe, eds. 1998).

Consider also the Etoro (Kelly 1976), a group of 400 people who subsisted by hunting and horticulture in the Trans-Fly region of Papua New Guinea. The Etoro illustrate the power of culture in molding human sexuality. The following account, based on ethnographic fieldwork by Raymond C. Kelly in the late 1960s, applies only to Etoro males and their beliefs. Etoro cultural norms prevented the male anthropologist who studied them from gathering comparable information about female attitudes and behavior. Note also that the activities described have been discouraged by missionaries. Because there has been no restudy of the Etoro specifically focusing on these activities, the extent to which these practices continue today is unknown. For this reason, I'll use the past tense in describing them.

Etoro opinions about sexuality were linked to their beliefs about the cycle of birth, physical growth, maturity, old age, and death. Etoro men believed that semen was necessary to give life force to a fetus, which was, they believed, implanted in a woman by an ancestral spirit. Sexual intercourse during pregnancy nourished the growing fetus. The Etoro believed that men had a limited lifetime supply of semen. Any sex act leading to ejaculation was seen as draining that supply, and as sapping a man's virility and vitality. The birth of children, nurtured by semen, symbolized a necessary sacrifice that would lead to the husband's eventual death. Male–female sexual intercourse, required only for reproduction, was discouraged. Women who wanted too much sex were viewed as witches, hazardous to their husbands' health. Etoro culture allowed male–female intercourse only about 100 days a year. The rest of the time it was tabooed. Seasonal birth clustering shows that the taboo was respected.

So objectionable was male–female sex that it was removed from community life. It could occur neither in sleeping quarters nor in the fields. Coitus could happen only in the woods, where it was risky because poisonous snakes, the Etoro believed, were attracted by the sounds and smells of male–female sex.

Although coitus was discouraged, sex acts between males were viewed as essential. Etoro believed that boys could not produce semen on their own. To grow into men and eventually give life force to their children, boys had to acquire semen orally from older men. From the age of 10 until adulthood, boys were inseminated by older men.

Anthropology Today   *The Global Gender Gap Index*

The World Economic Forum, based in Geneva, Switzerland, began publishing its annual Global Gender Gap Index in 2006 (see Hausmann, Tyson, and Zahidi 2012). This index is designed to measure gender inequality, and to assess progress in reducing it, in 135 countries for which comparable data are available. For each country, and their regions, the index measures the gap between males and females in four major categories: economic opportunity and participation, educational achievement, health and survival, and political empowerment.

German Chancellor Angela Merkel converses with French President François Hollande (on her right) and Belgian Prime Minister Elio Di Rupo during a March, 2013 summit meeting at the EU Headquarters in Brussels, Belgium. Is Merkel the world's most powerful woman?

The indexed countries represent more than 90 percent of the world's population, and most of them have made progress in closing the gender gap since the index's inception in 2006. Worldwide, 96 percent of the gender gap in health and survival has been closed, along with 93 percent of the gap in education. Only 60 percent of the economic gap, however, and a paltry 20 percent of the political gap between men and women have been closed.

With respect to political empowerment, the country that ranked highest for that variable (Iceland) had closed 73% of its gender gap by 2012, whereas the lowest-ranking country (Saudi Arabia) had closed none of its political gender gap. Clearly, women's political gains have lagged their advances in health and education. Worldwide, only about 20 women serve as elected heads of government (e.g., presidents, chancellors, or prime ministers). In 2012, *Forbes* magazine ranked Angela Merkel, Germany's chancellor, the world's second most powerful person (after President Barack Obama). Merkel, however, was the only woman in the top 10 and was 1 of only 3 women in the top 20 most powerful people in the world (see http://www.forbes.com/powerful-people/). In ministries, parliaments,

and houses of congress the global average is less than 20 percent female. (Finally, after the election of November 2012, the U.S. Senate had 20 female members—an all-time high. That still compares with 80 men in that chamber.)

The index ranked North America the world's most successful region in terms of correcting gender-based inequality, considering all four measures (health, education, economic, and political opportunities). Next came Europe and Central Asia, which had closed over 70 percent of their gender gaps. Latin America, Asia, and Africa followed—between 60 percent and 70 percent. The Middle East/North Africa ranked last, having closed just 59 percent of its gender gap.

Four Nordic countries consistently have held the top four positions in the index: Iceland, Finland, Norway, and Sweden. (Consider how this might relate to the happiness index discussed in this chapter.) Although no country has yet achieved full gender equality, those four countries have closed over 80 percent of their gender gaps, considering all criteria.

The lowest-ranking country, Yemen, has closed about half of its gender gap.

The United States ranked 22nd overall in the Global Gender Gap Index in 2012, down from 17th in 2011. The report found no gender gap in American educational attainment. U.S. literacy rates are high for both genders, and rates of female enrollment are comparable to male rates at all educational levels.

The United States fared less well in terms of economics and politics. The U.S. did rank 8th in the world in economic participation and opportunity, reflecting its high rate of female labor force participation. But it was only 61st in terms of equal pay for equal work. The United States did rise somewhat in political empowerment—from 66th place in 2006 to 55th place in 2012.

Let's summarize the progress that has been made globally in closing the gender gap. By 2012, 20 percent of the global political empowerment gap had been closed, versus 14 percent in 2006. In 2012, 60 percent of the economic participation gap had been closed, compared with 56 percent in 2006. In 2012, 93 percent of the educational achievement gap had been closed, up just a bit from 92 percent in 2006. In terms of health and survival, however, there was a small decline between 2006 and 2012, from 97 percent to 96 percent.

These rates of improvement strike me as being rather slow. There's still a lot of progress to be made. A country's gender equality is correlated with its overall economic development and its global competitiveness. Because women represent about half of any national talent base, a country's long-run competitiveness depends significantly on the opportunities it offers its women. How might your country act to reduce its gender gap?

No taboos were attached to this. This oral insemination could proceed in the sleeping area or garden. Every three years, a group of boys around the age of 20 were formally initiated into manhood. They went to a secluded mountain lodge, where they were visited and inseminated by several older men.

Male–male sex among the Etoro was governed by a code of propriety. Although sexual relations between older and younger males were considered culturally essential, those between boys of the same age were discouraged. A boy who took semen from other youths was believed to be sapping their life force and stunting their growth. A boy's rapid physical development could suggest he was getting semen from other boys. Like a sex-hungry wife, he could be shunned as a witch.

The sexual practices just described rested not on hormones or genes but on cultural beliefs and traditions. The Etoro, along with several other tribes in Papua New Guinea, especially in that country's Trans-Fly region, illustrate one extreme of a male–female avoidance pattern that is widespread in Papua New Guinea and indeed in many patrilineal–patrilocal societies.

Flexibility in sexual expression seems to be an aspect of our primate heritage. Both masturbation and same-sex sexual activity exist among chimpanzees and other primates.

Male bonobos (pygmy chimps) regularly engage in a form of mutual masturbation that has been called "penis fencing." Females get sexual pleasure from rubbing their genitals against those of other females (de Waal 1997). Our primate sexual potential is molded by culture, the environment, and reproductive necessity. Male–female coitus is practiced in all human societies—which, after all, must reproduce themselves—but alternatives also are widespread (Rathus, Nevid, and Fichner-Rathus 2013). Like our gender roles, the sexual component of human personality and identity—just how we express our "natural," or biological, sexual urges—is a matter that culture and environment influence and limit.

Summary

1. Gender roles are the tasks and activities that a culture assigns to each sex and to the genders it recognizes. Gender stereotypes are oversimplified ideas about attributes of males and females. Gender stratification describes an unequal distribution of rewards by gender, reflecting different positions in a social hierarchy.

2. Cross-cultural comparison reveals some recurrent patterns involving the division of labor by gender, as well as gender-based differences in reproductive strategies. Gender roles and gender stratification vary with environment, economy, adaptive strategy, system of kinship and descent, level of social complexity, and degree of participation in the world economy.

3. When gathering is prominent, gender status is more equal than when hunting or fishing dominates a foraging economy. Gender status also is more equal when the domestic and public spheres aren't sharply separated.

4. Gender stratification also is linked to descent and residence. Women's status in matrilineal societies tends to be high because overall social identity comes through female links. Women in many societies, especially matrilineal ones, wield power and make decisions. Scarcity of resources promotes intervillage warfare, patriliny, and patrilocality. The localization of related males is adaptive for military solidarity. Men may use their warrior role to symbolize and reinforce the social devaluation and oppression of women. Patriarchy describes a political system ruled by men in which women have inferior social and political status, including basic human rights.

5. Americans' attitudes about gender roles have varied with class and region, as well as historically. A declining need for female labor promotes the idea that women are unfit for many jobs, and vice versa. Countering the economic gains of many American women is the feminization of poverty. This has become a global phenomenon as impoverished female-headed households have increased worldwide. A cross-national survey revealed a correlation between degree of happiness and women's work outside the home.

6. Societies may recognize more than two genders. The term *intersex* describes a group of conditions, including chromosomal configurations, that may produce a discrepancy between external and internal genitals. Transgender individuals may or may not contrast biologically with ordinary males and females. Self-identified transgender

people tend to be individuals whose gender identity contradicts their biological sex at birth and the gender identity that society assigned to them in infancy.

7. Gender identity refers to whether a person feels, and is regarded as, male, female, or something else. One's gender identity does not dictate one's sexual orientation. Sexual orientation stands for a person's habitual sexual attraction to, and activities with, persons of the opposite sex (heterosexuality), the same sex (homosexuality), or both sexes (bisexuality). There has been a recent tendency to see sexual orientation as fixed and biologically based. However, anthropologists know that sexual norms vary widely from culture to culture and that, to some extent at least, erotic expression is influenced by culture.

Key Terms

domestic, *167*
domestic–public dichotomy, *167*
gender identity, *178*
gender roles, *161*
gender stereotypes, *161*
gender stratification, *161*
intersex, *175*
patriarchy, *170*
patrilineal–patrilocal complex, *169*
sexual dimorphism, *160*
sexual orientation, *178*
transgender, *176*

Chapter 9

Religion

Given the varied and worldwide scope of beliefs and behavior labeled "religious," anthropologists know how difficult it is to define **religion.** In his book *Religion: An Anthropological View,* Anthony F. C. Wallace offered this definition: "belief and ritual concerned with supernatural beings, powers, and forces" (1966, p. 5). By "supernatural" he referred to a nonmaterial realm beyond (but believed to impinge on) the observable world. This realm cannot be verified or falsified empirically and is inexplicable in ordinary terms. It must be accepted "on faith." Supernatural beings—deities, ghosts, demons, souls, and spirits—make their homes outside our material world, although they may visit it from time to time. There also are supernatural or sacred forces, some of them wielded by deities and spirits, others that simply exist. In many societies, people believe they can benefit from, become imbued with, or manipulate supernatural forces (see Bowen 2011; Bowie 2006; Crapo 2003; Hicks 2010; Lambek 2008; Stein and Stein 2011; Warms, Garber, and McGee, eds. 2009).

Wallace's definition of religion focuses on presumably universal categories (beings, powers, and forces) within the supernatural realm. For Emile Durkheim (1912/2001), one of the founders of the anthropology of religion, the key distinction was between the sacred and the profane. Like the supernatural for Wallace, Durkheim's "sacred" was the domain set off from the ordinary, or the mundane (he used the word *profane*). For Durkheim, every society had its sacred, but that domain was socially constructed; it varied from society to society. Durkheim focused on Native Australian societies, which he believed had preserved the most elementary, or basic, forms of religion. He noted that their most sacred objects, including plants and animals that served as totems, were not supernatural at all. Rather, they were "real-world" entities (e.g., kangaroos, grubs) that, over the generations, had acquired special meaning for the social groups that had made them sacred and continued to "worship" them.

Many definitions of religion focus on groups of people who gather together regularly for worship (see Reese 1999). These congregants or adherents internalize common beliefs and a shared system of meaning. They accept a set of doctrines involving the relationship between the individual and divinity, the sacred, or whatever is taken to be the ultimate nature of reality. Anthropologists like Durkheim have stressed the collective, social, shared, and enacted nature of religion, the emotions it generates, and the meanings it embodies. As Michael Lambek (2008, p. 5) remarks, "good anthropology understands that religious worlds are real, vivid, and significant to those who construct and inhabit them." Durkheim (1912/2001) highlighted religious effervescence, the bubbling up of collective emotional intensity generated by worship. Victor Turner (1969/1995) updated Durkheim's notion, using the term **communitas,** an intense community spirit, a feeling of great social solidarity, equality, and togetherness.

The word *religion* derives from the Latin *religare*—"to tie, to bind"—but it is not necessary for all members of a given religion to meet together as a common body. Subgroups meet regularly at local congregation sites. They may attend occasional meetings with adherents representing a wider region. And they may form an imagined community with people of similar faith throughout the world.

Participation in a collective religious act, such as singing in this choir, can strengthen social bonds among congregants, while promoting feelings of spiritual effervescence.

In studying religion cross-culturally, anthropologists pay attention to religion as a social phenomenon as well as to the meanings of religious doctrines, settings, acts, and events. Verbal manifestations of religious beliefs include prayers, chants, myths, texts, and statements about, including rules of, ethics and morality (see Hicks 2010; Klass 2003; Moro and Meyers 2012; Stein and Stein 2011). The anthropological study of religion also encompasses notions about purity and pollution (including taboos involving diet and physical contact), sacrifice, initiation, rites of passage, vision quests, pilgrimages, spirit possession, prophecy, study, devotion, and moral actions (Lambek 2008, p. 9).

Like ethnicity and language, religion is associated with social divisions within and between societies and nations. Religion both unites and divides. Participation in common rites may affirm, and thus maintain, the solidarity of a group of adherents. As we know from daily headlines, however, religious difference also may be associated with bitter enmity. Contacts and confrontations have increased between so-called world religions, such as Christianity and Islam, and the more localized forms of religion that missionaries typically lump together under the disparaging term "paganism." Increasingly, ethnic, regional, and class conflicts come to be framed in religious terms. Recent and contemporary examples of religion as a social and political force include the Iranian revolution, the rise of the religious right in the United States, and the worldwide spread of Pentecostalism.

Long ago, Edward Sapir (1928/1956) argued for a distinction between "a religion" and "religion." The former term would apply only to a formally organized religion, such as the world religions just mentioned. The latter—religion—is universal; it refers to religious beliefs and behavior, which exist in all societies, even if they don't stand out as a separate and clearly demarcated sphere. Indeed, many anthropologists (e.g., Asad 1983/2008) argue that such categories as "religion," "politics," and "the economy" are arbitrary constructs that apply best, and perhaps only, to Western, Christian, and modern societies. In such contexts religion can be seen as a specific domain, separate from politics and the economy. By contrast, in nonindustrial societies, religion typically is more embedded in society. Religious beliefs may help regulate the economy (e.g., astrologers determine when to plant) or permeate politics (e.g., divine right of kings).

Anthropologists agree that religion exists in all human societies; it is a cultural universal. However, we'll see that it isn't always easy to distinguish the sacred from the profane and that different societies conceptualize divinity, the sacred, the supernatural, and ultimate realities very differently.

Expressions of Religion

When did religion begin? No one knows for sure. There are suggestions of religion in Neandertal burials and on European cave walls, where painted stick figures may represent **shamans,** early religious specialists. Nevertheless, any statement about when, where, why, and how religion arose, or any description of its original nature, can only be speculative. Although such speculations are inconclusive, many have revealed important functions and effects of religious behavior. Several theories will be examined now.

Spiritual Beings

Another founder of the anthropology of religion was the Englishman Sir Edward Burnett Tylor (1871/1958). Religion arose, Tylor thought, as people tried to understand conditions and events they could not explain by reference to daily experience. Tylor believed that ancient humans—and contemporary nonindustrial peoples—were particularly intrigued with death, dreaming, and trance. People see images they may remember when they wake up or come out of a trance state. Tylor concluded that attempts to explain dreams and trances led early humans to believe that two entities inhabit the body. One is active during the day, and the other—a double or soul—is active during sleep and trance states. Although they never meet, they are vital to each other. When the double permanently leaves the body, the person dies. Death is departure of the soul. From the Latin for soul, *anima,* Tylor named this belief **animism.** The soul was one sort of spiritual entity; people remembered various images from their dreams and trances—other spirits. For Tylor, animism, the earliest form of religion, was a belief in spiritual beings.

Tylor proposed that religion evolved through stages, beginning with animism. **Polytheism** (the belief in multiple gods) and then **monotheism** (the belief in a single, all-powerful deity) developed later. Because religion originated to explain things, Tylor thought it would decline as science offered better explanations. To an extent, he was right. We now have scientific explanations for many things that religion once elucidated. Nevertheless, because religion persists, it must do something more than explain. It must, and does, have other functions and meanings.

Powers and Forces

In addition to animism—and sometimes coexisting with it in the same society—is a view of the supernatural as a domain of impersonal power, or force, which people can control under certain conditions. (You'd be right to think of *Star Wars.*) Such a conception has been particularly prominent in Melanesia, the area of the South Pacific that includes Papua New Guinea and adjacent islands. Melanesians traditionally believed in **mana,** a sacred impersonal force existing in the universe. Mana could reside in people, animals, plants, and objects.

Melanesian mana was similar to our notion of good luck. Objects with mana could change someone's luck. For example, a charm or an amulet belonging to a successful hunter could transmit the hunter's mana to the next person who held or wore it. A woman could put a rock in her garden, see her yields improve, and attribute the change to the force contained in the rock.

Beliefs in manalike forces have been widespread, although the specifics of the religious doctrines have varied. Consider the contrast between mana in Melanesia and Polynesia (the islands included in a triangular area marked by Hawaii to the north, Easter Island to the east, and New Zealand to the southwest). In Melanesia, anyone could acquire mana by chance, or by working hard to get it. In Polynesia, however, mana wasn't potentially available to everyone but was attached to political offices. Chiefs and nobles had more mana than ordinary people did.

So charged with mana were the highest chiefs that contact with them was dangerous to commoners. The mana of chiefs flowed out of their bodies. It could infect the ground, making it dangerous for others to walk in the chief's footsteps. It could permeate the containers and utensils chiefs used in eating. Because high chiefs had so much mana, their bodies and possessions were **taboo** (set apart as sacred and off-limits to ordinary people). Because ordinary people couldn't bear as much sacred current as royalty could, when commoners were accidentally exposed, purification rites were necessary.

One function of religion is to explain. As Horton (1993) and Lambek (2008) point out, there are universals in human thought and experience, common conditions and situations that call out for explanation. What happens in sleep and trance, and with death?—The soul leaves the body. Why do some people prosper, while others fail?—Blame it on such nonmaterial factors as luck, mana, sorcery, or being one of "God's chosen."

The beliefs in spiritual beings (e.g., animism) and supernatural forces (e.g., mana) fit within Wallace's definition of religion given at the beginning of this chapter. Most religions include both spirits and impersonal forces. Likewise the supernatural beliefs of contemporary North Americans include beings (gods, saints, souls, demons) and forces (charms, talismans, crystals, and sacred objects).

Magic and Religion

Magic refers to supernatural techniques intended to accomplish specific aims. These techniques include magical actions, offerings, spells, formulas, and incantations used with deities or with impersonal forces. Magicians employ *imitative magic* to produce a desired effect by imitating it. If magicians wish to harm someone, they may imitate that effect on an image of the victim. Sticking pins in "voodoo dolls" is an example. With *contagious magic,* whatever is done to an object is believed to affect a person who once had contact with it. Sometimes practitioners of contagious magic use body products from prospective victims—their nails or hair, for example. The spell performed on the body product is believed eventually to reach the person (see Stein and Stein 2011). Magic exists in societies with diverse religious beliefs, including animism, mana, polytheism, and monotheism.

Uncertainty, Anxiety, Solace

Religion and magic don't just explain things. They serve emotional needs as well as cognitive (e.g., explanatory) ones. Religion helps people face death and endure life crises. Magical techniques can dispel doubts that arise when outcomes are beyond human control. According to Malinowski, when people face uncertainty and danger, they often turn to magic. He observed that the Trobriand Islanders he studied used magic when sailing—a hazardous activity in which people lacked control over wind and weather (Malinowski 1931/1978). Only in situations they could not control did Trobrianders, out of psychological stress, turn from technology to magic.

Despite our improving technical skills, we still can't control every outcome, and magic persists in contemporary societies. Most of us still draw on magic and ritual in situations of uncertainty, such as before a test or perhaps a plane ride.

Rituals

Several features distinguish **rituals** from other kinds of behavior (Rappaport 1974, 1999). Rituals are formal—stylized, repetitive, and stereotyped. People perform them in special (sacred) places and at set times. Rituals include liturgical orders—sequences of words and actions invented prior to the current performance of the ritual in which they occur.

These features link rituals to plays, but there are important differences. Actors merely portray something, but ritual performers—who make up congregations—are in earnest. Rituals convey information about the participants and their traditions. Repeated year after year, generation after generation, rituals translate enduring messages, values, and sentiments into action.

Rituals are social acts. Inevitably, some participants are more committed than others are to the beliefs that lie behind the rites. However, just by taking part in a joint public act, the performers signal that they accept a common social and moral order, one that transcends their status as individuals.

Rites of Passage

Magic and religion, as Malinowski noted, can reduce anxiety and allay fears. Ironically, beliefs and rituals also can create anxiety and a sense of insecurity and danger (Radcliffe-Brown 1962/1965). Anxiety may arise because a rite exists. Indeed, participation in a collective ritual (e.g., circumcision of early teen boys, common among East African pastoralists) can produce stress, whose common reduction, once the ritual is completed, enhances the solidarity of the participants.

Rites of passage can be individual or collective. The traditional vision quests of Native Americans, particularly the Plains Indians, illustrate individual rites of passage (customs associated with the transition from one place or stage of life to another). To move from boyhood to manhood, a youth would temporarily separate from his community. After a period of isolation in the wilderness, often featuring fasting and drug consumption, the young man would see a vision, which would become his guardian spirit. He would return then to his community as an adult.

Contemporary rites of passage include confirmations, baptisms, bar and bat mitzvahs, initiations, weddings, and application for Medicare. Passage rites involve changes in social status, such as from boyhood to manhood and from nonmember to sorority sister. More generally, a rite of passage may mark any change in place, condition, social position, or age.

All rites of passage have three phases: separation, liminality, and incorporation. In the first phase, people withdraw from ordinary society. In the third phase, they reenter society, having completed a rite that changes their status. The second, or liminal, phase is the most interesting. It is the limbo or "time-out" during which people have left one status but haven't yet entered or joined the next (Turner 1967/1974).

Liminality always has certain characteristics. Liminal people exist apart from ordinary distinctions and expectations; they are living in a time out of time. A series of contrasts demarcate liminality from normal social life. For example, among the Ndembu of Zambia, a chief underwent a rite of passage before taking office. During the liminal

TABLE 9.1   **Oppositions between Liminality and Normal Social Life**

Source: Victor Turner, *The Ritual Process.* Copyright © 1969 by Victor W. Turner. Renewed 1997 by Edith Turner. Reprinted by permission of Aldine Transaction, a division of Transaction Publishers.

Liminality	Normal Social Structure
transition	state
homogeneity	heterogeneity
communitas	structure
equality	inequality
anonymity	names
absence of property	property
absence of status	status
nakedness or uniform dress	dress distinctions
sexual continence or excess	sexuality
minimization of sex distinctions	maximization of sex distinctions
absence of rank	rank
humility	pride
disregard of personal appearance	care for personal appearance
unselfishness	selfishness
total obedience	obedience only to superior rank
sacredness	secularity
sacred instruction	technical knowledge
silence	speech
simplicity	complexity
acceptance of pain and suffering	avoidance of pain and suffering

period, his past and future positions in society were ignored, even reversed. He was subjected to a variety of insults, orders, and humiliations.

Passage rites often are collective. Several individuals—boys being circumcised, fraternity or sorority initiates, men at military boot camps, football players in summer training camps, women becoming nuns—pass through the rites together as a group. Table 9.1 summarizes the contrasts, or oppositions, between liminality and normal social life. Most notable is the social aspect of collective liminality called communitas (Turner 1967/1974), an intense community spirit, a feeling of great social solidarity, equality, and togetherness. Liminal people experience the same treatment and conditions and must act alike. Liminality may be marked ritually and symbolically by reversals of ordinary behavior. For example, sexual taboos may be intensified; conversely, sexual excess may be encouraged. Liminal symbols, such as special clothing or body paint, mark the condition as extraordinary—beyond ordinary society and everyday life.

Liminality is basic to all passage rites. Furthermore, in certain societies, including our own, liminal symbols may be used to set off one (religious) group from another and from society as a whole. Such "permanent liminal groups" (e.g., sects, brotherhoods, and cults) are found most characteristically in nation-states. Such liminal features as humility, poverty, equality, obedience, sexual abstinence, and silence (see Table 9.1) may be required for all sect or cult members. Those who join such a group agree to its rules. As if they were undergoing a passage rite—but in this case a never-ending

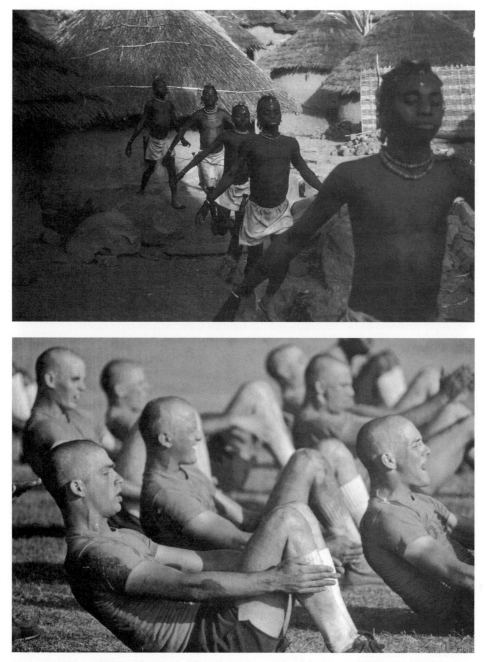

Passage rites are often collective. A group—such as these initiates in Senegal or these Navy trainees in San Diego—passes through the rites as a unit. Such liminal people experience the same treatment and conditions and must act alike. They share communitas, an intense community spirit, a feeling of great social solidarity or togetherness.

one—they may have to abandon their previous possessions and social ties, including those with family members. Is liminality compatible with Facebook?

Members of a sect or cult often wear uniform clothing. Often they adopt a common hairstyle (shaved head, short hair, or long hair). Liminal groups submerge the individual in the collective. This may be one reason Americans, whose core values include individuality and individualism, are so fearful and suspicious of "cults."

Not all collective rites are rites of passage. Most societies observe occasions on which people come together to worship or celebrate and, in doing so, affirm and reinforce their solidarity. Rituals such as the totemic ceremonies described below are *rites of intensification:* They intensify social solidarity. The ritual creates communitas and produces emotions (the collective spiritual effervescence described by Durkheim 1912/2001) that enhance social solidarity.

Totemism

Totemism was a key ingredient in the religions of the Native Australians. **Totems** could be animals, plants, or geographical features. In each tribe, groups of people had particular totems. Members of each totemic group believed themselves to be descendants of their totem. They customarily neither killed nor ate it, but this taboo was lifted once a year, when people assembled for ceremonies dedicated to the totem. These annual rites were believed to be necessary for the totem's survival and reproduction.

Totemism uses nature as a model for society. The totems usually are animals and plants, which are part of nature. People relate to nature through their totemic association with natural species. Because each group has a different totem, social differences mirror natural contrasts. Diversity in the natural order becomes a model for diversity in the social order. However, although totemic plants and animals occupy different niches in nature, on another level they are united because they all are part of nature. The unity of the human social order is enhanced by symbolic association with and imitation of the natural order (Durkheim 1912/2001; Lévi-Strauss 1963; Radcliffe-Brown 1962/1965).

Totemic principles continue to demarcate groups, including clubs, teams, and universities, in modern societies. Badgers and wolverines are animals, and (it is said in Michigan) buckeyes are some kind of nut (more precisely, buckeye nuts come from the buckeye tree). Differences between natural species (e.g., lions, tigers, and bears) distinguish sports teams, and even political parties (donkeys and elephants). Although the modern context is more secular, one can still witness, in intense college football rivalries, some of the effervescence Durkheim noted in Australian totemic religion and other rites of intensification.

Totems are sacred emblems symbolizing common identity. This is true not just among Native Australians but also among Native American groups of the North Pacific Coast of North America, whose totem poles are well known. Their totemic carvings, which commemorated and told visual stories about ancestors, animals, and spirits, were also associated with ceremonies. In totemic rites, people gather together to honor their totem. In so doing, they use ritual to maintain the social oneness that the totem symbolizes.

Social Control

Religion means a lot to people. It helps them cope with uncertainty, adversity, fear, and tragedy. It offers hope that things will get better. Lives can be transformed through spiritual healing. Sinners can repent and be saved—or they can go on sinning and be damned. If the faithful truly internalize a system of religious rewards and punishments, their religion becomes a powerful influence on their attitudes and behavior, as well as what they teach their children.

Many people engage in religious activity because it works for them. Prayers get answered. Faith healers heal. Many Native American people in southwestern Oklahoma use faith healers at high monetary costs, not just because it makes them feel better but also because they think it works (Lassiter 1998). Each year legions of Brazilians visit a church, Nosso Senhor do Bomfim, in the city of Salvador, Bahia. They vow to repay "Our Lord" (Nosso Senhor) if healing happens. Showing that the vows work, and are repaid, are the thousands of *ex votos,* plastic impressions of every conceivable body part, that adorn the church, along with photos of people who have been cured.

Religion can work by getting inside people and mobilizing their emotions—their joy, their wrath, their certainty, their righteousness. People can feel a deep sense of shared joy, meaning, experience, communion, belonging, and commitment to their religion. The power of religion affects action. When religions meet, they can coexist peacefully, or their differences can be a basis for enmity and disharmony, even battle. Religious fervor has inspired Christians on crusades against the infidel and has led Muslims to wage holy wars against non-Islamic peoples. Throughout history, political leaders have used religion to promote and justify their views and policies.

How may leaders mobilize communities and, in so doing, gain support for their own policies? One way is by persuasion; another is by hatred or fear. Consider witchcraft accusations. Witch hunts can be powerful means of social control by creating a climate of danger and insecurity that affects everyone. No one wants to seem deviant, to be accused of being a witch. Witch hunts often take aim at socially marginal people who can be accused and punished with least chance of retaliation. During the great European witch craze of the 15th, 16th, and 17th centuries (Harris 1974), most accusations and convictions were against poor women with little social support.

To ensure proper behavior, religions offer rewards (e.g., the fellowship of the religious community) and punishments (e.g., the threat of being cast out or excommunicated). Religions, especially the formal, organized ones

This 19th-century woodcut depicts the trial of Anne Hutchinson, an outspoken woman who was tried as a heretic and banished from the Massachusetts Bay Colony in 1637.

typically found in state societies, often prescribe a code of ethics and morality to guide behavior. Moral codes are ways of maintaining order and stability that are constantly reinforced in religious sermons, catechisms, and the like. They become internalized psychologically. They guide behavior and produce regret, guilt, shame, and the need for forgiveness, expiation, and absolution when they are not followed.

Kinds of Religion

Although religion is a cultural universal, religions exist in particular societies, and cultural differences show up systematically in religious beliefs and practices. For example, the religions of stratified, state societies differ from those of societies with less marked social contrasts—societies without kings, lords, and subjects. What can a given society afford in terms of religion? Churches, temples, and other full-time religious establishments, with their monumental structures and hierarchies of officials, must be supported in some consistent way, such as by tithes and taxes. What kinds of societies can support such hierarchies and architecture?

All societies have religious figures—those believed capable of mediating between humans and the supernatural. More generally, all societies have medico-magico-religious specialists. Modern societies can support both priesthoods and health care professionals. Lacking the resources for such specialization, foraging societies typically have only part-time specialists, who often have both religious and healing roles. *Shaman,* as defined on p. 186, is the general term encompassing curers ("witch doctors"), mediums, spiritualists, astrologers, palm readers, and other independent diviners. In foraging societies, shamans are usually part-time; that is, they also hunt or gather.

Societies with productive economies (based on agriculture and trade) and large, dense populations (nation-states) can support full-time religious specialists—professional priesthoods. Like the state itself, priesthoods are hierarchically and bureaucratically organized. Anthony Wallace (1966) describes the religions of such stratified societies as "ecclesiastical" (pertaining to an established church and its hierarchy of officials) and "Olympian," after Mount Olympus, home of the classical Greek gods. In such religions, powerful anthropomorphic gods have specialized functions, for example, gods of love, war, the sea, and death. Such *pantheons* (collections of deities) were prominent in the religions of many nonindustrial nation-states, including the Aztecs of Mexico, several African and Asian kingdoms, and classical Greece and Rome. Greco-Roman religions were polytheistic, featuring many deities. In monotheism, all supernatural phenomena are believed to be manifestations of, or under the control of, a single eternal, omniscient, omnipotent, and omnipresent being. In the ecclesiastical monotheistic religion known as Christianity, a single supreme being is manifest in a trinity.

Protestant Values and Capitalism

Notions of salvation and the afterlife dominate Christian ideologies. However, most varieties of Protestantism lack the hierarchical structure of earlier monotheistic religions, including Roman Catholicism. With a diminished role for the priest (minister), salvation is directly available to individuals, who have unmediated access to the supernatural.

In his influential book *The Protestant Ethic and the Spirit of Capitalism* (1904/1958), the social theorist Max Weber linked the spread of capitalism to the values preached by early Protestant leaders. He saw Protestants as more successful financially than Catholics and attributed this difference to the values stressed by their religions. Weber viewed Protestants as more ascetic, entrepreneurial, and future oriented than Catholics. Protestantism placed a premium on hard work, an ascetic life, and profit seeking. Early Protestants saw success on Earth as a sign of divine favor and probable salvation.

Weber also argued that rational business organization required the removal of production from the home. Protestantism made such a separation possible by emphasizing individualism: Individuals, not families or households, would be saved or not. Today, of course, in North America as throughout the world, people of many religions and with diverse worldviews are successful capitalists. Furthermore, traditional Protestant values often have little to do with today's economic maneuvering. Still, there is no denying that the individualistic focus of Protestantism was compatible with the severance of ties to land and kin that industrialism demanded.

World Religions

Information on the world's major religions as of 2010 is provided in Figure 9.1, based on a recent comprehensive study by the Pew Research Center (2012b). Considering data from more than 230 countries, that study estimated that the world contains about 5.8 billion religiously affiliated people—84 percent of its population of 6.9 billion in 2010.

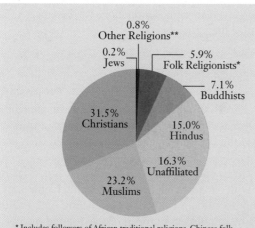

FIGURE 9.1   Major World Religions by Percentage of World Population, 2010

Source: www.adherents.com. Reprinted by permission.

* Includes followers of African traditional religions, Chinese folk religions, Native American religions, and Australian aboriginal religions.
** Includes Bahai's, Jains, Sikhs, Shintoists, Taoists, followers of Tenrikyo, Wiccans, Zoroastrians, and many other faiths.
Percentage may not add to 100 due to rounding.

That study found 2.2 billion Christians (32 percent of the global population), 1.6 billion Muslims (23 percent), 1 billion Hindus (15 percent), nearly 500 million Buddhists (7 percent), and 14 million Jews (0.2 percent). In addition, more than 400 million people (6 percent) practice various folk or traditional religions. These include the traditional or folk religions of Africa and China as well as those of Native Americans and Australians. Some 58 million people, a bit less than 1 percent of the world's population, belong to other religions, including Baha'i, Jainism, Sikhism, Shintoism, Taoism, Tenrikyo, Wicca, and Zoroastrianism.

The same study found that about 1.1 billion people—16 percent of the world's population—lacked any religious affiliation. The unaffiliated therefore constitute the third-largest group worldwide with respect to religious affiliation, behind Christians and Muslims. There are about as many unaffiliated people in the world as there are Roman Catholics. Many of the unaffiliated, however, hold some religious or spiritual beliefs, even if they don't identify with a particular religion (Pew Research Center 2012*b*).

Worldwide, Islam is growing at a rate of about 2.9 percent annually, compared with 2.3 percent for Christianity. Within Christianity, the growth rate varies. There were an estimated 680 million "born-again" Christians (e.g., Evangelicals/Pentecostals) in the world in 2001, with an estimated annual worldwide growth rate of 7 percent, versus just 2.3 percent for Christianity overall. (This would translate into 1.6 billion Evangelicals/Pentecostals by 2014.) The global growth rate of Roman Catholics has been estimated at only 1.3 percent, compared with an overall Protestant growth rate of 3.3 percent per year (Winter 2001).

Religion and Change

Like political organization, religion helps maintain social order. And like political mobilization, religious energy can be harnessed not just for change but also for revolution. Reacting to conquest or to actual or perceived foreign domination, for instance, religious leaders may seek to alter or revitalize their society.

Cargo Cults

Revitalization movements are social movements that occur in times of change, in which religious leaders emerge and undertake to alter or revitalize a society. Christianity originated as a revitalization movement. Jesus was one of several prophets who preached new religious doctrines while the Middle East was under Roman rule. It was a time of social unrest, when a foreign power ruled the land. Jesus inspired a new, enduring, and major religion. His contemporaries were not so successful.

Revitalization movements known as **cargo cults** have arisen in colonial situations in which local people have regular contact with outsiders but lack their wealth, technology, and living standards. Cargo cults attempt to explain European domination and wealth and to achieve similar success magically by mimicking European behavior and manipulating symbols of the desired lifestyle. The cargo cults of Melanesia and Papua New Guinea are hybrid creations that weave Christian doctrine with aboriginal beliefs. They take their name from their focus on cargo—European goods of the sort natives have seen unloaded from the cargo holds of ships and airplanes.

In one early cult, members believed that the spirits of the dead would arrive in a ship. These ghosts would bring manufactured goods for the natives and would kill all the Whites. More recent cults replaced ships with airplanes (Worsley 1959/1985). Many cults have used elements of European culture as sacred objects. The rationale is that Europeans use these objects, have wealth, and therefore must know the "secret of cargo." By mimicking how Europeans use or treat objects, natives hope also to come upon the secret knowledge needed to gain cargo.

For example, having seen Europeans' reverent treatment of flags and flagpoles, the members of one cult began to worship flagpoles. They believed the flagpoles were sacred towers that could transmit messages between the living and the dead. Other natives built airstrips to entice planes bearing canned goods, portable radios, clothing, wristwatches, and motorcycles. Some cargo cult prophets proclaimed that success would come through a reversal of European domination and native subjugation. The day was near, they preached, when natives, aided by God, Jesus, or native ancestors, would turn the tables. Native skins would turn white, and those of Europeans would turn brown; Europeans would die or be killed.

Cargo cults blend aboriginal and Christian beliefs. Melanesian myths told of ancestors shedding their skins and changing into powerful beings and of dead people returning to life. Christian missionaries also preached resurrection. The cults' preoccupation with cargo is related to traditional Melanesian big-man systems. In the chapter "Political Systems," we saw that a Melanesian big man had to be generous. People worked for the big man, helping him amass wealth, but eventually he had to give a feast and give away all that wealth.

A cargo cult in Vanuatu, a country in Melanesia. In this photo, followers of John Frumm, a cargo cult leader, stage a military band parade, trying to mimic American and British soldiers. Does anything in your own society remind you of a cargo cult?

Because of their experience with big-man systems, Melanesians believed that all wealthy people eventually had to give their wealth away. For decades they had attended Christian missions and worked on plantations. All the while they expected Europeans to return the fruits of their labor as their own big men did. When the Europeans refused to distribute the wealth or even to let natives know the secret of its production and distribution, cargo cults developed.

Like arrogant big men, Europeans would be leveled, by death if necessary. However, natives lacked the physical means of doing what their traditions said they should do. Thwarted by well-armed colonial forces, natives resorted to magical leveling. They called on supernatural beings to intercede, to kill or otherwise deflate the European big men and redistribute their wealth.

Cargo cults are religious responses to the expansion of the world capitalist economy. However, this religious mobilization had political and economic results. Cult participation gave Melanesians a basis for common interests and activities and thus helped pave the way for political parties and economic interest organizations. Previously separated by geography, language, and customs, Melanesians started forming larger groups as members of the same cults and followers of the same prophets. The cargo cults paved the way for political action through which the indigenous peoples eventually regained their autonomy.

New and Alternative Religious Movements

The New Age movement, which emerged in the 1980s, draws on and blends cultural elements from multiple traditions. It advocates change through individual personal transformation. In the United States and Australia, respectively, some people who are not Native Americans or Native Australians have appropriated the symbols, settings, and purported religious practices of Native Americans and Native Australians for New Age religions. Native American activists decry the appropriation and commercialization of their spiritual beliefs and rituals, as when "sweat lodge" ceremonies are held on cruise ships, with wine and cheese served. They see the appropriation of their ceremonies and traditions as theft.

New religious movements have varied origins. Some have been influenced by Christianity, others by Eastern (Asian) religions, still others by mysticism and spiritualism. Religion also evolves in tandem with science and technology. For example, the Raelian movement, a religious group centered in Switzerland and Montreal, promotes cloning as a way of achieving eternal life (Palmer 2001).

Many contemporary nations contain unofficial religions. One example is "Yoruba religion," a term applied to perhaps 15 million adherents in Africa as well as to millions of practitioners of *syncretic,* or blended, religions (with elements of Catholicism and spiritism) in the Western Hemisphere. Forms of Yoruba religion include *santeria* (in the Spanish Caribbean and the United States), *candomblé* (in Brazil), and *vodoun* (in the French Caribbean). Yoruba religion, with roots in precolonial nation-states of West Africa, has spread far beyond its religion of origin, as part of the African diaspora. It remains an influential, identifiable religion today, despite suppression, such as by Cuba's communist government. There are perhaps 3 million practitioners of santeria in Cuba, plus another 800,000 in the United States. At least 1 million Brazilians participate in candomblé, also known as macumba. Voodoo (*vodoun*) has between 2.8 and 3.2 million practitioners (Ontario Consultants 2011), many (perhaps most) of whom would name something else, such as Catholicism, as their religion.

Religion and Cultural Globalization

Evangelical Protestantism and Pentecostalism

The rapid spread of Evangelical Protestantism, which originated in Europe and North America, constitutes a highly successful form of contemporary cultural globalization. A century ago, more than 90 percent of the then approximately 80 million Evangelicals in the world lived in Europe and North America (Pew Research Center 2011). Today, estimates of the number of Evangelicals worldwide range from 400 million to over 1 billion, with most living outside Europe and North America—in sub-Saharan Africa, the Middle East and North Africa, Latin America, and Asia.

The growth of Evangelical Protestantism has been particularly explosive in Brazil—traditionally (and still) the world's most Catholic country. In 1980, when Pope John Paul II visited the country, 89 percent of Brazil's population claimed to be Roman Catholic. Since then, Evangelical Protestantism has spread like wildfire. Having made small inroads during the first half of the 20th century, Evangelical Protestantism grew exponentially in Brazil during the second half. Protestants accounted for fewer than 5 percent of the population through the 1960s. By 2000 Evangelical Protestants comprised more than 15 percent of Brazilians affiliated with a church. The current estimate of the Evangelical share of Brazil's population is between 20 and 25 percent and growing. Evangelical Protestantism's penetration of Brazil has been mainly at the expense of Catholicism. Among the factors that have worked against Catholicism are these: a declining priesthood overly dependent on foreigners, sharply contrasting political agendas of many of its clerics, and its reputation as mainly a women's religion.

Evangelical Protestantism stresses conservative morality, the authority of the Bible, and a personal ("born-again") conversion experience. Most Brazilian evangelicals are Pentecostals, who additionally embrace glossolalia (speaking in tongues) and beliefs in

Throughout Latin America, the Catholic Church has found it difficult to compete with an exploding Evangelical/ Pentecostal movement. Shown here, Evangelical Christians hold their hands out in prayer during the annual "March for Jesus" in downtown Rio de Janeiro, Brazil, on May 19, 2012.

faith healing, spirits, exorcism, and miracles. São Paulo, Brazil's largest city, has been called the Pentecostal world capital, with over 4 million adherents.

Like members of a liminal sect, converts to Pentecostalism are expected to separate themselves both from their pasts and from the secular social world that surrounds them. In Arembepe, Brazil, for example, the *crentes* ("true believers," as members of the local Pentecostal community are called) set themselves apart by their beliefs, behavior, and lifestyle (Kottak 2006). They worship, chant, and pray. They dress simply and forgo such worldly temptations (seen as vices) as tobacco, alcohol, gambling, and extramarital sexuality, along with dancing, movies, and other forms of popular culture. Wherever Pentecostalism exists, the converted observe an ascetic moral code and view the surrounding social world as a realm governed by Satan (Robbins 2004).

Pentecostalism strengthens family and household through a moral code that enjoins respect for marriage and prohibits adultery, gambling, drinking, and fighting. These activities were valued mainly by men in preconversion culture. Pentecostalism has appeal for men, however, because it does not publicly question their authority and even solidifies it within the household. Although Pentecostal ideology is strongly patriarchal, with women expected to subordinate themselves to men, women tend to be more active church members than men are. Pentecostalism promotes services and prayer groups by and for women. In such settings women develop leadership skills, as they also extend their social-support network beyond family and kin.

In its focus on ecstatic and exuberant worship, Pentecostalism has been heavily influenced by—and shares features with—African American Protestantism. In Brazil it shares features with candomblé, which also features chanting and spirit possession. Pentecostalism's habitual ritual engagement with spirits distinguishes it from other forms of Christianity (Casanova 2001; Meyer 1999).

Peter Berger (2010) suggests that modern Pentecostalism may be the fastest growing religion in human history and focuses on its social dimensions to explain why. According to Berger, Pentecostalism promotes strong communities while offering practical and psychological support to people whose circumstances are changing. My own experience in Brazil supports Berger's hypothesis; most new Pentecostals I encountered came from underprivileged, poor, and otherwise marginalized groups in areas undergoing rapid social change.

The British sociologist David Martin (1990) argues that Pentecostalism is spreading so rapidly because its adherents embody Max Weber's Protestant ethic—valuing self-discipline, hard work, and thrift. Others see Pentecostalism as a kind of cargo cult, built on the belief that magic and ritual activity can promote material success (Freston 2008; Meyer 1999). Berger (2010) suggests that today's Pentecostals probably include both types—Weberian Protestants working to produce material wealth as a sign of their salvation along with people who believe that magic and ritual will bring them good fortune.

Homogenization, Indigenization, or Hybridization?

Any cultural form that spreads from one society to another—be it a McDonald's or a form of religion—has to fit into the country and culture it enters. We can use the rapid spread of Pentecostalism as a case study of the process of adaptation of foreign cultural forms to local settings.

Joel Robbins (2004) has examined the extent to which what he calls Pentecostal/ charismatic Christianity preserves its basic form and core beliefs as it spreads and adapts to various national and local cultures. Pentecostalism is a Western invention: Its beliefs, doctrines, organizational features, and rituals originated in the United States, following the European rise and spread of Protestantism. The core doctrines of acceptance of Jesus as one's savior, baptism with the Holy Spirit, faith healing, and belief in the second coming of Jesus have spread across nations and cultures without losing their basic shape.

Scholars have argued about whether the global spread of Pentecostalism is best understood as (1) a process of Western cultural domination and homogenization (perhaps supported by a right-wing political agenda) or (2) one in which diffused cultural forms respond to local needs and are differentiated and indigenized. Joel Robbins (2004) takes a middle ground position, viewing the spread of Pentecostalism as a form of cultural hybridization. Robbins (2004) argues that global and local features appear with equal intensity within these Pentecostal cultures. Churches retain certain core Pentecostal beliefs and behaviors while responding to the local culture and being organized at the local level.

Reviewing the literature, Robbins (2004) finds little evidence that a Western political agenda is propelling the global spread of Pentecostalism. It is true that foreigners (including American pastors and televangelists) have helped introduce Pentecostalism to countries outside North America. There is little evidence, however, that overseas churches are largely funded and ideologically shaped from North America. Pentecostal churches typically are staffed from top to bottom with locals, who run them as organizations that are attentive and responsive to local situations. Conversion is typically a key feature of that agenda. Once converted, a Pentecostal is expected to be an active Evangelist, seeking to bring in new members. This Evangelization is one of the most important activities in Pentecostal culture and certainly aids its expansion.

Pentecostalism spreads as other forces of globalization displace people and disrupt local lives (Martin 1990). To people who feel socially adrift, Pentecostal evangelists offer tightly knit communities and a weblike structure of personal connections within and between Pentecostal communities. Such networks can facilitate access to health care, job placement, educational services, and other resources.

Unlike Catholicism, which is hierarchical, Pentecostalism is egalitarian. Adherents need no special education—only spiritual inspiration—to preach or to run a church. Based on his research in Brazil, John Burdick (1993) notes that many Afro-Brazilians are drawn to the Pentecostal community because others who are socially and racially like them are in the congregation, some serving as preachers. Opportunities for participation and leadership are abundant, for example, as lay preachers, deacons, and leaders of various men's, women's, and youth groups. The churches fund outreach to the needy and other locally relevant social services.

Antimodernism and Fundamentalism

Antimodernism is the rejection of the modern (including secular forces of globalization) in favor of what is perceived as an earlier, purer, and better way of life. This viewpoint arose out of disillusionment with the Industrial Revolution and with subsequent

developments in science, technology, and consumption patterns. Antimodernists typically consider the use of modern technology to be misguided or think technology should
have a lower priority than religious and cultural values.

Religious *fundamentalism* describes antimodernist movements in various religions,
including Christianity, Islam, and Judaism. Ironically, religious fundamentalism itself is
a modern phenomenon, based on its adherents' strong feelings of alienation from the
perceived secularism of the surrounding (modern) culture. Fundamentalists separate
from a larger religious group, whose founding principles, they believe, have been corrupted or abandoned. Fundamentalists advocate return and strict fidelity to the "true"
(fundamental) religious principles of the larger religion.

Fundamentalists also seek to rescue religion from absorption into modern, Western
culture, which they see as having corrupted mainstream religions. In Christianity, fundamentalists are "born-again Christians" as opposed to "mainline Protestants." In Islam
they are jama'at (in Arabic, enclaves based on close fellowship) engaged in jihad (struggle) against a Western culture hostile to Islam and the God-given (shariah) way of life.
In Judaism they are Haredi, "Torah-true" Jews. All such groups see a sharp divide between themselves and other religions, as well as between a "sacred" view of life and the
"secular" world (see Antoun 2008).

Both Pentecostalism and Christian fundamentalism preach ascetic morality, the duty
to convert others, and respect for the Bible. Fundamentalists, however, tend to cite their
success in living a moral life as proof of their salvation, whereas Pentecostals find assur-
ance of their salvation in exuberant, ecstatic experience. Fundamentalists also seek to
remake the political sphere along religious lines, whereas Pentecostals tend to have less
interest in politics (Robbins 2004).

The Spread of Islam

Islam—whose 1.6 billion followers constitute over a fifth of the world's population—is
another rapidly spreading global religion that can be used to illustrate cultural globalization. The globalization of Islam also illustrates cultural hybridization. Islam has adapted
successfully to the many nations and cultures it has entered, adopting architectural
styles, linguistic practices, and even religious beliefs from host cultures.

For example, while Mosques (Islamic houses of worship) all share certain characteristics (e.g., they face Mecca and have some common architectural features), they
also incorporate architectural and decorative elements from their national setting.
Although Arabic is Islam's liturgical language, used for prayer, most Muslims' discussion of their faith occurs in their local language. In China, Islamic concepts have
been influenced by Confucianism. In India and Bangladesh, the Islamic idea of the
prophet has blended with the Hindu notion of the avatar, a deity who takes mortal
form and descends to Earth to fight evil and guide the righteous. Islam entered
Indonesia by means of Muslim merchants who devised devotional exercises that fit
in with preexisting religions—Hinduism and Buddhism in Java and Sumatra and
animism in the eastern islands, which eventually became Christian. In Bali, Hinduism
survived as the dominant religion.

Both Pentecostalism and Islam, we have learned, hybridize and become locally relevant as they spread globally. Although certain core features endure, local people always

Indonesian Muslims pray at the historic Sunda Kelapa port in Jakarta on August 19, 2012. Muslims around the world were celebrating the end of Ramadan, the Muslim calendar's ninth and holiest month.

assign their own meanings to the messages and social forms they receive from outside, including religion. Such meanings reflect their cultural backgrounds, experiences, and prior belief systems. We must consider the processes of hybridization and indigenization in examining and understanding any form of cultural diffusion or globalization.

Secular Rituals

In concluding this chapter on religion, we may recognize some problems with the definitions of religion given at the beginning of this chapter. The first problem: If we define religion with reference to the sacred and/or supernatural beings, powers, and forces, how do we classify ritual-like behaviors that occur in secular contexts? Some anthropologists believe there are both sacred and secular rituals. Secular rituals include formal, invariant, stereotyped, earnest, repetitive behavior and rites of passage that take place in nonreligious settings.

A second problem: If the distinction between the supernatural and the natural is not consistently made in a society, how can we tell what is religion and what isn't? The Betsileo of Madagascar, for example, view witches and dead ancestors as real people who play roles in ordinary life. However, their occult powers are not empirically demonstrable.

Anthropology Today   *Baseball Magic*

Have you ever noticed how much baseball players spit? Outside baseball—even among other male sports figures—spitting is considered impolite. Football players, with their customary headgear, don't spit, nor do basketball players, who might slip on the court. No spitting by tennis players, gymnasts, or swimmers—not even Mark Spitz (a swimmer turned dentist). But watch any baseball game for a few minutes and you'll see spitting galore. Since pitchers appear to be the spitting champions, the custom likely originated on the mound. It continues today as a carryover from the days when pitchers routinely chewed tobacco, believing that nicotine enhanced their concentration and effectiveness. The spitting custom

spread to other players, who unabashedly spew saliva from the outfield to the dugout steps.

For the student of custom, ritual, and magic, baseball is an especially interesting game, to which lessons from anthropology are easily applied. The pioneering anthropologist Bronislaw Malinowski, writing about Pacific Islanders rather than baseball players, noted they had developed all sorts of magic to use in sailing, a hazardous activity. He proposed that when people face conditions they can't control (e.g., wind and weather), they turn to magic.

Magic, in the form of rituals, taboos, and sacred objects, is particularly evident in baseball. Like sailing magic, baseball magic reduces psychological stress,

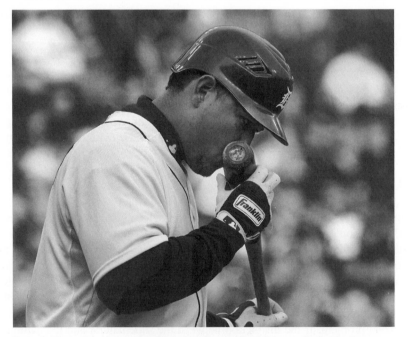

Detroit Tiger third baseman Miguel Cabrera kisses his maple bat before hitting his 42nd home run of 2012 at Comerica Park. Sometimes baseball magic works: Cabrera went on that year to achieve baseball's Triple Crown and win the American League's MVP award.

creating an illusion of control when real control is lacking.

In several publications about baseball, the anthropologist George Gmelch makes use of Malinowski's observation that magic is most common in situations dominated by chance and uncertainty. All sorts of magical behaviors surround pitching and batting, which are full of uncertainty. There are fewer rituals for fielding, over which players have more control. (Batting averages of .350 or higher are very rare after a full season, but a fielding percentage below .900 is a disgrace.)

Especially obvious are the rituals (like the spitting) of pitchers, who may tug their cap between pitches, spit in a particular direction, magically manipulate the resin bag, talk to the ball, or wash their hands after giving up a run. Batters have their rituals, too. It isn't uncommon to see outfielder Carlos Gomez kiss his bat, which he likes to talk to, smell, threaten—and reward when he gets a hit. Another batter routinely would spit, then ritually touch his gob with his bat, to enhance his success at the plate.

Humans use tools to accomplish a lot, but technology still doesn't let us "have it all." To keep hope alive in situations of uncertainty, and for outcomes we can't control, all societies draw on magic and religion as sources of nonmaterial comfort, explanation, and control. What are your rituals?

A third problem: The behavior considered appropriate for religious occasions varies tremendously from culture to culture. One society may consider drunken frenzy the surest sign of faith, whereas another may inculcate quiet reverence. Who is to say which is "more religious"?

It is possible for apparently secular settings, things, and events to acquire intense meaning for individuals who have grown up in their presence. For example, identities and loyalties based on fandom, football, baseball, and soccer can be powerful indeed. Rock stars and bands can mobilize many. Italians and Brazilians are rarely, if ever, as nationally focused and emotionally unified as they are when their teams are competing in the World Cup. The collective effervescence that Durkheim found so characteristic of religion can equally well describe what Brazilians experience when their country wins a World Cup.

In the context of comparative religion, the idea that the secular can become sacred isn't surprising. Long ago, Durkheim (1912/2001) pointed out that almost everything, from the sublime to the ridiculous, has in some societies been treated as sacred. The distinction between sacred and profane doesn't depend on the intrinsic qualities of the sacred symbol. In Australian totemic religion, for example, sacred beings include such humble creatures as ducks, frogs, rabbits, and grubs, whose inherent qualities could hardly have given rise to the religious sentiment they inspire.

Madagascar's tomb-centered ceremonies are times when the living and the dead are joyously reunited, when people get drunk, gorge themselves, and have sexual license. Perhaps the gray, sober, ascetic, and moralistic aspects of many official religious events, in taking the fun out of religion, force us to find religion (i.e., truth, beauty, meaning, passionate involvement) in fun.

Summary

1. Given the varied and worldwide scope of beliefs and behavior labeled "religious," anthropologists recognize the difficulty of defining religion. Religion, a cultural universal, describes beliefs and behavior concerned with supernatural beings, powers, and forces. Religion also encompasses the feelings, meanings, and congregations associated with such beliefs and behavior. Religious worlds are real, vivid, and significant to those who construct and inhabit them. Anthropological studies have revealed many forms, expressions, and functions of religion.

2. Tylor considered animism—the belief in spirits or souls—to be religion's earliest and most basic form. He focused on religion's explanatory role, arguing that religion would eventually disappear as science provided better explanations. Besides animism, another view of the supernatural also occurs in nonindustrial societies, seeing the supernatural as a domain of raw, impersonal power or force (called mana in Polynesia and Melanesia). People can manipulate and control mana under certain conditions.

3. When ordinary technical and rational means of doing things fail, people may turn to magic. Often they use magic when they lack control over outcomes. Religion offers comfort and psychological security at times of crisis. On the other hand, rites can also create anxiety. Rituals are formal, invariant, stylized, earnest acts in which people subordinate their beliefs to a social collectivity. Rites of passage have three stages: separation, liminality, and incorporation. Such rites can mark any change in social status, age, place, or social condition. Collective rites are often cemented by communitas, a feeling of intense solidarity.

4. Religion establishes and maintains social control through a series of moral and ethical beliefs and real and imagined rewards and punishments, internalized in individuals. Religion also achieves social control by mobilizing its members for collective action.

5. Religions exist in particular societies, and cultural differences show up systematically in religious beliefs and practices. The ecclesiastical and monotheistic religions of stratified, state societies, for example, differ from those of societies that lack hierarchies and specialized officials. The world's major religions vary in their growth rates, with Islam expanding more rapidly than Christianity.

6. Religion helps maintain social order, but it also can promote change. Cargo cults are revitalization movements that hybridize beliefs and that have helped people adapt to changing conditions. Among contemporary, "new" religious movements, some have been influenced by Christianity, others by Eastern (Asian) religions, still others by mysticism and spiritualism, or by science and technology.

7. The spread of Evangelical/Pentecostal Protestantism worldwide illustrates contemporary cultural globalization. Evangelical Protestantism stresses conservative morality, the authority of the Bible, and a personal ("born-again") conversion experience. To people who feel socially adrift, Pentecostalism offers tightly knit communities and a weblike structure of personal connections. Antimodernism is the rejection of the

modern, including globalization, in favor of what is perceived as an earlier, purer, and better way of life. Religious fundamentalism describes antimodernist movements in Christianity, Islam, and Judaism. The rapid spread of Islam also illustrates cultural globalization and hybridization. Although certain core features endure, local people always assign their own meanings to the messages and social forms they receive from outside, including religion. The processes of hybridization and indigenization are always associated with cultural diffusion and globalization.

8. There are secular as well as religious rituals. It is possible for apparently secular settings, things, and events to acquire intense meaning for individuals who have grown up in their presence.

Key Terms

animism, *187*
cargo cults, *196*
communitas, *185*
liminality, *189*
magic, *188*
mana, *187*

monotheism, *187*
polytheism, *187*
religion, *184*
revitalization
   movements, *196*
rites of passage, *189*

rituals, *189*
shaman, *186*
taboo, *188*
totem, *192*

Chapter 10

Ethnicity and Race

Ethnicity is based on cultural similarities (with members of the same ethnic group) and differences (between that group and others) in a society or nation. Ethnic groups must deal with other such groups in the nation or region they inhabit. Interethnic relations are important in the study of any nation or region, especially because of contemporary and recent international migration. (Table 10.1 lists American ethnic groups, based on U.S. Census Bureau estimates for 2011.)

Ethnic Groups and Ethnicity

As with any cultural identity, members of an **ethnic group** *share* certain beliefs, values, habits, customs, and norms because of their common background. They define themselves as different and special because of cultural features. This distinction may arise from language, religion, historical experience, geographic placement, kinship, or "race" (see Spickard, ed. 2004, 2012). Markers of an ethnic group may include a collective

TABLE 10.1   **Racial/Ethnic Identification in the United States, 2011 (U.S. Census Bureau estimates for 2011)**

Source: http://quickfacts.census.gov/qfd/states/00000.html.

Claimed Identity	Number (millions)	Percentage
White (non-Hispanic)	197.5	63.4
Hispanic	52.0	16.7
Black	40.8	13.1
Asian	15.6	5.0
American Indian	3.8	1.2
Pacific Islander	0.7	0.2
Two or more races	7.3	2.3
Total population	311.6	100.0

name, belief in common descent, a sense of solidarity, and an association with a specific territory, which the group may or may not hold (Ryan 1990, pp. xiii, xiv).

According to Fredrik Barth (1969), ethnicity can be said to exist when people claim a certain ethnic identity for themselves and are defined by others as having that identity. **Ethnicity** means identification with, and feeling part of, an ethnic group and exclusion from certain other groups because of this affiliation. Ethnic feelings and associated behavior vary in intensity within ethnic groups and countries and over time. A change in the degree of importance attached to an ethnic identity may reflect political changes (Soviet rule ends—ethnic feeling rises) or individual life-cycle changes (young people relinquish, or old people reclaim, an ethnic background).

Shifting Status

Ethnicity is only one basis for group identity. Cultural differences may also be associated with class, region, or religion. Individuals often have more than one group identity. People may be loyal (depending on circumstances) to their neighborhood, school, town, state or province, region, nation, continent, religion, ethnic group, or interest group (Ryan 1990, p. xxii). In a complex society such as the United States or Canada, people constantly negotiate their social identities. All of us "wear different hats," presenting ourselves sometimes as one thing, sometimes as another.

Sometimes our identities (social statuses) are mutually exclusive. It's hard to be both Black and White or male and female. Sometimes, assuming an identity or joining a group requires a conversion experience, acquiring a new and overwhelming primary identity, such as becoming a "born-again" Christian.

Some statuses aren't mutually exclusive, but contextual. People can be both Black and Hispanic or both a mother and a senator. One identity is used in certain settings, another in different ones. We call this the *situational negotiation of social identity* (Leman 2001).

It is not uncommon for members of an ethnic group to shift their ethnic identities. Hispanics, for example, may use different ethnic labels (e.g., "Cuban" or "Latino") to describe themselves depending on context. In a recent study, half (51 percent) of American Hispanics surveyed preferred to identify using their family's country of origin (as in

FIGURE 10.1   American Hispanics/Latinos, 2012

Source: P. Taylor, M. H. Lopez, J. H. Martínez, and G. Velasco, "When Labels Don't Fit: Hispanics and Their Views of Identity," Pew Research Hispanic Center, April 4, 2012. http://www.pewhispanic.org/2012/04/04/when-labels-dont-fit-hispanics-and-their-views-of-identity/.

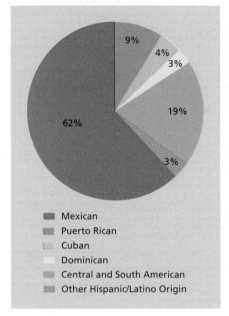

- ■ Mexican
- ■ Puerto Rican
- ■ Cuban
- ■ Dominican
- ■ Central and South American
- ■ Other Hispanic/Latino Origin

"Mexican," "Cuban," or "Dominican") rather than "Hispanic" or "Latino." Just one-quarter (24 percent) chose one of those two pan-ethnic terms, while 21 percent said they use the term "American" most often (Taylor, Lopez et al. 2012).

"Hispanics" are the fastest-growing ethnic group in the United States, increasing by 47 percent between 2000 and 2011—from 35.3 million to 52 million. "Hispanic" is a category based mainly on language. It includes Whites, Blacks, and "racially" mixed Spanish speakers and their ethnically conscious descendants. (There also are Native American and even Asian Hispanics.) The label "Hispanic" lumps together people of diverse geographic origin—Puerto Rico, Mexico, Cuba, El Salvador, Guatemala, the Dominican Republic, and other Spanish-speaking countries of Central and South America and the Caribbean. "Latino" is a broader category, which also can include Brazilians (who speak Portuguese). The national origins of American Hispanics/Latinos (excluding Brazilians) are shown in Figure 10.1.

Mexican Americans (Chicanos), Cuban Americans, and Puerto Ricans may mobilize to promote general Hispanic issues (e.g., opposition to "English-only" laws) but act as three separate interest groups in other contexts. Cuban Americans are richer on average than Chicanos and Puerto Ricans are, and their class interests and voting patterns differ. Cubans often vote Republican, but Puerto Ricans and Chicanos are more likely to favor Democrats. Some Mexican Americans whose families have lived in the United States for generations have little in common with new Hispanic immigrants, such as those from Central America. Many Americans (especially those fluent in English) claim Hispanic ethnicity in some contexts but shift to a general "American" identity in others.

Minority Groups and Stratification

In many societies a racial, ethnic, or caste status is associated with a position in the social–political hierarchy. Certain groups, called **minority groups,** are subordinate. They have inferior power and less secure access to resources than do **majority groups** (which are superordinate, dominant, or controlling). Often ethnic groups are minorities.

Minority groups are obvious features of stratification in the United States. The 2009 poverty rate was 9.4 percent for non-Hispanic Whites, 25.8 percent for Blacks, and 25.3 percent for Hispanics (U.S. Census Bureau 2010). Inequality shows up consistently in unemployment figures and in median household income. The median

"Hispanic" and "Latino" are ethnic categories that cross-cut "racial" contrasts such as between "Black" and "White." Note the physical diversity among these children in Trinidad, Cuba.

wealth of White households is 20 times that of Black households and 18 times that of Hispanic households (Kochhar, Fry, and Taylor 2011).

Human Biological Diversity and the Race Concept

Historically, scientists have approached the study of human biological diversity in two main ways: (1) racial classification (now largely abandoned) versus (2) the current explanatory approach, which focuses on understanding specific differences. First we'll consider problems with **racial classification** (the attempt to assign humans to discrete categories [purportedly] based on common ancestry). Then we'll offer some explanations for specific aspects of human biological diversity. *Biological differences are real, important, and apparent to us all.* Modern scientists find it most productive to seek explanations for this diversity, rather than trying to pigeonhole people into categories called races. Certainly, human groups do vary biologically—for example, in their genetic attributes. But often we observe gradual, rather than abrupt, shifts in gene frequencies between neighboring groups. Such gradual genetic shifts are called **clines,** and they are incompatible with discrete and separate races (see Mukhopadhyay et al. 2007).

What is race, anyway? In theory, a biological race would be a geographically isolated subdivision of a species. Such a *subspecies* would be capable of interbreeding with other subspecies of the same species, but it would not actually do so because of its geographic isolation. Some biologists also use "race" to refer to "breeds," as of dogs or roses. Thus, a pit bull and a chihuahua would be different races of dogs.

Such domesticated "races" have been bred by humans for generations. Humanity (*Homo sapiens*) lacks such races because human populations have not been isolated enough from one another to develop into such discrete groups. Nor have humans experienced controlled breeding like that which has created the various kinds of dogs and roses.

A race is supposed to reflect shared genetic material (inherited from a common ancestor), but early scholars instead used phenotypical traits (usually skin color) for racial classification. **Phenotype** refers to an organism's evident traits, its "manifest biology"—anatomy and physiology. Humans display hundreds of evident (detectable) physical traits. They range from skin color, hair form, eye color, and facial features (which are visible) to blood groups, color blindness, and enzyme production (which become evident through testing) (see Anemone 2011).

Racial classifications based on phenotype raise the problem of deciding which trait(s) should be primary. Should races be defined by height, weight, body shape, facial features, teeth, skull form, or skin color? Like their fellow citizens, early European and American scientists gave priority to skin color. Many schoolbooks and encyclopedias still proclaim the existence of three great races: the white, the black, and the yellow. This overly simplistic classification was compatible with the political use of race during the colonial period of the late 19th and early 20th centuries. Such a tripartite scheme kept White Europeans neatly separate from their African, Asian, and Native American subjects. Colonial empires began to break up, and scientists began to question established racial categories, after World War II (see Molnar 2006).

Races Are Not Biologically Distinct

History and politics aside, one obvious problem with "color-based" racial labels is that the terms don't accurately describe skin color. "White" people are more pink, beige, or tan than white. "Black" people are various shades of brown, and "yellow" people are tan or beige. But these terms have also been dignified by more scientific-*sounding* synonyms: Caucasoid, Negroid, and Mongoloid.

Another problem with the tripartite scheme is that many populations don't fit neatly into any one of the three "great races." For example, where would one put the Polynesians? *Polynesia* is a triangle of South Pacific islands formed by Hawaii to the north, Easter Island to the east, and New Zealand to the southwest. Does the "bronze" skin color of Polynesians connect them to the Caucasoids or to the Mongoloids? Some scientists, recognizing this problem, enlarged the original tripartite scheme to include the Polynesian "race." Native Americans presented a similar problem. Were they red or yellow? Some scientists added a fifth race—the "red," or Amerindian—to the major racial groups.

Many people in southern India have dark skin, but scientists have been reluctant to classify them with "black" Africans because of their Caucasoid facial features and hair form. Some, therefore, have created a separate race for these people. What about the Australian aborigines, hunters and gatherers native to what has been, throughout human history, the most isolated continent? By skin color, one might place some Native Australians in the same race as tropical Africans. However, similarities to Europeans in hair color (light or reddish) and facial features have led some scientists to classify them as Caucasoids. But there is no evidence that Australians are closer genetically or historically to either of these groups than they are to Asians. Recognizing this problem, scientists often regard Native Australians as a separate race.

The photos in this chapter illustrate only a small part of the range of human biological diversity. Shown above is a woman from Guangzhou province, People's Republic of China.

A young man from the Marquesas Islands in Polynesia.

A Native American: a Chiquitanos Indian woman from Bolivia.

A Native Australian man from Cloncurry, Queensland, Australia.

Finally, consider the San ("Bushmen") of the Kalahari Desert in southern Africa. Scientists have perceived their skin color as varying from brown to yellow. Some who regard San skin as "yellow" have placed them in the same category as Asians. In theory, people of the same race share more recent common ancestry with each other than they do with any others. But there is no evidence for recent common ancestry between San and Asians. Somewhat more reasonably, some scholars assign the San to the Capoid race (from the Cape of Good Hope), which is seen as being different from other groups inhabiting tropical Africa.

Similar problems arise when any single trait is used as a basis for racial classification. An attempt to use facial features, height, weight, or any other phenotypical trait is fraught with difficulties. For example, consider the *Nilotes,* natives of the upper Nile region of Uganda and Sudan. Nilotes tend to be tall and to have long, narrow noses. Certain Scandinavians are also tall, with similar noses. Given the distance between their homelands, to classify them as members of the same race makes little sense. There is no reason to assume that Nilotes and Scandinavians are more closely related to each other than either is to shorter and nearer populations with different kinds of noses.

Would it be better to base racial classifications on a combination of physical traits? This would avoid some of the problems mentioned earlier, but others would arise. First, skin color, stature, skull form, and facial features (nose form, eye shape, lip thickness) don't go together as a unit. For example, people with dark skin may be tall or short and have hair ranging from straight to very curly. Dark-haired populations may have light or dark skin, along with various skull forms, facial features, and body sizes and shapes. The number of combinations is very large, and the amount that heredity (versus environment) contributes to such phenotypical traits often is unclear.

Among contemporary humans, phenotypical similarities and differences aren't precisely or even necessarily correlated with genetic relationships (see this chapter's "Anthropology Today"). Because of changes in the environment that affect individuals during growth and development, the range of phenotypes characteristic of a population may change without any genetic change whatsoever. There are several examples. In the early 20th century, the anthropologist Franz Boas (1940/1966) described changes in skull form (e.g., toward rounder heads) among the children of Europeans who had migrated to North America. The reason for this was not a change in genes, for the European immigrants tended to marry among themselves. Also, some of their children had been born in Europe and merely raised in the United States. Something in the environment, probably in the diet, was producing this change. We know now that changes in average height and weight produced by dietary differences in a few generations are common and may have nothing to do with race or genetics.

Explaining Skin Color

Traditional racial classification assumed that biological characteristics such as skin color were determined by heredity and that they were stable (immutable) over many generations. We now know that a biological similarity doesn't necessarily indicate recent common ancestry. Dark skin color, for example, can be shared by tropical Africans and indigenous Australians for reasons other than common heredity. Scientists have made considerable progress in explaining variation in human skin color, along with many other features of human biological diversity. We shift now from classification to explanation, in which natural selection plays a key role (see also Anemone 2011).

Natural selection is the process by which the forms most fit to survive and reproduce in a given environment do so. Over the generations, the less fit organisms die out, and the favored types survive by producing more offspring. The role of natural selection in producing variation in skin color will illustrate the explanatory approach to human biological diversity. Comparable explanations have been provided for many other aspects of human biological variation.

Skin color is a complex biological trait—influenced by several genes. Just how many genes is not known. *Melanin,* the primary determinant of human skin color, is a chemical substance manufactured in the epidermis, or outer skin layer. The melanin cells of darker-skinned people produce more and larger granules of melanin than do those of lighter-skinned people. By screening out ultraviolet (UV) radiation from the sun, melanin offers protection against a variety of maladies, including sunburn and skin cancer.

Prior to the 16th century, most of the world's very dark-skinned peoples lived in the *tropics,* a belt extending about 23 degrees north and south of the equator, between the Tropic of Cancer and the Tropic of Capricorn. The association between dark skin color and a tropical habitat existed throughout the Old World, where humans and their ancestors have lived for

Before the 16th century, almost all the very dark-skinned populations of the world lived in the tropics, as does this Samburu woman from Kenya.

How would you describe Prince Harry's phenotype?

millions of years. The darkest populations of Africa evolved not in shady equatorial forests but in sunny, open grassland, or savanna, country.

Outside the tropics, skin color tends to be lighter. Moving north in Africa, for example, there is a gradual transition from dark brown to medium brown. Average skin color continues to lighten as one moves through the Middle East, into southern Europe, through central Europe, and to the north. South of the tropics skin color also is lighter. In the Americas, by contrast, tropical populations don't have very dark skin. This is the case because the settlement of the New World by light-skinned Asian ancestors of Native Americans was relatively recent, probably dating back no more than 20,000 years.

How, aside from migrations, can we explain the geographic distribution of human skin color? Natural selection provides an answer. In the tropics, intense UV radiation poses a series of threats, including severe sunburn, that make light skin color an adaptive disadvantage (Table 10.2 summarizes those threats). By damaging sweat glands, sunburn reduces the body's ability to perspire and thus to regulate its own temperature (thermoregulation). Sunburn also can increase susceptibility to disease. Melanin, nature's own sunscreen, confers a selective advantage (i.e., a better chance to survive and reproduce) on darker-skinned people living in the tropics. Yet another disadvantage of having light skin color in the tropics is that exposure to UV radiation can cause skin cancer (Blum 1961).

When and why might light skin color be advantageous? Years ago, W. F. Loomis (1967) focused on the role of UV radiation in stimulating the manufacture (synthesis) of vitamin D by the human body. The unclothed human body can produce its own vitamin D when exposed to sufficient sunlight. However, in a cloudy environment that also is so cold that people have to wear clothing much of the year (such as northern Europe, where very light skin color evolved), clouds and clothing impede the body's manufacture of vitamin D. Vitamin D deficiency diminishes the absorption of calcium in the intestines. A nutritional disease known as *rickets,* which softens and deforms the bones, may develop. In women, deformation of the pelvic bones from rickets can interfere with childbirth. In cold northern areas, light skin color maximizes the absorption of UV radiation and the synthesis of vitamin D by the few parts of the body that are exposed to direct sunlight. There has been selection against dark skin color in northern areas because melanin screens out UV radiation.

This natural selection continues today: East Asians who have migrated recently to northern areas of the United Kingdom have a higher incidence of rickets and osteoporosis (also related to vitamin D and calcium deficiency) than the general British population. A related illustration involves Eskimos (Inuit) and other indigenous inhabitants of northern Alaska and northern Canada. According to Nina Jablonski (quoted in Iqbal 2002), "Looking at Alaska, one would think that the native people should be pale as ghosts." One reason they aren't is that they haven't inhabited this region very long in terms of geological time. Even more important, their traditional diet, which is rich in seafood, including fish oils, supplies sufficient vitamin D so as to make a reduction in pigmentation unnecessary. However, and again illustrating natural selection at work today, "when these people don't eat their aboriginal diets of fish and marine mammals, they suffer tremendously high rates of vitamin D-deficiency diseases such as rickets in children and osteoporosis in adults" (Jablonski quoted in Iqbal 2002). Far from being immutable, skin color can become an evolutionary liability very quickly.

TABLE 10.2 **Advantages and Disadvantages (Depending on Environment) of Dark and Light Skin Color**
Also shown are cultural alternatives that can make up for biological disadvantages and examples of natural selection (NS) operating today in relation to skin color.

		Cultural Alternatives	NS in Action Today
DARK SKIN COLOR			
Advantage	Melanin is natural sunscreen.		
	In tropics: screens out UV		
	Reduces susceptibility to folate destruction and thus to neural tube defects (NTDs), including spina bifida		
	Prevents sunburn and thus enhances sweating and thermoregulation		
	Reduces disease susceptibility		
	Reduces risk of skin cancer		
Disadvantage	Outside tropics: Reduces UV absorption		
	Increases susceptibility to rickets, osteoporosis	Foods, vitamin D supplements	East Asians in northern UK Inuit with modern diets
LIGHT SKIN COLOR			
Advantage	No natural sunscreen		
	Outside tropics: admits UV		
	Body manufactures vitamin D and thus prevents rickets and osteoporosis.		
Disadvantage	Especially in tropics: increases susceptibility to folate destruction and thus to NTDs, including spina bifida	Folic acid/folate supplements	Whites still have more NTDs.
	Impaired spermatogenesis		
	Increases susceptibility to sunburn and thus to impaired sweating and poor thermoregulation	Shelter, sunscreens, lotions, etc.	
	Increases disease susceptibility		
	Increases susceptibility to skin cancer		

According to Jablonski and George Chaplin (2000), another key factor explaining the geographic distribution of skin color involves the effects of UV on folate, an essential nutrient that the human body manufactures from folic acid. Pregnant women require large amounts of folate to support rapid cell division in the embryo, and there is a direct connection between folate and individual reproductive success. Folate deficiency causes neural tube defects (NTDs) in human embryos. NTDs are marked by the incomplete closure of the neural tube, so the spine and spinal cord fail to develop completely. One NTD, anencephaly (with the brain an exposed mass), results in stillbirth or death soon after delivery. With spina bifida, another NTD, survival rates are higher, but babies have severe disabilities, including paralysis. NTDs are the second most common human birth defect after cardiac abnormalities. Today, women of reproductive age are advised to take folate supplements to prevent serious birth defects such as spina bifida.

Natural sunlight and UV radiation destroy folate in the human body. Because melanin, as we have seen, protects against UV hazards, such as sunburn and its consequences, dark skin coloration is adaptive in the tropics. Now we see that melanin also is adaptive because it conserves folate in the human body and thus protects against NTDs, which are much more common in light-skinned than in darker-skinned populations (Jablonski 2006; Jablonski and Chaplin 2000). Africans and African Americans rarely demonstrate severe folate deficiency, even among individuals with marginal nutritional status. Folate also plays a role in another key reproductive process, spermatogenesis—the production of sperm. In mice and rats, folate deficiency can cause male sterility; it may well play a similar role in humans.

Today, of course, cultural alternatives to biological adaptation permit light-skinned people to survive in the tropics and darker-skinned people to live in the far north. People can clothe themselves and seek shelter from the sun; they can use artificial sunscreens if they lack the natural protection that melanin provides. Dark-skinned people living in the north can, indeed must, get vitamin D from their diet or take supplements. Today, pregnant women are routinely advised to take folic acid or folate supplements as a hedge against NTDs. Even so, light skin color still is correlated with a higher incidence of spina bifida.

Jablonski and Chaplin (2000) explain variation in human skin color as resulting from a balancing act between the evolutionary needs to (1) protect against all UV hazards (thus favoring dark skin in the tropics) and (2) have an adequate supply of vitamin D (thus favoring lighter skin outside the tropics). We see that common ancestry, the presumed basis of race, is not the only reason for biological similarities. Natural selection, still at work today, makes a major contribution to variations in human skin color, as well as to many other human biological differences and similarities.

Race and Ethnicity

When an ethnic group is assumed to have a biological basis (distinctively shared "blood" or genes), it is called a **race.** Discrimination against such a group is called **racism** (Gotkowitz 2011; Kuper 2006; Scupin 2012). Race, like ethnicity in general, is a cultural category rather than a biological reality. That is, ethnic groups, including "races," derive from contrasts perceived and perpetuated in particular societies, rather than from scientific classifications based on common genes (see Wade 2002).

It is not possible to define human races biologically. Only cultural constructions of race are possible—even though the average person conceptualizes "race" in biological terms. Most Americans, for example, believe (incorrectly) that their population includes biologically based races to which various labels can be applied. These labels include "White," "Black," "yellow," "red," "Caucasoid," "Negroid," "Mongoloid," "Amerindian," "Euro-American," "African American," "Asian American," and "Native American."

In American culture, we hear the words *ethnicity* and *race* frequently, without clear distinctions made between them. Consider a *New York Times* article published on May 29, 1992. Discussing the changing ethnic composition of the United States, the article explained (correctly) that Hispanics "can be of any race" (Barringer 1992, p. A12). In other words, "Hispanic" is an ethnic category that cross-cuts racial contrasts such as that between "Black" and "White." However, another *Times* article published the same day reported that during Los Angeles riots in spring 1992, "hundreds of Hispanic residents were interrogated about their immigration status on the basis of their *race* alone [emphasis added]" (Mydans 1992*a*, p. A8). Use of *race* here seems inappropriate because "Hispanic" usually is perceived as referring to a linguistically based (Spanish-speaking) ethnic group, rather than a biologically based race. Since these Los Angeles residents were being interrogated because they were Hispanic, the article is actually reporting on ethnic, not racial, discrimination.

In a more recent case, consider a speech delivered by then Appeals Court Judge Sonia Sotomayor, newly nominated (in May 2009; confirmed in August 2009) for the U.S. Supreme Court by President Barack Obama. In a 2001 lecture titled "A Latina Judge's Voice," delivered as the Judge Mario G. Olmos Memorial Lecture at the University of California, Berkeley, School of Law, Sotomayor declared (as part of a much longer speech):

> I would hope that a wise Latina woman with the richness of her experiences would more often than not reach a better conclusion than a white male who hasn't lived that life. (Sotomayor 2001/2009)

Conservatives, including former House speaker Newt Gingrich and radio talk show host Rush Limbaugh, seized on this declaration as evidence that Sotomayor was a "racist" or a "reverse racist." Again, however, "Latina" is an ethnic (and gendered-female) rather than a racial category. I suspect that Sotomayor also was using "white male" as an ethnic-gender category, to refer to nonminority men.

These examples illustrate the difficulty in drawing a precise distinction between race and ethnicity. It probably is better to use the term *ethnic group* rather than *race* to describe *any* such social group, for example, African Americans, Asian Americans, Anglo Americans, Hispanics, Latinos, Latinas, and even non–Hispanic Whites.

The Social Construction of Race

Although races are assumed (by members of a particular culture) to have a biological basis, race actually is socially constructed. The "races" we hear about every day are cultural, or social, rather than biological categories. There is no clear genetic difference between people commonly regarded as being of different races.

Hypodescent: Race in the United States

In American culture, one acquires one's racial identity at birth, as an ascribed status, but race isn't based on biology or on simple ancestry. Take the case of the child of a "racially mixed" marriage involving one Black and one White parent. We know that 50 percent of the child's genes come from one parent and 50 percent from the other. Still, American culture overlooks heredity and classifies this child as Black. This rule is arbitrary. On the basis of genotype (genetic composition), it would be just as logical to classify the child as White.

American rules for assigning racial status can be even more arbitrary. In some states, anyone known to have any Black ancestor, no matter how remote, is classified as a member of the Black race. This is a rule of **descent** (it assigns social identity on the basis of ancestry), but of a sort that is rare outside the contemporary United States. It is called **hypodescent** (Harris and Kottak 1963), because it automatically places the children of a union between members of different groups in the minority group (*hypo* means "lower"). Hypodescent divides American society into groups that have been unequal in their access to wealth, power, and prestige.

The rule of hypodescent affects Blacks, Asians, Native Americans, and Hispanics differently (see Hunter 2005). It's easier to negotiate Native American or Hispanic identity than Black identity. The ascription rule isn't as definite, and the assumption of a biological basis isn't as strong. To be considered Native American, one ancestor out of eight (great-grandparents) or out of four (grandparents) may suffice. This depends on whether the assignment is by federal or state law or by a Native American tribal council.

Former Oklahoma quarterback and Heisman trophy winner Sam Bradford is a registered Cherokee Indian, but with significant non-Indian ancestry. In this photo Bradford has just been chosen by the St. Louis Rams as the first overall pick in the 2010 NFL Draft.

The child of a Hispanic may (or may not, depending on context) claim Hispanic identity. Many Americans with a Native American or Latino grandparent consider themselves White and lay no claim to minority group status.

Race in the Census

The U.S. Census Bureau has gathered data by race since 1790. Figure 10.2 shows that the 2010 census asked about both race and Hispanic origin. What do you think of the racial categories included?

Attempts to add a "multiracial" category to the U.S. Census have been opposed by the National Association for the Advancement of Colored People (NAACP) and the National Council of La Raza (a Hispanic advocacy group). Racial classification is a political issue (Goldberg 2002) involving access to resources, including jobs, voting districts, and federal funding of programs aimed at minorities.

FIGURE 10.2   Questions on Race and Hispanic Origin from U.S. Census 2010

Source: U.S. Census Bureau, Census 2010 questionnaire.

5. **Is this person of Hispanic, Latino, or Spanish origin?**

☐ No, not of Hispanic, Latino, or Spanish origin

☐ Yes, Mexican, Mexican Am., Chicano

☐ Yes, Puerto Rican

☐ Yes, Cuban

☐ Yes, another Hispanic, Latino, or Spanish origin — *Print origin, for example, Argentinean, Colombian, Dominican, Nicaraguan, Salvadoran, Spaniard, and so on.* ↗

6. **What is this person's race?** *Mark* ☒ *one or more boxes.*

☐ White

☐ Black, African Am., or Negro

☐ American Indian or Alaska Native — *Print name of enrolled or principal tribe.* ↗

☐ Asian Indian   ☐ Japanese   ☐ Native Hawaiian

☐ Chinese   ☐ Korean   ☐ Guamanian or Chamorro

☐ Filipino   ☐ Vietnamese   ☐ Samoan

☐ Other Asian — *Print race, for example, Hmong, Laotian, Thai, Pakistani, Cambodian, and so on.* ↗   ☐ Other Pacific Islander — *Print race, for example, Fijian, Tongan, and so on.* ↗

☐ Some other race — *Print race.* ↗

The hypodescent rule results in all the population growth being attributed to the minority category. Minorities fear their political clout will decline if their numbers go down.

But things are changing. Choice of "some other race" in the U.S. Census tripled from 1980 (6.8 million) to 2010 (over 19 million)—suggesting imprecision in and dissatisfaction with the existing categories. In the 2000 census, 2.4 percent of Americans—almost 7 million people—chose a first-ever option of identifying themselves as belonging to two or more races. This figure rose to 2.9 percent in the 2010 census. The number of interracial marriages and children is increasing, with implications for the traditional system of American racial classification. "Interracial," "biracial," or "multiracial" children who grow up with both parents undoubtedly identify with particular qualities of either parent. It is troubling for many of them to have so important an identity as race dictated by the arbitrary rule of hypodescent. It may be especially discordant when racial identity doesn't parallel gender identity, for instance, a boy with a White father and a Black mother or a girl with a White mother and a Black father.

Rather than race, the Canadian census asks about "visible minorities." That country's Employment Equity Act defines such groups as "persons, other than Aboriginal peoples [First Nations in Canada, Native Americans in the United States], who are non-Caucasian in race or non-white in colour" (Statistics Canada 2001). "South Asian" and "Chinese" are Canada's largest visible minorities (see Figure 10.3). Canada's visible minority population of 16.2 percent (in 2006, up from 13.4 percent in 2001) contrasts with an American minority population of 37 percent in 2012 (up from 25 percent in 2000).

As in the United States, Canada's minority population has been growing much faster than the country's overall population. In 1981, visible minorities accounted for only 4.7 percent of the Canadian population, versus 16.2 percent in 2006 (the most recent census data available as of this writing). Between 2001 and 2006, Canada's total population increased 5 percent, while visible minorities grew by 27 percent. If recent immigration trends continue, by 2031 visible minorities will comprise almost one-third (31 percent) of the Canadian population (Statistics Canada 2010).

Not Us: Race in Japan

American culture ignores considerable diversity in biology, language, and geographic origin as it socially constructs race in the United States. North Americans also overlook diversity by seeing Japan as a nation that is homogeneous in race, ethnicity, language,

FIGURE 10.3
Visible Minority Population of Canada, 2006 Census

Source: From Statistics Canada, 2006 Census, http://www12 .statcan.ca/english/census06/data /highlights/ethnic.

Percent	100.0% Total population: 31,241,030	
	4.0% South Asian	1,262,865
	3.9% Chinese	1,216,515
	2.5% Black	783,795
	1.3% Filipino	410,695
	1.2% Arab/West Asian	374,835
	1.0% Latin American	304,245
	0.8% Southeast Asian	239,935
	0.5% Korean	141,890
	0.3% Japanese	83,300
	0.4% Other visible minority	116,895
	0.4% Multiple visible minority	133,120
	16.2% Total visible minority population:	5,068,090
	83.8% Not visible minority (i.e. majority): 26,172,940	

and culture—an image the Japanese themselves cultivate. Scholars estimate, however, that 10 percent of Japan's national population are minorities of various sorts. These include aboriginal Ainu, annexed Okinawans, outcast *burakumin,* children of mixed marriages, and immigrant nationalities, especially Koreans, who number more than 700,000 (Lie 2001; Ryang and Lie 2009).

How is race culturally constructed in Japan? The (majority) Japanese define themselves by opposition to others, whether minority groups in their own nation or outsiders—anyone who is "not us." The "not us" should stay that way; assimilation generally is discouraged. Cultural mechanisms, especially residential segregation and taboos on "interracial" marriage, work to keep minorities "in their place."

In its construction of race, Japanese culture regards certain ethnic groups as having a biological basis, when there is no evidence that they do. The best example is the *burakumin,* a stigmatized group of at least 4 million outcasts, sometimes compared to India's untouchables. The burakumin are physically and genetically indistinguishable from other Japanese. Many of them "pass" as (and marry) majority Japanese, but a deceptive marriage can end in divorce if burakumin identity is discovered (Aoki and Dardess, eds. 1981).

Burakumin are perceived as standing apart from majority Japanese. Based on their ancestry, (and thus, it is assumed, their "blood" or genetics), burakumin are considered "not us." Majority Japanese try to keep their lineage pure by discouraging mixing. The burakumin are residentially segregated in neighborhoods (rural or urban) called *buraku,*

Japan's stigmatized burakumin are physically and genetically indistinguishable from other Japanese. In response to burakumin political mobilization, Japan has dismantled the legal structure of discrimination against burakumin. This Sports Day for burakumin children is one kind of mobilization.

from which the racial label is derived. Compared with majority Japanese, the burakumin are less likely to attend high school and college. When burakumin attend the same schools as majority Japanese, they face discrimination. Majority children and teachers may refuse to eat with them, because burakumin are considered unclean.

In applying for university admission or a job and in dealing with the government, Japanese must list their address, which becomes part of a household or family registry. This list makes residence in a buraku, and likely burakumin social status, evident. Schools and companies use this information to discriminate. (The best way to pass is to move so often that the buraku address eventually disappears from the registry.) Majority Japanese also limit "race" mixture by hiring marriage mediators to check out the family histories of prospective spouses. They are especially careful to check for burakumin ancestry (De Vos, Wetherall, and Stearman 1983).

The origin of the burakumin lies in a historical, tiered system of stratification (from the Tokugawa period—1603–1868). The top four ranked categories were warrior-administrators (*samurai*), farmers, artisans, and merchants. The ancestors of the burakumin were below this hierarchy, an outcast group who did unclean jobs such as animal slaughter and disposal of the dead. Burakumin still do similar jobs, including work with leather and other animal products. The burakumin are more likely than majority Japanese to do manual labor (including farm work) and to belong to the national lower class. Burakumin and other Japanese minorities also are more likely to have careers in crime, prostitution, entertainment, and sports (De Vos, Wetherall, and Stearman 1983).

Like Blacks in the United States, the burakumin are class-stratified. Because certain jobs are reserved for the burakumin, people who are successful in those occupations (e.g., shoe factory owners) can be wealthy. Burakumin also have found jobs as government bureaucrats. Financially successful burakumin can temporarily escape their stigmatized status by travel, including foreign travel.

Discrimination against the burakumin is strikingly like the discrimination that Blacks have experienced in the United States. The burakumin often live in villages and neighborhoods with poor housing and sanitation. They have limited access to education, jobs, amenities, and health facilities. In response to burakumin political mobilization, Japan has dismantled the legal structure of discrimination against burakumin and has worked to improve conditions in the buraku. (The website http://blhrri.org/index_e.htm is sponsored by the Buraku Liberation and Human Rights Research Institute and includes the most recent information about the buraku liberation movement.) Still Japan has yet to institute American-style affirmative action programs for education and jobs. Discrimination against nonmajority Japanese is still the rule in companies. Some employers say that hiring burakumin would give their company an unclean image and thus create a disadvantage in competing with other businesses (De Vos, Wetherall, and Stearman 1983).

Phenotype and Fluidity: Race in Brazil

There are more flexible, less exclusionary ways of socially constructing race than those used in the United States and Japan. Along with the rest of Latin America, Brazil has less exclusionary categories, which permit individuals to change their racial classification. Brazil shares a history of slavery with the United States, but it lacks the hypodescent rule.

Brazilians use many more racial labels—over 500 were once reported (Harris 1970)—than Americans or Japanese do. In northeastern Brazil, I found 40 different racial terms in use in Arembepe, then a village of only 750 people (Kottak 2006). Through their traditional classification system Brazilians recognize and attempt to describe the physical variation that exists in their population. The system used in the United States, by recognizing only three or four races, blinds Americans to an equivalent range of evident physical contrasts. The system Brazilians use to construct social race has other special features. In the United States one's race is an ascribed status; it is assigned automatically by hypodescent and usually doesn't change. In Brazil racial identity is more flexible, more of an achieved status. Brazilian racial classification pays attention to phenotype. A Brazilian's phenotype and racial label may change because of environmental factors, such as the tanning rays of the sun or the effects of humidity on the hair.

A Brazilian can change his or her "race" (say, from "Indian" to "mixed") by changing his or her manner of dress, language, location (e.g., rural to urban), and even attitude (e.g., by adopting urban behavior). Two racial/ethnic labels used in Brazil are *indio* (indigenous, Native American) and *cabôclo* (someone who "looks *indio*" but wears modern clothing and participates in Brazilian culture, rather than living in an indigenous community). Similar shifts in racial/ethnic classification occur in other parts of Latin America, for example, Guatemala (see Wade 2010). The perception of biological race is influenced not just by the physical phenotype but also by how one dresses and behaves.

Furthermore, racial differences in Brazil may be so insignificant in structuring community life that people may forget the terms they have applied to others. Sometimes they even forget the ones they've used for themselves. In Arembepe, I made it a habit to ask the same person on different days to tell me the races of others in the village (and my own). In the United States I am always "White" or "Euro-American," but in Arembepe I got lots of terms besides *branco* ("White"). I could be *claro* ("light"), *louro* ("blond"), *sarará* ("light-skinned redhead"), *mulato claro* ("light mulatto"), or *mulato* ("mulatto"). The racial term used to describe me or anyone else varied from person to person, week to week, even day to day. My best informant, a man with very dark skin color, changed the term he used for himself all the time—from *escuro* ("dark") to *preto* ("Black") to *moreno escuro* ("dark brunet").

For centuries the United States and Brazil have had mixed populations, with ancestors from Native America, Europe, Africa, and Asia. Although races have mixed in both countries, Brazilian and American cultures have constructed the results differently. The historical reasons for this contrast lie mainly in the different characteristics of the settlers of the two countries. The mainly English early settlers of the United States came as women, men, and families, but Brazil's Portuguese colonizers were mainly men— merchants and adventurers. Many of these Portuguese men married Native American women and recognized their racially mixed children as their heirs. Like their North American counterparts, Brazilian plantation owners had sexual relations with their slaves. But the Brazilian landlords more often freed the children that resulted—for demographic and economic reasons. (Sometimes these were their only children.) Freed offspring of master and slave became plantation overseers and foremen and filled many intermediate positions in the emerging Brazilian economy. They were not classed with the slaves, but were allowed to join a new intermediate category. No hypodescent rule developed in Brazil to ensure that Whites and Blacks remained separate (see Degler 1970; Harris 1964).

In today's world system, Brazil's system of racial classification is changing in the context of international identity politics and rights movements. Just as more and more Brazilians claim indigenous (Native Brazilian) identities, an increasing number now

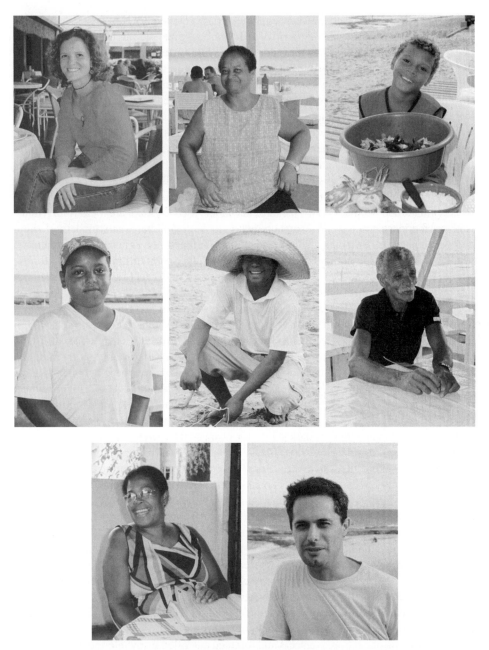

These photos, taken in Brazil in 2003 and 2004, give just a glimpse of the spectrum of phenotypical diversity encountered among contemporary Brazilians.

assert their Blackness and self-conscious membership in the African diaspora. Particularly in such northeastern Brazilian states as Bahia, where African demographic and cultural influence is strong, public universities have instituted affirmative action programs aimed at indigenous peoples and especially at Blacks. Racial identities firm up in the context of international (e.g., pan-African and pan-Indian) mobilization and access to strategic resources based on race.

Ethnic Groups, Nations, and Nationalities

The term **nation** once was synonymous with *tribe* or *ethnic group*. All three of these terms have been used to refer to a single culture sharing a single language, religion, history, territory, ancestry, and kinship. Thus, one could speak interchangeably of the Seneca (Native American) nation, tribe, or ethnic group. Now *nation* has come to mean state—an independent, centrally organized political unit, or a government. *Nation* and *state* have become synonymous. Combined in **nation-state** they refer to an autonomous political entity, a country—like the United States, "one nation, indivisible" (see Farner, ed. 2004; Gellner 1997).

Because of migration, conquest, and colonialism, most nation-states are not ethnically homogeneous. A 2003 study by James Fearon found that about 70 percent of all countries have an ethnic group that forms an absolute majority of the population; the average population share of such groups is 65 percent. The average size of the *second* largest group, or largest ethnic minority, is 17 percent. Only 18 percent of all countries, including Brazil and Japan, have a single ethnic group that accounts for 90 percent or more of its population.

There is substantial regional variation in countries' ethnic structures. Strong states, particularly in Europe (e.g., France), have deliberately and actively worked to homogenize their diverse premodern populations to a common national identity and culture (see Beriss 2004; Gellner 1983). Although countries with no ethnic majority are fairly rare in the rest of the world, this is the norm in Africa. The average African country has a plurality group of about 22 percent, with the second largest slightly less than this. Rwanda, Burundi, Lesotho, Swaziland, and Zimbabwe are exceptions; each has a large majority group and a minority that makes up almost all the rest of the population. Botswana has a large majority (the Tswana) and a set of smaller minorities (Fearon 2003).

Most Latin American and Caribbean countries contain a majority group (speaking a European language, such as Portuguese in Brazil, Spanish in Argentina) and a single minority group—"indigenous peoples." "Indigenous peoples" is a catch-all category encompassing several small Native American tribes or remnants. Exceptions are Guatemala and the Andean countries of Bolivia, Peru, and Ecuador, with large indigenous populations (see Gotkowitz 2011; Wade 2010).

Most countries in Asia and the Middle East/North Africa have ethnic majorities. The Asian countries of Myanmar, Laos, Vietnam, and Thailand contain a large lowland majority edged by more fragmented mountain folk. Several oil-producing countries in the Middle East, including Saudi Arabia, Bahrain, United Arab Emirates, Oman, and Kuwait, contain an ethnically homogeneous group of citizens who form either a plurality or a bare majority; the rest of the population consists of ethnically diverse noncitizen workers. Several countries in the Middle East/North Africa contain two principal ethnic or ethnoreligious groups: Arabs and Berbers in Morocco, Algeria, Libya, and Tunisia; Muslims and Copts in Egypt; Turks and Kurds in Turkey; Greeks and Turks in Cyprus; and Palestinians and TransJordan Arabs in Jordan (Fearon 2003).

Nationalities and Imagined Communities

Ethnic groups that once had, or wish to have or regain, autonomous political status (their own country) are called **nationalities.** In the words of Benedict Anderson (1991/2006), they are "imagined communities." Even when they become nation-states, they remain imagined communities because most of their members, though feeling comradeship, will never meet (Anderson 1991, pp. 6–10). They can only imagine they all participate in the same unit.

Anderson traces Western European nationalism, which arose in imperial powers such as England, France, and Spain, back to the 18th century. He stresses that language and print played a crucial role in the growth of European national consciousness. The novel and the newspaper were "two forms of imagining" communities (consisting of all the people who read the same sources and thus witnessed the same events) that flowered in the 18th century (Anderson 1991, pp. 24–25).

Over time, political upheavals, wars, and migration have divided many imagined national communities that arose in the 18th and 19th centuries. The German and Korean homelands were artificially divided after wars, according to communist and capitalist ideologies. World War I split the Kurds, who remain an imagined community, forming a majority in no state. Kurds are a minority group in Turkey, Iran, Iraq, and Syria.

In creating multitribal and multiethnic states, colonialism often erected boundaries that corresponded poorly with preexisting cultural divisions. But colonial institutions also helped create new "imagined communities" beyond nations. A good example is the idea of *négritude* ("Black identity") developed by African intellectuals in Francophone (French-speaking) West Africa. Négritude can be traced to the association and common experience in colonial times of youths from Guinea, Mali, Ivory Coast, and Senegal at the William Ponty school in Dakar, Senegal (Anderson 1991, pp. 123–124).

Ethnic Tolerance and Accommodation

Ethnic diversity may be associated either with positive group interaction and coexistence or with conflict (discussed beginning on p. 233). There are nation-states in which multiple cultural groups live together in reasonable harmony, including some less-developed countries.

Assimilation

Assimilation describes the process of change that a minority ethnic group may experience when it moves to a country where another culture dominates. By assimilating, the minority adopts the patterns and norms of its host culture. It is incorporated into the dominant culture to the point that it no longer exists as a separate cultural unit. Some countries, such as Brazil, are more assimilationist than others. Germans, Italians, Japanese, Middle Easterners, and East Europeans started migrating to Brazil late in the 19th century. These immigrants have assimilated to a common Brazilian culture, which has Portuguese, African, and Native American roots. The descendants of these immigrants speak the national language (Portuguese) and participate in the national culture. (During World War II, Brazil, which was on the Allied side, forced assimilation by banning instruction in any language other than Portuguese—especially in German.)

The Plural Society

Assimilation isn't inevitable, and there can be ethnic harmony without it. Ethnic distinctions can persist despite generations of interethnic contact. Through a study of three ethnic groups in Swat, Pakistan, Fredrik Barth (1958/1968) challenged an old idea that interaction always leads to assimilation. He showed that ethnic groups can be in contact for generations without assimilating. Barth (1958/1968, p. 324) defines **plural society** (an idea he extended from Pakistan to the Middle East) as a society combining ethnic contrasts, ecological specialization (i.e., use of different environmental resources by each ethnic group), and the economic interdependence of those groups.

In Barth's view, ethnic boundaries are most stable and enduring when the groups occupy different ecological niches. That is, they make their living in different ways and don't compete. Ideally, they should depend on each other's activities and exchange with one another. When different ethnic groups exploit the *same* ecological niche, the militarily more powerful group will normally replace the weaker one. If they exploit more or less the same niche, but the weaker group is better able to use marginal environments, they also may coexist (Barth 1958/1968, p. 331). Given niche specialization, ethnic boundaries and interdependence can be maintained, although the specific cultural features of each group may change. By shifting the analytic focus from individual cultures or ethnic groups to *relationships* between cultures or ethnic groups, Barth (1958/1968, 1969) has made important contributions to ethnic studies (see also Kamrava 2011).

Multiculturalism

The view of cultural diversity in a country as something good and desirable is called **multiculturalism** (see Kottak and Kozaitis 2012). The multicultural model is the opposite of the assimilationist model, in which minorities are expected to abandon their cultural traditions and values, replacing them with those of the majority population. The multicultural view encourages the practice of cultural–ethnic traditions. A multicultural society socializes individuals not only into the dominant (national) culture but also into an ethnic culture. Thus, in the United States today millions of people speak both English and another language, eat both "American" (apple pie, steak, hamburgers) and "ethnic" foods, and celebrate both national (July 4, Thanksgiving) and ethnic–religious holidays.

Multiculturalism seeks ways for people to understand and interact that don't depend on sameness but rather on respect for differences. Multiculturalism stresses the interaction of ethnic groups and their contribution to the country. It assumes that each group has something to offer to and learn from the others. Several forces have propelled North America away from the assimilationist model toward multiculturalism. First, multiculturalism reflects the fact of recent large-scale migration, particularly from the "less-developed countries" to the "developed" nations of North America and Western Europe. The global scale of modern migration introduces unparalleled ethnic variety to host nations. Multiculturalism is related to globalization: People use modern means of transportation to migrate to nations whose lifestyles they learn about through the media and from tourists who increasingly visit their own countries (see Inda and Rosaldo, eds. 2008).

Migration also is fueled by rapid population growth, coupled with insufficient jobs (both for educated and uneducated people), in the less-developed countries. As traditional rural economies decline or mechanize, displaced farmers move to cities, where they and their children often are unable to find jobs. As people in the less-developed countries get better educations, they seek more skilled employment. They hope to partake of an international culture of consumption that includes such modern amenities as refrigerators, televisions, and automobiles (Ahmed 2004).

Changing Demographics

In October 2006, the population of the United States reached 300 million people, just 39 years after reaching 200 million and 91 years after reaching the 100 million mark (in 1915). Consider how much the country's ethnic composition has changed in the past 40 years. The 1970 census, the first to attempt an official count of Hispanics, found they represented no more than 4.7 percent of the American population. By the 2010 census this figure had risen to 16.3 percent—over 50 million Hispanics. The number of African Americans grew from 11.1 percent in 1967 to 12.6 percent in 2010, while (non-Hispanic) Whites ("Anglos") declined from 83 to 63.7 percent. In 1967 fewer than 10 million people in the United States (5 percent of the population) had been born elsewhere, compared with more than 38 million foreign born today (12.5 percent) (all data from U.S. Census Bureau). In 2011, for the first time in American history, minorities (including Hispanics, Blacks, Asians, Native Americans, and those of mixed race) accounted for more than half (50.4 percent) of all births in the United States (Tavernise 2012).

In 1973, 78 percent of the students in American public schools were White, and 22 percent were minorities: Blacks, Hispanics, Asians, Pacific Islanders, and "others." By 2004, only 57 percent of public school students were White, and 43 percent were minorities. Minority students are projected to outnumber (non-Hispanic) White students by 2015. They already do in California, Hawaii, Mississippi, New Mexico, and Texas (Dillon 2006).

Immigration, mainly from southern and eastern Europe, had a similar effect on classroom diversity, at least in the largest American cities, a century ago. A study of American public schools in 1908–1909 found that only 42 percent of those urban students were native born, while 58 percent were immigrants. In a very different context (multicultural now versus assimilationist then), today's American classrooms have regained the ethnic diversity they demonstrated in the early 1900s, when my German-speaking Austro-Hungarian-born father and grandparents immigrated to the United States.

The Gray and the Brown

Drawing on a 2010 Brookings Institution report titled "State of Metropolitan America: On the Front Lines of Demographic Transformation," Ronald Brownstein (2010) analyzes an intensifying confrontation between groups he describes as "the gray and the brown." Brownstein and demographer William Frey, an author of the Brookings report, focus on two key U.S. demographic trends:

1. Ethnic/racial diversity is increasing, especially among the young.
2. The country is aging, and most of the senior population is White.

Frey (in Brookings Institution 2010, pp. 26, 63) sees these trends as creating a "cultural generation gap"—a sharp contrast in the attitudes, priorities, and political leanings of younger and older Americans. Whites now constitute 80 percent of older Americans, but only 56 percent of children.

Politically the two groups—the gray (older) and the brown (younger)—are poles apart. The aging White population appears increasingly resistant to taxes and public spending, while younger people and minorities value government support of education, health, and social welfare. In the 2008 and 2012 elections, young people, especially minorities, strongly supported President Barack Obama. Seniors, especially White ones, voted solidly for Republicans John McCain and Mitt Romney. These differences have persisted thereafter in measures of approval for President Obama's job performance—consistently highest among non-Whites and young people.

The gray and the brown are more interdependent economically than either usually realizes. If minority children benefit disproportionately from public education today, minority workers will pay a growing share of the payroll taxes needed to sustain Social Security and Medicare in the future. These are government programs that most directly benefit old White people.

The history of U.S. national immigration policy helps us understand how the gap between the gray and the brown arose. Federal policies established in the 1920s severely curtailed immigration from areas other than northern Europe. In 1965, Congress loosened restrictions—resulting in an eventual influx of immigrants from southern Europe, Asia, Africa, the Caribbean, and Latin America (see Vigil 2012).

Note the ethnic diversity between generations in this recent American photo.

Non-Hispanic Whites constituted the overwhelming majority of Americans through the mid–20th century, including the post–World War II Baby Boom (1946–1964). Most baby boomers grew up and have lived much of their lives in White suburbs, residentially isolated from minorities (Brownstein 2010). As they age and retire, many older White Americans are reconstituting such communities in racially homogeneous enclaves in the Southeast and Southwest.

In such communities, except for their yard and construction workers and house cleaners, older White people live apart from multicultural America and the minorities who represent a growing share of the national population. Since 1965, expanded immigration and higher fertility rates among minorities have transformed American society. As recently as 1980, minorities made up only 20 percent of the total population (versus over 35 percent today) and 25 percent of children under 18 (versus over 44 percent today). If recent demographic trends continue, the ethnic composition of the United States will change even more dramatically (see Figure 10.4). Similar trends are evident in western Europe and are everyday expressions of globalization.

FIGURE 10.4   **Ethnic Composition of the United States**
The proportion of the American population that is White and non-Hispanic is declining. The projection for 2050 shown here comes from a 2008 U.S. Census Bureau report. Note especially the dramatic rise in the Hispanic portion of the American population between 2011 and 2050.

Source: Based on 2010 data from U.S. Census Bureau, decennial census, and a 2008 projection by the U.S. Census Bureau, http://www.census.gov/population/www/projections/analytical-document09.pdf, Table 1, p. 17.

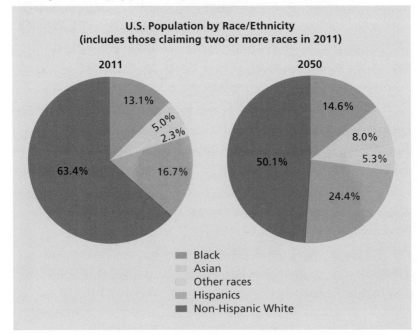

Roots of Ethnic Conflict

Ethnicity, based on perceived cultural similarities and differences in a society or nation, can be expressed in peaceful multiculturalism or in discrimination or violent interethnic confrontation. The roots of ethnic differentiation—and therefore, potentially, of ethnic conflict—can be political, economic, religious, linguistic, cultural, or racial (see Kuper 2006). Why do ethnic differences often lead to conflict and violence? The causes include a sense of injustice because of resource distribution, economic or political competition, and reaction to discrimination, prejudice, and other expressions of devalued identity (see Donham 2011; Friedman 2003; Ryan 1990, p. xxvii).

In Iraq, under the dictator Saddam Hussein, there was discrimination by one Muslim group (Sunnis) against others (Shiites and Kurds). Sunnis, although a numeric minority within Iraq's population, enjoyed privileged access to power, prestige, and position. After the elections of 2005, which many Sunnis chose to boycott, Shiites gained political control. A civil war developed out of "sectarian violence" (conflicts among sects of the same religion) as Sunnis (and their foreign supporters) fueled an insurgency against the new government and its foreign supporters, including the United States. Shiites retaliated against Sunni attacks and a history of Sunni privilege and perceived discrimination against Shiites, as Shiite militias engaged in ethnic (sectarian) cleansing of their own.

Prejudice and Discrimination

Ethnic conflict often arises in reaction to prejudice (attitudes and judgments) or discrimination (action). **Prejudice** means devaluing (looking down on) a group because of its assumed behavior, values, capabilities, or attributes. People are prejudiced when they hold stereotypes about groups and apply them to individuals. (**Stereotypes** are fixed ideas—often unfavorable—about what the members of a group are like.) Prejudiced people assume that members of the group will act as they are "supposed to act" (according to the stereotype) and interpret a wide range of individual behaviors as evidence of the stereotype. They use this behavior to confirm their stereotype (and low opinion) of the group.

Discrimination refers to policies and practices that harm a group and its members. Discrimination may be *de facto* (practiced, but not legally sanctioned) or *de jure* (part of the law). An example of de facto discrimination is the harsher treatment that American minorities (compared with other Americans) tend to get from the police and the judicial system. This unequal treatment isn't legal, but it happens, anyway. Segregation in the southern United States and *apartheid* in South Africa provide two examples of de jure discrimination, which no longer are in existence. In both systems, by law, Blacks and Whites had different rights and privileges. Their social interaction ("mixing") was legally curtailed.

Chips in the Mosaic

Although the multicultural model is increasingly prominent in North America, ethnic competition and conflict also are evident. There is conflict between newer arrivals, for instance, Central Americans and Koreans, and longer-established ethnic groups, such as African Americans. Ethnic antagonism flared in South-Central Los Angeles in spring 1992 in rioting that followed the acquittal of four White police officers who were tried for the videotaped beating of Rodney King (see Abelmann and Lie 1995).

Angry Blacks attacked Whites, Koreans, and Latinos. This violence expressed frustration by African Americans about their prospects in an increasingly multicultural society. A *New York Times* CBS News poll conducted just after the Los Angeles riots found that Blacks had a bleaker outlook than Whites about the effects of immigration on their lives. Only 23 percent of the Blacks felt they had more opportunities than recent immigrants, compared with twice that many Whites (Toner 1992).

Aftermaths of Oppression

Fueling ethnic conflict are such forms of discrimination as genocide, forced assimilation, ethnocide, and cultural colonialism. The most extreme form of ethnic discrimination is **genocide,** the deliberate elimination of a group (such as Jews in Nazi Germany, Muslims in Bosnia, or Tutsi in Rwanda) through mass murder (see Hinton and O'Neill 2011). A dominant group may try to destroy the cultures of certain ethnic groups **(ethnocide)** or force them to adopt the dominant culture (*forced assimilation*). Many countries have penalized or banned the language and customs of an ethnic group (including its religious observances). One example of forced assimilation is the anti-Basque campaign that the dictator Francisco Franco (who ruled between 1939 and 1975) waged in Spain. Franco banned Basque books, journals, newspapers, signs, sermons, and tombstones and imposed fines for using the Basque language in schools (Ryan 1990). His policies led to the formation of a Basque terrorist group and spurred strong nationalist sentiment in the Basque region.

A policy of *ethnic expulsion* aims at removing groups who are culturally different from a country. There are many examples, including Bosnia-Herzegovina in the 1990s. Uganda expelled 74,000 Asians in 1972. The neofascist parties of contemporary Western Europe advocate repatriation (expulsion) of immigrant workers (West Indians in England, Algerians in France, and Turks in Germany) (see Friedman 2003; Ryan 1990, p. 9). A policy of expulsion may create **refugees**—people who have been forced (involuntary refugees) or who have chosen (voluntary refugees) to flee a country, to escape persecution or war.

In many countries, colonial nation-building left ethnic strife in its wake. Thus, over a million Hindus and Muslims were killed in the violence that accompanied the division of the Indian subcontinent into India and Pakistan. Problems between Arabs and Jews in Palestine began during the British mandate period (see Kamrava 2011).

Multiculturalism may be growing in the United States and Canada, but the opposite is happening in the former Soviet Union, where ethnic groups (nationalities) want their own nation-states. The flowering of ethnic feeling and conflict as the Soviet empire disintegrated illustrates that years of political repression and ideology provide insufficient common ground for lasting unity. **Cultural colonialism** refers to internal domination— by one group and its culture or ideology over others. One example is the domination over the former Soviet empire by Russian people, language, and culture and by communist ideology. The dominant culture makes itself the official culture. This is

Two faces of ethnic difference in the former Soviet empire. Above, a propaganda poster depicts a happy mix of nationalities that make up the population of Kyrgyzstan, Central Asia. Below, in 2008, in the troubled republic of Georgia, refugees wait to be registered for humanitarian aid in the town of Gori, northwest of Tbilisi, Georgia's capital.

Anthropology Today   *AAA Statement on Race*

There is considerable public confusion about the meaning and relevance of "race." Recognizing that false claims about "racial" differences continue to be made, the American Anthropological Association (AAA) adopted the following statement. This statement represents the thinking and scholarly positions of most anthropologists (see also http:// www.understandingrace.org/).

In the United States both scholars and the general public have been conditioned to viewing human races as natural and separate divisions within the human species based on visible physical differences. With the vast expansion of scientific knowledge in this century, however, it has become clear that human populations are not unambiguous, clearly demarcated, biologically distinct groups. Evidence from the analysis of genetics (e.g., DNA) indicates that most physical variation, about 94%, lies within so-called racial groups. Conventional geographic "racial" groupings differ from one another only in about 6% of their genes. This means that there is greater variation within "racial" groups than between them. In neighboring populations there is much overlapping of genes and their phenotypic (physical) expressions. Throughout history whenever different groups have come into contact, they have interbred. The continued sharing of genetic materials has maintained all of humankind as a single species.

Physical variations in any given trait tend to occur gradually rather than abruptly over geographic areas. And because physical traits are inherited independently of one another, knowing the range of one trait does not predict the presence of others. For example, skin color varies largely from light in the temperate areas in the north to dark in the tropical areas in the south; its intensity is not related to nose shape or hair texture. Dark skin may be associated with frizzy or kinky hair or curly or wavy or straight hair, all of which are found among different indigenous peoples in tropical regions. These facts render any attempt to establish lines of division among biological populations both arbitrary and subjective.

Historical research has shown that the idea of "race" has always carried more meanings than mere physical differences; indeed, physical variations in the human species have no meaning except the social ones that humans put on them. Today scholars in many fields argue that "race" as it is understood in the United States of America was a social mechanism invented during the 18th century to refer to those populations brought together in colonial America: the English and other European settlers, the conquered Indian (Native American) peoples, and those peoples of Africa brought in to provide slave labor.

From its inception, this modern concept of "race" was modeled after an ancient theorem of the Great Chain of Being, which posited natural categories on a hierarchy established by God or nature. Thus "race" was a mode of classification linked specifically to peoples in the colonial situation. It subsumed a growing ideology of inequality devised to rationalize European attitudes and treatment of the conquered and enslaved peoples. Proponents of slavery in particular during the 19th century used "race" to justify the retention of slavery. The ideology magnified the differences among Europeans, Africans, and Indians (Native Americans), established a rigid hierarchy of socially exclusive categories, underscored and bolstered unequal rank and status differences, and provided the rationalization that the inequality was natural or God-given. The different physical traits of African-Americans and Indians (Native Americans) became markers or symbols of their status differences.

As they were constructing US society, leaders among European-Americans fabricated the cultural/behavioral characteristics associated with each "race," linking superior traits with Europeans and negative and inferior ones to blacks and Indians (Native Americans). Numerous arbitrary and fictitious beliefs about the different peoples were institutionalized and deeply embedded in American thought. . . .

Ultimately "race" as an ideology about human differences was subsequently spread to other areas of the world. It became a strategy for dividing, ranking, and controlling colonized people used by colonial powers everywhere. But it was not limited to the colonial situation. In the latter part of the 19th century it was employed by Europeans to rank one another and to justify social, economic, and political inequalities among their peoples. During World War II, the Nazis under Adolf Hitler enjoined the expanded ideology of "race" and "racial" differences and took them to a logical end: the extermination of 11 million people of "inferior races" (e.g., Jews, Gypsies, Africans, homosexuals, and so forth) and other unspeakable brutalities of the Holocaust.

"Race" thus evolved as a world view, a body of prejudgments that distorts our ideas about human differences and group behavior. Racial beliefs constitute myths about the diversity in the human species and about the abilities and behavior of people homogenized into " racial"

categories. The myths fused behavior and physical features together in the public mind, impeding our comprehension of both biological variations and cultural behavior, implying that both are genetically determined. Racial myths bear no relationship to the reality of human capabilities or behavior. . . .

We now understand that human cultural behavior is learned, conditioned into infants beginning at birth, and always subject to modification. No human is born with a built-in culture or language. Our temperaments, dispositions, and personalities, regardless of genetic propensities, are developed within sets of meanings and values that we call "culture." . . .

It is a basic tenet of anthropological knowledge that all normal human beings have the capacity to learn any cultural behavior. The American experience with immigrants from hundreds of different language and cultural backgrounds who have acquired some version of American culture traits and behavior is the clearest evidence of this fact. Moreover, people of all physical variations have learned different cultural behaviors and continue to do so as modern transportation moves millions of immigrants around the world.

How people have been accepted and treated within the context of a given society or culture has a direct impact on how they perform in that society. The "racial" world view was invented to assign some groups to perpetual low status, while others were permitted access to privilege, power, and wealth. The tragedy in the United States has been that the policies and practices stemming from this world view succeeded all too well in constructing

continued

Anthropology Today *continued*

unequal populations among Europeans, Native Americans, and peoples of African descent. Given what we know about the capacity of normal humans to achieve and function within any culture, we conclude that present-day inequalities between so-called "racial" groups are not consequences of their biological inheri-

tance but products of historical and contemporary social, economic, educational, and political circumstances.

Source: From the American Anthropological Association (AAA) Statement on "Race" (May 1998). http://www.aaanet.org/stmts/racepp. htm. Reprinted with permission of the American Anthropological Association.

reflected in schools, the media, and public interaction. Under Soviet rule, ethnic minorities had very limited self-rule in republics and regions controlled by Moscow. All the republics and their peoples were to be united by the oneness of "socialist internationalism." One common technique in cultural colonialism is to flood ethnic areas with members of the dominant ethnic group. Thus, in the former Soviet Union, ethnic Russian colonists were sent to many areas, to diminish the cohesion and clout of the local people.

The Commonwealth of Independent States (CIS), founded in 1991 and headquartered in Minsk, Belarus, is what remains of the once-powerful Soviet Union (see Yurchak 2005). In Russia and other formerly Soviet nations, ethnic groups (nationalities) have sought to forge separate and viable nation-states based on cultural boundaries. This celebration of ethnic autonomy is part of an ethnic florescence that—as surely as globalization and transnationalism—is a trend of the late 20th and early 21st centuries.

Summary

1. An ethnic group consists of members of a particular culture in a nation or region that contains others. Ethnicity is based on actual, perceived, or assumed cultural similarities (among members of the same ethnic group) and differences (between that group and others). Ethnic distinctions can be based on language, religion, history, geography, kinship, or race. A race is an ethnic group assumed to have a biological basis. Usually, race and ethnicity are ascribed statuses; people are born members of a group and remain so all their lives.

2. Because of a range of problems involved in classifying humans into racial categories, the study of human biological diversity now focuses on specific differences and attempts to explain them. *Homo sapiens* has not evolved subspecies or distinct races. Biological similarities between human groups may reflect—rather than common ancestry—similar but independent adaptations to similar natural selective forces, such as degrees of ultraviolet radiation from the sun in the case of skin color.

3. Human races are cultural rather than biological categories. Such races derive from contrasts perceived in particular societies, rather than from scientific classifications based on common genes. In the United States, racial labels such as "White" and "Black" designate socially constructed categories defined by American culture. American racial classification, governed by the rule of hypodescent, is based neither on phenotype nor on genes. Children of mixed unions, no matter what their appearance, are classified with the minority group parent.

4. Racial attitudes in Japan illustrate intrinsic racism—the belief that a perceived racial difference is a sufficient reason to value one person less than another. The valued group is majority (pure) Japanese, who are believed to share the same blood. Majority Japanese define themselves by opposition to others, such as Koreans and burakumin. These may be minority groups in Japan or outsiders—anyone who is "not us."

5. Such exclusionary racial systems are not inevitable. Although Brazil shares a history of slavery with the United States, it lacks the hypodescent rule. Brazilian racial identity is more of an achieved status. It can change during someone's lifetime, reflecting phenotypical changes.

6. The term *nation* once was synonymous with *ethnic group*. Now *nation* has come to mean a state—a centrally organized political unit. Because of migration, conquest, and colonialism, most nation-states are not ethnically homogeneous. Ethnic groups that seek autonomous political status (their own country) are nationalities. Political upheavals, wars, and migrations have divided many imagined national communities.

7. Assimilation describes the process of change an ethnic group may experience when it moves to a country where another culture dominates. By assimilating, the minority adopts the patterns and norms of its host culture. Assimilation isn't inevitable, and there can be ethnic harmony without it. A plural society combines ethnic contrasts and economic interdependence between ethnic groups. The view of cultural diversity in a nation-state as good and desirable is multiculturalism. A multicultural society socializes individuals not only into the dominant (national) culture but also into an ethnic one.

8. In the United States, ethnic/racial diversity is increasing, especially among the young. Simultaneously, the country is aging, and most of the senior population is White. These trends are associated with contrasting attitudes, priorities, and political leanings of younger and older Americans. Minorities now constitute over 35 percent of the total U.S. population and 44 percent of children under 18.

9. Ethnicity can be expressed either in peaceful multiculturalism or in discrimination or violent confrontation. Ethnic conflict often arises in reaction to prejudice (attitudes and judgments) or discrimination (action). The most extreme form of ethnic discrimination is genocide, the deliberate elimination of a group through mass murder. A dominant group may try to destroy certain ethnic practices (ethnocide), or to force ethnic group members to adopt the dominant culture (forced assimilation). A policy of ethnic expulsion may create refugees. Cultural colonialism is internal domination—by one group and its culture or ideology over others.

Key Terms

assimilation, *228*
clines, *211*
cultural
  colonialism, *234*
descent, *220*
discrimination, *233*
ethnic group, *208*
ethnicity, *209*
ethnocide, *234*
genocide, *234*
hypodescent, *220*

majority
  groups, *210*
minority
  groups, *210*
multiculturalism,
  229
nation, *227*
nation-state, *227*
nationalities, *228*
natural
  selection, *215*

phenotype, *212*
plural society, *229*
prejudice, *233*
race, *218*
racial
  classification, *211*
racism, *218*
refugees, *234*
stereotypes, *233*

Chapter 11

Applying Anthropology

As we learned in Chapter 1, applied anthropology is the use of anthropological data, perspectives, theory, and methods to identify, assess, and solve contemporary problems (see Ervin 2005; Wasson, Butler, and Copeland-Carson 2012; Nolan 2013). Applied anthropologists help make anthropology relevant and useful to the world beyond anthropology. Medical anthropologists, for instance, have worked as cultural interpreters in public health programs, helping such programs fit into local culture. Development anthropologists work for or with international development agencies, such as the World Bank and the U.S. Agency for International Development (USAID). The findings of garbology, the archaeological study of waste, are relevant to the Environmental Protection Agency, the paper industry, and packaging and trade associations. Archaeology also is applied in cultural resource management and historic preservation. Biological anthropologists apply their expertise in programs aimed at public health, nutrition, genetic counseling, aging, substance abuse, and mental health. Forensic anthropologists work with the police, medical examiners, the courts, and international organizations to identify victims of crimes, accidents, wars, and terrorism. Linguistic anthropologists study physician–patient communication and show how speech differences influence classroom learning. Most applied anthropologists seek humane and effective ways of helping local people.

The ethnographic method is a particularly valuable tool in applying anthropology. Remember that ethnographers study societies firsthand, living with, observing, and learning from ordinary people. Nonanthropologists working in social-change programs often are content to converse with officials, read reports, and copy statistics. However, the applied anthropologist's likely early request is some variant of "take me to the local people." Anthropologists know that people must play an active role in the changes that affect them and that "the people" have information that "the experts" lack.

Anthropological *theory,* the body of findings and generalizations of the four sub-fields, also guides applied anthropology. Just as theory aids practice, application fuels theory (see Rylko-Bauer, Singer, and Van Willigen 2006). As we compare social-change programs, our understanding of cause and effect increases. We add new generalizations about culture change to those discovered in traditional and ancient cultures.

The Role of the Applied Anthropologist

Early Applications

Application was a central concern of early anthropology in Great Britain (in the context of colonialism) and the United States (in the context of Native American policy). Before turning to the new, we should consider some problems with the old. For the British empire, specifically its African colonies, Bronislaw Malinowski (1929) proposed that "practical anthropology" (his term for colonial applied anthropology) should focus on Westernization, the diffusion of European culture into tribal societies. Malinowski did not question the legitimacy of colonialism or the anthropologist's role in making it work. He saw nothing wrong with aiding colonial regimes by studying land tenure and land use, to recommend how much of their land local people should be allowed to keep and how much Europeans should be permitted to take. Malinowski's views exemplify a historical association between early anthropology, particularly in Europe (especially England, France, and Portugal), and colonialism (see also Duffield and Hewitt, eds. 2009; Lange 2009; Rylko-Bauer, Singer, and Van Willigen 2006).

During World War II, American anthropologists studied Japanese and German "culture at a distance" in an attempt to predict the behavior of the enemies of the United States. After that war, applied anthropologists worked on Pacific islands to promote local-level cooperation with American policies in various trust territories. The American Anthropological Association (AAA) has raised strong ethical objections to applying anthropology in war zones and for military intelligence. Such concerns were voiced during the Vietnam War. More recently they have emerged in criticisms of anthropologists' participation in the Human Terrains System (HTS) project in Iraq and Afghanistan, as discussed in Chapter 3. Anthropological research should not harm the people anthropologists study.

Academic and Applied Anthropology

After World War II, the baby boom, which began in 1946 and peaked in 1957, fueled a tremendous expansion of the American educational system. New junior, community, and four-year colleges opened, and anthropology became a standard part of the college curriculum. During the 1950s and 1960s, most American anthropologists were college professors, although some still worked in agencies and museums.

The growth of academic anthropology continued through the early 1970s. Especially during the Vietnam War, undergraduates flocked to anthropology classes to learn about other cultures. Students were especially interested in Southeast Asia, whose indigenous societies were being disrupted by war. Many anthropologists protested the superpowers' apparent disregard for non-Western lives, values, customs, and social systems.

Most anthropologists still worked in colleges and museums during the 1970s and 1980s. However, an increasing number of anthropologists were employed by international organizations, governments, businesses, hospitals, and schools. The AAA estimates that nowadays more than half of anthropology PhDs seek nonacademic employment. This shift toward application has benefited the profession. It has forced anthropologists to consider the wider social value and implications of their research.

Applied Anthropology Today

Most contemporary applied anthropologists see their work as radically removed from the colonial enterprise. Modern applied anthropology usually is seen as a helping profession, devoted to assisting local people, as anthropologists speak up for the disenfranchised. However, applied anthropologists also have clients that are neither poor nor powerless. An applied anthropologist working as a market researcher for a business is concerned with discovering how to expand profits for his or her employer or client. Such goals can pose ethical dilemmas, as can work in cultural resource management (CRM). The CRM anthropologist helps decide how to preserve significant remains when sites are threatened by development or public works. A CRM firm typically is hired by someone seeking to build a road or a factory. That client may have a strong interest in an outcome in which no sites are found that need protecting. Even if they don't work for colonial powers or the military, applied anthropologists still face ethical questions: To whom does the researcher owe loyalty? How does one criticize programs in which one has participated (see Escobar 1991, 1994)? Anthropology's professional organizations have addressed such questions by establishing codes of ethics and ethics committees. As Karen Tice (1997) notes, attention to ethical issues has become paramount in the teaching of applied anthropology.

Anthropologists are experts on human problems and social change, who study, understand, and respect diverse cultural values. Given this background, anthropologists are highly qualified to suggest, plan, and implement social policy affecting people. Proper roles for applied anthropologists include (1) identifying needs for change that local people perceive, (2) working with those people to design culturally appropriate and socially sensitive change, and (3) protecting local people from harmful policies and projects that may threaten them.

Development Anthropology

Development anthropology is the branch of applied anthropology that focuses on social issues in, and the cultural dimension of, economic development. Development anthropologists don't just carry out development policies planned by others; they also plan and guide policy. (For more detailed discussions of issues in development anthropology, see Edelman and Haugerud 2005; Escobar 2012; Ferguson 1995; Nolan 2002.)

Still, ethical dilemmas often confront development anthropologists (Escobar 1991, 2012). Foreign aid, including funds for economic development, usually doesn't go where need and suffering are greatest. Rather, such funds are spent on political, economic, and strategic priorities as international donors, political leaders, and powerful interest groups perceive them. Planners' interests don't always coincide with the best interests of the local people. Although the stated aim of most development projects is to enhance the quality of life, living standards often decline in the affected area.

Equity

A commonly stated goal of recent development policy is to promote equity. **Increased equity** means reduced poverty and a more even distribution of wealth. However, if projects are to increase equity, they must have the support of reform-minded governments. Wealthy and powerful people typically resist projects that threaten their vested interests.

Some development projects actually widen wealth disparities; that is, they have a negative equity impact. An initial uneven distribution of resources often becomes the basis for even greater inequality after the project. In Bahia, Brazil (Kottak 2006), for example, sailboat owners (but not nonowners) got loans to buy motors for their boats. To repay the loans, the owners increased the percentage of the catch they took from the men who fished in their boats. Over the years, they used their rising profits to buy larger and more expensive boats. The result was stratification—the creation of a group of wealthy people within a formerly more egalitarian community. New boats became so expensive that ambitious young men, who once would have sought careers in fishing, no longer could afford to buy a boat of their own. They sought wage labor on land instead. To avoid such results, credit-granting agencies must seek out and invest in enterprising young fishers, rather than giving loans only to owners and established businesspeople.

Strategies for Innovation

Development anthropologists should work closely with local people to assess, and help them realize, their own wishes and needs for change. Funding development projects in area A that are inappropriate there but needed in area B, or that are unnecessary anywhere, is a waste of money when so many true local needs cry out for a solution. Development anthropology can help sort out the needs of the As and Bs and fit projects accordingly. Projects that put people first by consulting with them and responding to their expressed needs must be identified (Cernea, ed. 1991). Thereafter, development anthropologists can work to ensure socially compatible ways of implementing a good project.

In a comparative study of 68 rural development projects from around the world, I found the culturally compatible economic development projects to be twice as successful financially as the incompatible ones (Kottak 1990*b*, 1991). This finding suggests that using anthropological expertise in planning, to ensure cultural compatibility, is cost effective. To maximize social and economic benefits, projects must (1) be culturally compatible, (2) respond to locally perceived needs, (3) involve men and women in planning

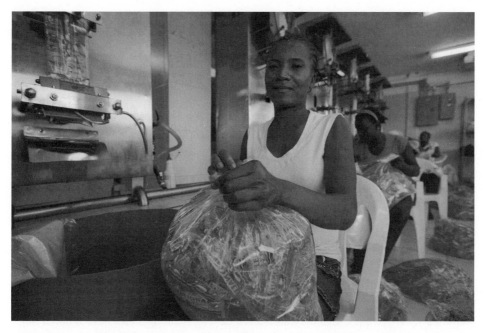

Shown here, a worker at Eau Nationale, a Haitian bottled water plant. Production at this plant, which produces clean water meeting international standards, slowed down after a massive earthquake hit Haiti in 2010. In an unforeseen and unfortunate consequence of international aid, the bottled water imported by NGOs reduced demand for the local product, threatening the survival of Eau Nationale. What's an NGO?

and carrying out the changes that affect them, (4) harness traditional organizations, and (5) be flexible.

Consider a recent example of a development initiative that failed because it ignored local culture. Working in Afghanistan after the fall of the Taliban, ethnographer Noah Coburn (2011) studied Istalif, a village of potters. During his fieldwork there Coburn discovered that an NGO had spent $20,000 on an electric kiln that could have greatly enhanced the productivity of local potters. The only problem was that the kiln was donated to a women's center that men could not enter. The misguided donors ignored the fact that Istalif's men did the work—pot-making and firing—that a kiln could facilitate. Women's role in pottery came later—in glazing and decorating.

Overinnovation

In my comparative study, the compatible and successful projects avoided the fallacy of **overinnovation** (too much change). People usually are willing to change just enough to maintain, or slightly improve on, what they already have. Motives for modifying behavior come from the traditional culture and the small concerns of ordinary life. Peasants' values are not such abstract ones as "learning a better way," "progressing," "increasing technical know-how," "improving efficiency," or "adopting modern techniques."

Their objectives are down-to-earth and specific—e.g., to enhance the productivity of their crops, amass resources for a ceremony, get a child through school, or have enough cash to pay the tax bill. The goals and values of subsistence producers differ from those of people who work for cash, just as they differ from those of development planners. Different value systems must be considered during planning.

Development projects that fail usually are either (or both) economically and culturally incompatible. For example, one South Asian project promoted the cultivation of onions and peppers, expecting this practice to fit into a preexisting labor-intensive system of rice-growing. Cultivation of these cash crops wasn't traditional in the area, and the labor peaks for pepper and onion production coincided with those for rice, to which the farmers gave priority.

Another naive and incompatible project was an overinnovative scheme in Ethiopia. Its major fallacy was to try to convert free-ranging nomadic herders into farm workers. Outsiders—commercial farmers—were to get much of the herders' territory, to convert to commercial farmland—plantations. The pastoralists were expected to settle down and start working on those plantations. The planners naively expected the herders to give up a generations-old way of life to work three times harder growing rice and picking cotton for bosses.

Underdifferentiation

The fallacy of **underdifferentiation** is planners' tendency to view "the less-developed countries" as more alike than they are. Often development agencies have ignored huge cultural contrasts (e.g., between Brazil and Burundi) and adopted a uniform approach to deal with very different sets of people. Planners also have tried to impose incompatible property concepts and social units.

Ethnocentrically, planners often assume that the individual and the nuclear family are key social units among the intended beneficiaries. This was true of one project in West Africa, where the extended family was the basic social unit. The project succeeded despite its faulty social design because the participants used their traditional extended family networks to attract additional settlers. Eventually, twice as many people as planned benefited as extended family members flocked to the project area. Here, settlers used the principles of their traditional society to modify the project design that had been imposed on them.

Another dubious social model that has been common in development planning is the cooperative. In the comparative study of rural development projects, new cooperatives fared badly. Cooperatives succeeded only when they harnessed preexisting local-level communal institutions. This is a corollary of a more general rule: *Participants' groups are most effective when they are based on traditional social organization or on a socioeconomic similarity among members.*

An alternative to such foreign models is needed: greater use of indigenous social models in economic development. These are traditional social units, such as the clans, lineages, and other extended kin groups of Africa, Oceania, and many other nations, with their communally held estates and resources. *The most humane and productive strategy for change is to base the social design for innovation on traditional social forms in each target area.*

Indigenous Models

Many governments are not genuinely, or realistically, committed to improving the lives of their citizens. Interference by major powers also has kept governments from enacting needed reforms. Occasionally, however, a government does act as an agent of and for its people. One historic example is Madagascar, whose people, the Malagasy, were organized into descent groups prior to indigenous state formation in the 18th century. The Merina, creators of the major precolonial state of Madagascar, wove descent groups into its structure, making members of important groups advisers to rulers—thus giving them authority in government. The Merina state collected taxes and organized labor for public works projects. In return, it redistributed resources to peasants in need. It also granted them some protection against war and slave raids and allowed them to cultivate their rice fields in peace. The government maintained the water works for rice cultivation. It opened to ambitious peasant boys the chance of becoming state bureaucrats, through hard work and study.

Throughout the history of the Merina state—and continuing to some extent in post-colonial Madagascar—there have been strong relationships between the individual, the descent group, and the state. Local Malagasy communities, where residence is based on descent, are more cohesive and homogeneous than are communities in Latin America or North America. Madagascar gained political independence from France in 1960. Its new government had an economic development policy aimed at increasing the ability of the Malagasy to feed themselves. Government policy emphasized increased production of rice, a subsistence crop, rather than cash crops. Furthermore, local communities, with their traditional cooperative patterns and solidarity based on kinship and descent, were treated as partners in, not obstacles to, the development process.

In a sense, the descent group is preadapted to equitable national development. In Madagascar, descent groups pooled their resources to educate their most ambitious members. Once educated, those men and women gained economically secure positions in the nation. They then shared the advantages of their new positions with their kin. For example, they gave room and board to rural cousins attending school and helped them find jobs.

This Madagascar example suggests that when government officials are of "the people" (rather than the elites) and have strong personal ties to common folk, they are more likely to promote democratic reform. In Latin America, by contrast, leaders and followers too often have been from different social classes, with no connections based on kinship, descent, marriage, or common background. When elites rule, elites usually prosper. Recently, however, Latin America has elected some nonelite leaders. Brazil's lower class (indeed the entire nation) benefited socioeconomically when one of its own was elected president. Luis Inácio da Silva, or Lula, a former factory worker with only a fourth-grade education, served two terms (ending in 2011) as one of the Western Hemisphere's most popular leaders.

Realistic development policies promote change but not overinnovation. Many changes are possible if the aim is to preserve things while making them work better. Successful economic development projects respect, or at least don't attack, local cultural patterns. Effective development draws on indigenous cultural practices and social structures. As nations become more tied to the world capitalist economy, it is not inevitable that indigenous forms of social organization will break down into nuclear family organization, impersonality, and alienation. Descent groups, with their traditional communalism and solidarity, have important roles to play in economic development.

Anthropology and Education

Attention to culture also is fundamental to **anthropology and education,** a field whose research extends from classrooms into homes, neighborhoods, and communities (see Anderson-Levitt 2012; Levinson and Pollock, eds. 2011; Spindler and Hammond 2006). In classrooms, anthropologists have observed interactions among teachers, students, parents, and visitors. Jules Henry's classic account of the American elementary school classroom (1955) shows how students learn to conform to and compete with their peers. Anthropologists view children as total, cultural creatures whose enculturation and attitudes toward education belong to a context that includes family and peers (see also Kontopodis, Wulf, and Fichtner 2011).

Sociolinguists and cultural anthropologists have worked side by side in education research. In one classic study of Puerto Rican seventh-graders in the urban Midwest, anthropologists uncovered some key misconceptions held by teachers (Hill-Burnett 1978). The teachers mistakenly had assumed that Puerto Rican parents valued education less than did non-Hispanics, but in-depth interviews revealed that the Puerto Rican parents valued it more. The anthropologists also identified certain practices that were preventing Hispanics from being adequately educated. For example, the teachers' union and the board of education had agreed to teach "English as a foreign language." However, they had provided no bilingual teachers to work with Spanish-speaking students. The school was assigning all students (including non-Hispanics) with low reading scores and behavior problems to the English-as-a-foreign-language classroom. This educational disaster brought together in the classroom a teacher who spoke no Spanish, children

Afghan girls attend a lesson at the secondary school in Sarkani village, Kunar Province, eastern Afghanistan. What do you see here that differs from classrooms in your country?

who barely spoke English, and a group of English-speaking students with reading and behavior problems. The Spanish speakers were falling behind not just in reading but in all subjects. They could at least have kept up in the other subjects if a Spanish speaker had been teaching them science, social studies, and math until they were ready for English-language instruction in those areas.

Urban Anthropology

For centuries, cities have been influenced by global forces, including world capitalism and colonialism (Smart and Smart 2003). However, the roles of cities in the world system have changed recently because of the time–space compression made possible by modern transportation and communication systems. That is, everything appears closer today because contact and movement are so much easier.

In the context of globalization, the mass media have joined local factors in guiding people's routines, dreams, and aspirations. Although people live in particular places, their imaginations are not locally confined (Appadurai 1996). Media-transmitted images and information help draw people to cities. People migrate partly for economic reasons, but also to be where the action is. Rural Brazilians routinely cite *movimento,* urban activity and excitement, as something to be valued. International migrants tend to settle in large cities, where a lot is going on and where they can feel at home in ethnic enclaves. Consider Canada, which, after Australia, is the country with the highest percentage of foreign-born population. Three-quarters of immigrants to Canada settle in Toronto, Vancouver, or Montreal. By 2031, it is estimated that nearly one-half (46%) of Canadians aged 15 and over will be foreign born or will have at least one foreign-born parent, up from 39% in 2006 (Statistics Canada 2010).

Urban living has increased steadily since the Industrial Revolution. The percentage of the world's population living in cities surpassed 50 percent for the first time in 2008 and is projected to rise to 70 percent by 2050 (Handwerk 2008). Only about 3 percent of people were city dwellers in 1800, compared with 13 percent in 1900, over 40 percent in 1980, and over 50 percent today (see Handwerk 2008; Smart and Smart 2003). The more-developed countries (MDCs) were 76 percent urbanized in 2000, compared with 39 percent for the less-developed countries (LDCs). However, the urbanization growth rate is much faster in the LDCs (Smart and Smart 2003). In Africa and Asia alone, a million people a week migrate to cities (Handwerk 2008). The world had only 16 cities with more than a million people in 1900, versus 314 such cities in 2005 (Butler 2005; Stevens 1992).

One billion people now live in urban slums, mostly without reliable water, sanitation, and public services (Handwerk 2008; Vidal 2003). If current trends continue, urban population increase and the concentration of people in slums will be accompanied by rising rates of crime, along with water, air, and noise pollution. These problems will be most severe in the LDCs.

As industrialization and urbanization spread globally, anthropologists increasingly study these processes and the social problems they create. **Urban anthropology,** which has theoretical (basic research) and applied dimensions, is the cross-cultural and

One-sixth of the Earth's population lives in urban slums. Roçinha (shown here) is a populous shantytown city within the city of Rio de Janeiro, Brazil. How might anthropologists study slums?

ethnographic study of urbanization and life in cities (see Gmelch, Kemper, and Zenner 2010; Pardo and Prato 2012; Smart and Smart 2003; Stevenson 2003). The United States and Canada have become popular arenas for urban anthropological research on topics such as immigration, ethnicity, poverty, class, and urban violence (Vigil 2003, 2010).

Urban versus Rural

An early student of urbanization, the anthropologist Robert Redfield, contrasted rural communities, whose social relations are on a face-to-face basis, with cities, where impersonality reigns. Redfield (1941) proposed that urbanization be studied along a rural–urban continuum. He described differences in values and social relations in four sites that spanned such a continuum. In Mexico's Yucatán peninsula, Redfield compared an isolated Maya-speaking Indian community, a rural peasant village, a small provincial city, and a large capital. Several studies in Africa (Little 1971) and Asia were influenced by Redfield's view that cities are centers through which cultural innovations spread to rural and tribal areas.

In any nation, urban and rural represent different social systems. However, cultural diffusion or borrowing occurs as people, products, images, and messages move from one to the other. Migrants bring rural practices and beliefs to cities and take urban patterns back home. The experiences and social forms of the rural area affect adaptation to city life. City folk also develop new institutions to meet specific urban needs.

An applied anthropology approach to urban planning starts by identifying key social groups in specific urban contexts—avoiding the fallacy of underdifferentiation. After identifying those groups, the anthropologist might elicit their wishes for change, convey those needs to funding agencies, and work with agencies and local people to realize those goals. In Africa relevant groups might include ethnic associations, occupational groups, social clubs, religious groups, and burial societies. Through membership in such groups, urban Africans maintain wide networks of personal contacts and support. The groups provide cash support and lodging for their rural relatives. Sometimes such groups think of themselves as a gigantic kin group that includes urban and rural members. Members may call one another "brother" and "sister." As in an extended family, richer members help their poorer relatives. A member's improper behavior, however, can lead to expulsion—an unhappy fate for a migrant in a large, ethnically heterogeneous city.

One role for the urban applied anthropologist is to help people deal with urban institutions, such as legal and social services, with which recent migrants may be unfamiliar. In certain North American cities, as in Africa, ethnic associations are relevant urban groups. One example comes from Los Angeles, which has the largest Samoan immigrant community in the United States (over 50,000 people). Samoans in Los Angeles draw on their traditional system of *matai* (*matai* means "chief"; the matai system now refers to respect for elders) to deal with modern urban problems. One example: When a White police officer killed two unarmed Samoan brothers, and the judge dismissed charges against the officer, local leaders used the matai system to calm angry youths. (Young Samoans have formed gangs, like other ethnic groups in the Los Angeles area.) Clan leaders and elders organized a well-attended community meeting, in which they urged young members to be patient. The Samoans then used the American judicial system. They brought a civil case against the officer in question and pressed the U.S. Justice Department to initiate a civil rights case in the matter (Mydans 1992*b*). Not all conflicts involving gangs and law enforcement end so peacefully.

James Vigil (2003, 2010) examines gang violence in the context of large-scale immigrant adaptation to American cities. He notes that before the 1970s most gangs were located in White ethnic enclaves in eastern and midwestern cities. Back then, gang incidents typically were brawls involving fists, sticks, and knives. Today, gangs more often are composed of non-White ethnic groups, and handguns have replaced less lethal weapons. Gangs still consist mostly of male adolescents who have grown up together, usually in a low-income neighborhood, where it's estimated that about 10 percent of young men join gangs (Vigil 2003, 2010).

The populations that include most of today's gang members settled originally in poor urban areas. On the East Coast these usually were run-down neighborhoods where a criminal lifestyle already was present. Around Los Angeles, urban migrants created squatterlike settlements in previously empty spaces. Immigrants tend to reside in neighborhoods apart from middle-class people, thus limiting their opportunities for integration (Vigil 2003). In addition, many industries and jobs have moved from American cities to distant suburbs and foreign nations. Given their limited access to entry-level jobs, many urban minority youth pursue informal and illegal economic arrangements, of which drug trafficking in particular has heightened gang violence (Singer 2008; Vigil

2003, 2010). How might an applied anthropologist approach the problem of urban violence? Which groups would have to be involved in the study (see Vigil 2010)?

Medical Anthropology

Medical anthropology is both academic and applied and includes anthropologists from all four subfields (see Brown and Barrett 2010; Dressler, Oths, and Gravlee 2005; Joralemon 2010; Singer 2012; Trevathan, Smith, and McKenna, eds. 2008; Wiley and Allen 2012). **Medical anthropology** is a biocultural field that studies variation in health care systems, including disease, illness, health standards, and disease theories. Medical anthropologists examine such questions as which diseases and health conditions affect particular populations (and why) and how illness is socially constructed, diagnosed, managed, and treated in various societies.

Disease refers to a scientifically identified health threat caused genetically or by a bacterium, virus, fungus, parasite, or other pathogen. **Illness** is a condition of poor health perceived or felt by an individual (Inhorn and Brown 1990). Perceptions of good and bad health are culturally constructed. Various cultures and ethnic groups recognize different illnesses, symptoms, and causes and have developed different health care systems and treatment strategies (Womack 2010).

The incidence and severity of *disease* vary as well (see Baer, Singer, and Susser 2013). Group differences are evident in the United States. One study examined health status indicators for groups named in the U.S. census: non-Hispanic Whites, African Americans, Hispanics, American Indians, and Asians or Pacific Islanders (Keppel, Pearch, and Wagener 2002). African Americans' rates for six measures (total mortality, heart disease, lung cancer, breast cancer, stroke, and homicide) exceeded those of the other groups by a factor ranging from 2.5 to almost 10. Whites had the highest suicide rates and Native Americans the highest rates for motor vehicle accidents. Asian Americans lived longest (see Dressler, Oths, and Gravlee 2005).

Magdalena Hurtado and colleagues (2005) note that the life expectancy at birth for indigenous South Americans was at least 20 years shorter than that of other South Americans. The life expectancy of indigenous peoples in Brazil and Venezuela was lower than that in Sierra Leone, which had the world's lowest national life expectancy (Hurtado et al. 2005). What can applied anthropologists do to help improve health conditions among indigenous peoples? Hurtado and colleagues (2005) suggest three steps: (1) Identify the most pressing health problems; (2) gather information on possible solutions; and (3) implement solutions in partnership with the agencies that are in charge of public health programs for indigenous populations.

In many areas, the world system and colonialism worsened the health of indigenous peoples by spreading diseases, warfare, servitude, and other stressors. Traditionally and in ancient times, hunter-gatherers, because of their small numbers, mobility, and relative isolation from other groups, lacked most of the epidemic infectious diseases that affect agrarian and urban societies (Cohen and Armelagos, eds. 1984; Inhorn and Brown 1990). Epidemic diseases such as cholera, typhoid, and bubonic plague thrive in dense populations, and thus among farmers and city dwellers. The spread of malaria has been linked to population growth and deforestation associated with food production.

Certain diseases, and physical conditions such as obesity, have spread with economic development and globalization (Baer, Singer, and Susser 2013; Inhorn and Wentzell 2012; Ulijaszek and Lofink 2006). Schistosomiasis, or bilharzia (liver flukes), is probably the fastest-spreading and most dangerous parasitic infection now known. It is propagated by snails that live in ponds, lakes, and waterways, usually ones created by irrigation projects. The applied anthropology approach to reducing such diseases is to see if local people perceive a connection between the vector (e.g., snails in the water) and the disease. If not, such information may be provided by enlisting active local groups, schools, and the media.

The highest global rates of HIV infection and AIDS-related deaths are in Africa, especially southern Africa. As it kills productive adults, AIDS leaves behind dependent children and seniors (Baro and Deubel 2006). In southern and eastern Africa, AIDS and other sexually transmitted diseases (STDs) have spread along highways, via encounters between truckers and prostitutes. STDs also are spread through prostitution as young men from rural areas seek wage work in cities, labor camps, and mines. When the men return home, they infect their wives. Cities also are prime sites of STD transmission in Europe, Asia, and North and South America. Cultural factors also affect the spread of HIV, which is less likely to be transmitted when men are circumcised.

The kinds of and incidence of disease vary among societies, and cultures perceive and treat illness differently. Health standards are cultural constructions that vary in time and space (Martin 1992). Still, all societies have what George Foster and Barbara Anderson call "disease-theory systems" to identify, classify, and explain illness. Foster and Anderson (1978) identified three basic theories about the causes of illness: personalistic, naturalistic, and emotionalistic. *Personalistic* disease theories blame illness on agents, such as sorcerers, witches, ghosts, or ancestral spirits.

Naturalistic disease theories explain illness in impersonal terms. One example is Western medicine, or biomedicine, which aims to link illness to scientifically demonstrated agents that bear no personal malice toward their victims (see Lupton 2012). Thus, Western medicine attributes illness to organisms (e.g., bacteria, viruses, fungi, or parasites), accidents, toxic materials, or genes. Other naturalistic systems blame poor health on unbalanced body fluids. Many Latin cultures classify food, drink, and environmental conditions as "hot" or "cold." People believe their health suffers when they eat or drink hot or cold substances together or under inappropriate conditions. For example, one shouldn't drink something cold after a hot bath or eat a pineapple (a "cold" fruit) when one is menstruating (a "hot" condition).

Emotionalistic disease theories assume that emotional experiences cause illness. For example, Latin Americans may develop *susto,* an illness caused by anxiety or fright (Bolton 1981; Finkler 1985). Its symptoms (lethargy, vagueness, distraction) are similar to those of "soul loss," a diagnosis of similar symptoms made by people in Madagascar. Modern psychoanalysis also focuses on the role of the emotions in physical and psychological well-being.

All societies have **health care systems** consisting of beliefs, customs, specialists, and techniques aimed at ensuring health and diagnosing and curing illness. A society's illness-causation theory is important for treatment. When illness has a personalistic cause, shamans may be effective curers. They draw on varied techniques (occult and practical) that are part of their special expertise. A shaman may cure soul loss by enticing the spirit back into the body. Shamans may ease difficult childbirths by asking spirits to travel up the birth canal to guide the baby out (Lévi-Strauss 1967). A shaman may cure a cough by counteracting a curse or removing a substance introduced by a sorcerer.

If there is a "world's oldest profession" besides hunter and gatherer, it is curer, often a shaman. The curer's role has some universal features (Foster and Anderson 1978). Thus, a **curer** emerges through a culturally defined process of selection (e.g., parental prodding, inheritance of the role, visions, dream instructions) and training (apprentice shamanship, medical school). Eventually, the curer is certified by older practitioners and acquires a professional image. Patients believe in the skills of the curer, whom they consult and compensate.

We should not lose sight, ethnocentrically, of the difference between **scientific medicine** and Western medicine per se. To be sure, there have been scientific advances in technology, genomics, molecular biology, pathology, surgery, diagnostics, and applications. However, many Western medical procedures have little justification in science, logic, or fact. Overprescription of drugs, unnecessary surgery, and the impersonality and inequality of the physician–patient relationship are questionable features of Western medical systems (see Briggs 2005 for linguistic aspects of this inequality). Also, overuse of antibiotics seems to be triggering an explosion of resistant microorganisms, which may pose a long-term global public health hazard.

Still, biomedicine surpasses tribal treatment in many ways. Although medicines such as quinine, coca, opium, ephedrine, and rauwolfia were discovered in nonindustrial societies, thousands of effective drugs are available today to treat myriad diseases. Today's surgical procedures are much safer and more effective than those of traditional societies.

But industrialization and globalization have spawned their own health problems. Modern stressors include uneven nutrition, dangerous machinery, impersonal work, isolation, poverty, homelessness, substance abuse, and noise, air, and water pollution (see McElroy and Townsend 2009). Health problems in industrial nations are caused as much by economic, social, political, and cultural factors as by pathogens. In modern North America, for example, poverty contributes to many illnesses, including arthritis, heart conditions, back problems, and hearing and vision impairment. Poverty also is a factor in the differential spread of infectious diseases.

In the United States and other developed countries, good health has become something of an ethical imperative (Foucault 1990). Individuals are expected to shape themselves in accordance with new medical knowledge. Those who do so acquire the status of *sanitary citizens*—people with proper, modern understanding of the body, health, and illness. Such citizens practice hygiene and look to health care professionals when they are sick. People who act differently (e.g., smokers, overeaters, those who avoid doctors) are blamed for their own health problems (Briggs 2005; Foucault 1990).

Even getting an epidemic disease such as cholera may be interpreted today as a moral failure. It's assumed that people who act rationally can avoid "preventable" diseases. Individuals are expected to follow scientifically based imperatives (e.g., "boil water," "don't smoke"). People can become objects of avoidance and discrimination simply by belonging to a group seen as having a greater risk of disease or poor health (e.g., gay men, smokers, veterans) (Briggs 2005).

In Serra Parima, Brazil, a Yanomami Indian is examined at a field hospital. Such hospitals and clinics provide antibiotics, antimalarials, surgery, and preventive medicine.

Health interventions always have to fit into local cultures and be accepted by local people. When Western medicine is introduced, people usually retain many of their old methods while accepting new ones. Native curers may continue to treat certain conditions (spirit possession), while physicians deal with others. When patients get better, the native curer and the physician share the credit.

A more personal treatment of illness that emulates the non-Western curer–patient–community relationship might benefit Western systems. Western medicine tends to draw a rigid line between biomedical and psychological causation. Non-Western theories usually lack this sharp distinction, recognizing that poor health has intertwined physical, emotional, and social causes. The mind–body opposition is part of Western folk taxonomy, not of science (see also Brown and Barrett 2010; Helman 2007; Joralemon 2010; Strathern and Stewart 2010).

Medical anthropology also considers the impact of new scientific and medical techniques on ideas about life, death, and *personhood* (what it means to be a person). For decades, disagreements about personhood—such as when life begins and ends—have been part of political and religious discussions of contraception, abortion, assisted suicide, and euthanasia (mercy killing). More recent additions to such discussions include stem cells, "harvested" embryos, assisted reproduction, genetic screening, cloning, and life-prolonging medical treatments. How long should a human body be kept alive if there is no hope of recovery?

Sharon Kaufman and Lynn Morgan (2005) emphasize the contrast between what they call low-tech and high-tech life events. A desperately poor young mother dies of

AIDS in Africa, while half a world away an American child of privilege is born as a result of a $50,000 in vitro fertilization procedure. Medical anthropologists increasingly are concerned with how the boundaries of life and death are being questioned and negotiated in the 21st century.

Anthropology and Business

For decades anthropologists have used ethnography to understand business settings (Jordan, A., 2003; Jordan, B., 2013). Ethnographic research in an auto factory, for example, may view workers, managers, and executives as different social categories participating in a common system. Each group has characteristic attitudes and behavior patterns. These are transmitted through *microenculturation,* the process by which people learn particular roles within a limited social system. The free-ranging nature of ethnography takes the anthropologist back and forth from worker to executive. Each employee is both an individual with a personal viewpoint and a cultural creature whose perspective is, to some extent, shared with other members of his or her group. Applied anthropologists have acted as "cultural brokers," translating managers' goals or workers' concerns to the other group (see Ferraro and Briody 2013).

Carol Taylor (1987) has stressed the value of an "anthropologist-in-residence" in a large, complex organization, such as a hospital or corporation (see also Briody and

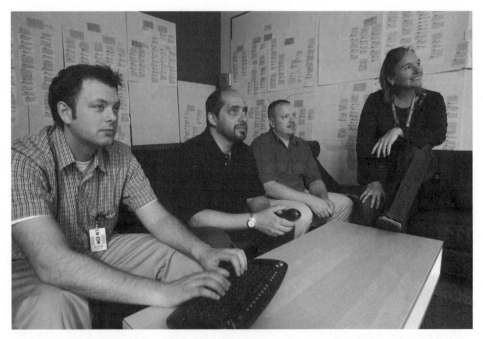

Motorola staff anthropologist Crysta Metcalf (right) and her team sample a new technology at Motorola in Schaumburg, Illinois. This innovation allows people easily to communicate with others while watching the same televised show or event from different locations.

Trotter 2008; Jordan 2013). A free-ranging ethnographer can be a perceptive oddball when information and decisions typically move through a rigid hierarchy. If allowed to observe and converse freely with all types and levels of personnel, the anthropologist may acquire a unique perspective on organizational conditions and problems. Such high-tech companies as Xerox, IBM, and Apple have employed anthropologists in various roles. Closely observing how people actually use computer products, anthropologists have worked with engineers to design products that are more user-friendly.

Key features of anthropology that are of value to business include (1) ethnography and observation as ways of gathering data, (2) a focus on diversity, and (3) cross-cultural expertise. Hallmark Cards has hired anthropologists to observe parties, holidays, and celebrations of ethnic groups to improve its ability to design cards for targeted audiences. Applied anthropologists routinely go into people's homes to see how they actually use products (see Sunderland and Denny 2007 and the "Anthropology Today" at the end of this chapter).

Careers and Anthropology

Many college students find anthropology interesting and consider majoring in it. However, their parents or friends may discourage them by asking, "What kind of job are you going to get with an anthropology degree?" The first step in answering that question is to consider the more general question "What do you do with any college major?" The answer is "Not much, without a good bit of effort, thought, and planning." A survey of graduates of the University of Michigan's literary college showed that few had jobs that were clearly linked to their majors. Most professions, including medicine and law, require advanced degrees. Although many colleges offer bachelor's degrees in engineering, business, accounting, and social work, master's degrees often are needed to get the best jobs in those fields. Anthropologists, too, need an advanced degree, almost always a PhD, to find gainful employment in academic, museum, or applied anthropology.

A broad college education, and even a major in anthropology, can be an excellent foundation for success in many fields. One survey of women executives showed that most had not majored in business but in the social sciences or humanities. Only after graduating from college did they study business, leading to a master's degree in business administration (MBA). Those executives felt that the breadth of their college educations had contributed to their business careers. Anthropology majors go on to medical, law, and business schools and find success in many professions that often have little explicit connection to anthropology.

Anthropology's breadth provides knowledge and an outlook on the world that are useful in many kinds of work. For example, an anthropology major combined with a master's degree in business is excellent preparation for work in international business. Breadth is anthropology's hallmark. Anthropologists study people biologically, culturally, socially, and linguistically, across time and space, in various countries, in simple and complex settings. Most colleges offer anthropology courses that compare cultures, along with others that focus on particular world areas, such as Latin America, Asia, Africa, the Middle East, and Eastern Europe. The knowledge of foreign areas

Anthropology Today *Culturally Appropriate Marketing*

Innovation succeeds best when it is culturally appropriate. This axiom of applied anthropology could guide the international spread not only of development projects but also of businesses, such as fast food. Each time McDonald's or Burger King expands to a new nation, it must devise a culturally appropriate strategy for fitting into the new setting.

McDonald's has been very successful internationally. Almost 70 percent of its current annual revenue comes from sales outside the United States. As the world's most successful restaurant chain, McDonald's has more than 33,000 restaurants in 119 countries. One place where McDonald's has expanded successfully is Brazil, where 100 million middle-class people, most living in densely packed cities, provide a concentrated market for a fast-food chain. Still,

it took McDonald's some time to find the right marketing strategy for Brazil.

In 1980 when I visited Brazil after a seven-year absence, I first noticed, as a manifestation of Brazil's growing participation in the world economy, the appearance of two McDonald's restaurants in Rio de Janeiro. There wasn't much difference between Brazilian and American McDonald's. The restaurants looked alike. The menus were more or less the same, as was the taste of the quarter-pounders. I picked up an artifact, a white paper bag with yellow lettering, exactly like the take-out bags then used in American McDonald's. An advertising device, it carried several messages about how Brazilians could bring McDonald's into their lives. However, it seemed to me that McDonald's Brazilian ad campaign was missing some important points about

A McDonald's restaurant in Kazan, capital of the Republic of Tatarstan, within Russia. Can you see any evidence that McDonald's is adapting to this cultural setting?

how fast food should be marketed in a culture that valued large, leisurely lunches.

The bag proclaimed, "You're going to enjoy the [McDonald's] difference," and listed several "favorite places where you can enjoy McDonald's products." This list confirmed that the marketing people were trying to adapt to Brazilian middle-class culture, but they were making some mistakes. "When you go out in the car with the kids" transferred the uniquely developed North American cultural combination of highways, affordable cars, and suburban living to the very different context of urban Brazil. A similar suggestion was "traveling to the country place." Even Brazilians who owned country places could not find McDonald's, still confined to the cities then, on the road. The ad creator had apparently never attempted to drive up to a fast-food restaurant in a neighborhood with no parking spaces.

Several other suggestions pointed customers toward the beach, where *cariocas* (Rio natives) do spend much of their leisure time. One could eat McDonald's products "after a dip in the ocean," "at a picnic at the beach," or "watching the surfers." These suggestions ignored the Brazilian custom of consuming cold things, such as beer, soft drinks, ice cream, and ham and cheese sandwiches, on the beach. Brazilians don't consider a hot, greasy hamburger proper beach food. They view the sea as "cold" and hamburgers as "hot"; they avoid "hot" foods at the beach.

Also culturally dubious was the suggestion to eat McDonald's hamburgers "lunching at the office." Brazilians prefer their main meal at midday, often eating at a leisurely pace with business associates. Many firms serve ample lunches to their employees. Other workers take advantage of a two-hour lunch break to go home to eat with the spouse and children. Nor did it make sense to suggest that children should eat hamburgers for lunch, since most kids attend school for half-day sessions and have lunch at home. Two other suggestions—"waiting for the bus" and "in the beauty parlor"—did describe common aspects of daily life in a Brazilian city. However, these settings have not proved especially inviting to hamburgers or fish filets.

The homes of Brazilians who can afford McDonald's products often have cooks and maids to do many of the things that fast-food restaurants do in the United States. The suggestion that McDonald's products be eaten "while watching your favorite television program" is culturally appropriate, because Brazilians watch TV a lot. However, Brazil's consuming classes can ask the cook to make a snack when hunger strikes. Indeed, much televiewing occurs during the light dinner served when the husband gets home from the office.

Most appropriate to the Brazilian lifestyle was the suggestion to enjoy McDonald's "on the cook's day off." Throughout Brazil, Sunday is that day. The Sunday pattern for middle-class families who live on the coast is a trip to the beach, liters of beer, a full midday meal around 3:00 P.M., and a light evening snack. McDonald's found its niche in the Sunday evening meal, when families flock to the fast-food restaurant.

McDonald's has expanded rapidly in Brazil, where, as in North America, young appetites have fueled the fast-food explosion. McDonald's outlets now dot urban neighborhoods throughout Brazil, and the cost of hiring in-home help has skyrocketed. Given these changes, Brazilian

continued

Anthropology Today   *continued*

teenagers increasingly use McDonald's for after-school snacks, and whole families have evening meals there. As an anthropologist could have predicted, the fast-food industry has not revolutionized Brazilian food and meal customs. Rather, McDonald's is succeeding because it has adapted to preexisting Brazilian cultural patterns.

Once McDonald's realized that more money could be made by fitting in with, rather than trying to Americanize, Brazilian meal habits, it started aiming its advertising at that goal.

acquired in such courses can be useful in many jobs. Anthropology's comparative outlook and its focus on diverse lifestyles combine to provide an excellent foundation for overseas employment (see Omohundro 2001).

For work in contemporary North America as well, anthropology's focus on culture is increasingly relevant. Every day we hear about cultural differences and about problems whose solutions require a multicultural viewpoint—an ability to recognize and reconcile ethnic differences (see Kottak and Kozaitis 2012). Government, schools, hospitals, and businesses constantly deal with people from different social classes, ethnic groups, and cultural backgrounds. Physicians, attorneys, social workers, police officers, judges, teachers, and students can all do a better job if they understand cultural differences in a nation that is one of the most ethnically diverse in history.

Knowledge of the traditions and beliefs of the groups that make up a modern nation is important in planning and carrying out programs that affect those groups. Experience in planned social change—whether community organization in North America or economic development overseas—shows that a proper social study should be done before a project or policy is implemented. When local people want the change and it fits their lifestyle and traditions, it has a better chance of being successful, beneficial, and cost effective.

People with anthropology backgrounds do well in many fields. Even if one's job has little or nothing to do with anthropology in a formal or obvious sense, a background in anthropology provides a useful orientation when we work with our fellow human beings. For most of us, this means every day of our lives.

Summary

1. Applied anthropology uses anthropological perspectives, theory, methods, and data to identify, assess, and solve problems. Applied anthropologists have a range of employers. Examples are government agencies; development organizations; NGOs; tribal, ethnic, and interest groups; businesses; hospitals; social services; and educational agencies. Applied anthropologists come from all four subfields. Ethnography is one of applied anthropology's most valuable research tools.

2. Development anthropology focuses on social issues in, and the cultural dimension of, economic development. Not all governments seek to increase equality and end poverty. Resistance by elites to reform is typical. At the same time, local people rarely cooperate with projects requiring major and risky changes in their daily lives. Many projects seek to impose inappropriate property notions and incompatible social units on their intended beneficiaries. The best strategy for change is to base the social design for innovation on traditional social forms in each target area.

3. Anthropology and education researchers work in classrooms, homes, and other settings relevant to education and make policy recommendations based on their findings. Both academic and applied anthropologists study migration from rural areas to cities and across national boundaries. North America has become a popular arena for urban anthropological research on migration, ethnicity, poverty, and related topics. Although rural and urban are different social systems, there is cultural diffusion from one to the other.

4. Medical anthropology is a biocultural field that studies variation in health care systems, including disease, illness, health standards, and disease theories. In a given setting, the characteristic diseases reflect diet, population density, economy, and social complexity. Native theories of illness may be personalistic, naturalistic, or emotionalistic. In applying anthropology to business, the key features are (1) ethnography and observation as ways of gathering data, (2) a focus on diversity, and (3) cross-cultural expertise.

5. A broad college education, including anthropology and foreign-area courses, offers an excellent background for many fields. Anthropology's comparative, cross-cultural outlook provides an excellent basis for overseas employment. Even for work in North America, a focus on culture and cultural diversity is valuable. Anthropology majors attend medical, law, and business schools and succeed in many fields, some of which have little explicit connection with anthropology.

Key Terms

anthropology and education, *248*
curer, *254*
development anthropology, *243*
disease, *252*
equity, increased, *244*
health care systems, *253*
illness, *252*
medical anthropology, *252*
overinnovation, *245*
scientific medicine, *254*
under-differentiation, *246*
urban anthropology, *249*

Chapter 12

The World System and Colonialism

Although fieldwork in small communities has been anthropology's hallmark, isolated groups are impossible to find today. Truly isolated human societies probably never have existed. For thousands of years, human groups have been in contact with one another. Local societies always have participated in a larger system, which today has global dimensions. We call it the *modern world system,* by which we mean a world in which nations are economically and politically interdependent.

The World System

A huge increase in international trade during and after the 15th century led to the **capitalist world economy** (Wallerstein 1982, 2004*b*), a single world system committed to production for sale or exchange, with the object of maximizing profits, rather than supplying domestic needs. The world system and the relations among the countries within it are shaped by the capitalist world economy. **Capital** refers to wealth or resources invested in business, with the intent of using the means of production to make a profit.

262

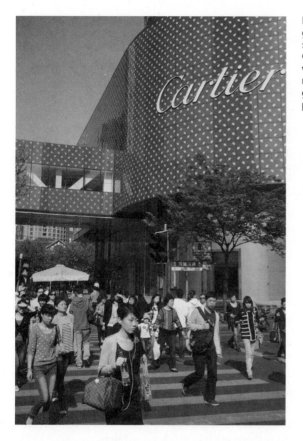

Illustrating the contemporary global spread of capitalism is this scene from central Shanghai, China. In April 2012, pedestrians walk near an upscale shopping mall. What evidence of globalization do you see in this photo?

World-system theory can be traced to the French social historian Fernand Braudel. In his three-volume work *Civilization and Capitalism, 15th–18th Century* (1981, 1982, 1992), Braudel argued that society consists of interrelated parts assembled into a system. Societies are subsystems of larger systems, with the world system the largest. The key claim of **world-system theory** is that an identifiable social system, featuring wealth and power differentials, extends beyond individual countries. That system has been formed by a set of economic and political relations that has characterized much of the globe since the 16th century, when the Old World established regular contact with the Americas (see Bodley 2008).

According to Wallerstein (1982, 2004b), countries within the world system occupy three different positions of economic and political power: core, periphery, and semiperiphery. The **core,** the dominant position, includes the strongest, most powerful, and technically most advanced industrial nations. In core nations, "the complexity of economic activities and the level of capital accumulation is the greatest" (Thompson 1983, p. 12). According to Arrighi (2010), the core monopolizes the most profitable activities, especially the control of world finance.

The **semiperiphery** is intermediate between the core and the periphery. Contemporary nations of the semiperiphery are industrialized. Like core nations, they export both industrial goods and commodities, but they lack the power and economic dominance of

Jobs continue to migrate from core nations to places in the semiperiphery, such as Chennai (formerly Madras), India. Shown here in February 2013, a worker in the Royal Enfield cycle company. How does this photo suggest both outsourcing and globalization?

core nations. Thus Brazil, a semiperiphery nation, exports automobiles to Nigeria (a periphery nation) and auto engines, orange juice extract, coffee, and shrimp to the United States (a core nation). The **periphery** includes the world's least privileged and powerful countries. Economic activities there are less mechanized than are those in the core and semiperiphery, although some degree of industrialization has reached even peripheral nations. The periphery produces raw materials, agricultural commodities, and, increasingly, human labor for export to the core and the semiperiphery (Shannon 1996).

In the United States and Western Europe today, immigration—legal and illegal—from the periphery and semiperiphery supplies cheap labor, especially for agriculture, construction, and paid domestic labor. U.S. states as distant as California, Michigan, and South Carolina make significant use of farm labor from Mexico. The availability of relatively cheap workers from noncore nations such as Mexico (in the United States) and Turkey (in Germany) benefits farmers and business owners in core countries while supplying remittances to families in the semiperiphery and periphery. As a result of 21st-century telecommunications technology, cheap labor doesn't even need to migrate to the United States. Thousands of families in India are being supported as American companies outsource jobs—from telephone assistance to software engineering—to nations outside the core (see Nadeem 2011).

The Emergence of the World System

By the 15th century, Europeans were profiting from a transoceanic trade-oriented economy, and people worldwide entered Europe's sphere of influence. What was new was the transatlantic component of a long history of Old World sailing and commerce. As early as 600 B.C.E., the Phoenicians/Carthaginians sailed around Britain on regular trade routes and circumnavigated Africa. Likewise, Indonesia and Africa have been linked in Indian Ocean trade for at least 2,000 years. In the 15th century, Europe established regular contact with Asia, Africa, and eventually the New World (the Caribbean and the Americas). Christopher Columbus's first voyage from Spain to the Bahamas and the Caribbean in 1492 was soon followed by additional voyages. These journeys opened the way for a major exchange of people, resources, products, ideas, and diseases, as the Old and New Worlds were forever linked (Crosby 2003; Diamond 1997; Fagan 1998; Mann 2011). Led by Spain and Portugal, Europeans extracted silver and gold, conquered the natives (taking some as slaves), and colonized their lands.

Previously in Europe as throughout the world, rural people had produced mainly for their own needs, growing their own food and making clothing, furniture, and tools from local products. People produced beyond their immediate needs in order to pay taxes and to purchase trade items such as salt and iron. As late as 1650 the English diet was based on locally grown starches (Mintz 1985). In the 200 years that followed, however, the English became extraordinary consumers of imported goods. One of the earliest and most popular of those goods was sugar (Mintz 1985).

Sugarcane, originally domesticated in Papua New Guinea, was first processed in India. Reaching Europe via the eastern Mediterranean, it was carried to the Americas by Columbus (Mintz 1985). The climate of Brazil and the Caribbean proved ideal for growing sugarcane, and Europeans built plantations there to supply the growing demand for sugar. This led to the development in the 17th century of a plantation economy based on a single cash crop—a system known as *monocrop* production.

The demand for sugar in a growing international market spurred the development of the transatlantic slave trade and New World plantation economies based on slave labor. By the 18th century, an increased English demand for raw cotton led to rapid settlement of what is now the southeastern United States and the emergence there of another slave-based monocrop production system. Like sugar, cotton was a key trade item that fueled the growth of the world system.

Industrialization

By the 18th century the stage had been set for the **Industrial Revolution**—the historical transformation (in Europe, after 1750) of "traditional" into "modern" societies through industrialization. The seeds of industrial society were planted well before the 18th century (Gimpel 1988). For example, a knitting machine invented in England in 1589 was so far ahead of its time that it played a profitable role in factories two and three centuries later. The appearance of cloth mills late in the Middle Ages foreshadowed the search for new sources of wind and water power that characterized the Industrial Revolution. Industrialization required capital for investment. The established system of transoceanic commerce supplied this capital from the profits it generated. As wealthy people invested in machines and engines to drive machines, capital and scientific innovation fueled invention. Industrialization increased production in both farming and manufacturing.

European industrialization developed from and eventually replaced the *domestic system* of manufacture (the home-handicraft system). In this system, an organizer–entrepreneur

The *Art of* STOCKING-FRAME-WORK-KNITTING.

Engrav'd for the Universal Magazine 1750 for J. Hinton at the Kings Arms in St. Pauls Church Yard LONDON.

In the home-handicraft, or domestic, system of production, an organizer supplied raw materials to workers in their homes and collected their products. Family life and work were intertwined, as in this English scene. Is there a modern equivalent to the domestic system of production?

supplied the raw materials to workers in their homes and collected the finished products from them. The entrepreneur, whose sphere of operations might span several villages, owned the materials, paid for the work, and arranged the marketing.

Causes of the Industrial Revolution

The Industrial Revolution began with cotton products, iron, and pottery. These were widely used items whose manufacture could be broken down into simple routine motions that machines could perform. When manufacturing moved from homes to factories, where machinery replaced handwork, agrarian societies evolved into industrial ones. As factories produced cheap staple goods, the Industrial Revolution led to a dramatic increase in production. Industrialization fueled urban growth and created a new kind of city, with factories crowded together in places where coal and labor were cheap.

The Industrial Revolution began in England, and, as its industrialization proceeded, Britain's population began to increase dramatically. It doubled during the 18th century (especially after 1750) and did so again between 1800 and 1850. This demographic explosion fueled consumption, but British entrepreneurs couldn't meet the increased demand with the traditional production methods. This spurred further experimentation, innovation, and rapid technological change.

English industrialization drew on national advantages in natural resources. Britain was rich in coal and iron ore and had navigable coats and waterways. It was a seafaring island-nation located at the crossroads of international trade. These features gave Britain a favored position for importing raw materials and exporting manufactured goods. Another factor in England's industrial growth was the fact that much of its 18th-century colonial empire was occupied by English settler families who looked to the mother country as they tried to replicate European civilization abroad. These colonies bought large quantities of English staples.

It also has been argued that particular cultural values and religion contributed to industrialization. Many members of the emerging English middle class were Protestant nonconformists. Their beliefs and values encouraged industry, thrift, the dissemination of new knowledge, inventiveness, and willingness to accept change (Weber 1904/1958).

Socioeconomic Effects of Industrialization

The socioeconomic effects of industrialization were mixed. English national income tripled between 1700 and 1815 and increased 30 times more by 1939. Standards of comfort rose, but prosperity was uneven. At first, factory workers got wages higher than those available in the domestic system. Later, however, owners started recruiting labor in places where living standards were low and labor (including that of women and children) was cheap. Filth and smoke polluted 19th-century cities. Housing was crowded and unsanitary. People experienced rampant disease and rising death rates. This was the world of Ebenezer Scrooge, Bob Cratchit, Tiny Tim—and Karl Marx.

Industrial Stratification

The social theorists Karl Marx and Max Weber focused on the stratification systems associated with industrialization. From his observations in England and his analysis of 19th-century industrial capitalism, Marx (Marx and Engels 1848/1976) saw socioeconomic stratification as a sharp and simple division between two opposed classes: the bourgeoisie (capitalists) and the proletariat (propertyless workers). The bourgeoisie traced its origins to overseas ventures and the world capitalist economy, which had created a wealthy commercial class (White 2009).

Industrialization shifted production from farms and cottages to mills and factories, where mechanical power was available and where workers could be assembled to operate heavy machinery. The **bourgeoisie** owned the factories, mines, estates, and other means of production. Members of the **working class, or proletariat,** had to sell their labor to survive.

Industrialization, and the rural to urban migration it fueled, hastened the process of *proletarianization*—the separation of workers from the means of production. Bourgeoisie domination extended to the means of communication, the schools, and other key institutions. *Class consciousness* (recognition of collective interests and personal identification with one's economic group) was a vital part of Marx's view of class. He saw bourgeoisie and proletariat as socioeconomic divisions with radically opposed interests. Marx viewed classes as powerful collective forces that could mobilize human energies to influence the course of history. On the basis of their common experience, workers, he thought, would develop class consciousness, which could lead to revolutionary change. Although no proletarian revolution was to occur in England, workers did develop organizations to protect their interests and increase their share of industrial profits. During the 19th century, trade unions and socialist parties emerged to express a rising anticapitalist spirit. The concerns of the English labor movement were to remove young children from factories and limit the hours during which women and children could work. The profile of stratification in industrial core nations gradually took shape. Capitalists controlled production, but labor was organizing for better wages and working conditions. By 1900 many governments had factory legislation and social-welfare programs. Mass living standards in core nations improved as population grew.

Today, the existence of publicly traded companies complicates the division between capitalists and workers. Through pension plans and personal investments, some workers have become part-owners rather than propertyless workers. Today's key capitalist isn't the factory owner, who may have been replaced by stockholders, but the CEO or the chair of the board of directors, neither of whom may actually own the corporation.

Modern stratification systems aren't simple and dichotomous. They include (particularly in core and semiperiphery nations) a middle class of skilled and professional workers. Gerhard Lenski (1966) argues that social equality tends to increase in advanced industrial societies. The masses improve their access to economic benefits and political power. In Lenski's scheme, the shift of political power to the masses reflects the growth of the middle class, which reduces the polarization between owning and working classes. The proliferation of middle-class occupations creates opportunities for social mobility and a more complex stratification system (Giddens 1973).

In the United States the complexity of this system goes largely unnoticed by many Americans. Most contemporary Americans, for example, think they belong to, and claim identity with, the middle class, which they tend to perceive as a vast, undifferentiated group. However, there are substantial socioeconomic differences between the richest and the poorest Americans, and the gap has been widening. According to U.S. Census data from 1970 to 2009, the top (richest) quintile (fifth) of American households increased its share of national income by 16 percent, while all other quintiles fell. The percentage share of the lowest fifth fell most dramatically—17 percent. In 2009 the top fifth got 50.3 percent of all national income, while the lowest fifth got only 3.4 percent. The 2009 ratio was 15:1, versus 14:1 in 2000 and 11:1 in 1970. In other words, by 2009 the richest fifth of American households, with a mean annual income of $170,844, had become 15 times wealthier than the poorest fifth, whose mean annual income was only $11,552 (DeNavas-Walt, Proctor, and Smith 2010).

Considering wealth (investments, property, possessions, etc.) rather than income, the contrast is even more striking (see Figure 12.1). The top 1 percent of American households hold over one-third (35.6 percent) of the nation's wealth (Allegretto 2011). Their net worth is 225 times greater than that of the median household. The top 1 percent owns more than the bottom 90 percent combined (Witt 2011, p. 229).

FIGURE 12.1
The Ratio of the Wealthiest 1 Percent to Median Wealth in the United States, 1962–2009.

Source: S. A. Allegretto, *The State of Working America's Wealth,* Briefing Paper no. 292, Economic Policy Institute, March 23, 2011. http://www.epi.org/page/-/BriefingPaper292.pdf.

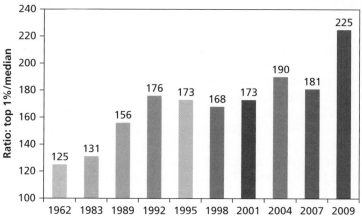

The Great Recession of December 2007–June 2009 increased inequality. While all Americans were affected, the poor suffered more than the rich did. Household wealth shrank by 16 percent for the richest quintile, versus 25 percent for the bottom 80 percent (four quintiles combined). Recognition of such disparities, and that the rich were getting richer and the poor, poorer, led to the Occupy movement of 2011. That movement began on Wall Street and quickly spread to many other cities in the United States and Canada.

Max Weber faulted Karl Marx for an overly simple and exclusively economic view of stratification. As we saw in the chapter "Political Systems," Weber (1922/1968) defined three dimensions of social stratification: wealth, power, and prestige. Although, as Weber showed, wealth, power, and prestige are separate components of social ranking, they tend to be correlated. Weber also believed that social identities based on ethnicity, religion, race, nationality, and other attributes could take priority over class (social identity based on economic status). In addition to class contrasts, the modern world system *is* cross-cut by collective identities based on ethnicity, religion, and nationality (Shannon 1996). Class conflicts tend to occur within nations, and nationalism has impeded global class solidarity, particularly of proletarians.

Although the capitalist class dominates politically in most countries, growing wealth made it easier for core nations to grant higher wages (Hopkins and Wallerstein 1982). However, the improvement in core workers' living standards wouldn't have occurred without the world system. Without the periphery, core capitalists would have trouble maintaining their profits and satisfying the demands of core workers. In the periphery, wages and living standards are much lower. The current *world stratification system* features a substantial contrast between both capitalists and workers in the core nations and workers on the periphery (see Kerbo 2006).

Colonialism

The major forces influencing global cultural interactions during the past 500 years have been commercial expansion, industrial capitalism, and the dominance of colonial and core nations (Wallerstein 1982, 2004*b*; Wolf 1982). As state formation had done previously, industrialization accelerated local participation in larger networks. According to Bodley (2008, 2012), perpetual expansion is a distinguishing feature of industrial economic systems.

During the 19th century, European business interests initiated a concerted search for markets. This process led to European imperialism in Africa, Asia, and Oceania. **Imperialism** refers to a policy of extending the rule of a country or an empire over foreign nations and of taking and holding foreign colonies. Imperialism goes back to early states, including Egypt in the Old World and the Incas in the New. A Greek empire was forged by Alexander the Great, and Julius Caesar and his successors spread the Roman empire. More recent examples include the British, French, and Soviet empires.

After 1850, European imperial expansion was aided by improved transportation, which facilitated the colonization of vast areas of sparsely settled lands in Australia and the interior of North and South America. The new colonies purchased goods from the industrial centers and shipped back wheat, cotton, wool, mutton, beef, and leather. The first phase of European colonialism had been the exploration and exploitation of the Americas and the Caribbean after Columbus. A second phase began as European nations competed for colonies between 1875 and 1914.

Colonialism is the political, social, economic, and cultural domination of a territory and its people by a foreign power for an extended time (see Bremen and Shimizu, eds. 1999; Stoler, McGranahan, and Perdue 2007). If imperialism is almost as old as the state, colonialism can be traced back to the Phoenicians, who established colonies along the eastern Mediterranean 3,000 years ago. The ancient Greeks and Romans were avid colonizers, as well as empire builders.

The first phase of modern colonialism began with the European "Age of Discovery"—of the Americas and of a sea route to the Far East. After 1492, the Spanish, the original conquerors of the Aztecs and the Incas, explored and colonized widely in the Caribbean, Mexico, the southern portions of what was to become the United States, and Central and South America. In South America, Portugal ruled over Brazil. Rebellions and wars aimed at independence ended the first phase of European colonialism by the early 19th century. Brazil declared independence from Portugal in 1822. By 1825 most of Spain's colonies were politically independent. Spain held on to Cuba and the Philippines until 1898 but otherwise withdrew from the colonial field. During the first phase of colonialism, Spain and Portugal, along with Britain and France, were major colonizing nations. The last two (Britain and France) dominated the second phase.

British Colonialism

At its peak about 1914, the British empire covered a fifth of the world's land surface and ruled a fourth of its population (see Figure 12.2). Like several other European nations, Britain had two stages of colonialism. The first began with the Elizabethan voyages of the 16th century. During the 17th century, Britain acquired most of the eastern coast of

FIGURE 12.2   **Map of the British Empire in 1765 and 1914**

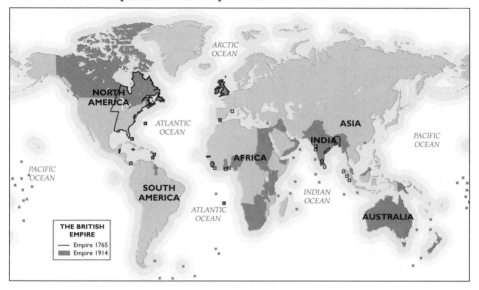

North America, Canada's St. Lawrence basin, islands in the Caribbean, slave stations in Africa, and interests in India.

The British shared the exploration of the New World with the Spanish, Portuguese, French, and Dutch. The British by and large left Mexico, along with Central and South America, to the Spanish and the Portuguese. The end of the Seven Years' War in 1763 forced a French retreat from most of Canada and India, where France previously had competed with Britain (Cody 1998; Farr 1980).

The American revolution ended the first stage of British colonialism. A second colonial empire, on which the "sun never set," rose from the ashes of the first. Beginning in 1788, but intensifying after 1815, the British settled Australia. Britain had acquired Dutch South Africa by 1815. The establishment of Singapore in 1819 provided a base for a British trade network that extended to much of South Asia and along the coast of China. By this time, the empires of Britain's traditional rivals, particularly Spain, had been severely diminished in scope. Britain's position as imperial power and the world's leading industrial nation was unchallenged (Cody 1998; Farr 1980).

During the Victorian Era (1837–1901), as Britain's colonial expansion continued, Prime Minister Benjamin Disraeli implemented a foreign policy justified by a view of imperialism as shouldering "the white man's burden"—a phrase coined by the poet Rudyard Kipling. People in the empire were seen as unable to govern themselves, so that British guidance was needed to civilize and Christianize them. This paternalistic and racist doctrine was used to legitimize Britain's acquisition and control of parts of central Africa and Asia (Cody 1998).

After World War II, the British empire began to fall apart, with nationalist movements for independence. India became independent in 1947, as did Ireland in 1949. Decolonization in Africa and Asia accelerated during the late 1950s. Today, the ties that

On January 1, 1900, a British officer in India receives a pedicure from a servant. What does this photo say to you about colonialism? Who gives pedicures in your society?

remain between Britain and its former colonies are mainly linguistic or cultural rather than political (Cody 1998).

French Colonialism

French colonialism also had two phases. The first began with the explorations of the early 1600s. Prior to the French revolution in 1789, missionaries, explorers, and traders carved out niches for France in Canada, the Louisiana territory, several Caribbean islands, and parts of India, which were lost along with Canada to Great Britain in 1763 (Harvey 1980).

The foundations of the second French empire were established between 1830 and 1870. In Great Britain the drive for profit led expansion, but French colonialism was spurred more by the state, church, and armed forces than by pure business interests. France acquired Algeria and part of what eventually became Indochina (Cambodia, Laos, and Vietnam). By 1914 the French empire covered 4 million square miles and included some 60 million people (see Figure 12.3). By 1893 French rule had been fully established in Indochina. Tunisia and Morocco became French protectorates in 1883 and 1912, respectively (Harvey 1980).

To be sure, the French, like the British, had substantial business interests in their colonies, but they also sought, again like the British, international glory and prestige. The French promulgated a *mission civilisatrice,* their equivalent of Britain's "white man's burden." The goal was to implant French culture, language, and religion, Roman Catholicism, throughout the colonies (Harvey 1980).

FIGURE 12.3   **Map of the French Empire at Its Height around 1914**

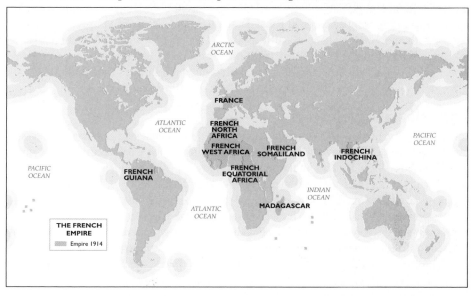

The French used two forms of colonial rule: *indirect rule,* governing through native leaders and established political structures, in areas with long histories of state organization, such as Morocco and Tunisia; and *direct rule* by French officials in many areas of Africa, where the French imposed new government structures to control diverse societies, many of them previously stateless. Like the British empire, the French empire began to disintegrate after World War II. France fought long—and ultimately futile—wars to keep its empire intact in Indochina and Algeria (Harvey 1980).

Colonialism and Identity

Many geopolitical labels in the news today had no equivalent meaning before colonialism. Whole countries, along with social groups and divisions within them, were colonial inventions. In West Africa, for example, by geographic logic, several adjacent countries could be one (Togo, Ghana, Ivory Coast, Guinea, Guinea-Bissau, Sierra Leone, Liberia). Instead, they are separated by linguistic, political, and economic contrasts promoted under colonialism.

Hundreds of ethnic groups and "tribes" are colonial constructions (see Ranger 1996). The Sukuma of Tanzania, for instance, were first registered as a single tribe by the colonial administration. Then missionaries standardized a series of dialects into a single Sukuma language, into which they translated the Bible and other religious texts. Thereafter, those texts were taught in missionary schools and to European foreigners and other non-Sukuma speakers. Over time this standardized the Sukuma language and ethnicity (Finnstrom 1997).

As in most of East Africa, in Rwanda and Burundi farmers and herders live in the same areas and speak the same language. Historically they have shared the same social world, although their social organization is "extremely hierarchical," almost "castelike"

(Malkki 1995, p. 24). There has been a tendency to see the pastoral Tutsis as superior to the agricultural Hutus. Tutsis have been presented as nobles, Hutus as commoners. Yet when distributing identity cards in Rwanda, the Belgian colonizers simply identified all people with more than 10 head of cattle as Tutsi. Owners of fewer cattle were registered as Hutus (Bjuremalm 1997). Years later, these arbitrary colonial registers were used systematically for "ethnic" identification during the mass killings (genocide) that took place in Rwanda in 1994 (as portrayed vividly in the film *Hotel Rwanda*).

Postcolonial Studies

In anthropology, history, and literature, the field of postcolonial studies has gained prominence since the 1970s (see Ashcroft, Griffiths, and Tiffin 1989; Chakrabarty 2007; Cooper and Stoler, eds. 1997). **Postcolonial** refers to the study of the interactions between European nations and the societies they colonized (mainly after 1800). In 1914, European empires, which broke up after World War II, ruled more than 85 percent of the world (Petraglia-Bahri 1996). The term *postcolonial* also has been used to describe the second half of the 20th century in general, the period succeeding colonialism. Even more generically, *postcolonial* may be used to signify a position against imperialism and Eurocentrism (Petraglia-Bahri 1996).

The former colonies (*postcolonies*) can be divided into settler, nonsettler, and mixed (Petraglia-Bahri 1996). The settler countries, with large numbers of European colonists and sparser native populations, include Australia and Canada. Examples of nonsettler countries include India, Pakistan, Bangladesh, Sri Lanka, Malaysia, Indonesia, Nigeria, Senegal, Madagascar, and Jamaica. All these had substantial native populations and relatively few European settlers. Mixed countries include South Africa, Zimbabwe, Kenya, and Algeria. Such countries had significant European settlement despite having sizable native populations.

Given the varied experiences of such countries, *postcolonial* has to be a loose term. The United States, for instance, was colonized by Europeans and fought a war for independence from Britain. Is the United States a postcolony? It usually isn't perceived as such, given its current world power position, its treatment of Native Americans (sometimes called internal colonization), and its annexation of other parts of the world (Petraglia-Bahri 1996). Research in postcolonial studies is growing, permitting a wide-ranging investigation of power relations in varied contexts. Broad topics in the field include the formation of an empire, the impact of colonization, and the state of the postcolony today.

Development

During the Industrial Revolution, a strong current of thought viewed industrialization as a beneficial process of organic development and progress. Many economists still assume that industrialization increases production and income. They seek to create in Third World ("developing") countries a process like the one that first occurred spontaneously in 18th-century Great Britain.

We have seen that Britain used the notion "a white man's burden" to justify its imperialist expansion and that France claimed to be engaged in a *mission civilisatrice,* a civilizing mission, in its colonies. Both these ideas illustrate an **intervention philosophy,** an ideological justification for outsiders to guide native peoples in specific directions.

Economic development plans also have intervention philosophies. John Bodley (2012) argues that the basic belief behind interventions—whether by colonialists, missionaries, governments, or development planners—has been the same for more than one hundred years. This belief is that industrialization, modernization, Westernization, and individualism are desirable evolutionary advances and that development schemes that promote them will bring long-term benefits to local people.

Neoliberalism

One currently influential intervention philosophy is neoliberalism. This term encompasses a set of assumptions that have become widespread during the last 30 years. Neoliberal policies are being implemented in developing nations, including postsocialist societies (e.g., those of the former Soviet Union). **Neoliberalism** is the current form of the classic economic liberalism laid out in Adam Smith's famous capitalist manifesto, *The Wealth of Nations,* published in 1776, soon after the Industrial Revolution. Smith advocated laissez-faire (hands-off) economics as the basis of capitalism: The government should stay out of its nation's economic affairs. Free trade, Smith argued, is the best way for a nation's economy to develop. There should be no restrictions on manufacturing, no barriers to commerce, and no tariffs. This philosophy is called "liberalism" because it aimed at liberating, or freeing, the economy from government controls. Economic liberalism encouraged "free" enterprise and competition, with the goal of generating profits. (Ironically, Adam Smith's liberalism is today's capitalist "conservatism.")

Economic liberalism prevailed in the United States until President Franklin Roosevelt's New Deal during the 1930s. The Great Depression produced a turn to Keynesian economics, which challenged liberalism. John Maynard Keynes (1927, 1936) insisted that full employment was necessary for capitalism to grow, that governments and central banks should intervene to increase employment, and that government should promote the common good.

Especially since the fall of Communism (1989–1991), there has been a revival of neoliberalism, which has been spreading globally. Around the world, neoliberal policies have been imposed by powerful financial institutions such as the International Monetary Fund (IMF), the World Bank, and the Inter-American Development Bank (see Edelman and Haugerud 2005). Neoliberalism entails open (tariff- and barrier-free) international trade and investment. Profits are sought through the lowering of costs, whether through improving productivity, laying off workers, or seeking workers who accept lower wages. In exchange for loans, the governments of postsocialist and developing nations have been required to accept the neoliberal premise that deregulation leads to economic growth, which will eventually benefit everyone through a process sometimes called "trickle down." Accompanying the belief in free markets and the idea of cutting costs is a tendency to impose austerity measures that cut government expenses. This can entail reduced public spending on education, health care, and other social services (Martinez and Garcia 2000).

The Second World

The labels "First World," "Second World," and "Third World" represent a common, although ethnocentric, way of categorizing nations. The *First World* refers to the "democratic West"—traditionally conceived in opposition to a "Second World" ruled by "Communism." The *Second World* refers to the former Soviet Union and the socialist and once-socialist countries of Eastern Europe and Asia. Proceeding with this classification, the "less-developed countries," or "developing nations," make up the *Third World*.

Communism

The two meanings of communism involve how it is written, whether with a lowercase (small) or an uppercase (large) *c*. Small-*c* **communism** describes a social system in which property is owned by the community and in which people work for the common good. Large-*C* **Communism** was a political movement and doctrine seeking to overthrow capitalism and to establish a form of communism such as that which prevailed in the Soviet Union (USSR) from 1917 to 1991. The heyday of Communism was a 40-year period from 1949 to 1989, when more Communist regimes existed than at any time before or after. Today only five Communist states remain—China, Cuba, Laos, North Korea, and Vietnam, compared with 23 in 1985.

Communism, which originated with Russia's Bolshevik Revolution in 1917 and took its inspiration from Karl Marx and Friedrich Engels, was not uniform over time or among countries. All Communist systems were *authoritarian* (promoting obedience to authority rather than individual freedom). Many were *totalitarian* (banning rival parties and demanding total submission of the individual to the state). The Communist Party monopolized power in every Communist state, and relations within the party were highly centralized and strictly disciplined. Communist nations had state ownership, rather than private ownership, of the means of production. Finally, all Communist regimes, with the goal of advancing communism, cultivated a sense of belonging to an international movement (Brown 2001).

Postsocialist Transitions

Social scientists have tended to refer to "Second World" societies as socialist rather than Communist. Today research by anthropologists is thriving in *postsocialist* societies—those that once emphasized bureaucratic redistribution of wealth according to a central plan (Verdery 1997, 2001). In the postsocialist period, states that once had planned economies have been following the neoliberal agenda, by divesting themselves of state-owned resources in favor of privatization. Some of them have moved toward formal liberal democracy, with political parties, elections, and a balance of powers (Grekova 2001).

Neoliberal economists assumed that dismantling the Soviet Union's planned economy would raise gross domestic product (GDP) and living standards. The goal was to enhance production by substituting a free market system and providing incentives through privatization. In October 1991, Boris Yeltsin, who had been elected president of Russia that June, announced a program of radical market-oriented reform, pursuing a changeover to capitalism. Yeltsin's program of "shock therapy" cut subsidies to farms and industries and ended price controls. Since then, postsocialist Russia has faced many problems. After the fall of the Soviet Union, Russia's GDP fell by half. Life expectancy and the birth rate declined, and poverty increased.

The World System Today

The spread of industrialization continues today, although nations have shifted their positions within the world system. By 1900, the United States had become a core nation, having overtaken Great Britain in iron, coal, and cotton production. In a few decades (1868–1900), Japan changed from a medieval handicraft economy to an industrial one, joining the semiperiphery by 1900 and moving to the core between 1945 and 1970. India and China have joined Brazil as leaders of the semiperiphery. The map in Figure 12.4 shows the world system today.

Twentieth-century industrialization added hundreds of new industries and millions of new jobs. Production increased, often beyond immediate demand, spurring strategies, such as advertising, to sell everything industry could churn out. Mass production gave rise to a culture of consumption, which valued acquisitiveness and conspicuous consumption.

How do things stand today? Worldwide, young people are abandoning traditional subsistence pursuits and seeking cash. A popular song once queried "How're you gonna keep 'em down on the farm after they've seen Paree?" Nowadays most people *have* seen Paree—Paris, that is—along with other world capitals, maybe not in person but in print or on-screen. Young people today are better educated and wiser in the ways of the world than ever before. Increasingly they are exposed to the material and cultural promises of a better life away from the farm. They seek paying jobs, but work is scarce, spurring migration within and across national boundaries. If they can't get cash legally, they seek it illegally.

FIGURE 12.4   The World System Today

Source: Conrad Kottak, *Anthropology,* 10th ed., fig 23.5, p. 660. Reprinted by permission of The McGraw-Hill Companies.

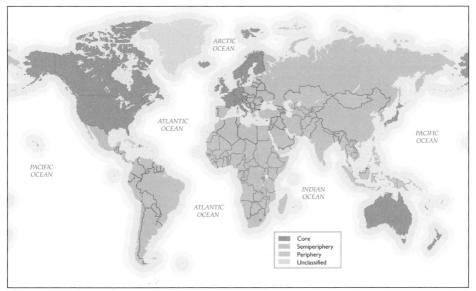

Recently work has been scarce as well in the industrial world, including the United States and Western Europe. As the United States struggled to emerge from the recession of 2007–2009, its stock market more than doubled between March 2009 and October 2012. In what many saw as a "jobless recovery," corporations held on to their profits, rather than using them to hire new workers. The goal of capitalism, after all, is to maintain profitability. In a global economy, profitability doesn't necessarily come from hiring workers who are fellow citizens. Jobs continue to be outsourced. Machines and information technology continue to replace people. Corporations, from airlines to banks, offer their customers incentives to bypass humans. Even outside the industrial world, but especially within it, the Internet allows an increasing number of people to buy plane tickets, print boarding passes, rent cars, reserve hotel rooms, move money, or pay bills online. Amazon as a virtual bookstore and, increasingly a department store as well, threatens to send not only "mom and pop" shops but even national chains such as Sears and Radio Shack into oblivion. Borders bit the dust in 2011. Nowadays, when one does manage to speak by phone to a human, that person is as likely to be in Mumbai or Manila as Minneapolis or Miami.

Companies claim, with some justification, that labor unions limit their flexibility, adaptability, and profitability. American corporations (and the politicians who represent them) have become more ideologically opposed to unions and more aggressive in discouraging unionization. Unions still bring benefits to their workers. Median weekly earnings for union members—$917 in 2010—remain higher than those of nonunion workers—$717 (Greenhouse 2011). Still, union membership in the United States has fallen to its lowest point in more than 70 years. The unionized percentage of the American workforce fell to 11.9 percent in 2010, compared with 20.1 percent in 1983 and a high of 35 percent during the mid-1950s. The number of unionized private sector workers stood at 7.1 million in 2010, versus a larger share—7.6 million workers—in the public sector (Greenhouse 2011). What jobs do you know that are unionized? How likely is it that you will join a union?

Neoliberalism and NAFTA's Economic Refugees

In recent decades, many of the migrants seeking work in the United States have come from Mexico. Most Americans are aware of recent large-scale Mexican immigration, often of undocumented workers. Most Americans are unaware, however, of the extent to which international forces, including new technologies and the neoliberal North American Free Trade Agreement (NAFTA), are responsible for this migration. Ana Aurelia López (2011) shows how such forces have destroyed traditional Mexican farming systems, degraded agricultural land, and displaced Mexican farmers and small-business people—thereby fueling the migration of millions of undocumented Mexicans to the United States. The following account is a synopsis of her findings.

To understand what is happening in North America today, we need to be aware of an agricultural tradition that began at least 7,000 years ago. For thousands of years, Mexican farmers have grown corn (maize) in a sustainable manner. For all those millennia, Mexican farmers planted corn, beans, and squash (known as "the three sisters") together. This polyculture (cultivation of multiple crops) results in corn yields higher than those obtained when corn is cultivated by itself (monoculture). To preserve the fertility

of the soil, a "three sisters" plot was allowed to "rest" for five years after being cultivated for two.

Over the generations Mexican farmers selected diverse strains of corn well adapted
to a huge variety of specific microclimates. Mexico became a repository of corn genetic
diversity for the world. When corn grown elsewhere developed disease or pest susceptibility or was of poor quality, Mexico could provide other countries with genetically
superior plants.

Prior to NAFTA, Mexico supported its farmers by buying a portion of their harvest
each year at an elevated cost through price supports. This corn went to a countrywide
chain of successful CONASUPO (Compañía Nacional de Subsistencias Populares)
stores, which sold corn and other staple foodstuffs below market price to the urban and
rural poor. Border tariffs protected Mexican farmers from the entrance of foreign corn,
such as that grown in the United States.

The first assault on Mexico's sustainable farming culture began in the 1940s when
"Green Revolution" technologies were introduced, including seeds that require chemical inputs (e.g., fertilizer). The Mexican government encouraged farmers to replace their
traditional, genetically diverse *maíz crillo* ("creole corn") with the genetically homogenized *maíz mejorado* ("improved corn"), a hybrid from the United States. Agrochemi-
cal companies initially supplied the required chemical inputs free of charge.

Company representatives visited rural villages and offered free samples of seeds and
agrochemicals to a few farmers. As news of unusually large first-year crops spread,
other farmers abandoned their traditional corn strains for the "improved," chemically
dependent corn. As the transition accelerated, the price of both the new seeds and associated inputs rose gradually. Eventually farmers no longer could afford either the seeds
or the required agrochemicals. When cash-strapped farmers tried to return to planting
their former *maíz criollo* seeds, the plants would grow but corn would not appear. Only
the hybrid seeds from the United States would produce corn on the chemically altered
soils. Today over 60 percent of Mexico's farmland is degraded due to the spread of agrochemicals—chemical fertilizers and pesticides. (This chapter's "Anthropology Today" describes another case of environmental degradation due to chemical pollution,
with mining as the culprit.)

The second major assault on traditional Mexican farming came when NAFTA went
into effect in 1994. The World Bank granted Mexico a loan to restructure its economy
to fit the neoliberal "free trade" agreement. The loan required Mexico to end corn price
supports for its small-scale corn farmers. Also ended were Mexico's CONASUPO food
stores, which had benefited the rural and urban poor.

While small-scale Mexican farmers have suffered, American agricultural industries
have profited from NAFTA. The U.S. government continues to subsidize its own corn
farmers, who otherwise would go out of business. Prior to NAFTA, Mexico's border
tariffs made the sale of U.S. corn in Mexico unprofitable. Under NAFTA, Mexican corn
tariffs were supposed to be phased out over 15 years, providing time for small farmers to
adjust to the NAFTA economy. In fact, the Mexican corn tariffs mysteriously disappeared
after only 30 months. Corn from the United States began flooding the Mexican markets.

The NAFTA economy offers Mexico's small-scale corn farmers few options: (1) stay
in rural Mexico and suffer, (2) look for work in a Mexican city, or (3) migrate to the

Anthropology Today *Mining Giant Compatible with Sustainability Institute?*

The spread of industrialization, illustrated by the mining described here, has contributed to the destruction of indigenous economies, ecologies, and populations. Today, multinational corporations, along with the governments of nations such as Papua New Guinea (PNG) as described here, are accelerating the process of resource depletion that began with the Industrial Revolution. Fortunately, however, today's world also contains environmental watchdogs, including concerned anthropologists, lawyers, and NGOs. Described here is a conundrum confronting a major university. Are multinational corporations whose operations have destroyed the landscapes and livelihoods of indigenous peoples proper advisers for an institute devoted to ecological sustainability?

In the 1990s, the giant mining company now known as BHP Billiton drew worldwide condemnation for the environmental damage caused by its copper and gold mine in Papua New Guinea. Its mining practices destroyed the way of life of thousands of farming and fishing families who lived along and subsisted on the rivers polluted by the mine, and it was only after being sued in a landmark class-action case that the company agreed to compensate them.

Today several activists and academics who work on behalf of indigenous people around the world say the company continues to dodge responsibility for the problems its mines create. . . .

Yet at the University of Michigan at Ann Arbor, BHP Billiton . . . is one of 14 corporate members of an External Advisory Board for the university's new Graham Environmental Sustainability Institute.

Critics at and outside the university contend that Michigan's decision to enlist BHP Billiton as an adviser to an institute devoted to sustainability reflects badly on the institution and allows the company to claim [an undeserved] mantle of environmental and social responsibility. . . .

The arguments echo the discussions about corporate "greenwashing" that have arisen at Stanford University and the University of California at Berkeley over major research grants from ExxonMobil and BP, respectively. . . .

For one BHP Billiton critic at Michigan, the issue is personal. Stuart Kirsch, an associate professor of anthropology, has spent most of his academic career documenting the damage caused by BHP Billiton's Ok Tedi mine in Papua New Guinea. . . .

Mr. Kirsch, who first visited some of the affected communities as a young ethnographer in 1987, became involved in the class-action lawsuit brought against the company and helped villagers participate in the 1996 legal settlement. "I put my career on hold while being an activist," he says.

He subsequently published several papers related to his work with the Yonggom people as they fought for recognition and compensation from mine operators—scholarship that helped him win tenure. . . . He remains involved with the network of activists and academics who follow mining and its impact on undeveloped communities around the world. . . .

The company's practices polluted the Ok Tedi and Fly Rivers and caused thousands of people to leave their homes because the mining-induced flooding made it impossible for them to grow food to feed themselves, says Mr. Kirsch.

BHP Billiton, based in Australia, later acknowledged that the mine was "not compatible with our environmental values," and spun it off to an independent company

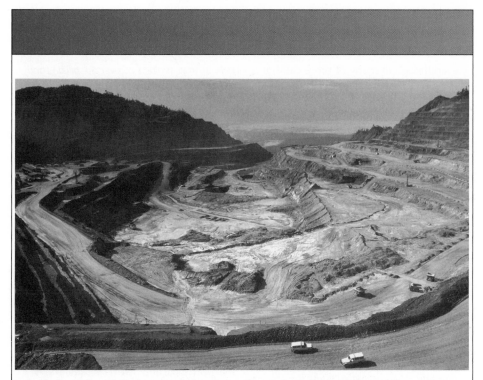

This photo of the Ok Tedi copper mine shows the ecological devastation of the native landscape.

that pays all of its mining royalties to the government of Papua New Guinea.

But Mr. Kirsch says that in doing so, the company skirted responsibility for ameliorating the damage it caused. BHP Billiton says it would have preferred to close the mine, but the Papua New Guinea government, in need of the mine revenues, pressed to keep it open. The deal freed BHP Billiton from any future liabilities for environmental damage. . . .

Illtud Harri, a BHP Billiton spokesman, says the company regrets its past with Ok Tedi but considers its pullout from the mine "a responsible exit" that left in place a system that supports educational, agricultural, and social programs for the people of the community. . . .

Mr. Talbot, the interim director of the two-year-old sustainability institute, says . . .

"We intentionally selected a cross-sector group of organizations" for the advisory board from a list of about 140 nominees, . . . and several companies that "weren't making any serious efforts" toward sustainability were rejected. . . .

BHP Billiton, a company formed from the 2001 merger of the Australian mining enterprise Broken Hill Proprietary Company with London-based Billiton, is now the world's largest mining company, with more than 100 operations in 25 countries. . . .

The BHP Billiton charter includes a statement that the company has "an overriding commitment to health, safety, environmental responsibility, and sustainable development." But its critics say the company continues to play a key role in mining projects with questionable records on environmental and human rights,
continued

Anthropology Today   *continued*

even though in many of those cases, it is not directly responsible. . . .

BHP Billiton has the resources to present itself as the "golden boy," but, says Mr. Kirsch, "it's much harder to see the people on the Ok Tedi and Fly rivers."

A forum could help to right that imbalance, he says. "Let the students and faculty decide whether this is an appropriate company to advise the University of Michigan," says Mr. Kirsch. "It would be an educational process for everyone involved."

Update: As of this writing (2013) BHP Billiton no longer is listed as a member of the advisory board of Michigan's Graham Institute. And in PNG, after BHP Billiton transferred its ownership of the mine to Ok Tedi Mining Limited, that independent company has spent more than a billion dollars on environmental remediation. The 1996 settlement decreed that BHP would be spared future legal claims in return for giving all its shares to the people of Papua New Guinea. Those shares are now held in trust (valued at over $1 billion, and growing) in a Singapore-based entity, PNG Sustainable Development Program Limited. The mission of that trust is to promote development in PNG's Western Province, where the mine is located, and across PNG. Today, the provincial and national governments of PNG and the PNG Sustainable Development Program are the only shareholders of Ok Tedi Mining Limited, which pays all its royalties to the PNG government. For hundreds of miles down the Fly River, fishers and farmers still complain about the destruction of their habitat, even as the Ok Tedi mine supplies 16 percent of PNG's national revenue.

Sources: Goldie Blumenstyk, "Mining Company Involved in Environmental Disaster Now Advises Sustainability Institute at U. of Michigan," *Chronicle of Higher Education,* December 7, 2007. Copyright © 2007, The Chronicle of Higher Education. Reprinted with permission; http://www.radioaustralia.net.au/pacific/radio/program/pacific-beat/documentary-special-ok-tedi/1069558; Stuart Kirsch (personal communication).

United States in search of work. NAFTA did not create a common labor market (i.e., the ability of Mexicans, Americans, and Canadians to move freely across each country's borders and work legally anywhere in North America.) Nor did NAFTA make provisions for the predicted 15 million Mexican corn farmers who would be forced off the land as a result of the trade agreement. As could have been expected (and planned for), millions of Mexicans migrated to the United States.

Because of NAFTA and neoliberalism, Mexico's 7,000-year-old traditional farming culture is disappearing. Corn farmers have fled the countryside, and U.S.-subsidized corn has flooded the Mexican market. A declining number of traditional farmers remain to plant and conserve Mexico's unique corn varieties. Between one-third and one-half of Mexico's corn now is imported from the United States, much of it by U.S.-based Archer-Daniels-Midland, the world's largest corporate corn exporter. NAFTA also has facilitated the entrance of other giant U.S. corporations into Mexico: Walmart, Dow Agribusiness, Monsanto, Marlboro cigarettes, and Coca-Cola. These multinationals, in turn, have displaced many small Mexican businesses, creating yet another wave of immigrants—former shopkeepers and their employees—to the United States.

In this summary of Ana Aurelia López's (2011) insightful analysis, we see how farmers and small-business men and women have been forced, by decisions beyond their control, to leave Mexico for the United States. In migrating, these millions of economic refugees continue to face daunting challenges, including separation from their families and homeland, dangerous border crossings, and the ever-present possibility of deportation from the United States.

Within today's world system, comparable effects of neoliberal policies extend well beyond Mexico. As forces of globalization transform rural landscapes throughout the world, rural–urban and transnational migration have become global phenomena. Over and over again, Green Revolution technologies have transformed subsistence into cash economies, fueling a need for money to acquire foreign inputs, while hooking the land on chemicals, reducing genetic diversity and sustainability, and forcing the poorest farmers off the land. Few Americans are aware, specifically, of NAFTA's role in ending a 7,000-year-old sustainable farming culture and displacing millions of Mexicans, and, more generally, that comparable developments are happening all over the world. The next chapter considers several other forces of globalization and anthropology's role in a globalizing world.

Summary

1. Local societies increasingly participate in wider systems—regional, national, and global. The capitalist world economy depends on production for sale, with the goal of maximizing profits. The key claim of world-system theory is that an identifiable social system, based on wealth and power differentials, extends beyond individual countries. That system is formed by a set of economic and political relations that has characterized much of the globe since the 16th century. World capitalism has political and economic specialization at the core, semiperiphery, and periphery.

2. Columbus's voyages opened the way for a major exchange between the Old and New Worlds. Seventeenth-century plantation economies in the Caribbean and Brazil were based on sugar. In the 18th century, plantation economies based on cotton arose in the southeastern United States.

3. The Industrial Revolution began in England around 1760. Transoceanic commerce supplied capital for industrial investment. Industrialization hastened the separation of workers from the means of production. Marx saw a sharp division between the bourgeoisie and the proletariat. Class consciousness was a key feature of Marx's view of this stratification. Weber believed that social solidarity based on ethnicity, religion, race, or nationality could take priority over class. Today's capitalist world economy maintains the contrast between those who own the means of production and those who don't, but the division is now worldwide. There is a substantial contrast between not only capitalists but workers in the core nations and workers on the periphery.

4. Imperialism is the policy of extending the rule of a nation or an empire over other nations and of taking and holding foreign colonies. Colonialism is the domination

of a territory and its people by a foreign power for an extended time. European colonialism had two main phases. The first started in 1492 and lasted through 1825. For Britain this phase ended with the American Revolution. For France it ended when Britain won the Seven Years' War, forcing the French to abandon Canada and India. For Spain, it ended with Latin American independence. The second phase of European colonialism extended approximately from 1850 to 1950. The British and French empires were at their height around 1914, when European empires controlled 85 percent of the world. Britain and France had colonies in Africa, Asia, Oceania, and the New World.

5. Many geopolitical labels and identities were created under colonialism that had little or nothing to do with existing social demarcations. The new ethnic or national divisions were colonial inventions, sometimes aggravating conflicts.

6. Like colonialism, economic development has an intervention philosophy that provides a justification for outsiders to guide native peoples toward particular goals. Development usually is justified by the idea that industrialization and modernization are desirable evolutionary advances. Neoliberalism revives and extends classic economic liberalism: the idea that governments should not regulate private enterprise and that free market forces should rule. This intervention philosophy currently dominates aid agreements with postsocialist and developing nations.

7. Spelled with a lowercase *c*, communism describes a social system in which property is owned by the community and in which people work for the common good. Spelled with an uppercase *C*, Communism indicates a political movement and doctrine seeking to overthrow capitalism and to establish a form of communism such as that which prevailed in the Soviet Union from 1917 to 1991. The heyday of Communism was between 1949 and 1989. The fall of Communism can be traced to 1989–1990 in Eastern Europe and 1991 in the Soviet Union. Postsocialist states have followed the neoliberal agenda, through privatization, deregulation, and democratization.

8. By 1900 the United States had become a core nation. Mass production gave rise to a culture that valued acquisitiveness and conspicuous consumption. As subsistence economies yield increasingly to cash, job seeking and unemployment have become global problems. One effect of industrialization has been an accelerated rate of resource depletion.

Key Terms

bourgeoisie, *267*
capital, *262*
capitalist world
    economy, *262*
colonialism, *270*
communism, *276*
Communism, *276*
core, *263*

imperialism, *270*
Industrial
    Revolution, *265*
intervention
    philosophy, *274*
neoliberalism, *275*
periphery, *264*
postcolonial, *274*

semiperiphery, *263*
working class, or
    proletariat, *267*
world-system
    theory, *263*

Chapter 13

Anthropology's Role in a Globalizing World

This chapter applies an anthropological perspective to contemporary global issues. We begin by considering different meanings of the term *globalization*. The fact that certain risks now have global implications leads to a discussion of energy consumption and environmental degradation, including climate change, or global warming. Also considered are the threats that deforestation and emerging diseases pose to global biodiversity and human life. The second half of this chapter turns from ecology to the contemporary flows of people, technology, finance, information, images, and ideology that contribute to a global culture of consumption. Globalization promotes intercultural communication, through the media, travel, and migration, which bring people from different societies into direct contact. Finally, we'll consider how such contacts and external linkages affect indigenous peoples and how those groups have organized to confront and deal with national and global issues.

It would be impossible in a single chapter to discuss all or even most of the global issues that are salient today and that anthropologists have studied. Some such issues (e.g., war, displacement, terrorism, NGOs) have been considered in previous chapters. For timely anthropological analysis of a range of global issues, see recent books by John H. Bodley (2008, 2012) and Richard H. Robbins (2011).

Globalization: Its Meanings and Its Nature

Chapter 2 characterized globalization as a series of processes that promote change in a world in which nations and people are increasingly interlinked. Forces of globalization include international manufacture, commerce, and finance; travel and tourism; transnational migration; and the media, the Internet, and other high-tech information flows.

Mark Smith and Michele Doyle (2002) distinguish between two meanings of globalization:

1. *Globalization as fact:* the spread and connectedness of production, communication, and technologies across the world. This meaning is like the one described above and in Chapter 2.
2. *Globalization as ideology and policy:* efforts by the International Monetary Fund (IMF), the World Bank, and other international financial powers to create a global free market for goods and services.

In this second sense, for neoliberal economists, globalization is the way the world should go. For their opponents—anti-neoliberals—it is the way the world should *not* go (Lewellen 2010). It is this neoliberal view of globalization that has generated the protests described in Chapter 2.

The first meaning is more neutral. Globalization as *systemic connectedness* reflects the relentless and ongoing growth of the world system. In its current form, that system has some radical new aspects. Especially noteworthy are the *speed* of global communication, the *scale* (size and complexity) of global networks, and the *volume* of international transactions.

The fall of the Soviet empire (in 1989–1990) allowed a truly global economy to emerge (Lewellen 2010). Consider three key features of this new economy: (1) it is based on knowledge and information; (2) its networks are transnational; and (3) its core activities, no matter where they take place, can proceed as a unit in real time (Castells 2001).

The Internet makes possible the very rapid global transmission of information and resources. Activities that once involved face-to-face contact are now conducted impersonally and coordinated across vast distances. The computers that take and process your order from Amazon can be on different continents, and the products you order can come from a warehouse anywhere in the world. The average food product now travels 1,300 miles and changes hands a dozen times before it reaches an American consumer (Lewellen 2010). When you order something from the Internet, the only human being you might speak to is the delivery driver (Smith and Doyle 2002).

People increasingly live their lives across borders, maintaining social, financial, cultural, and political connections with more than one nation-state (see Lugo 1997). Examples of such "multiplaced" people include business and intellectual leaders, development workers, and members of multinational corporations, as well as migratory domestic, agricultural, and construction workers (see Lewellen 2010).

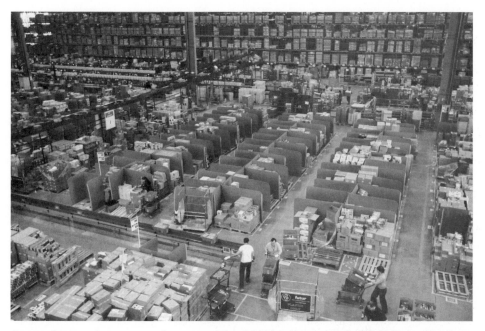

A scene from an Amazon warehouse on Cyber Monday, December 5, 2011, the busiest day of the year for online shoppers. This warehouse could be in a lot of places, but it happens to be in Great Britain.

By the year 2000, multinational corporations accounted for a third of global output and two-thirds of world trade (Gray 1999, p. 62). Profit-seeking multinationals move their operations to places where labor and materials are cheap. This globalization of labor creates unemployment "back home" as industries relocate and outsource abroad.

Multinationals seek out new markets and strive to create new needs among specific target groups. Young people, for example, increasingly construct their identities around consumption, especially of brand-name products. Successful multinationals, including Nike, Apple, Coca-Cola, and McDonald's, invest huge sums in promoting their brands. The goal is to make a particular brand an integral part of the way people see themselves (Klein 2000; Smith and Doyle 2002).

Multinational companies attempt to forge beneficial alliances with politicians and government officials, especially those who are most concerned with world trade. The influence of multinationals extends to key transnational players, such as the European Union and the World Bank. With the globalization of financial markets, nations have less control over their own economies. Such institutions as the World Bank, the International Monetary Fund, the European Union, and the European Central Bank routinely constrain and dictate national economic policies.

As capitalism has spread globally, the gap between rich and poor has widened both within and between nations. The widening gap in the United States was discussed in the chapter "The World System and Colonialism." David Landes (1999) calculated the difference in per capita income between the world's richest nation (he cited Switzerland) and the poorest nation (Mozambique) as 400 to 1, versus around 5 to 1 when the Industrial Revolution began. The key role of knowledge in today's global economy has accelerated this gap, because knowledge tends to be concentrated in core countries and certain regions within them. Knowledge has commercial value as new ideas are converted into products and services that consumers want (Leadbeater 1999).

Energy Consumption and Industrial Degradation

Industrialization entailed a shift from reliance on renewable resources to the use of fossil fuels. Oil, gas, and coal are being depleted rapidly to support a previously unknown level of consumption. Americans are the world's foremost consumers of nonrenewable energy. The average American consumes about 35 times more energy than the average forager or tribesperson (Bodley 1985, 2008).

Table 13.1 compares energy consumption, per capita and total, in the United States and selected other countries. Overall the United States represents 20.4 percent of the world's annual energy consumption, compared with China's 17.3 percent, but the average American consumes 5 times the energy used by the average Chinese and 18 times the energy used by the average inhabitant of India.

Industrialization and factory labor have spread to Asia, Latin America, Africa, and the Pacific. One result of industrial expansion has been the destruction of indigenous economies, ecologies, and populations. Two centuries ago, as industrialization was developing, 50 million people still lived in politically independent bands, tribes, and chiefdoms. Occupying vast areas, those nonstate societies, although not totally isolated, were only marginally affected by nation-states and the world capitalist economy. In 1800, bands, tribes, and chiefdoms controlled half the globe and 20 percent of its population (Bodley 2008). Industrialization tipped the balance in favor of states (see Hornborg and Crumley, eds. 2007).

Globally many contemporary nations are repeating—at an accelerated rate—the process of resource depletion that started in Europe and the United States during the

TABLE 13.1
Energy Consumption in Selected Countries, 2008

Source: Based on data in *Statistical Abstract of the United States*, 2012 (Table 1383), p. 864.

	Total	Per Capita
World	493.0*	74[†]
United States	100.6	330
China	85.1	65
Russia	30.4	216
India	20.0	18
Germany	14.4	174
Canada	14.0	422
France	11.3	180
United Kingdom	9.3	151

*462.8 quadrillion (462,800,000,000,000,000) Btu.
[†]70 million Btu.

Industrial Revolution. Fortunately, however, today's world has some environmental watchdogs that did not exist during the first centuries of the Industrial Revolution. Given national and international cooperation and sanctions, the modern world may benefit from the lessons of the past (see Hornborg, McNeill, and Martinez-Alier, eds. 2007).

A key component of globalization is the globalization of risk (Smith and Doyle 2002). Hazards linked to industrial production, emerging diseases, or a cyber attack can spread quickly beyond their point of origin. Climate risks clearly have become globalized, as each consumer of fossil fuels makes his or her individual contribution (the consumer's "carbon footprint") to global climate change, to which we now turn.

Global Climate Change

Globally, the year 2010 tied 2005 as the hottest ever recorded by NASA's Goddard Institute for Space Studies (GISS), whose analysis covers 131 years (2011 was the second hottest). For the United States (but not the globe), 2012 was the hottest year since record-keeping began in 1895 (Gillis 2013; Zaborenko 2012). Earth's surface temperatures have risen about 1.48°F (0.78°C) since the early 20th century (see Johansen 2008). (This chapter's "Anthropology Today" discusses how this rise has affected an indigenous group in Alaska.) About two-thirds of this increase has been since 1978 (Figure 13.1). Scientific measurements confirm that global warming is not due to increased solar radiation. As most scientists recognize, the causes are mainly *anthropogenic*—caused by humans and their activities. Who can reasonably deny that 7 billion people, along with their animals, crops, machines, and increasing use of fossil fuels, have a greater environmental impact than the 5 million or so pre-Neolithic hunter-gatherers who lived on our planet 12,000 years ago?

FIGURE 13.1   Global Temperature Change
Global annual-mean surface air temperature derived from measurements at meteorological stations has increased by 1.4°F (0.7°C) since the early 20th century, with about 0.9°F (0.5°C) of the increase occurring since 1978.

Source: Goddard Institute for Space Studies, from "Understanding and Responding to Climate Change: Highlights of National Academy of Sciences Reports," http://dels.nas.edu/basc/Climate-HIGH.pdf.

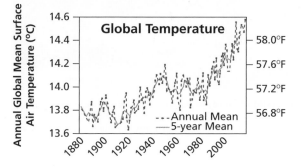

The **greenhouse effect** is a natural phenomenon that keeps the Earth's surface warm. Without greenhouse gases—water vapor (H_2O), carbon dioxide (CO_2), methane (CH_4), nitrous oxide (N_2O), halocarbons, and ozone (O_3)—life as we know it wouldn't exist. Like a greenhouse window, such gases allow sunlight to enter and then trap heat from escaping the atmosphere. All those gases have increased since the Industrial Revolution. Today, the atmospheric concentration of greenhouse gases is at its highest level in 400,000 years. It will continue to rise—as will global temperatures—without actions to slow it down (National Academy of Sciences 2008; National Research Council 2011).

Scientists prefer the term **climate change** to *global warming.* The former term points out that, beyond rising temperatures, there have been changes in sea levels, precipitation, storms, and ecosystem effects. The precise effects of climate change on regional weather patterns have yet to be fully determined. Land areas are predicted to warm more than oceans, with the greatest warming in higher latitudes, such as Canada, the northern United States, and northern Europe. Climate change may benefit these areas, offering milder winters and extended growing seasons. However, many more people worldwide probably will be harmed (see Cribb 2010). Already we know that in the Arctic, temperatures have risen almost twice as much as the global average. Arctic landscapes and ecosystems are changing rapidly and perceptibly, as this chapter's "Anthropology

In the global economy, India and China (shown here) in particular have increased their use of fossil fuels, and consequently their emissions of CO_2. This scene, near Beijing, shows the Shougang steel plant, a major source of air pollution. What's the most polluted place you've ever been to?

Today" illustrates. Coastal communities worldwide can anticipate increased flooding and more severe storms and surges. At risk are people, animals, plants, freshwater supplies, and such industries as tourism and farming (Crate and Nuttall 2008; National Academy of Sciences 2008).

Meeting global energy demand is the single greatest obstacle to slowing climate change. In the United States, about 80 percent of all energy used comes from fossil fuels. Worldwide, energy use continues to grow with economic and population expansion. China and India, in particular, are rapidly increasing their use of energy, mainly from fossil fuels, and consequently their emissions (Figure 13.2). Among the alternatives to fossil fuels are nuclear power and such renewable energy technologies as solar, wind, and biomass generators.

FIGURE 13.2
Projected Emission of Greenhouse Gases, 2025
This figure compares CO_2 emissions per nation in 2000 and projections for 2025. In 2000, the largest emitter of CO_2 was the United States, which was responsible for 25 percent of global emissions. In 2025, China and the developing world may significantly increase their CO_2 emissions relative to the United States.

Source: K. Baumert, T. Herzog, and J. Pershing 2005. Navigating the Numbers: Greenhouse Gas Data and International Climate Policy. World Resources Institute. http://www.wri.org/publication/navigating-the-numbers. Baumert, Harzog, and Pershing 2005.

Trillions of tons of carbon equivalent

World — 57%
Developed — 35%
Developing — 84%

U.S. — 39%
China — 118%
EU — 19%
Former Soviet Union — 42%
India — 70%
Africa — 80%
Brazil — 68%
Japan — 26%
Mexico — 124%

■ 2000 emissions
● Projected emissions, 2025
50% Projected increase from 2000 levels

Greenhouse gases do not include CO_2 from land use change.

Worldwide, energy consumption continues to grow (24 percent between 2000 and 2008) with economic and population expansion. China, in particular, is rapidly increasing its use of energy, mainly from fossil fuels, and consequently its emissions (Figure 13.2). Between 2000 and 2008, per capita energy consumption more than doubled in China, while declining 7 percent in the United States. China now accounts for over 17 percent of world energy consumption, versus 9 percent in 2000. The U.S. share fell from 25 percent in 2000 to 20 percent in 2008 (*Statistical Abstract of the United States 2012*, Table 1383, p. 864).

Environmental Anthropology

Anthropology always has been concerned with how environmental forces influence humans and how human activities affect the environment. The 1950s–1970s witnessed the emergence of an area of study known as cultural ecology, or **ecological anthropology** (see Haenn and Wilk 2006). That field focused on how cultural beliefs and practices helped human populations adapt to their environments, as well as how people used elements of their culture to maintain their ecosystems. Ecological anthropologists showed that many indigenous groups did a reasonable job of managing their resources and preserving their ecosystems (see Menzies 2006). Such groups had traditional ways of categorizing resources and using them sustainably. The term **ethnoecology** describes a society's set of environmental perceptions and practices.

Outside forces increasingly challenge indigenous ethnoecologies. Given national and international incentives to exploit and degrade, ethnoecological systems that once preserved local and regional environments increasingly are ineffective or irrelevant (see Dove, Sajise, and Doolittle 2011). Anthropologists routinely witness threats to the people they study and their environments. Among such threats are commercial logging, industrial pollution, and the imposition of external management systems on local ecosystems (see Johnston 2009). Today's ecological anthropology, *environmental anthropology,* attempts not only to understand but also to find solutions to environmental problems. As aspects of the globalization of risk, such problems must be tackled at the national and international levels (e.g., global warming).

Local people and their landscapes, ideas, values, and traditional management systems face attacks from all sides (see Hornborg, Clark, and Hermele 2011). Outsiders attempt to remake native landscapes and cultures in their own image. The aim of many agricultural development projects, for example, seems to be to make the world as much like a midwestern American agricultural state as possible. Often there is an attempt to impose mechanized farming and nuclear family ownership, even though these institutions may be inappropriate in areas far removed from the midwestern United States. Anthropologists know that development projects usually fail when they try to replace indigenous institutions with culturally alien concepts (Kottak 1990*b*).

Global Assaults on Local Autonomy

A clash of cultures related to environmental change may occur when development threatens indigenous peoples and their environments. A second clash of cultures related to environmental change may occur when external regulation aimed at conservation confronts indigenous peoples and their ethnoecologies. Like development projects, conservation schemes may ask people to change their ways in order to satisfy planners' goals rather than local goals. In places as different as Madagascar, Brazil, and the Pacific Northwest of the United States, people have been asked, told, or forced to abandon basic economic activities because to do so is good for "nature" or "the globe." "Good for the globe" doesn't play very well in Brazil, whose Amazon region has been a focus of international environmentalist attention. Brazilians complain that outsiders (e.g., Europeans and North Americans) promote "global needs" and "saving the Amazon" after having destroyed their own forests for economic growth. Well-intentioned conservation plans can be as insensitive as development schemes that promote radical changes without involving local people in planning and carrying out the policies that affect them. When people are asked to give up the basis of their livelihood, they usually resist.

The spread of environmentalism may reveal radically different notions about the "rights" and value of plants and animals versus humans. In Madagascar, many intellectuals and officials complain that foreigners seem more concerned about lemurs and other endangered species than about the people of Madagascar (the Malagasy). As a geographer there remarked to me, "The next time you come to Madagascar, there'll be no more Malagasy. All the people will have starved to death, and a lemur will have to meet you at the airport." Most Malagasy perceive human poverty as a more pressing problem than animal and plant survival.

On the other hand, who can doubt that conservation, including the preservation of biodiversity, is a worthy goal? The challenge for applied ecological anthropology is to devise culturally appropriate strategies for achieving biodiversity conservation in the face of unrelenting population growth and commercial expansion. How does one get people to support conservation measures that may, in the short run at least, diminish their access to resources? Like development plans in general, the most effective conservation strategies pay attention to the needs and wishes of the local people.

Deforestation

Generations of anthropologists have studied how human economic activities (ancient and modern) affect the environment. Anthropologists know that food producers (farmers and herders) typically do more to degrade the environment than foragers do. Population increase and the need to expand farming caused deforestation in many parts of the ancient Middle East and Mesoamerica (see Hornborg and Crumley, eds. 2007). Even today, many farmers think of trees as giant weeds to be removed and replaced with productive fields.

Often, deforestation is demographically driven—caused by population pressure. For example, Madagascar's population is growing at a rate of 3 percent annually, doubling every generation. Population pressure leads to migration, including rural–urban migration. Madagascar's capital, Antananarivo, had just 100,000 people in 1967. The population stands at about 2 million today. Urban growth promotes deforestation if city dwellers rely on fuelwood from the countryside, as is true in Madagascar. As forested watersheds disappear, crop productivity declines. Madagascar is known as the "great red island," after the color of its soil. On that island, the effects of soil erosion and water runoff are visible to the naked eye. From the look of its rivers, Madagascar appears to be bleeding to death. Increasing runoff of water no longer trapped by trees causes erosion of low-lying rice fields near swollen rivers as well as siltation in irrigation canals (Kottak 2007).

Causes of deforestation include demographic pressure (from births or immigration) on subsistence economies, commercial logging, road building, cash cropping, fuelwood needs associated with urban expansion, and clearing and burning associated with livestock and grazing. The fact that forest loss has several causes has a policy implication: Different deforestation scenarios require different conservation strategies.

What can be done? On this question applied anthropology weighs in, spurring policy makers to think about new conservation strategies. The traditional approach has been to restrict access to forested areas designated as parks, then employ park guards and punish violators. Modern strategies are more likely to consider the needs, wishes, and abilities of the people (often impoverished) living in and near the forest. Since effective conservation depends on the cooperation of the local people, their concerns must be addressed in devising conservation strategies.

Reasons to change behavior must make sense to local people (see Sillitoe 2007). In Madagascar, the economic value of the forest for agriculture (as an antierosion mechanism and reservoir of potential irrigation water) provides a much more powerful

Applied anthropology uses anthropological perspectives to identify and solve contemporary problems that affect humans. Deforestation is one such problem. Here, women take part in a reforestation project in coastal Tanzania near Dar es Salaam.

incentive against forest degradation than do such global goals as "preserving biodiversity." Most Malagasy have no idea that lemurs and other endemic species exist only in Madagascar. Nor would such knowledge provide much of an incentive for them to conserve the forests if doing so jeopardized their livelihoods.

To curb the global deforestation threat, we need conservation strategies that work. Laws and enforcement may help reduce commercially driven deforestation caused by burning and clear-cutting. But local people also use and abuse forested lands. A challenge for the environmentally oriented applied anthropologist is to find ways to make forest preservation attractive to local people and ensure their cooperation. Applied anthropologists must work to make "good for the globe" good for the people.

Emerging Diseases

When humans modify or destroy environments and ecosystems, nature has a way of striking back. Most or all infectious diseases that have emerged in the last few decades are due to human encroachment on wild lands, particularly forests, and to changes in demography (human population increase and changing settlement patterns). In the Amazon, one study showed that an increase in deforestation of just 4 percent produced a 50 percent increase in the incidence of malaria. This is because mosquitoes, which transmit malaria, thrive in the right mix of sunlight and water in recently deforested areas (Robbins 2012; see also Livingstone 1969). The recent emergence and spread of infectious diseases like HIV/AIDS, Ebola, West Nile, SARS (severe acute respiratory syndrome), and Lyme disease are all the result of things people have done to their environments.

The spread of disease from wild to domesticated animals and then to humans has been going on since the Neolithic, when animals were first domesticated. Diseases that spread from animals to humans are known as *zoonotic* diseases, and they pose a huge threat today because of human population increase and forces of globalization. Emerging diseases kill more than two million people annually, and 60 percent of those diseases originate in animals (Robbins 2012).

Especially since the Neolithic, infectious diseases, including malaria and plague, have moved from woods and wildlife to humans, often through their domesticated animals. One such disease, the Nipah virus, began its migration from fruit bats to humans in South Asia. Because fruit bats have co-evolved with the Nipah virus for millions of years, it does little damage to their health. When the virus moves from bats into other species, however, it can be lethal. Fruit bats eat the pulp of fruit and spit out the residue. In rural Malaysia in 1999, an infected bat appears to have dropped a piece of chewed fruit into the food supply of a swine herd (a scenario depicted in the movie *Contagion*). The virus then spread from those pigs to humans. Of 276 people infected in Malaysia, 106 died. Eleven more people died in Singapore, when the virus was exported there via live pigs. South Asia has experienced a dozen smaller Nipah outbreaks in recent years.

Spillovers from wildlife to humans have quadrupled in the last half-century, reflecting increasing human encroachment on disease hotspots, especially in the tropics (Robbins 2012). Wildlife trafficking and modern air travel contribute to the potential for a serious outbreak or pandemic among humans. (A *pandemic* is an epidemic with global scope.) The zero patient for the HIV/AIDS pandemic (in North America, at least) is reputed to have been a flight attendant who flew internationally. HIV/AIDS originally jumped from chimpanzees to humans through bush-meat hunters in Africa, who kill and butcher chimps.

The threat posed by zoonotic diseases has been recognized by biologists and doctors. One international project, called PREDICT, funds teams of veterinarians, conservation biologists, medical doctors, and epidemiologists to identify disease-causing organisms in wildlife before they spread to humans (see http://www.vetmed.ucdavis.edu/ohi/predict/index.cfm). PREDICT, which is financed by the United States Agency for International Development (USAID), attempts to "predict," spot, and prevent the spread of zoonotic diseases in global geographic hotspots with high potential for disease transmission. At least 24 countries in Africa, Latin America, and Asia participate in the program. PREDICT scientists monitor areas where deadly viruses are known to exist and where humans are encroaching. One such locale is a new highway being built to link the Atlantic and Pacific Oceans in South America, traversing Brazil and the Peruvian Andes.

PREDICT scientists also gather blood, saliva, and other samples from high-risk wildlife species to create a "library" of viruses, in order to facilitate identification when a threat is imminent. This library focuses on the animals most likely to carry diseases that affect people, such as primates, rats, and bats. PREDICT scientists also study ways of preventing disease spillovers and the pandemics that might follow. Sometimes solutions can be remarkably simple. In Bangladesh, for example, outbreaks of the Nipah virus were contained by placing bamboo screens (which cost 8 cents each) over the containers used to collect date palm sap (Robbins 2012). Because human groups create the conditions that allow zoonotic pathogens to jump species and to spread, anthropologists have a key role to play in studying the cultural (including economic) causes of environmental encroachment and in suggesting culturally appropriate and workable solutions.

Interethnic Contact

Since at least the 1920s anthropologists have studied the changes that arise from contact between industrial and nonindustrial societies. *Acculturation* refers to changes that result when groups come into continuous firsthand contact—changes in the cultural patterns of either or both groups (Redfield, Linton, and Herskovits 1936, p. 149). Acculturation differs from *diffusion,* or cultural borrowing, which can occur without firsthand contact. For example, most North Americans who eat hot dogs ("frankfurters") have never been to Frankfurt, Germany, nor have most North American Toyota owners or sushi eaters ever visited Japan. Although *acculturation* can be applied to any case of sustained cultural contact and change, the term most often has described **Westernization**—the influence of Western expansion on indigenous peoples and their cultures. Thus, local people who wear store-bought clothes, learn Indo-European languages, and otherwise adopt Western customs are called acculturated.

Acculturation may be voluntary or forced, and there may be considerable resistance to the process.

Different degrees of destruction, domination, resistance, survival, adaptation, and modification of native cultures may follow interethnic contact. In the most destructive encounters, subordinate cultures face obliteration. Often, when powerful outsiders (e.g., colonialists) threaten or conquer indigenous peoples, a "shock phase" follows the initial encounter (Bodley 2008). Outsiders may attack or exploit the local people. Such exploitation may increase mortality, disrupt subsistence, fragment kin groups, damage social support systems, and inspire new religious movements (Bodley 2008). During the shock phase, there may be civil repression backed by military force. Such factors may lead to the group's cultural collapse (ethnocide) or physical extinction (genocide).

Cultural Imperialism and Indigenization

Cultural imperialism refers to the spread or advance of one culture at the expense of others, or its imposition on other cultures, which it modifies, replaces, or destroys—usually because of differential economic or political influence. Thus, children in the French colonial empire learned French history, language, and culture from standard textbooks also used in France. Tahitians, Malagasy, Vietnamese, and Senegalese learned the French language by reciting from books about "our ancestors the Gauls."

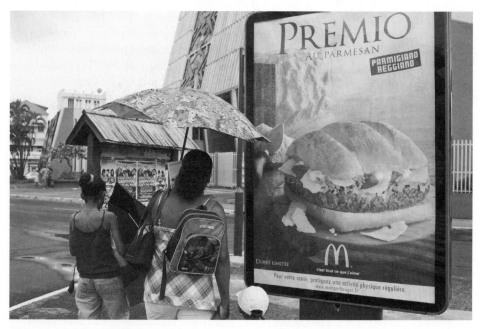

Illustrating both globalization and indigenization, McDonalds's now routinely tries to tailor its offerings to specific cultural appetites. Shown here in downtown Fort de France, Martinique (French West Indies), is a billboard advertising a hamburger topped with Italian cheese (Parmigiano-Reggiano).

To what extent do contemporary global forces promote cultural imperialism? Some commentators see the spread of modern technology, the media, and global brands as erasing cultural differences, as homogeneous products reach more people worldwide. Others note that certain innovations have allowed social groups (local cultures) to express themselves and to survive (Marcus and Fischer 1999). For example, modern radio, TV, film, digital media, and increasingly the Internet (e.g., YouTube) constantly bring local happenings to the attention of a larger public. Susan Boyle's rendition of "I Dreamed a Dream" on a British TV show soon became an Internet sensation and made her a global star. Without YouTube, appreciation of Boyle's voice might have been confined to the United Kingdom. Contemporary media play a role in stimulating and organizing local and community activities of many sorts. Think of ways in which this is done by YouTube, Facebook, and Twitter—global networks all.

In Brazil, local practices, celebrations, and performances have changed in the context of outside forces, including the mass media and tourism. In the town of Arembepe (Kottak 2006), TV coverage stimulated increased participation in a traditional annual performance, the Chegança. This is a danceplay that reenacts the Portuguese discovery of Brazil. Arembepeiros have traveled to the state capital to perform the Chegança before television cameras, for a nationally televised program featuring traditional performances from many rural communities, and cameras have gone to Arembepe to record it.

In several towns along the Amazon River, annual folk ceremonies now are staged more lavishly for TV and video cameras. In the Amazon town of Parantíns, for example, boatloads of tourists arriving any time of year are shown a video recording of the town's annual Bumba Meu Boi festival. This is a costumed performance mimicking bullfighting, parts of which have been shown on national TV. This pattern, in which local communities preserve, revive, and intensify the scale of traditional ceremonies to perform for the media and tourists, is expanding. To see whether I could, I just managed to watch snippets of these annual events in Arembepe and Parantíns on YouTube!

In the process of globalization, people constantly make and remake culture as they assign their own meanings to the information, images, and products they receive from outside. One example of such a process of **indigenization**—how a globally spreading Evangelical Protestantism adapts to local circumstances—was discussed in the chapter "Religion." Indigenization occurs in cultural domains as different as fast food, music, housing styles, science, religion, terrorism, celebrations, and political ideas and institutions (Appadurai 1990; Fiske 2011; Wilk 2006).

A Global System of Images

With globalization more people in many more places imagine "a wider set of 'possible' lives than they ever did before. One important source of this change is the mass media . . ." (Appadurai 1991, p. 197). The United States as a global media center has been joined by Canada, Japan, Western Europe, Brazil, Mexico, Nigeria, Egypt, India, and Hong Kong. Like print (see Anderson 1991), the electronic mass media can diffuse the cultures of different countries within (and often beyond) their own boundaries, thus enhancing national cultural identity. For example, millions of Brazilians who once were cut off (by geographic isolation or illiteracy) from urban, national, and international events and information now participate in a larger "mediascape" (Appadurai 1991) through mass media and the Internet (Kottak 1990*a*, 2009).

Brazil's most popular network (Rede Globo) relies heavily on its own productions, especially *telenovelas* (nightly serial programs often compared to American soap operas). Globo plays each night to the world's largest and most devoted audience (perhaps 80 million viewers throughout the nation and beyond—via satellite TV). The programs that attract this horde are made by Brazilians, for Brazilians.

The mass media and the Internet also play a prominent role in maintaining ethnic and national identities among people who lead transnational lives. Arabic-speaking Muslims, including migrants in several countries, follow the TV network Al Jazeera, based in Qatar, which helps reinforce ethnic and religious identities. As groups move, they can stay linked to each other and to their homeland through global media. **Diasporas** (people who have spread out from an original, ancestral homeland) have enlarged the markets for media, communication, brands, and travel services targeted at specific ethnic, national, or religious groups who now live in various parts of the world.

A Global Culture of Consumption

Besides the electronic media, other key global forces are production, commerce, and finance. As Arjun Appadurai (1991, p. 194) puts it, "money, commodities, and persons unendingly chase each other around the world." Residents of many Latin American communities now depend on outside cash, remitted from international labor migration. The American economy is increasingly influenced by foreign investment and dependent on foreign labor—whether through the immigration of laborers or the export of jobs.

Business, technology, and the media have increased the craving for commodities and images throughout the world (Gottdiener, ed. 2000). This has forced nation-states to accept a global culture of consumption. Almost everyone today participates in this culture. Few people have never seen a T-shirt advertising a Western product. American and English rock stars' recordings blast through the streets of Rio de Janeiro, while taxi drivers from Toronto to Madagascar play Brazilian music. Peasants and tribal people participate in the global economy, not only because they have been hooked on cash but also because their products and images are appropriated by world capitalism (Root 1996). They are commercialized by others (like the Quileute nation in the *Twilight* series). Furthermore, indigenous peoples also market their own images and products, through outlets like Cultural Survival (see Mathews 2000).

People in Motion

Globalization has both enlarged and erased old boundaries and distinctions. Arjun Appadurai (1990, p. 1) characterizes today's world as a "translocal" "interactive system" that is "strikingly new." Whether as refugees, migrants, tourists, pilgrims, proselytizers, laborers, businesspeople, development workers, politicians, terrorists, soldiers, sports figures, or media-borne images, people travel more than ever.

The scale of human movement has expanded dramatically. So important has transnational migration become that many Mexican villagers find "their most important kin and friends are as likely to be living hundreds or thousands of miles away as immediately around them" (Rouse 1991). Most migrants maintain their ties with their native land (phoning, Skyping, texting, e-mailing, visiting, sending money, watching home videos or "ethnic TV"). In a sense, they live multilocally—in different places at once. Dominicans in New York City, for example, have been characterized as living "between two islands": Manhattan and Hispaniola, where the Dominican Republic is located (Grasmuck and Pessar 1991). With so many people "in motion," the unit of anthropological study expands from the local community to the diaspora. Anthropologists increasingly follow descendants of the villages we have studied as they move from rural to urban areas and across national boundaries.

Postmodernity describes our time and situation: today's world in flux, these people on the move who have learned to manage multiple identities depending on place

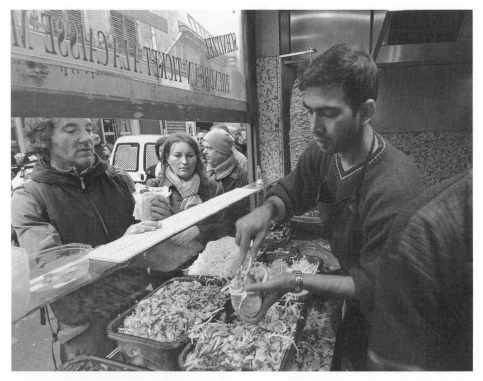

With so many people on the move, the unit of anthropological study has expanded from the local community to the diaspora. This refers to the offspring of an area who have spread to many lands, such as the owners of this falafel shop in Paris, France.

and context. In its most general sense, **postmodern** refers to the blurring and breakdown of established canons (rules or standards), categories, distinctions, and boundaries. The word is taken from **postmodernism**—a style and movement in architecture that succeeded modernism, beginning in the 1970s. Postmodern architecture rejected the rules, geometric order, and austerity of modernism. Modernist buildings were expected to have a clear and functional design. Postmodern design is "messier" and more playful. It draws on a diversity of styles from different times and places—including popular, ethnic, and non-Western cultures. Postmodernism extends "value" globally—well beyond classic, elite, and Western cultural forms. *Postmodern* now is used to describe comparable developments beyond architecture—in music, literature, and visual art. From this origin, postmodernity describes a world in which traditional standards, contrasts, groups, boundaries, and identities are opening up, reaching out, and breaking down.

New kinds of political and ethnic units have emerged along with globalization. In some cases, cultures and ethnic groups have banded together in larger associations. There is a growing pan-Native-American identity (Nagel 1996) and an international pantribal movement as well. Thus, in June 1992, the World Conference of Indigenous Peoples met in Rio de Janeiro concurrently with UNCED (the United Nations Conference on the Environment and Development). Along with diplomats, journalists, and environmentalists came 300 representatives of the tribal diversity that survives under globalization—from Lapland to Mali (Brooke 1992; see also Maybury-Lewis 2002; Maybury-Lewis, Macdonald, and Maybury-Lewis 2009). In May 2012, the United Nations sponsored a high-level commemoration of the fifth anniversary of the adoption of the UN Declaration on the Rights of Indigenous Peoples.

Indigenous Peoples

All too often, conquest, annexation, and development have been associated with genocide—the deliberate extermination of a specific ethnic group. Examples include the Holocaust, Rwanda in 1994, and Bosnia in the early 1990s. Bodley (2008) estimates that an average of 250,000 indigenous people perished annually between 1800 and 1950. The causes included warfare, outright murder, introduced diseases, slavery, land grabbing, and other forms of dispossession and impoverishment.

The indigenous groups that have survived now live within nation-states. Often they maintain a distinct ethnic identity, despite having lost their ancestral cultures to varying degrees. Many such groups aspire to autonomy. As the original inhabitants of their territories, they are called indigenous peoples (see Maybury-Lewis 2002).

The term *indigenous people* entered international law in 1982 with the creation of the United Nations Working Group on Indigenous Populations (WGIP). This group meets annually and has members from six continents. The UN General Assembly adopted its Declaration of Indigenous Rights in 2007. Convention 169, a document supporting cultural diversity and indigenous empowerment, was approved by the International Labor Organization (ILO) in 1989. Such documents, along with the global work of the WGIP,

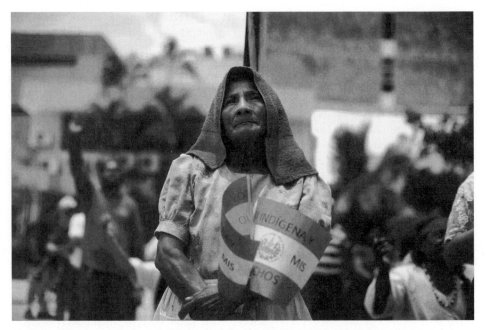

Seeking official recognition of el Salvador's indigenous peoples, a member of one such group, the Lenca, participates in a 2013 demonstration in the national capital, San Salvador. In 1932, dictator Maximiliano Hernandez Martinez, suppressing a peasant uprising, massacred up to 30,000 natives. The survivors, as a result, stopped using their language and hid their traditional customs. Here, as throughout Latin America, things have been changing.

have influenced governments, NGOs, and international agencies to adopt policies favorable to indigenous peoples. Social movements worldwide now use *indigenous people* as a self-identifying label in their quests for social, cultural, and political rights (Brower and Johnston 2007; de la Peña 2005).

In Spanish-speaking Latin America, social scientists and politicians now favor the term *indígena* (indigenous person) over *indio* (Indian), the colonial term that European conquerors used for Native Americans (de la Peña 2005). Until the mid- to late 1980s, Latin American public policy emphasized assimilation. During the past 30 years, the emphasis has shifted from assimilation—*mestizaje*—to cultural difference. In Ecuador, groups seen previously as Quichua-speaking peasants are classified now as indigenous communities with their own territories. Brazil has recognized 30 new indigenous communities in the northeast, a region previously seen as having lost its native population. Guatemala, Nicaragua, Brazil, Colombia, Mexico, Paraguay, Ecuador, Argentina, Bolivia, Peru, and Venezuela now are officially multicultural (Jackson and Warren 2005). Several national constitutions recognize the rights of indigenous peoples to cultural distinctiveness and political representation (de la Peña 2005).

Anthropology Today *Engulfed by Climate Change, Town Seeks Lifeline*

The United Nations' Intergovernmental Panel on Climate Change estimates that 150 million people worldwide could become environmental refugees by 2050 (York 2009). The Alaskan villagers described in this news story are among the first climate change refugees in the United States. During the past 50 years, the state of Alaska has warmed at more than twice the rate of the rest of the United States (York 2009). Residents of Newtok, Alaska, belong to a federally recognized American Indian tribe. Decades ago, the U.S. government mandated that they (and other Alaskan natives) abandon a nomadic life based on hunting and fishing and settle down in what used to be a winter camp. What obligations does government have to local people whose lives have been disrupted not only by government decree but also by global warming?

NEWTOK, Alaska—The earth beneath much of Alaska is not what it used to be. The permanently frozen subsoil, known as permafrost, upon which Newtok and so many other Native Alaskan villages rest is melting, yielding to warming air temperatures and a warming ocean. Sea ice that would normally protect coastal villages is forming later in the year, allowing fall storms to pound away at the shoreline.

Erosion has made Newtok an island, caught between the ever widening Ninglick River and a slough to the north. The village is below sea level, and sinking. Boardwalks squish into the spring muck. Human waste, collected in "honey buckets" that many residents use for toilets, is often dumped within eyeshot in a village where no point is more than a five-minute walk from any other. The ragged wooden houses have to be adjusted regularly to level them on the shifting soil.

Studies say Newtok could be washed away within a decade. Along with the villages of Shishmaref and Kivalina farther to the north, it has been the hardest hit of about 180 Alaska villages that suffer some degree of erosion. Some villages plan to hunker down behind sea walls built or planned by the Army Corps of Engineers, at least for now. Others, like Newtok, have no choice but to abandon their patch of tundra. The corps has estimated that to move Newtok could cost $130 million because of its remoteness, climate and topography. That comes to almost $413,000 for each of the 315 residents. . . .

Newtok's leaders say the corps' relocation estimates are inflated, that they intend to move piecemeal rather than in one collective migration, which they say will save money. But they say government should pay, no matter the cost—if only there were a government agency charged with doing so. There is not a formal process by which a village can apply to the government to relocate.

"They grossly overestimate it, and that's why federal and state agencies are afraid to step in," said Stanley Tom, the current tribal administrator. . . . "They don't want to spend that much money." Still, Newtok has made far more progress toward moving than other villages, piecing together its move grant by grant.

Through a land swap with the U.S. Fish and Wildlife Service, it has secured a new site, on Nelson Island, nine miles south. It is safe from the waves on a windy rise above the Ninglick River. They call it Mertarvik, which means "getting water from the spring." They tell their children they will grow up in a place where E. coli does not thrive in every puddle, the way it does here.

With the help of state agencies, it won a grant of about $1 million to build a
continued

Anthropology Today *continued*

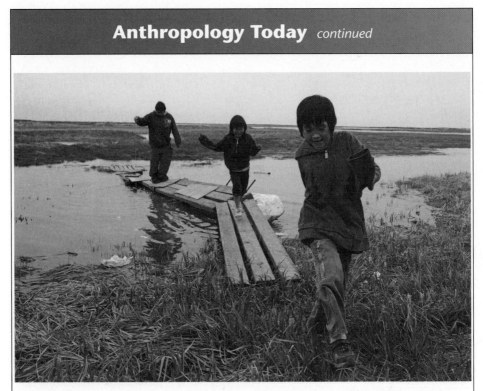

Children of Newtok, Alaska, make their way across improvised boardwalks on a soggy landscape created by thawing permafrost. Rising sea levels and temperatures are eroding the land at a rapid pace. Newtok's 350 residents have become global climate change refugees.

barge landing at the new site. Bids go out this summer, and construction could be complete next year, providing a platform to unload equipment for building roads, water and sewer systems, houses and a new landing strip. . . .

The administrative leaders of Newtok are mostly men in their 40s, nearly all of them related. They are widely praised by outsiders for their initiative and determination to relocate.

Yet nearly any place would seem an improvement over Newtok as it exists today, and not all of its problems are rooted in climate change. Some are almost universal to Alaskan villages, which have struggled for decades to reconcile their culture of subsistence hunting and fishing with the expectations and temptations of the world outside.

Excrement dumped from honey buckets is piled on the banks of the slow-flowing Newtok River, not far from wooden shacks where residents take nightly steam baths. An elderly man drains kerosene into a puddle of snowmelt. Children pedal past a walrus skull left to rot, tusks intact, in the mud beside a boardwalk that serves as a main thoroughfare. There are no cars here, just snow machines, boats and all-terrain vehicles that tear up the tundra. Village elders speak their native Yupik more often than they speak English. They remember when the village was a collection of families who moved with the seasons, making houses from sod, fishing from Nelson Island in the summer, hunting caribou far away in the winter.

Many men still travel with the seasons to hunt and fish. Some will take boats into Bristol Bay this summer to catch salmon alongside commercial fishermen from out of state. But the waterproof jacket sewn from seal gut that Stanley Tom once wore is now stuffed inside a display case at Newtok School next to other relics.

Now Mr. Tom puts on a puffy parka to walk the few hundred feet he travels to work. He checks his e-mail messages to see if there is news from the corps . . . while his brother, Nick, sketches out a budget proposal for a nonprofit corporation to help manage the relocation, presuming the money arrives. . [The projected move to the new site described in this story is proceeding as of 2013].

The indigenous rights movement exists in the context of globalization, including transnational movements focusing on human rights, women's rights, and environmentalism. Transnational organizations have helped indigenous peoples to influence legislation. Since the 1980s there has been a general shift in Latin America from authoritarian to democratic rule. Still, inequality and discrimination persist, including assassinations of indigenous leaders and their supporters (Jackson and Warren 2005).

Ceuppens and Geschiere (2005) explore a recent upsurge, in multiple world areas, of the notion of *autochthony* (being native to, or formed in, the place where found), with an implicit call for excluding strangers. The terms *autochthony* and *indigenous* both go back to classical Greek history, with similar implications. "Autochthony" refers to self and soil. "Indigenous" literally means born inside, with the connotation in classical Greek of being born "inside the house." Both notions stress the rights of first-comers to privileged status and protection versus later immigrants—legal or illegal (Ceuppens and Geschiere 2005; Hornborg, Clark, and Hermele 2011).

During the 1990s, autochthony became an issue in many parts of Africa, inspiring violent efforts to exclude (European and Asian) "strangers." Simultaneously, autochthony became a key notion in debates about immigration and multiculturalism in Europe. European majority groups have claimed the label *autochthon*. This term highlights the prominence that the exclusion of strangers has assumed in day-to-day politics worldwide (Ceuppens and Geschiere 2005). One familiar example is the United States, as represented in debates over illegal immigration.

Identity in Indigenous Politics

Essentialism describes the process of viewing an identity as established, real, and frozen, thus ignoring the historical processes within which that identity was forged.

Identities, however, are not fixed. We saw in the chapter "Ethnicity and Race" that identities can be fluid and multiple. People draw on particular, sometimes competing, self-labels and identities. Some Peruvian groups, for instance, self-identify as *mestizos* but still see themselves as indigenous. Identity is a fluid, dynamic process, and there are multiple ways of being indigenous. Neither speaking an indigenous language nor wearing "native" clothing is required (Jackson and Warren 2005).

Anthropology's Lessons

Anthropology teaches us that the adaptive responses of humans can be more flexible than those of other species because our main adaptive means are sociocultural. However, in the face of globalization, the cultural institutions of the past always influence subsequent adaptation, producing continued diversity in the actions and reactions of different groups as they indigenize global inputs. In our globalizing world, anthropology offers a people-centered vision of social change. The existence of anthropology is itself a tribute to the continuing need to understand similarities and differences among human beings throughout the world.

Anthropology offers relevant, indeed powerful, ways of understanding how the world actually works. Lessons of the past can and should be applied to the present and future, hopefully to benefit humanity. Anthropologists know that civilizations and world powers rise and fall, and that social transformations typically follow major innovations, such as the Neolithic and the Industrial Revolution. There is no guarantee that the current world system and the power relations within it will last forever. What will happen if humans do survive and find themselves living in entirely new systems? Try to answer this question using your new knowledge of anthropology.

Summary

1. Fueling global climate change are human population growth and use of fossil fuels, which produce greenhouse gases. The atmospheric concentration of those gases has increased since the Industrial Revolution, and especially since 1978. Climate change encompasses global warming along with changing sea levels, precipitation, storms, and ecosystem effects. Coastal communities can anticipate increased flooding and more severe storms and surges.

2. Anthropology always has been concerned with how environmental forces influence humans and how human activities affect the biosphere. Many indigenous groups did a reasonable job of preserving their ecosystems. An ethnoecology is any society's set of environmental practices and perceptions. Indigenous ethnoecologies increasingly are being challenged by global forces that work to exploit and degrade—and that sometimes aim to protect—the environment. The challenge for applied ecological anthropology is to devise culturally appropriate strategies

for conservation in the face of unrelenting population growth and commercial expansion.

3. Deforestation is a major factor in the loss of global biodiversity. Causes of deforestation include demographic pressure (from births or immigration) on subsistence economies; commercial logging; road building; cash cropping; fuelwood needs associated with urban expansion; and clearing and burning associated with livestock and grazing. The fact that forest loss has several causes has a policy implication: Different deforestation scenarios require different conservation strategies. Applied anthropologists must work to make "good for the globe" good for the people.

4. The recent emergence and spread of infectious diseases like HIV/AIDS, Ebola, West Nile, SARS, and Lyme disease are all the result of things people have done to their environments. The spread of zoonotic diseases from wild to domesticated animals and then to humans has been going on since the Neolithic. Because human groups create the conditions that allow zoonotic pathogens to jump species and to spread, anthropologists have a key role to play in studying the causes of environmental encroachment and in suggesting culturally appropriate solutions.

5. Cultural imperialism is the spread of one culture and its imposition on other cultures, which it modifies, replaces, or destroys—usually because of differential economic and political power. Some worry that modern technology, including the mass media, is destroying traditional cultures. But others see an important role for new technology in allowing local cultures to express themselves. As the forces of globalization spread, they are modified (indigenized) to fit local cultures. The mass media can help diffuse a national culture within and beyond its own boundaries. The media, including the Internet, also play a role in preserving ethnic and national identities among people who lead transnational lives.

6. People travel more than ever. But migrants also maintain ties with home, so they live multilocally. With so many people "in motion," the unit of anthropological study expands from the local community to the diaspora. Postmodernity describes this world in flux, such people on the move who manage multiple social identities depending on place and context. With globalization, new kinds of political and ethnic units are emerging as others break down or disappear.

7. The term and concept *indigenous people* has gained legitimacy within international law. Governments, NGOs, and international agencies have adopted policies designed to recognize and benefit indigenous peoples. Social movements worldwide have adopted this term as a self-identifying and political label based on past oppression but now signaling a search for social, cultural, and political rights.

8. In Latin America, emphasis has shifted from assimilation to identities that value difference. Transnational organizations have helped indigenous peoples influence national legislative agendas. Recent use of the notion of autochthony (being native to, or formed in, the place where found) includes a call to exclude strangers, such as recent and illegal immigrants. Identity is a fluid, dynamic process, and there are multiple ways of being indigenous. No social movement exists apart from the nation and world that include it.

Key Terms

climate change, *290*
cultural
    imperialism, *297*
diaspora, *299*
ecological
    anthropology, *292*

essentialism, *305*
ethnoecology, *292*
greenhouse
    effect, *290*
indigenization *298*

postmodern, *301*
postmodernism, *301*
postmodernity, *300*
Westernization, *296*

Glossary

A

acculturation   The exchange of cultural features that results when groups come into continuous firsthand contact; the original cultural patterns of either or both groups may be altered, but the groups remain distinct. (34)

achieved status   Social status that comes through talents, actions, efforts, activities, and accomplishments, rather than ascription. (116)

adaptation   The process by which organisms cope with environmental stresses. (3)

age set   Group uniting all men or women (usually men) born during a certain time span; this group controls property and often has political and military functions. (118)

agriculture   Nonindustrial system of plant cultivation characterized by continuous and intensive use of land and labor. (88)

animism   Belief in souls or doubles. (187)

anthropology   The study of the human species and its immediate ancestors. (2)

anthropology and education   Anthropological research in classrooms, homes, and neighborhoods, viewing students as total cultural creatures whose enculturation and attitudes toward education belong to a larger context that includes family, peers, and society. (248)

applied anthropology   The application of anthropological data, perspectives, theory, and methods to identify, assess, and solve contemporary social problems. (12)

archaeological anthropology   The branch of anthropology that reconstructs, describes, and interprets human behavior and cultural patterns through material remains; best known for the study of prehistory. Also known as "archaeology." (7)

ascribed status   Social status (e.g., race or gender) that people have little or no choice about occupying. (115)

assimilation   The process of change that a minority group may experience when it moves to a country where another culture dominates; the minority is incorporated into the dominant culture to the point that it no longer exists as a separate cultural unit. (228)

authority   The formal, socially approved use of power, e.g., by government officials. (108)

B

balanced reciprocity   See *generalized reciprocity*. (101)

band   Basic unit of social organization among foragers. A band includes fewer than one hundred people; it often splits up seasonally. (87)

big man   Figure often found among tribal horticulturalists and pastoralists. The big man occupies no office but creates his reputation through entrepreneurship and generosity to others. Neither his wealth nor his position passes to his heirs. (115)

biocultural   Referring to the inclusion and combination (to solve a common problem) of both biological and cultural approaches—one of anthropology's hallmarks. (5)

biological anthropology   The branch of anthropology that studies human biological diversity in time and space—for instance, hominid evolution, human genetics, human biological adaptation; also includes primatology (behavior and evolution of monkeys and apes). Also called *physical anthropology*. (10)

Black English Vernacular (BEV)   A rule-governed dialect of American English with roots in southern English. BEV is spoken by African American youth and by many adults in their casual, intimate speech—sometimes called *ebonics*. (75)

bourgeoisie   One of Karl Marx's opposed classes; owners of the means of production (factories, mines, large farms, and other sources of subsistence). (267)

C

call systems   Systems of communication among nonhuman primates, composed of a limited number of sounds that vary in intensity and duration. Tied to environmental stimuli. (59)

capital   Wealth or resources invested in business, with the intent of producing a profit. (262)

capitalist world economy   The single world system, which emerged in the 16th century, committed to production for sale, with the object of maximizing profits rather than supplying domestic needs. (262)

cargo cults   Postcolonial, acculturative, religious movements common in Melanesia that attempt to explain European domination and wealth and to achieve similar success magically by mimicking European behavior. (196)

caste system   Closed, hereditary system of stratification, often dictated by religion; hierarchical social status is ascribed at birth, so that people are locked into their parents' social position. (148)

chiefdom   Form of sociopolitical organization intermediate between the tribe and the state; kin-based with differential access to resources and a permanent political structure. (110)

clan   Unilineal descent group based on stipulated descent. (143)

climate change   Global warming, plus changing sea levels, precipitation, storms, and ecosystem effects. (290)

colonialism   The political, social, economic, and cultural domination of a territory and its people by a foreign power for an extended time. (270)

communism   Spelled with a lowercase *c*, describes a social system in which property is owned by the community and in which people work for the common good. (276)

Communism   Spelled with a capital *C*, a political movement and doctrine seeking to overthrow capitalism and to establish a form of communism such as that which prevailed in the Soviet Union (USSR) from 1917 to 1991. (276)

communitas   Intense community spirit, a feeling of great social solidarity, equality, and togetherness; characteristic of people experiencing liminality together. (185)

conflict resolution   The means by which disputes are socially regulated and settled; found in all societies, but the resolution methods tend to be more formal and effective in states than in nonstates. (112)

core   Dominant structural position in the world system; consists of the strongest and most powerful states with advanced systems of production. (263)

core values   Key, basic, or central values that integrate a culture and help distinguish it from others. (21)

correlation   An association between two or more variables such that when one changes (varies), the other(s) also change(s) (covaries); for example, temperature and sweating. (87)

cultural anthropology   The study of human society and culture; describes, analyzes, interprets, and explains social and cultural similarities and differences. (7)

cultural colonialism   Within a nation or empire, domination by one ethnic group or nationality and its culture/ideology over others—e.g., the dominance of Russian people, language, and culture in the former Soviet Union. (234)

cultural consultant   Someone the ethnographer gets to know in the field, who teaches him or her about their society and culture, aka *informant*. (46)

cultural imperialism   The rapid spread or advance of one culture at the expense of others, or its imposition on other cultures, which it modifies, replaces, or destroys—usually because of differential economic or political influence. (297)

cultural relativism   The position that the values and standards of cultures differ and deserve respect. Anthropology is characterized by methodological rather than moral relativism: In order to understand another culture fully, anthropologists try to understand its members' beliefs and motivations. Methodological relativism does not preclude making moral judgments or taking action. (32)

cultural resource management (CRM)   The branch of applied archaeology aimed at preserving sites threatened by dams, highways, and other projects. (15)

cultural rights   Doctrine that certain rights are vested not in individuals but in identifiable groups, such as religious and ethnic minorities and indigenous societies. (33)

cultural transmission   A basic feature of language; transmission through learning. (61)

culture   Traditions and customs that govern behavior and beliefs; distinctly human; transmitted through learning. (2)

curer   Specialized role acquired through a culturally appropriate process of selection, training, certification, and acquisition of a professional image; the curer is consulted by patients, who believe in his or her special powers, and receives some form of special consideration; a cultural universal. (254)

D

daughter languages   Languages developing out of the same parent language; for example, French and Spanish are daughter languages of Latin. (77)

descent   Rule assigning social identity on the basis of some aspect of one's ancestry. (220)

descent group   A permanent social unit whose members claim common ancestry; fundamental to tribal society. (141)

descriptive linguistics   The scientific study of a spoken language, including its phonology, morphology, lexicon, and syntax. (64)

development anthropology   The branch of applied anthropology that focuses on social issues in, and the cultural dimension of, economic development. (243)

diaspora   The offspring of an area who have spread to many lands. (299)

differential access   Unequal access to resources; basic attribute of chiefdoms and states. Superordinates have favored access to

such resources, while the access of subordinates is limited by superordinates. (110)

diffusion   Borrowing between cultures either directly or through intermediaries. (34)

diglossia   The existence of "high" (formal) and "low" (familial) dialects of a single language, such as German. (72)

discrimination   Policies and practices that harm a group and its members. (233)

disease   An etic or scientifically identified health threat caused by a bacterium, virus, fungus, parasite, or other pathogen. (252)

displacement   A linguistic capacity that allows humans to talk about things and events that are not present. (62)

domestic   Within or pertaining to the home. (167)

domestic–public dichotomy   Contrast between women's role in the home and men's role in public life, with a corresponding social devaluation of women's work and worth. (167)

dowry   A marital exchange in which the wife's group provides substantial gifts to the husband's family. (151)

E

ecological anthropology   Study of cultural adaptations to environments. (292)

economy   A population's system of production, distribution, and consumption of resources. (94)

emic   The research strategy that focuses on native explanations and criteria of significance. (46)

enculturation   The social process by which culture is learned and transmitted across the generations. (18)

endogamy   Marriage between people of the same social group. (147)

equity, increased   A reduction in absolute poverty and a fairer (more even) distribution of wealth. (244)

essentialism   The process of viewing an identity as established, real, and frozen, so as to hide the historical processes and politics within which that identity developed. (305)

estrus   Period of maximum sexual receptivity in female baboons, chimpanzees, and other primates, signaled by vaginal area swelling and coloration. (26)

ethnic group   Group distinguished by cultural similarities (shared among members of that group) and differences (between that group and others); ethnic group members share beliefs, values, habits, customs, and norms, and a common language, religion, history, geography, kinship, and/or race. (208)

ethnicity   Identification with, and feeling part of, an ethnic group, and exclusion from certain other groups because of this affiliation. (209)

ethnocentrism   The tendency to view one's own culture as best and to judge the behavior and beliefs of culturally different people by one's own standards. (31)

ethnocide   Destruction by a dominant group of the culture of an ethnic group. (234)

ethnoecology   A culture's set of environmental practices and perceptions. (292)

ethnography   Field work in a particular culture. (7)

ethnology   The theoretical, comparative study of society and culture; compares cultures in time and space. (7)

etic   The research strategy that emphasizes the observer's rather than the natives' explanations, categories, and criteria of significance. (46)

exogamy   Mating or marriage outside one's kin group; a cultural universal. (145)

extended family household   Expanded household including three or more generations. (138)

F

family   A group of people (e.g., parents, children, siblings, grandparents, grandchildren, uncles, aunts, nephews, nieces, cousins, spouses, siblings-in-law, parents-in-law, children-in-law) who are considered to be related in some way, for example, by "blood" (common ancestry or descent) or marriage. (134)

family of orientation   Nuclear family in which one is born and grows up. (135)

family of procreation   Nuclear family established when one marries and has children. (135)

fiscal   Pertaining to finances and taxation. (124)

focal vocabulary   A set of words and distinctions that are particularly important to certain groups (those with particular foci of experience or activity), such as types of snow to Eskimos or skiers. (69)

food production   Plant cultivation and animal domestication. (4, 83)

G

gender identity   Identity based on whether a person feels, and is regarded as, male, female, or something else. (178)

gender roles   The tasks and activities that a culture assigns to each sex. (161)

gender stereotypes   Oversimplified but strongly held ideas about the characteristics of males and females. (161)

gender stratification   Unequal distribution of rewards (socially valued resources, power, prestige, and personal freedom) between men and women, reflecting their different positions in a social hierarchy. (161)

genealogical method   Procedures by which ethnographers discover and record connections of kinship, descent, and marriage, using diagrams and symbols. (45)

general anthropology   The field of anthropology as a whole, consisting of cultural, archaeological, biological, and linguistic anthropology. (4)

generality   Culture pattern or trait that exists in some but not all societies. (27)

generalized reciprocity   Principle that characterizes exchanges between closely related individuals. As social distance increases, reciprocity becomes balanced and finally negative. (100)

genocide   Policies aimed at, and/or resulting in, the physical extinction (through mass murder) of a people perceived as a racial group, that is, as sharing defining physical, genetic, or other biological characteristics. (234)

globalization   The accelerating interdependence of nations in a world system linked economically and through mass media and modern transportation systems. (34)

greenhouse effect   Warming from trapped atmospheric gases. (290)

H

head, village   See *village head*. (114)

health care systems   Beliefs, customs, and specialists concerned with ensuring health and preventing and curing illness; a cultural universal. (253)

hegemony   The internalization of a dominant ideology. (125)

historical linguistics   Subdivision of linguistics that studies languages over time. (77)

holistic   Interested in the whole of the human condition past, present, and future; biology, society, language, and culture. (2)

hominid   A member of the taxonomic family that includes humans and the African apes and their immediate ancestors. (23)

hominin   A member of the human lineage after its split from ancestral chimps; used to describe all the human species that ever have existed, including the extinct ones, but excluding chimps and gorillas. (23)

horticulture   Nonindustrial system of plant cultivation in which plots lie fallow for varying lengths of time. (88)

human rights   Doctrine that invokes a realm of justice and morality beyond and superior to particular countries, cultures, and religions. Human rights, usually seen as vested in individuals, would include the right to speak freely, to hold religious beliefs without persecution, and not to be enslaved. (32)

hypodescent   A rule that automatically places the children of a union or mating between members of different socioeconomic groups in the less privileged group. (220)

I

illness   An emic condition of poor health felt by individual. (252)

imperialism   A policy of extending the rule of a nation or empire over foreign nations and of taking and holding foreign colonies. (270)

incest   Sexual relations with a close relative. (145)

increased equity   See *equity, increased*. (244)

independent invention   Development of the same culture trait or pattern in separate cultures as a result of comparable needs and circumstances. (34)

indigenization   Process by which cultural items introduced from outside are modified to fit the local culture. (298)

indigenous peoples   The original inhabitants of particular territories; often descendants of tribespeople who live on as culturally distinct colonized peoples, many of whom aspire to autonomy. (227)

Industrial Revolution   The historical transformation (in Europe, after 1750) of "traditional" into "modern" societies through industrialization of the economy. (265)

informed consent   An agreement sought by ethnographers from community members to take part in research. (53)

intellectual property rights (IPR)   Each society's cultural base—its core beliefs and principles. IPR is claimed as a group right—a cultural right, allowing indigenous groups to control who may know and use their collective knowledge and its applications. (33)

international culture   Cultural traditions that extend beyond national boundaries. (30)

intersex   Pertaining to a group of conditions reflecting a discrepancy between the external genitals (penis, vagina, etc.) and the internal genitals (testes, ovaries, etc.). (175)

intervention philosophy   Guiding principle of colonialism, conquest, missionization, or development; an ideological justification for outsiders to guide native peoples in specific directions. (274)

interview schedule   Ethnographic tool for structuring a formal interview. A prepared form (usually printed) that guides interviews with households or individuals being compared systematically. Contrasts with a questionnaire because the researcher has personal contact and records people's answers. (45)

K

key cultural consultant   An expert on a particular aspect of local life who helps the ethnographer understand that aspect. (46)

kinesics   The study of communication through body movements, stances, gestures, and facial expressions. (63)

L

law   A legal code, including trial and enforcement; characteristic of state-organized societies. (112)

levirate   Custom by which a widow marries the brother of her deceased husband. (153)

lexicon   Vocabulary; a dictionary containing all the morphemes in a language and their meaning. (64)

life history   Of a cultural consultant; provides a personal cultural portrait of existence or change in a culture. (46)

liminality   The critically important marginal or in-between phase of a rite of passage. (189)

lineage   Unilineal descent group based on demonstrated descent. (143)

linguistic anthropology   The branch of anthropology that studies linguistic variation in time and space, including interrelations between language and culture; includes *historical linguistics* and *sociolinguistics*. (11)

lobola   A customary gift before, at, or after marriage from the husband and his kin to the wife and her kin. (151)

longitudinal research   Long-term study of a community, society, culture, or other unit, usually based on repeated visits. (50)

M

magic   Use of supernatural techniques to accomplish specific aims. (188)

majority groups   Superordinate, dominant, or controlling groups in a social-political hierarchy. (210)

mana   Sacred impersonal force in Melanesian and Polynesian religions. (187)

market principle   Profit-oriented principle of exchange that dominates in states, particularly industrial states. Goods and services are bought and sold, and values are determined by supply and demand. (99)

matrilineal descent   Unilineal descent rule in which people join the mother's group automatically at birth and stay members throughout life. (141)

matrilocality   Customary residence with the wife's relatives after marriage, so that children grow up in their mother's community. (144)

means (or factors) of production   Land, labor, technology, and capital—major productive resources. (95)

medical anthropology   Unites biological and cultural anthropologists in the study of disease, health problems, health care systems, and theories about illness in different cultures and ethnic groups. (252)

minority groups   Subordinate groups in a social–political hierarchy, with inferior power and less secure access to resources than majority groups have. (210)

mode of production   Way of organizing production—a set of social relations through which labor is deployed to wrest energy from nature by means of tools, skills, and knowledge. (94)

monotheism   Worship of an eternal, omniscient, omnipotent, and omnipresent supreme being. (187)

morphology   The study of form; used in linguistics (the study of morphemes and word construction) and for form in general—for example, biomorphology relates to physical form. (64)

multiculturalism   The view of cultural diversity in a country as something good and desirable; a multicultural society socializes individuals not only into the dominant (national) culture, but also into an ethnic culture. (229)

N

nation   Once a synonym for "ethnic group," designating a single culture sharing a language, religion, history, territory, ancestry, and kinship; now usually a synonym for "state" or "nation-state." (227)

nation-state   An autonomous political entity, a country like the United States or Canada. (227)

national culture   Cultural experiences, beliefs, learned behavior patterns, and values shared by citizens of the same nation. (30)

nationalities   Ethnic groups that once had, or wish to have or regain, autonomous political status (their own country). (228)

natural selection   Originally formulated by Charles Darwin and Alfred Russel Wallace; the process by which nature selects the forms most fit to survive and reproduce in a given environment, such as the tropics. (215)

negative reciprocity   See *generalized reciprocity*. (101)

neoliberalism   Revival of Adam Smith's classic economic liberalism, the idea that governments should not regulate private enterprise and that free market forces should rule; a currently dominant intervention philosophy. (275)

neolocality   Postmarital residence pattern in which a couple establishes a new place of residence rather than living with or near either set of parents. (138)

norms   Cultural standards or guidelines that enable individuals to distinguish between appropriate and inappropriate behavior in a given society. (112)

O

office   Permanent political position. (121)

overinnovation   Characteristic of development projects that require major changes in people's daily lives, especially ones that interfere with customary subsistence pursuits. (245)

P

pantribal sodality   A non-kin-based group that exists throughout a tribe, spanning several villages. (117)

participant observation   A characteristic ethnographic technique; taking part in the events one is observing, describing, and analyzing. (42)

particularity   Distinctive or unique culture trait, pattern, or integration. (27)

pastoral nomadism   Movement throughout the year by the whole pastoral group (men, women, and children) with their animals; more generally, such constant movement in pursuit of strategic resources. (93)

pastoralists   People who use a food-producing strategy of adaptation based on care of herds of domesticated animals. (92)

patriarchy   Political system ruled by men in which women have inferior social and political status, including basic human rights. (170)

patrilineal descent   Unilineal descent rule in which people join the father's group automatically at birth and stay members throughout life. (141)

patrilineal–patrilocal complex   An interrelated constellation of patrilineality, patrilocality, warfare, and male supremacy. (169)

patrilocality   Customary residence with the husband's relatives after marriage, so that children grow up in their father's community. (144)

peasant   Small-scale agriculturist living in a state, with rent fund obligations. (99)

periphery   Weakest structural position in the world system. (264)

phenotype   An organism's evident traits, its "manifest biology"—anatomy and physiology. (212)

phoneme   Significant sound contrast in a language that serves to distinguish meaning, as in minimal pairs. (65)

phonemics   The study of the sound contrasts (phonemes) of a particular language. (66)

phonetics   The study of speech sounds in general; what people actually say in various languages. (66)

phonology   The study of sounds used in speech. (64)

physical anthropology   See *biological anthropology*. (10)

plural marriage   Marriage of a man to two or more women (polygyny) or marriage of a woman to two or more men (polyandry)—at the same time; see also *polygamy*. (152)

plural society   A society that combines ethnic contrasts, ecological specialization (i.e., use of different environmental resources by each ethnic group), and the economic interdependence of those groups. (229)

polyandry   Variety of plural marriage in which a woman has more than one husband. (152)

polygamy   Marriage with three or more spouses, at the same time; see also *plural marriage*. (152)

polygyny   Variety of plural marriage in which a man has more than one wife. (152)

polytheism   Belief in several deities who control aspects of nature. (187)

postcolonial   Referring to interactions between European nations and the societies they colonized (mainly after 1800); more generally, "postcolonial" may be used to signify a position against imperialism and Eurocentrism. (274)

postmodern   In its most general sense, describes the blurring and breakdown of established canons (rules, standards), categories, distinctions, and boundaries. (301)

postmodernism   A style and movement in architecture that succeeded modernism. Compared with modernism, postmodernism is less geometric, less functional, less austere, more playful, and more willing to include elements from diverse times and cultures; *post-modern* now describes comparable developments in music, literature, and visual art. (301)

postmodernity   Condition of a world in flux, with people on-the-move, in which established groups, boundaries, identities, contrasts, and standards are reaching out and breaking down. (300)

potlatch   Competitive feast among Indians on the North Pacific Coast of North America. (102)

power   The ability to exercise one's will over others—to do what one wants; the basis of political status. (108)

prejudice   Devaluing (looking down on) a group because of its assumed behavior, values, capabilities, or attributes. (233)

prestige   Esteem, respect, or approval for acts, deeds, or qualities considered exemplary. (122)

productivity   The ability to use the rules of one's language to create new expressions comprehensible to other speakers; a basic feature of language. (61)

proletariat   See *working class*. (267)

protolanguage   Language ancestral to several daughter languages. (77)

R

race   An ethnic group assumed to have a biological basis. (218)

racial classification   The attempt to assign humans to discrete categories (purportedly) based on common ancestry. (211)

racism   Discrimination against an ethnic group assumed to have a biological basis. (218)

reciprocity   One of the three principles of exchange. Governs exchange between social equals; major exchange mode in band and tribal societies. (100)

reciprocity continuum   Regarding exchanges, a range running from general-ized reciprocity (closely related/deferred return) through balanced reciprocity to negative reciprocity (strangers/immediate return). (100)

redistribution   Major exchange mode of chiefdoms, many archaic states, and some states with managed economies. (100)

refugees   People who have been forced (involuntary refugees) or who have chosen (voluntary refugees) to flee a country, to escape persecution or war. (234)

religion   Beliefs and rituals concerned with supernatural beings, powers, and forces. (184)

revitalization movements   Movements that occur in times of change, in which religious leaders emerge and undertake to alter or revitalize a society. (196)

rites of passage   Culturally defined activities associated with the transition from one place or stage of life to another. (189)

ritual   Behavior that is formal, stylized, repetitive, and stereotyped, performed earnestly as a social act; rituals are held at set times and places and have liturgical orders. (189)

S

sample   A smaller study group chosen to represent a larger population. (45)

Sapir-Whorf hypothesis   Theory that different languages produce different ways of thinking. (67)

science   A systematic field of study or body of knowledge that aims, through experiment, observation, and deduction, to produce reliable explanations of phenomena, with reference to the material and physical world. (11)

scientific medicine   As distinguished from Western medicine, a health care system based on scientific knowledge and procedures, encompassing such fields as pathology, microbiology, biochemistry, surgery, diagnostic technology, and applications. (254)

semantics   A language's meaning system. (70)

semiperiphery   Structural position in the world system intermediate between core and periphery. (263)

sexual dimorphism   Marked differences in male and female biology besides the contrasts in breasts and genitals. (160)

sexual orientation   A person's habitual sexual attraction to, and activities with persons of the opposite sex (*heterosexuality*),

the same sex (*homosexuality*), or both sexes (*bisexuality*). (178)

shaman   A part-time religious practitioner who mediates between ordinary people and supernatural beings and forces. (186)

social control   Those fields of the social system (beliefs, practices, and institutions) that are most actively involved in the maintenance of any norms and the regulation of any conflict. (125)

society   Organized life in groups; typical of humans and other animals. (2)

sociolinguistics   Study of relationships between social and linguistic variation; study of language in its social context. (11, 71)

sociopolitical typology   Classification scheme based on the scale and complexity of social organization and the effectiveness of political regulation; includes band, tribe, chiefdom, and state. (110)

sodality   See *pantribal sodality*. (117)

sororate   Custom by which a widower marries the sister of his deceased wife. (152)

state (nation-state)   Complex sociopolitical system that administers a territory and populace with substantial contrasts in occupation, wealth, prestige, and power. An independent, centrally organized political unit, a government. (110)

status   Any position that determines where someone fits in society; may be ascribed or achieved. (115)

stereotypes   Fixed ideas—often unfavorable—about what members of a group are like. (233)

style shifts   Variations in speech in different contexts. (72)

subcultures   Different cultural symbol-based traditions associated with subgroups in the same complex society. (31)

subgroups   Languages within a taxonomy of related languages that are most closely related. (77)

subordinate   The lower, or underprivileged, group in a stratified system. (123)

superordinate The upper, or privileged, group in a stratified system. (123)

survey research Characteristic research procedure among social scientists other than anthropologists. Studies society through sampling, statistical analysis, and impersonal data collection. (51)

symbol Something, verbal or non-verbal, that arbitrarily and by convention stands for something else, with which it has no necessary or natural connection. (18)

syntax The arrangement and order of words in phrases and sentences. (64)

T

taboo Prohibition backed by supernatural sanctions. (188)

totem An animal, plant, or geographic feature associated with a specific social group, to which that totem is sacred or symbolically important. (193)

transgender A category of varied individuals whose gender identity contradicts their biological sex at birth and the gender identity that society assigned to them in infancy. (176)

transhumance One of two variants of pastoralism; part of the population moves seasonally with the herds while the other part remains in home villages. (93)

tribe Form of sociopolitical organization usually based on horticulture or pastoralism. Socioeconomic stratification and centralized rule are absent in tribes, and there is no means of enforcing political decisions. (110)

tropics Geographic belt extending about 23 degrees north and south of the equator, between the Tropic of Cancer (north) and the Tropic of Capricorn (south). (215)

typology, sociopolitical See *sociopolitical typology*. (110)

U

underdifferentiation Planning fallacy of viewing less developed countries as an undifferentiated group; ignoring cultural diversity and adopting a uniform approach (often ethnocentric) for very different types of project beneficiaries. (246)

unilineal descent Matrilineal or patrilineal descent. (142)

universal Something that exists in every culture. (27)

urban anthropology The anthropological study of life in and around world cities, including urban social problems, differences between urban and other environments, and adaptation to city life. (249)

V

variables Attributes (e.g., age, occupation, income) that differ from one person or case to the next. (52)

village head Leadership position in a village (as among the Yanomami, where the head is always a man); has limited authority; leads by example and persuasion. (114)

W

wealth All a person's material assets, including income, land, and other types of property; the basis of economic status. (122)

Westernization The acculturative influence of Western expansion on other cultures. (296)

working class (or proletariat) Those who must sell their labor to survive; the antithesis of the bourgeoisie in Marx's class analysis. (267)

world-system theory Argument for the historic and contemporary social, political, and economic significance of an identifiable global system, based on wealth and power differentials, that extends beyond individual countries. (263)

Photo Credits

Page xxii: © Juliet Kottak Mavromatis

Chapter 1: page 5: © National Anthropological Archives, Smithsonian Institution, Neg. #906-B; p. 6: © Buda Mendes/LatinContent/Getty Images; p. 9: © Randy Olson/Aurora Photos; p. 13: © AP Photo/Obama Presidential Campaign

Chapter 2: p. 22 (top): © William Gottlieb/Corbis; p. 22 (bottom): © St. Petersburg Times/Skip O'Rourke/The Image Works; p. 25: © Clive Bromhall; p. 33: © Louise Gubb/Corbis; p. 35: © Tauseef Mustafa/AFP/Getty Images; p. 36: © Alan Bailey/Getty Images RF

Chapter 3: p. 41: © AP Photo; p. 44: © Amy Toensing/National Geographic Stock; p. 48: © Mary Evans Picture Library/The Image Works; p. 51: © Christopher M. O'Leary; p. 55: © Michael Gurven

Chapter 4: p. 60: © Michael Nichols/Getty Images; p. 65: © Lucas Film/Topham/The Image Works; p. 68: © Lonny Shavelson; p. 69: © Louis Lopez/NewSport/Corbis; p. 72: © Larry Downing/Corbis; p. 75: © Jim Goldberg/Magnum Photos; p. 76: © Joshua Roberts/Bloomberg via Getty Images; p. 79: © Chris Rainier/Enduring Voices Project

Chapter 5: p. 89: © Tyrone Turner/National Geographic Society/Corbis; p. 90: © Earl & Nazima Kowall/Corbis; p. 96: © AP Photo/Imaginechina; p. 102: © American Museum of Natural History Neg. #336116; p. 105: © Carl D. Walsh/Aurora Photos

Chapter 6: p. 109: © Sarah L. Voisin/The Washington Post via Getty Images; p. 111: © Joy Tessman/Getty Images; p. 116: © Burt Glinn/Magnum Photos; p. 120: © John A. Novak/Animals Animals;

p. 122: © Damian Dovarganes//AP/Corbis; p. 128: © Everett Collection/Newscom; p. 130: © Apichart Weerawong//AP/Corbis

Chapter 7: p. 136: © Brenninger/Sueddeutsche Zeitung Photo/The Image Works; p. 137: © Katja Heinemann/Aurora Photos; p. 150: © Marmaduke St. John/Alamy; p. 155 (left): © AP Photo/Mike Hutchings; p. 155 (right): © Stan Honda/AFP/Getty Images

Chapter 8: p. 162: © Robert Harding World Imagery/Alamy; p. 168: © Lindsay Hebberd/Corbis; p. 169: © Hemis.fr/SuperStock; p. 171: National Archives; p. 174: © Karsten Schoene/laif/Redux; p. 177: © Maciej Dakowicz/Alamy; p. 180: © Bartrand Langlois/AFP/Getty Images

Chapter 9: p. 185: © Jose Luis Palaez inc./Blend Images/Getty Images RF; p. 191 (top): © Danita Delimont/Alamy; p. 191 (bottom): © Bob Krist/Corbis; p. 193: © North Wind Picture Archives via AP Images; p. 199: © Victor R. Caivano//AP/Corbis; p. 197: © Thierry Falise/LightRocket via Getty Images; p. 203: © Chicarito/AFP/Getty Images; p. 204: © Stan Grossfeld/The Boston Globe via Getty Images

Chapter 10: p. 211: © Paul Bucknall/Alamy; p. 213 (China): © Ed George/Getty Images; p. 213 (Polynesia): © Darrell Gulin/Corbis; p. 213 (Bolivia): © imagebroker/Alamy; p. 213 (Australia): © Holger Leue/Getty Images; p. 215 (left): © Jan Spieczny/Getty Images; p. 215 (right): © Press Association/The Image Works; p. 220: © Shannon Stapleton/Reuters/Corbis; p. 223: © Philip Jones Griffiths/Magnum Photos; p. 226 (all): © Conrad Kottak; p. 231: © James Marshall/Corbis/Age Fotostock; p. 235 (top): © Bradley Mayhew/Getty Images; p. 235 (bottom): © AP Photo/Sergei Grits

Bibliography

Abelmann, N., and J. Lie 1995. *Blue Dreams: Korean Americans and the Los Angeles Riots.* Cambridge, MA: Harvard University Press.

Ahmed, A. S. 2004. *Postmodernism and Islam: Predicament and Promise,* rev. ed. New York: Routledge.

Allegretto, S. A. 2011. The State of Working America's Wealth, Briefing Paper no. 292, Economic Policy Institute, March 23. http://www.epi.org/page/-/BriefingPaper292.pdf.

Amadiume, I. 1987. *Male Daughters, Female Husbands.* Atlantic Highlands, NJ: Zed.

Anderson, B. 1991. *Imagined Communities: Reflections on the Origin and Spread of Nationalism,* rev. ed. London: Verso.

————. 2006. *Imagined Communities: Reflections on the Origin and Spread of Nationalism,* rev. ed. New York: Verso.

Anderson, R. 1996. *Magic, Science, and Health: The Aims and Achievements of Medical Anthropology.* Fort Worth, TX: Harcourt Brace.

Anderson-Levitt, K. M. 2012 *Anthropologies of Education: A Global Guide to Ethnographic Studies of Learning and Schooling.* New York: Berghahn Books.

Anthropology Newsletter. Published 9 times annually by the American Anthropological Association, Washington, DC.

Antoun, R. T. 2008. *Understanding Fundamentalism: Christian, Islamic, and Jewish Movements,* 2nd ed. Lanham, MD: AltaMira.

Aoki, M. Y., and M. B. Dardess, eds. 1981. *As the Japanese See It: Past and Present.* Honolulu: University Press of Hawaii.

Appadurai, A. 1990. Disjuncture and Difference in the Global Cultural Economy. *Public Culture* 2(2):1–24.

————. 1991. Global Ethnoscapes: Notes and Queries for a Transnational Anthropology. In *Recapturing Anthropology: Working in the Present,* R. G. Fox, ed., pp. 191–210. Santa Fe, NM: School of American Research Advanced Seminar Series.

————. 1996. *Modernity at Large. Cultural Dimensions of Globalization.* Minneapolis: University of Minnesota Press.

Appadurai, A., ed. 2001. *Globalization.* Durham, NC: Duke University Press.

Arrighi, G. 2010. *The Long Twentieth Century: Money, Power, and the Origins of Our Times,* new and updated ed. New York: Verso.

Arnold, J. E., et al. 2012. *Life at Home in the Twenty-first Century: 32 Families Open Their Doors.* Los Angeles: Cotsen Institute of Archaeology Press.

Asad, T. 2008 (orig. 1983). The Construction of Religion as an Anthropological Category. In *A Reader in the Anthropology of Religion,* M. Lambek, ed., pp. 110–132. Malden, MA: Blackwood.

Ashcroft, B., G. Griffiths, and H. Tiffin 1989. *The Empire Writes Back: Theory and Practice in Post-colonial Literatures.* New York: Routledge.

Baer, H. A., M. Singer, and I. Susser 2013. *Medical Anthropology and the World System,* 3rd ed. Santa Barbara, CA: Praeger.

Bailey, R. C. 1990. *The Behavioral Ecology of Efe Pygmy Men in the Ituri Forest, Zaire.* Ann Arbor: Anthropological Papers, Museum of Anthropology, University of Michigan, no. 86.

Bailey, R. C., G. Head, M. Jenike, B. Owen, R. Rechtman, and E. Zechenter 1989. Hunting and Gathering in Tropical Rain Forests: Is It Possible? *American Anthropologist* 91:59–82.

Barnaby, F., ed. 1984. *Future War: Armed Conflict in the Next Decade.* London: M. Joseph.

Barnard, A., ed. 2004. *Hunter-Gatherers in History, Archaeology and Anthropology.* New York: Oxford University Press.

Baro, M., and T. F. Deubel 2006. Persistent Hunger: Perspectives on Vulnerability, Famine, and Food Security in Sub-Saharan Africa. *Annual Review of Anthropology* 35:521–538.

Baron, D. E. 2009. *A Better Pencil: Readers, Writers, and the Digital Revolution.* New York: Oxford University Press.

Barringer, F. 1992. New Census Data Show More Children Living in Poverty. *New York Times,* May 29, pp. A1, A12–A13.

Barth, F. 1968. (orig. 1958). Ecologic Relations of Ethnic Groups in Swat, North Pakistan. In *Man in Adaptation: The Cultural Present,* Yehudi Cohen, ed., pp. 324–331. Chicago: Aldine.

Beeman, W. 1986. *Language, Status, and Power in Iran.* Bloomington: Indiana University Press.

Behar, R. 1993. *Translated Woman: Crossing the Border with Esperanza's Study.* Boston: Beacon Press.

Benedict, R. F. 1946. *The Chrysanthemum and the Sword.* Boston: Houghton Mifflin.

Bennett, J. W. 1969. *Northern Plainsmen: Adaptive Strategy and Agrarian Life.* Chicago: Aldine.

Berger, P. 2010. Pentecostalism—Protestant Ethic or Cargo Cult? Peter Berger's blog, July 29. http://blogs.the-american-interest.com/berger/2010/07/29/pentecostalism-%E2%80%93-protestant-ethic-or-cargo-cult/.

Beriss, D. 2004. *Black Skins, French Voices: Caribbean Ethnicity and Activism in Urban France.* Boulder, CO: Westview.

Berlin, B., and P. Kay 1992 (orig. 1969). *Basic Color Terms: Their Universality and Evolution,* 2nd ed. Berkeley: University of California Press.

Bernard, H. R. 2011. *Research Methods in Anthropology: Qualitative and Quantitative Approaches.* 5th ed. Lanham, MD: AltaMira.

Bernard, H. R., ed. 1998. *Handbook of Methods in Cultural Anthropology,* Walnut Creek, CA: AltaMira.

Bicker, A., P. Sillitoe, and J. Pottier, eds. 2004. *Investigating Local Knowledge: New Directions, New Approaches.* Burlington, VT: Ashgate.

Bird-David, N. 1992. Beyond "The Original Affluent Society": A Culturalist Reformulation. *Current Anthropology* 33(1):25–47.

Bjuremalm, H. 1997. Rattvisa kan skippas i Rwanda: Folkmordet 1994 gar attt forklara och analysera pa samma satt som forintelsen av judarna. *Dagens Nyheter* [06-03-19777, p. B3].

Blackwood, E. 2010. *Falling into the Lesbi World: Desire and Difference in Indonesia.* Honolulu: University of Hawaii Press.

Blau, S., and D. Ubelaker, eds. 2009. *Handbook of Forensic Anthropology and Archaeology.* Walnut Creek, CA: Left Coast Press.

Blommaert, J. 2010. *Sociolinguistics of Globalization.* New York: Cambridge University Press.

Bodley, J. H. 2008. *Victims of Progress,* 5th ed. Lanham, MD: AltaMira.

———. 2012. *Anthropology and Contemporary Human Problems,* 6th ed. Lanham, MD: AltaMira.

Boellstorff, T. 2007. Queer Studies in the House of Anthropology. *Annual Review of Anthropology* 36:375–389.

Bolton, R. 1981. Susto, Hostility, and Hypoglycemia. *Ethnology* 20(4): 227–258.

Bonvillain, N. 2007 *Women and Men: Cultural Constructs of Gender,* 4th ed. Upper Saddle River, NJ: Prentice Hall.

———. 2012. *Language, Culture, and Communication: The Meaning of Messages,* 7th ed. Boston: Pearson Prentice Hall.

Bourdieu, P. 1977. *Outline of a Theory of Practice.* R. Nice (trans.). Cambridge: Cambridge University Press.

———. 1982. *Ce Que Parler Veut Dire.* Paris: Fayard.

———. 1984. *Distinction: A Social Critique of the Judgment of Taste.* R. Nice (trans.). Cambridge, MA: Harvard University Press.

Bourque, S. C., and K. B. Warren 1987. Technology, Gender and Development. *Daedalus* 116(4): 173–197.

Bowen, J. R. 2011. *Religion in Practice: An Approach to Anthropology of Religion,* 5th ed. Boston: Pearson/Allyn and Bacon.

Bowie, F. 2006. *The Anthropology of Religion: An Introduction*. Malden, MA: Blackwell.

Braudel, F. 1981. *Civilization and Capitalism, 15th–18th Century,* Volume I, *The Structure of Everyday Life: The Limits*. S. Reynolds (trans.). New York: Harper and Row.

———. 1982. *Civilization and Capitalism, 15th–18th Century,* Volume II, *The Wheels of Commerce*. New York: Harper and Row.

———. 1992. *Civilization and Capitalism, 15th–18th Century,* Volume III, *The Perspective of the World*. Berkeley: University of California Press.

Bremen, J., and A. Shimizu, eds. 1999. *Anthropology and Colonialism in Asia and Oceania*. London: Curzon.

Brenneis, D. 1988. Language and Disputing. *Annual Review of Anthropology* 17:221–237.

Brettell, C. B., and C. F. Sargent, eds. 2009. *Gender in Cross-Cultural Perspective*, 5th ed. Upper Saddle River, NJ: Pearson/Prentice Hall.

Briggs, C. L. 2005. Communicability, Racial Discourse, and Disease. *Annual Review of Anthropology* 34:269–291.

Briody, E. K., and R. T. Trotter II 2008. *Partnering for Organizational Performance; Collaboration and Culture in the Global Workplace*. Lanham, MD: Rowman & Littlefield.

Brooke, J. 1992. Rio's New Day in Sun Leaves Laplander Limp. *New York Times,* June 1, p. A7.

Brookings Institution 2010. *State of Metropolitan America: On the Front Lines of Demographic Transition*. The Brookings Institution Metropolitan Policy Program. http://www.brookings.edu/~/media/Files/Programs/Metro/state_of_metro_america/metro_america_report1.pdf.

Brower, B., and B. R. Johnston 2007. *Disappearing Peoples? Indigenous Groups and Ethnic Minorities in South and Central Asia*. Walnut Creek, CA: Left Coast Press.

Brown, A. 2001. Communism. *International Encyclopedia of the Social & Behavioral Sciences,* pp. 2323–2326. New York: Elsevier.

Brown, D. 1991. *Human Universals*. New York: McGraw-Hill.

Brown, M. F. 2003. *Who Owns Native Culture?* Cambridge, MA: Harvard University Press.

Brown, P. J., and R. L. Barrett 2010. *Understanding and Applying Medical Anthropology*, 2nd ed. New York: McGraw-Hill.

Brownstein, R. 2010. The Gray and the Brown: The Generational Mismatch. *National Journal*, July 24. http://www.nationaljournal.com/njmagazines/cs_20100724_3946php.

———. 2003. Invisible Clues to New World Domestication. *Science* 299 (February 14) 1029–1030.

———. 2007a. Artifact: Maize Pollen. *Archaeology* 60(4). www.archaeology.org/0707/etc/artifact.html.

———. 2007b. Little Things Mean a Lot: The Search for Starch Grains at Archaeological Sites. *Mammoth Trumpet* 22(4):3–4, 16.

Buikstra, J. E., and C. A. Roberts, eds. 2012. *The Global History of Paleopathology: Pioneers and Prospects*. Oxford, NY: Oxford University Press.

Burdick, J. 1993. *Looking for God in Brazil: The Progressive Catholic Church in Urban Brazil's Religious Arena*. Berkeley: University of California Press.

Butler, R. 2005. World's Largest Cities: [Ranked by City Population]. http://www.mongabay.com/cities_pop_01.htm.

Buvinic, M. 1995. The Feminization of Poverty? Research and Policy Needs. In *Reducing Poverty through Labour Market Policies*. Geneva: International Institute for Labour Studies.

Campbell, C. J., ed. 2011. *Primates in Perspective,* 2nd ed. New York: Oxford University Press.

Carey, B. 2007. Washoe, a Chimp of Many Words Dies at 42. *New York Times,* November 1. http://www.nytimes.com.

Carneiro, R. L. 1956. Slash-and-Burn Agriculture: A Closer Look at Its Implications for Settlement Patterns. In *Men and Cultures*. Selected Papers of the Fifth International Congress of Anthropological and Ethnological Sciences, pp. 229–234. Philadelphia: University of Pennsylvania Press.

———. 1968. (orig. 1961). Slash-and-Burn Cultivation among the Kuikuru and Its Implications for Cultural Development in the Amazon Basin. In *Man in Adaptation: The Cultural Present,* Y. A. Cohen, ed., pp. 131–145. Chicago: Aldine.

———. 1970. A Theory of the Origin of the State. *Science* 69:733–738.

Carsten, J. 2004. *After Kinship*. New York: Cambridge University Press.

Carter, J. 1988. Freed from Keepers and Cages, Chimps Come of Age on Baboon Island. *Smithsonian,* June, pp. 36–48.

Casanova, J. 2001. Religion, the New Millennium, and Globalization. *Sociology of Religion* 62:415-441.

Castells, M. 2001. Information Technology and Global Capitalism. In *On the Edge: Living with Global Capitalism*, W. Hutton and A. Giddens, eds. London: Vintage.

Cernea, M., ed. 1991. *Putting People First: Sociological Variables in Rural Development,* 2nd ed. New York: Oxford University Press (published for the World Bank).

Ceuppens, B., and P. Geschiere 2005. Autochthony: Local or Global? New Modes in the Struggle over Citizenship and Belonging in Africa and Europe. *Annual Review of Anthropology* 34:385–407.

Chagnon, N. A. 1992 (orig. 1983). *Yanomamo: The Fierce People,* 4th ed. New York: Harcourt Brace.

———. 1997. *Yanomamo,* 5th ed. Fort Worth, TX: Harcourt Brace.

Chakrabarty, D. 2007. *Provincializing Europe: Postcolonial Thought and Historical Difference.* Princeton, NJ: Princeton University Press.

Chambers, E. 1987. Applied Anthropology in the Post-Vietnam Era: Anticipations and Ironies. *Annual Review of Anthropology* 16:309–337.

Chapais, B. 2008. *Primeval Kinship: How Pair Bonding Gave Birth to Human Society.* Cambridge, MA: Harvard University Press.

Chatterjee, P. 2004. *The Politics of the Governed: Reflections on Popular Politics in Most of the World*. New York: Columbia University Press.

Chibnik, M. 2011. *Anthropology, Economics, and Choice*. Austin: University of Texas Press.

Childe, V.G. 1951. *Man Makes Himself.* New York: New American Library.

Choi, C. Q. 2011. Savanna, Not Forest, Was Human Ancestors' Proving Ground. *Live Science*, August 3. http://www.livescience.com/15377-savannas-human-ancestors-evolution.html.

Chomsky, N. 1957. *Syntactic Structures.* The Hague: Mouton.

Clark, G. 2010. *African Market Women: Seven Life Stories from Ghana*. Indianapolis: Indiana University Press.

Clifford, J. 1982. *Person and Myth: Maurice Leenhardt in the Melanesian World*. Berkeley: University of California Press.

———. 1988. *The Predicament of Culture: Twentieth-Century Ethnography, Literature and Art*. Cambridge, MA: Harvard University Press.

Coburn, N. 2011. *Bazaar Politics: Power and Pottery in an Afghan Market Town*. Stanford, CA: Stanford University Press.

Cody, D. 1998. British Empire. http://www.stg.brown.edu/projects/hypertext/landow/victorian/history/Empire.html, May 18.

Cohen, M. N., and G. J. Armelagos, eds. 1984. *Paleopathology at the Origins of Agriculture*. New York: Academic Press.

Cohen, P. 2008. The Pentagon Enlists Social Scientists to Study Security Issues. *New York Times,* June 18.

Cohen, R. 1967. *The Kanuri of Bornu.* New York: Holt, Rinehart & Winston.

Cohen, Y. 1974. Culture as Adaptation. In *Man in Adaptation: The Cultural Present,* 2nd ed., Y. A. Cohen, ed., pp. 45–68. Chicago: Aldine.

Colson, E., and T. Scudder 1975. New Economic Relationships between the Gwembe Valley and the Line of Rail. In *Town and Country in Central and Eastern Africa,* David Parkin, ed., pp. 190–210. London: Oxford University Press.

———. 1988. *For Prayer and Profit: The Ritual, Economic, and Social Importance of Beer in Gwembe District, Zambia, 1950–1982.* Stanford, CA: Stanford University Press.

Cooper, F., and A. L. Stoler, eds. 1997. *Tensions of Empire: Colonial Cultures in a Bourgeois World.* Berkeley: University of California Press.

Crapo, R. H. 2003. *Anthropology of Religion: The Unity and Diversity of Religions.* Boston: McGraw-Hill.

Crate, S. A., and M. Nuttall 2008. *Anthropology and Climate Change: From Encounters to Actions.* Walnut Creek, CA: Left Coast Press.

Cresswell, T. 2006. *On the Move: Mobility in the Modern West.* New York: Routledge.

Cribb, J. 2010. *The Coming Famine: The Global Food Crisis and What We Can Do to Avoid It.* Berkeley: University of California Press.

Crosby, A. W., Jr. 2003. *The Columbian Exchange: Biological and Cultural Consequences of 1492.* Westport, CT: Praeger.

Cultural Survival Quarterly. Quarterly journal. Cambridge, MA: Cultural Survival, Inc.

Dalton, R. 2006. Ethiopia: Awash with Fossils. http://www.nature.com/news/2006/060102/full/439014a.html.

DaMatta, R. 1991. *Carnivals, Rogues, and Heroes: An Interpretation of the Brazilian Dilemma.* Translated from the Portuguese by John Drury. Notre Dame, IN: University of Notre Dame Press.

D'Andrade, R. 1984. Cultural Meaning Systems. In *Culture Theory: Essays on Mind, Self, and Emotion,* R. A. Shweder and R. A. Levine, eds., pp. 88–119. Cambridge: Cambridge University Press.

Das, V., and D. Poole, eds. 2004. *Anthropology in the Margins of the State.* Santa Fe, NM: School of American Research Press.

Degler, C. 1970. *Neither Black nor White: Slavery and Race Relations in Brazil and the United States.* New York: Macmillan.

de la Peña, G. 2005. Social and Cultural Policies toward Indigenous Peoples: Perspectives from Latin America. *Annual Review of Anthropology* 34:717–739.

DeNavas-Walt, C., B. D. Proctor, and J. C. Smith 2010. *Income, Poverty, and Health Insurance Coverage in the United States: 2009.* U.S. Census Bureau, Current Population Reports, P60-238. Washington, DC: U.S. Government Printing Office. http://www.census.gov/prod/2010pubs/p60-238.pdf.

Dentan, R. K. 1979. *The Semai: A Nonviolent People of Malaya,* Fieldwork edn. New York: Harcourt Brace.

———. 2008. *Overwhelming Terror: Love, Fear, Peace and Violence among the Semai of Malaysia.* Lanham, MD: Rowman & Littlefield.

De Vos, G. A., W. O. Wetherall, and K. Stearman 1983. *Japan's Minorities: Burakumin, Koreans, Ainu and Okinawans.* Report no. 3. London: Minority Rights Group.

DeWaal F.B.M. 1997. *Bonobo: The Forgotten Ape.* Berkeley: University of California Press.

———. 1998. *Chimpanzee Politics: Power and Sex among Apes,* rev. ed. Baltimore: Johns Hopkins University Press.

Diamond, J. M. 1990. A Pox upon Our Genes. *Natural History,* February, pp. 26–30.

———. 1997. *Guns, Germs, and Steel: The Fates of Human Societies.* New York: Norton.

Di Leonardo, M., ed., 1991a. *Gender at the Crossroads of Knowledge: Feminist Anthropology in the Postmodern Era.* Berkeley: University of California Press.

———. 1991b. *Toward a New Anthropology of Gender.* Berkeley: University of California Press.

Dillon, S. 2006. In School across U.S., the Melting Pot Overflows. *New York Times,* August 27. http://www.nytimes.com.

Divale, W. T., and M. Harris 1976. Population, Warfare, and the Male Supremacist Complex. *American Anthropologist* 78:521–538.

Donham, D. L. 2011. *Violence in a Time of Liberation: Murder and Ethnicity at a South African Gold Mine, 1994.* Durham, NC: Duke University Press.

Dorward, D. C., ed. 1983. *The Igbo "Women's War" of 1929: Documents Relating to the Aba Riots in Eastern Nigeria.* Wakefield, England: East Ardsley.

Dove, M. R., and C. Carpenter, eds. 2008. *Environmental Anthropology: A Historical Reader*. Malden, MA: Blackwell.

Dove, M. R., P. E. Sajise, and A. A. Doolittle, eds. 2011. *Beyond the Sacred Forest: Complicating Conservation in Southeast Asia*. Durham, NC: Duke University Press.

Dressler, W. W., K. S. Oths, and C. C. Gravlee 2005. Race and Ethnicity in Public Health Research. *Annual Review of Anthropology* 34:231–252.

Duffield, M., and V. Hewitt, eds. 2009. *Empire, Development, and Colonialism: The Past in the Present*. Rochester, NY: James Currey.

Duranti, A., ed. 2009. *Linguistic Anthropology: A Reader*. Malden, MA: Wiley Blackwell.

Durkheim, E. 1951 (orig. 1897). *Suicide: A Study in Sociology*. Glencoe, IL: Free Press.

———. 2001 (orig. 1912). *The Elementary Forms of the Religious Life*. Translated by Carol Cosman. Abridged with an introduction and notes by Mark S. Cladis. New York: Oxford University Press.

Dwyer, K. 1982. *Moroccan Dialogues: Anthropology in Question*. Baltimore: Johns Hopkins University Press.

Earle, T. K. 1987. Chiefdoms in Archaeological and Ethnohistorical Perspective. *Annual Review of Anthropology* 16:279–308.

———. 1997. *How Chiefs Come to Power: The Political Economy in Prehistory*. Stanford, CA: Stanford University Press.

Eckert, P. 1989. *Jocks and Burnouts: Social Categories and Identity in the High School*. New York: Teachers College Press, Columbia University.

———. 2000. *Linguistic Variation as Social Practice: The Linguistic Construction of Identity in Belten High*. Malden, MA: Blackwell.

Eckert, P., and S. McConnell-Ginet 2013. *Language and Gender*, 2nd ed. Cambridge, UK: Cambridge University Press.

Eckert, P., and N. Mendoza-Denton 2002. Getting real in the golden state. *Language*, March. 29.

Edelman, M., and A. Haugerud 2005. *The Anthropology of Development and Globalization: From Classical Political Economy to Contemporary Neoliberalism*. Malden, MA: Blackwell.

Errington, F., and D. Gewertz 1987. *Cultural Alternatives and a Feminist Anthropology: An Analysis of Culturally Constructed Gender Interests in Papua New Guinea*. New York: Cambridge University Press.

Ervin, A. M. 2005. *Applied Anthropology: Tools and Perspectives for Contemporary Practice,* 2nd ed. Boston: Pearson/Allyn & Bacon.

Escobar, A. 1991. Anthropology and the Development Encounter: The Making and Marketing of Development Anthropology. *American Ethnologist* 18:658–682.

———. 1994. Welcome to Cyberia: Notes on the Anthropology of Cyberculture. *Current Anthropology* 35(3):211–231.

———. 2012. *Encountering Development: The Making and Unmaking of the Third World*. Princeton, NJ: Princeton University Press.

Eskridge, W. N., Jr. 1996. *The Case for Same-Sex Marriage: From Sexual Liberty to Civilized Commitment*. New York: Free Press.

Evans-Pritchard, E. E. 1970. Sexual Inversion among the Azande. *American Anthropologist* 72:1428–1433.

———. 1998. *World Prehistory: A Brief Introduction,* 4th ed. New York: Longman.

———. 2012. *Archeology: A Brief Introduction,* 11th ed. Upper Saddle River, NJ: Prentice Hall.

Farner, R. F., ed. 2004. *Nationalism, Ethnicity, and Identity: Cross-National and Comparative Perspectives*. New Brunswick, NJ: Transaction.

Farr, D. M. L. 1980. British Empire. *Academic American Encyclopedia*. Princeton, NJ: Arete, volume 3, pp. 495–496.

Fasold, R. W., and J. Connor-Linton 2006. *An Introduction to Language and Linguistics*. New York: Cambridge University Press.

Fearon, James D. 2003. Ethnic and Cultural Diversity by Country. *Journal of Economic Growth* 8:2 (June 2003):195–222.

Ferguson, R. B. 1995. *Yanomami Warfare: A Political History*. Santa Fe, NM: School of American Research Press.

———. 2002. *The State, Identity, and Violence: Political Disintegration in the Post-Cold War Era*. New York: Routledge.

Ferraro, G., and E. Briody 2013. *The Cultural Dimension of Global Business,* 7th ed. Boston: Pearson.

Feuer, J. 2012. The Clutter Culture, *UCLA Magazine Online*, July 1, 2012, http://magazine.ucla.edu/features/the-clutter-culture/.

Fields, J. M. 2004. America's Families and Living Arrangements: 2003. U.S. Census Bureau. *Current Population Reports,* P20–553, November. http://www.census.gov.

Finkler, K. 1985. *Spiritualist Healers in Mexico: Successes and Failures of Alternative Therapeutics*. South Hadley, MA: Bergin and Garvey.

Finnstrom, S. 1997. Postcoloniality and the Postcolony: Theories of the Global and the Local. http://www.stg.brown.edu/projects/hypertext/landow/post/poldiscourse/finnstrom/finnstrom1.html.

Fiske, J. 1989. *Understanding Popular Culture*. Boston: Unwin Hyman.

———. 2011. *Reading the Popular,* 2nd ed. New York: Routledge.

———. 2003b. The Origin of War: New ^{14}C Dates from Ancient Mexico. *Proceedings of the National Academy of Sciences of the United States of America,* 100(20):11801–11805.

Fleisher, M. L. 2000. *Kuria Cattle Raiders: Violence and Vigilantism on the Tanzania/Kenya Frontier*. Ann Arbor: University of Michigan Press.

Ford, C. S., and F. A. Beach 1951. *Patterns of Sexual Behavior*. New York: Harper Torchbooks.

Fortes, M. 1950. Kinship and Marriage among the Ashanti. In *African Systems of Kinship and Marriage,* A. R. Radcliffe-Brown and D. Forde, eds., pp. 252–284. London: Oxford University Press.

Fortier, J. 2009. The Ethnography of South Asian Foragers. *Annual Review of Anthropology* 39:99–114.

Foster, G. M., and B. G. Anderson 1978. *Medical Anthropology*. New York: McGraw-Hill.

Foucault, M. 1979. *Discipline and Punish: The Birth of the Prison*. A. Sheridan (trans.). New York: Vintage Books.

———. 1990. *The History of Sexuality,* Volume 2, *The Use of Pleasure*. R. Hurley (trans.). New York: Vintage.

Fouts, R. S. 1997. *Next of Kin: What Chimpanzees Have Taught Me about Who We Are*. New York: William Morrow.

Fouts, R. S., D. H. Fouts, and T. E. Van Cantfort 1989. The Infant Loulis Learns Signs from Cross-Fostered Chimpanzees. In *Teaching Sign Language to Chimpanzees,* R. A. Gardner, B. T. Gardner, and T. E. Van Cantfort, eds., pp. 280–292. Albany: State University of New York Press.

Freilich, M., D. Raybeck, and J. Savishinsky 1991. *Deviance: Anthropological Perspectives*. Westport, CT: Bergin and Garvey.

Freston, P., ed. 2008. *Evangelical Christianity and Democracy in Latin America*. New York: Oxford University Press.

Fricke, T. 1994. *Himalayan Households: Tamang Demography and Domestic Processes,* 2nd ed. New York: Columbia University Press.

Fried, M. H. 1960. On the Evolution of Social Stratification and the State. In *Culture in History,* S. Diamond, ed., pp. 713–731. New York: Columbia University Press.

———. 1967. *The Evolution of Political Society: An Essay in Political Anthropology*. New York: McGraw-Hill.

Friedl, E. 1962 *Vasilika: A Village in Modern Greece*. New York: Holt, Rinehart, and Winston.

———. 1975. *Women and Men: An Anthropologist's View*. New York: Holt, Rinehart & Winston.

Friedman, J., ed. 2003. *Globalization, the State, and Violence*. Walnut Creek, CA: AltaMira.

Friedman, K. E., and J. Friedman 2008. *The Anthropology of Global Systems*. Lanham, MD: AltaMira.

Gal, S. 1989. Language and Political Economy. *Annual Review of Anthropology* 18:345–367.

Gardner, R. A., B. T. Gardner, and T. E. Van Cantfort, eds. 1989. *Teaching Sign Language to Chimpanzees*. Albany: State University of New York Press.

Geertz, C. 1973. *The Interpretation of Cultures*. New York: Basic Books.

Geis, M. L. 1987. *The Language of Politics*. New York: Springer-Verlag.

Gellner, E. 1983. *Nations and Nationalism*. Ithaca, NY: Cornell University Press.

———. 1997. *Nationalism*. New York: New York University Press.

Giddens, A. 1973. *The Class Structure of the Advanced Societies*. New York: Cambridge University Press.

Gillis, J. 2012. It's Official: 2012 Was Hottest Year Ever in U.S. *New York Times*, January 8. http://www.nytimes.com/2013/01/09/science/earth/2012-was-hottest-year-ever-in-us.html?hp&_r=0.

Gilmore, D. D. 1987. *Aggression and Community: Paradoxes of Andalusian Culture*. New Haven, CT: Yale University Press.

Gimpel, J. 1988. *The Medieval Machine: The Industrial Revolution of the Middle Ages,* 2nd ed. Aldershot, Hants, England: Wildwood House.

Gmelch, G., R. V. Kemper, and W. P. Zenner, eds. 2010. *Urban Life: Readings in the Anthropology of the City*, 5th ed. Long Grove, IL: Waveland.

Goldberg, D. T. 2002. *The Racial State*. Malden, MA: Blackwell.

Goleman, D. 1992. Anthropology Goes Looking for Love in All the Old Places. *New York Times,* November 24, 1992, p. B1.

Goodall, J. 1996. *My Life with the Chimpanzees*. New York: Pocket Books.

Gotkowitz, L., ed. 2011. *Histories of Race and Racism: The Andes and Mesoamerica from Colonial Times to the Present*. Durham, NC: Duke University Press.

Gottdiener, M., ed. 2000. *New Forms of Consumption: Consumers, Culture, and Commodification*. Lanham, MD: Rowman & Littlefield.

Gough, E. K. 1959. The Nayars and the Definition of Marriage. *Journal of the Royal Anthropological Institute* 89:23–34.

Gramsci, A. 1971. *Selections from the Prison Notebooks*. Q. Hoare and G. N. Smith, ed. and trans. London: Wishart.

Grasmuck, S., and P. Pessar 1991. *Between Two Islands: Dominican International Migration*. Berkeley: University of California Press.

Gray, J. 1999. *False Dawn. The Delusions of Global Capitalism.* London: Granta.

Greaves, T. C. 1995. Problems Facing Anthropologists: Cultural Rights and Ethnography. *General Anthropology* 1(2):1, 3–6.

Green, G. M., and R. W. Sussman 1990. Deforestation History of the Eastern Rain Forests of Madagascar from Satellite Images. *Science* 248 (April 13):212–215.

Greenhouse, S. 2011. Union Membership in U.S. Fell to a 70-Year Low Last Year. *New York Times,* January 21.

Greenwood, D. J. 1976. *Unrewarding Wealth: The Commercialization and Collapse of Agriculture in a Spanish Basque Town*. Cambridge: Cambridge University Press.

Grekova, M. 2001. Postsocialist Societies. *International Encyclopedia of the Social & Behavioral Sciences,* pp. 11877–11881. New York: Elsevier.

Gremaux, R.1993. Woman Becomes Man in the Balkans. In *Third Sex, Third Gender: Beyond Sexual Dimorphism in Culture and History,* G. Herdt, ed. Cambridge, MA: MIT Press.

Griffin, P. B., and A. Estioko-Griffin, eds. 1985. *The Agta of Northern Luzon: Recent Studies*. Cebu City, Philippines: University of San Carlos.

Gu, S. 2012. *Language and Culture in the Growth of Imperialism*. Jefferson, NC: McFarland.

Gudeman, S., ed. 1999. *Economic Anthropology*. Northhampton, MA: E. Elgar.

Gugliotta, G. 2005. Tools Found in Britain Show Much Earlier Human Existence. *Washington Post,* December 15, p. A24.

Gumperz, J. J., and S. C. Levinson, eds. 1996. *Rethinking Linguistic Relativity*. New York: Cambridge University Press.

Gupta, A., and J. Ferguson 1997a. Culture, Power, Place: Ethnography at the End of an Era. In *Culture, Power, Place: Explorations in Critical Anthropology,* A. Gupta and J. Ferguson, eds., pp. 1–29. Durham, NC: Duke University Press.

————. 1997b. Beyond "Culture": Space, Identity, and the Politics of Difference. In *Culture, Power, Place,* A. Gupta and J. Ferguson, eds., pp. 33–51. Durham, NC: Duke University Press.

Haenn, N., and R. R. Wilk, eds. 2006. *The Environment in Anthropology: A Reader in Ecology, Culture, and Sustainable Living.* New York: New York University Press.

Hallowell, A. I. 1955. *Culture and Experience.* Philadelphia: University of Pennsylvania Press.

Handwerk, B. 2008. Half of Humanity Will Live in Cities by Year's End. *National Geographic News,* March 13. www.national geographic.com/news/pf30472163.html.

Handwerker, W. P. 2009. *The Origins of Cultures: How Individual Choices Make Cultures Change*. Walnut Creek, CA: Left Coast Press.

Hann, C., and K. Hart 2011. *Economic Anthropology: History, Ethnography, Critique.* Malden, MA: Polity Press.

Hann, C., and K. Hart, eds. 2009. *Market and Society: The Great Transformation Today.* New York: Cambridge University Press

Harlow, H. F. 1971. *Learning to Love.* San Francisco: Albion.

Harris, M. 1964. *Patterns of Race in the Americas.* New York: Walker.

————. 1970. Referential Ambiguity in the Calculus of Brazilian Racial Identity. *Southwestern Journal of Anthropology* 26(1):1–14.

————. 1974. *Cows, Pigs, Wars, and Witches: The Riddles of Culture*. New York: Random House.

————. 1978. *Cannibals and Kings*. New York: Vintage Books.

————. 2001 (orig. 1968). *The Rise of Anthropological Theory:* Walnut Creek, CA: AltaMira.

Harris, M., and C. P. Kottak 1963. The Structural Significance of Brazilian Racial Categories. *Sociologia* 25:203–209.

Harrison, G. G., W. L. Rathje, and W. W. Hughes 1994. Food Waste Behavior in an Urban Population. In *Applying Anthropology: An Introductory Reader,* 3rd ed., A. Podolefsky and P. J. Brown, eds., pp. 107–112. Mountain View, CA: Mayfield.

Harrison, K. D. 2007. *When Languages Die: The Extinction of the World's Languages and the Erosion of Human Knowledge.* New York: Oxford University Press.

————. 2010. *The Last Speakers: The Quest to Save the World's Most Endangered Languages*. Washington: National Geographic.

Hart, C. W. M., A. R. Pilling, and J. C. Goodale 1988. *The Tiwi of North Australia* 3rd ed. Fort Worth, TX: Harcourt Brace.

Harvey, D. J. 1980. French Empire. *Academic American Encyclopedia*. Princeton, NJ: Arete, volume 8, pp. 309–310.

Haugerud, A., M. P. Stone, and P. D. Little, eds. 2011. *Commodities and Globalization: Anthropological Perspectives.* Lanham, MD: Rowman & Littlefield.

Hausmann, R., L. D. Tyson, and S. Zahidi 2012. *The Global Gender Gap Report*. World Economic Forum. http://www3.weforum.org/docs/WEF_GenderGap_Report_2012.pdf.

Hawkes, K., J. O'Connell, and K. Hill 1982. Why Hunters Gather: Optimal Foraging and the Aché of Eastern Paraguay. *American Ethnologist* 9:379–398.

Helman, C. 2007. *Culture, Health, and Illness* 5th ed. New York: Oxford University Press.

Henry, J. 1955. Docility, or Giving Teacher What She Wants. *Journal of Social Issues* 2:33–41.

Herdt, G. H. 2006. *The Sambia: Ritual, Sexuality, and Change in Papua New Guinea.* Belmont, CA: Thomson/Wadsworth.

Herskovits, M. 1937. *Life in a Haitian Valley.* New York: Knopf.

Hess, E. 2008. *Nim Chimpsky: The Chimp Who Would Be Human.* New York: Bantam Books.

Hicks, D., ed. 2010. *Ritual and Belief: Readings in the Anthropology of Religion,* 3rd ed. Lanham, MD: AltaMira.

Hill, J. H. 1978. Apes and Language. *Annual Review of Anthropology* 7:89–112.

Hill, K., H. Kaplan, K. Hawkes, and A. Hurtado 1987. Foraging Decisions among Ache Hunter-Gatherers: New Data and Implications for Optimal Foraging Models. *Ethology and Sociobiology* 8:1–36.

Hill, K. R., R. S. Walker, et al. 2011. Coresidence Patterns in Hunter-Gatherer Societies Show Unique Human Social Structure. *Science* (March 11):1286–1289.

Hill-Burnett, J. 1978. Developing Anthropological Knowledge through Application. In *Applied Anthropology in America,* E. M. Eddy and W. L. Partridge, eds., pp. 112–128. New York: Columbia University Press.

Hinton, A. L., and K. L. O'Neill, eds. 2009. *Genocide: Truth, Memory, and Representation.* Durham, NC: Duke University Press.

Hobhouse, L. T. 1915. *Morals in Evolution,* rev. ed. New York: Holt.

Hoebel, E. A. 1954. *The Law of Primitive Man.* Cambridge, MA: Harvard University Press.

————. 1968 (orig. 1954). The Eskimo: Rudimentary Law in a Primitive Anarchy. In *Studies in Social and Cultural Anthropology,* J. Middleton, ed., pp. 93–127. New York: Crowell.

Hoge, W. 2001. Kautokeino Journal; Reindeer Herders, at Home on a (Very Cold) Range. *New York Times,* March 26, late ed.—final, sec. A, p. 4.

Holden, A. 2005. *Tourism Studies and the Social Sciences.* New York: Routledge.

Hornborg, A., B. Clark, and K. Hermele, eds. 2011. *Ecology and Power: Struggles over Land and Material Resources in the Past, Present and Future.* New York; Routledge.

Hornborg, A., and C. L. Crumley, eds. 2007. *The World System and the Earth System: Global Socioenvironmental Change and Sustainability since the Neolithic.* Walnut Creek, CA: Left Coast Press.

Hornborg, A., J. R. McNeill, and J. Martinez-Alier, eds. 2007. *Rethinking Environmental History: World-System History and Global Environmental Change.* Lanham, MD: AltaMira.

Horton, R. 1993. *Patterns of Thought in Africa and the West: Essays on Magic, Religion, and Science.* Cambridge: Cambridge University Press.

Hunt, R. C. 2007. *Beyond Relativism: Comparability in Cultural Anthropology.* Lanham, MD: AltaMira.

Hunter, M. L. 2005. *Race, Gender, and the Politics of Skin Tone.* New York: Routledge.

Hurtado, A. M., C. A. Lambourne, P. James, K. Hill, K. Cheman, and K. Baca 2005. Human Rights, Biomedical Science, and Infectious Diseases among South American Indigenous Groups. *Annual Review of Anthropology* 34:639–665.

Inda, J. X., and R. Rosaldo, eds. 2008. *The Anthropology of Globalization: A Reader.* Malden, MA: Blackwell.

Ingraham, C. 2008. *White Weddings: Romancing Heterosexuality in Popular Culture,* 2nd ed. New York: Routledge.

Inhorn, M. C., and P. J. Brown 1990. The Anthropology of Infectious Disease. *Annual Review of Anthropology* 19:89–117.

Inhorn, M. C., and E. A. Wentzell, eds. 2012. *Medical Anthropology at the Intersections: Histories, Activisms, and Futures.* Durham, NC: Duke University Press.

Jackson, J., and K. B. Warren 2005. Indigenous Movements in Latin America, 1992–2004: Controversies, Ironies, New Directions. *Annual Review of Anthropology* 34:549–573.

Jenks, C. 2005. *Culture,* 2nd ed. New York: Routledge.

Johansen, B. E. 2008. *Global Warming 101.* Westport, CT: Greenwood.

Johnson, A. W. 1978. *Quantification in Cultural Anthropology: An Introduction to Research Design.* Stanford, CA: Stanford University Press.

Johnson, A. W., and T. K. Earle 2000. *The Evolution of Human Societies: From Foraging Group to Agrarian State,* 2nd ed. Stanford, CA: Stanford University Press.

Johnston, B. R. 2009. *Life and Death Matters: Human Rights, Environment, and Social Justice,* 2nd ed. Walnut Creek, CA: Left Coast Press.

Jordan, A. 2003. *Business Anthropology.* Prospect Heights, IL: Waveland.

Jordan, B., ed. 2013. *Advancing Ethnography in Corporate Environments: Challenges and Emerging Opportunities.* Walnut Creek, CA: Left Coast Press.

Kamrava, M. 2011. T*he Modern Middle East: A Political History since the First World War,* 2nd ed. Berkeley: University of California Press.

Kan, S. 1986. The 19th-Century Tlingit Potlatch: A New Perspective. *American Ethnologist* 13:191–212.

———. 1989. *Symbolic Immortality: The Tlingit Potlatch of the Nineteenth Century.* Washington, DC: Smithsonian Institution Press.

Kaneshiro, N. K. 2009. Intersex. Medline Plus. National Institutes of Health, U.S. National Library of Medicine. http://www.nlm. nih.gov/medlineplus/ency/article/001669.htm.

Katzenberg, M. A., and S. R. Saunders 2007. *Biological Anthropology of the Human Skeleton,* 2nd ed. Hoboken, NJ: Wiley.

Kaufman, S. R., and L. M. Morgan 2005. The Anthropology of the Beginnings and Ends of Life. *Annual Review of Anthropology* 34:317–341.

Kearney, M. 1996. *Reconceptualizing the Peasantry: Anthropology in Global Perspective.* Boulder, CO: Westview Press.

Kellenberger, J. 2008. *Moral Relativism: A Dialogue.* Lanham, MA: Rowman & Littlefield.

Kelly, R. C. 1976. Witchcraft and Sexual Relations: An Exploration in the Social and Semantic Implications of the Structure of Belief. In *Man and Woman in the New Guinea Highlands,* P. Brown and G. Buchbinder, eds., pp. 36–53. Special Publication no. 8. Washington, DC: American Anthropological Association.

Kelly, R. L. 1995. *The Foraging Spectrum: Diversity in Hunter-Gatherer Lifeways.* Washington, DC: Smithsonian Institution Press.

Kent, S. 1992. The Current Forager Controversy: Real versus Ideal Views of Hunter-gatherers. *Man* 27:45–70.

———. 1996. *Cultural Diversity among Twentieth-Century Foragers: An African Perspective.* New York: Cambridge University Press.

Kent, S., ed. 2002. *Ethnicity, Hunter-Gatherers, and the "Other": Association or Assimilation in Africa.* Washington: Smithsonian Institution Press.

Kent, S., and H. Vierich 1989. The Myth of Ecological Determinism: Anticipated Mobility and Site Organization of Space. In *Farmers as Hunters: The Implications of Sedentism,* S. Kent, ed., pp. 96–130. New York: Cambridge University Press.

Keppel, K. G., J. N. Pearch, and D. K. Wagener 2002. Trends in Racial and Ethnic-Specific Rates for the Health Status Indicators: United States, 1990–98. *Healthy People Statistical Notes No. 23.* Hyattsville, MD: National Center for Health Statistics.

Kershaw, S. 2009. For Teenagers, Hello Means 'How About a Hug?' *New York Times,* May 28.

Keynes, J. M. 1927. *The End of Laissez-Faire.* London: L and Virginia Woolf.

———. 1936. *General Theory of Employment, Interest, and Money.* New York: Harcourt Brace.

Kimmel, M. S. 2007. *The Gendered Society,* 3rd ed. New York: Oxford University Press.

King, E. 2012. Stanford linguists seek to identify the elusive California accent. *Stanford Report*, August 6. http://news.stanford.edu/news/2012/august/california-dialect-linguistics-080612.html.

Kinsey, A. C., W. B. Pomeroy, and C. E. Martin 1948. *Sexual Behavior in the Human Male*. Philadelphia: W. B. Saunders.

Kjaerulff, J. 2010. *Internet and Change: An Ethnography of Knowledge and Flexible Work*. Walnut Creek, CA: Left Coast Press.

Klass, M. 2003. *Mind over Mind: The Anthropology and Psychology of Spirit Possession*. Lanham, MA: Rowman & Littlefield.

Klein, N. 2000. *No Logo*. London: Flamingo.

Kluckhohn, C. 1944. *Mirror for Man: A Survey of Human Behavior and Social Attitudes*. Greenwich, CT: Fawcett.

Kochhar, R., R. Fry, and P. Taylor 2011. *Wealth Gaps Rise to Record Highs between Whites, Blacks, Hispanics*. Pew Research Center. Pew Social and Economic Trends. http://www.pewsocialtrends.org/2011/07/26/wealth-gaps-rise-to-record-highs-between-whites-blacks-hispanics/.

Komar, D. A., and J. E. Buikstra 2008. *Forensic Anthropology: Contemporary Theory and Practice*. New York: Oxford University Press.

Kontopodis, M., C. Wulf, and B. Fichtner, eds. 2011. *Children, Development, and Education: Cultural, Historical, and Anthropological Perspectives*. New York: Springer.

Kottak, C. P. 1980. *The Past in the Present: History, Ecology, and Social Organization in Highland Madagascar*. Ann Arbor: University of Michigan Press.

———. 1990a. Culture and "Economic Development." *American Anthropologist* 93(3):723–731.

———. 1990b. *Prime-Time Society: An Anthropological Analysis of Television and Culture*. Belmont, CA: Wadsworth.

———. 1991. When People Don't Come First: Some Lessons from Completed Projects. In *Putting People First: Sociological Variables in Rural Development,* 2nd ed., M. Cernea, ed., pp. 429–464. New York: Oxford University Press.

———. 1999. The New Ecological Anthropology. *American Anthropologist* 101(1):23–35.

———. 2006. *Assault on Paradise: The Globalization of a Little Community in Brazil,* 4th ed. New York: McGraw-Hill.

———. 2007. Return to Madagascar: A Forty Year Retrospective. *General Anthropology: Bulletin of the General Anthropology Division of the American Anthropological Association* 14(2):1–10.

———. 2009. *Prime-Time Society: An Anthropological Analysis of Television and Culture,* updated ed. Walnut Creek, CA: Left Coast Press.

Kottak, C. P., and K. A. Kozaitis 2012. *On Being Different: Diversity and Multiculturalism in the North American Mainstream,* 4th ed. New York: McGraw-Hill.

Kottak, C. P., L. L. Gezon, and G. Green 1994. Deforestation and Biodiversity Preservation in Madagascar: The View from Above and Below. *CIESIN Human Dimensions Kiosk*—an electronic publication. http://www.ciesin.com.

Kottak, N. C. 2002. *Stealing the Neighbor's Chicken: Social Control in Northern Mozambique.* PhD dissertation. Department of Anthropology, Emory University, Atlanta, GA.

Kreider, R. M., and R. Ellis 2011. Number, Timing, and Duration of Marriages and Divorces: 2009, *Current Population Reports*, P70-125. http://www.census.gov/prod/2011pubs/p70-125.pdf.

Kulick, D. 1998. *Travesti: Sex, Gender, and Culture among Brazilian Transgendered Prostitutes*. Chicago: University of Chicago Press.

Kuper, L. 2006. *Race, Class, and Power: Ideology and Revolutionary Change in Plural Societies*. New Brunswick, NJ: Transaction Publishers.

Kurtz, D. V. 2001. *Political Anthropology: Power and Paradigms*. Boulder, CO: Westview Press.

Kutsche, P. 1998. *Field Ethnography: A Manual for Doing Cultural Anthropology*. Upper Saddle River, NJ: Prentice Hall.

Labov, W. 1972a. *Language in the Inner City: Studies in the Black English Vernacular.* Philadelphia: University of Pennsylvania Press.

———. 1972b. *Sociolinguistic Patterns.* Philadelphia: University of Pennsylvania Press.

———. 2006. *The Social Stratification of English in New York City.* New York: Cambridge University Press.

———. 2012. *Dialect Diversity in America: The Politics of Language Change.* Charlottesville: University of Virginia Press.

Lakoff, G. 2008. *The Political Mind: Why You Can't Understand 21st-century Politics with an 18th-century Brain.* New York: Viking.

Lakoff, R. T. 2004. *Language and Women's Place: Text and Commentaries,* rev. ed., M. Bucholtz, ed. New York: Oxford University Press.

Lambek, M., ed. 2008. *A Reader in the Anthropology of Religion.* Malden, MA: Blackwell.

Landes, D. 1999. *The Wealth and Poverty of Nations. Why Some Are So Rich and Some Are So Poor.* London: Abacus.

Lange, M. 2009. *Lineages of Despotism and Development: British Colonialism and State Power.* Chicago: University of Chicago Press.

Larsen, C. S. 2000. *Skeletons in Our Closet: Revealing Our Past through Bioarchaeology.* Princeton, NJ: Princeton University Press.

Lassiter, L. E. 1998. *The Power of Kiowa Song: A Collaborative Ethnography.* Tucson: University of Arizona Press.

Leach, E. R. 1955. Polyandry, Inheritance and the Definition of Marriage. *Man* 55:182–186.

———. 1961. *Rethinking Anthropology.* London: Athlone Press.

Leadbeater, C. 1999. *Europe's New Economy.* London: Centre for European Reform.

Lee, R. B. 1979. *The !Kung San: Men, Women, and Work in a Foraging Society.* New York: Cambridge University Press.

———. 1984. *The Dobe !Kung.* New York: Harcourt Brace.

———. 2003. *The Dobe Ju/'hoansi,* 3rd ed. Belmont, CA: Wadsworth.

———. 2012. The !Kung and I: Reflections on My Life and Times with the Ju/Hoansi People. *General Anthropology* 19(1):1–4.

Lee, R. B., and R. H. Daly 1999. *The Cambridge Encyclopedia of Hunters and Gatherers.* New York: Cambridge University Press.

Lenski, G. 1966. *Power and Privilege: A Theory of Social Stratification.* New York: McGraw-Hill.

Levine, N. E. 2008. Alternative Kinship, Marriage, and Reproduction. *Annual Review of Anthropology* 37:17–35.

Levinson, B. A. U., and M. Pollock, eds. 2011. *A Companion to the Anthropology of Education.* Malden, MA: Blackwell.

Lévi-Strauss, C. 1963. *Totemism.* R. Needham (trans.). Boston: Beacon Press.

———. 1967. *Structural Anthropology.* New York: Doubleday.

Levy, F. 2010. The World's Happiest Countries. *Forbes,* July 14. http://www.forbes.com/2010/07/14/world-happiest-countries-lifestyle-realestate-gallup.html.

Levy, J. E., with B. Pepper 1992. *Orayvi Revisited: Social Stratification in an "Egalitarian" Society.* Santa Fe, NM: School of American Research Press, and Seattle: University of Washington Press.

Lewellen, T. C. 2003. *Political Anthropology: An Introduction,* 3rd ed. Westport, CT: Praeger.

———. 2010. Groping toward Globalization: In Search of Anthropology without Boundaries. *Reviews in Anthropology* 31(1):73–89.

Lie, J. 2001. *Multiethnic Japan.* Cambridge, MA: Harvard University Press.

Lindenbaum, S. 1972. Sorcerers, Ghosts, and Polluting Women: An Analysis of Religious Belief and Population Control. *Ethnology* 11:241–253.

Little, K. 1971. Some Aspects of African Urbanization South of the Sahara. Reading, MA: Addison-Wesley, McCaleb Modules in Anthropology.

Livingstone, F. B. 1969. Gene Frequency Clines of the b Hemoglobin Locus in Various Human Populations and Their Similarities by Models Involving Differential Selection. *Human Biology* 41:223–236.

Lockwood, W. G. 1975. *European Moslems: Economy and Ethnicity in Western Bosnia.* New York: Academic Press.

López, A. A. 2011. New Questions in the Immigration Debate. *Anthropology Now* 3(1):47–53.

Lowie, R. H. 1961 (orig. 1920). *Primitive Society.* New York: Harper & Brothers.

Lugo, Alejandro. "Reflections on Border Theory, Culture, and the Nation." *Border Theory: The Limits of Cultural Politics.* ed. S. Michaelsen and D. Johnson, pp. 43–67. Minneapolis: University of Minnesota Press.

Lugo, A. 1997. Reflections on Border Theory, Culture, and the Nation. *Border Theory: The Limits of Cultural Politics.* Ed. Scott Michaelsen and David Johnson. Minneapolis: University of Minnesota Press, 1997. 43–67.

Lugo, A., and B. Maurer 2000. *Gender Matters: Rereading Michelle Z. Rosaldo.* Ann Arbor, University of Michigan Press.

Lupton, D. 2012. *Medicine as Culture: Illness, Disease, and the Body.* Los Angeles: Sage.

Madra, Y. M. 2004. Karl Polanyi: Freedom in a Complex Society. *Econ-Atrocity Bulletin: In the History of Thought.* http://www.fguide.org/Bulletin/polanyi.htm.

Malinowski, B. 1927. *Sex and Repression in Savage Society.* London and New York: International Library of Psychology, Philosophy and Scientific Method.

———. 1929. Practical Anthropology. *Africa* 2:23–38.

———. 1961 (orig. 1922). *Argonauts of the Western Pacific.* New York: Dutton.

———. 1978 (orig. 1931). The Role of Magic and Religion. In *Reader in Comparative Religion: An Anthropological Approach,* 4th ed., W. A. Lessa and E. Z. Vogt, eds., pp. 37–46. New York: Harper and Row.

Malkki, L. H. 1995. *Purity and Exile: Violence, Memory, and National Cosmology among Hutu Refugees in Tanzania.* Chicago: University of Chicago Press.

Mann, C. C. 2011. *1493: Uncovering the New World Columbus Created.* New York: Knopf.

Marcus, G. E., and D. Cushman. 1982. Ethnographies as Texts. *Annual Review of Anthropology* 11:25–69.

Marcus, G. E., and M. M. J. Fischer. 1986. *Anthropology as Cultural Critique: An Experimental Moment in the Human Sciences.* Chicago: University of Chicago Press.

———. 1999. *Anthropology as Cultural Critique: An Experimental Moment in the Human Sciences,* 2nd ed. Chicago: University of Chicago Press.

Margolis, M. L. 1984. *Mothers and Such: American Views of Women and How They Changed.* Berkeley: University of California Press.

———. 2000. *True to Her Nature: Changing Advice to American Women.* Prospect Heights, IL: Waveland.

Marshall, R. C., ed. 2011. *Cooperation in Economy and Society.* Lanham, MD: Rowman & Littlefield.

Martin, D. 1990. *Tongues of Fire: The Explosion of Protestantism in Latin America.* Cambridge, MA: Blackwell.

Martin, E. 1992. The End of the Body? *American Ethnologist* 19:121–140.

Martin, K., and B. Voorhies 1975. *Female of the Species.* New York: Columbia University Press.

Martin, S. M. 1988. *Palm Oil and Protest: An Economic History of the Ngwa Region, South-Eastern Nigeria, 1800–1980.* New York: Cambridge University Press.

Martinez, E., and A. Garcia 2000. What Is "Neo-Liberalism"? A Brief Definition. http://www.globalexchange.org/campaigns/econ101/neoliberalDefined.html.pdf.

Marx, K., and F. Engels 1976 (orig. 1848). *Communist Manifesto*. New York: Pantheon.

Mascia-Lees, F. 2010. *Gender & Difference in a Globalizing World: Twenty-First Century Anthropology*. Long Grove, IL: Waveland.

Mathews, G. 2000. *Global Culture/Individual Identity: Searching for Home in the Cultural Supermarket*. New York: Routledge.

Maugh, T. H., III 2007. One Language Disappears Every 14 Days; About Half of the World's Distinct Tongues Could Vanish This Century, Researchers Say. *Los Angeles Times,* September 19.

Maybury-Lewis, D. 2002. *Indigenous Peoples, Ethnic Groups, and the State,* 2nd ed. Boston: Allyn & Bacon.

Maybury-Lewis, D., T. Macdonald, and B. Maybury-Lewis, eds. 2009. *Manifest Destinies and Indigenous Peoples*. Cambridge, MA: David Rockefeller Center for Latin American Studies and Harvard University Press.

Mayell, H. 2003. Orangutans Show Signs of Culture, Study Says. *National Geographic News*, January 3. http://news.nationalgeo-graphic.com/news/2002/12/1220_021226_orangutan.html.

Mba, N. E. 1982. *Nigerian Women Mobilized: Women's Political Activity in Southern Nigeria, 1900–1965*. Berkeley: University of California Press.

McConnell-Ginet, S. 2010. *Gender, Sexuality, and Meaning: Linguistic Practice and Politics*. New York: Oxford University Press.

McElroy, A., and P. K. Townsend. 2009 *Medical Anthropology in Ecological Perspective*, 5th ed. Boulder, CO: Westview Press.

McKinnon, S. 2005. On Kinship and Marriage: A Critique of the Genetic and Gender Calculus of Evolutionary Psychology. In *Complexities: Beyond Nature and Nurture,* S. McKinnon and S. Silverman, eds., pp. 106–131. Chicago: The University of Chicago Press.

Mead, M. 1937. *Cooperation and Competition among Primitive Peoples*. New York: McGraw-Hill.

———. 1950 (orig. 1935). *Sex and Temperament in Three Primitive Societies*. New York: New American Library.

Meigs, A., and K. Barlow 2002. Beyond the Taboo: Imagining Incest. *American Anthropologist* 104(1):38–49.

Menzies, C. R., ed. 2006. *Traditional Ecological Knowledge and Natural Resource Management*. Lincoln: University of Nebraska Press.

Mercader, J., M. Panger, and C. Boesch 2002. Excavation of a Chimpanzee Stone Tool Site in the African Rainforest. *Science* 296 (May 24): 1452–1455.

Merry, S. E. 2006. Anthropology and International Law. *Annual Review of Anthropology* 35:99–116.

Meyer, B. 1999. *Translating the Devil: Religion and Modernity among the Ewe in Ghana*. Trenton, NJ: Africa World Press.

Miles, H. L. 1983. Apes and Language: The Search for Communicative Competence. In *Language in Primates,* J. de Luce and H. T. Wilder, eds., pp. 43–62. New York: Springer Verlag.

Mintz, S. 1985. *Sweetness and Power: The Place of Sugar in Modern History*. New York: Viking Penguin.

Mitani, J. C., and D. P. Watts 1999. Demographic Influences on the Hunting Behavior of Chimpanzees. *American Journal of Physical Anthropology* 109:439–454.

Mooney, A. 2011. *Language, Society, and Power*. New York: Routledge.

Moro, P. A., and J. E. Myers 2012. *Magic, Witchcraft, and Religion: A Reader in the Anthropology of Religion*, 9th ed. New York: McGraw-Hill.

Morrill, C., D. A. Snow, and C. H. White, eds. 2005. *Together Alone: Personal Relationships in Public Places*. Berkeley: University of California Press.

Motseta, S. 2006. Botswana Gives Bushmen Tough Conditions. *Washington Post,* December 14. http://www.washingtonpost.com/wp-dyn/content/article/2006/12/14/.

Murdock, G. P. 1957. World Ethnographic Sample. *American Anthropologist* 59:664–687.

Murdock, G. P., and C. Provost 1973. Factors in the Division of Labor by Sex: A Cross-Cultural Analysis. *Ethnology* 12(2):203–225.

Murray, S. O., and W. Roscoe, eds. 1998. *Boy-wives and Female Husbands: Studies in African Homosexualities.* New York: St. Martin's Press.

Mydans, S. 1992a. Criticism Grows over Aliens Seized during Riots. *New York Times,* May 29, p. A8.

———. 1992b. Judge Dismisses Case in Shooting by Officer. *New York Times,* June 4, p. A8.

Nadeem, S. 2011. *Dead Ringers: How Outsourcing Is Changing the Way Indians Understand Themselves.* Princeton, NJ: Princeton University Press.

Nagel, J. 1996. *American Indian Ethnic Renewal: Red Power and the Resurgence of Identity and Culture.* New York: Oxford University Press.

Nanda, S. 1996. Hijras: An Alternative Sex and Gender Role in India, ed. G. Herdt. *Third Sex Third Gender: Beyond Sexual Dimorphism in Culture and History,* pp. 373–418. New York: Zone Books.

———. 1998 *Neither Man nor Woman: The Hijras of India.* Belmont, CA: Thomson/Wadsworth.

———. 2000. *Gender Diversity: Crosscultural Variations.* Prospect Heights, IL: Waveland.

National Academy of Sciences 2008. *Understanding and Responding to Climate Change: Highlights of National Academies Reports.* http://dels.nas.edu/dels/rpt_briefs/climate_change_2008_final.pdf.

National Research Council 2011. *America's Climate Choices.* http://nas-sites.org/americas-climatechoices/sample-page/panel-reports/americas-climate-choices-final-report/.

Naylor, L. L. 1996. *Culture and Change: An Introduction.* Westport, CT: Bergin and Garvey.

Nazarea, V. D. 2006. Local Knowledge and Memory in Biodiversity Conservation. *Annual Review of Anthropology* 35:317–335.

Nolan, R., ed. 2013. *Handbook of Practicing Anthropology.* Hoboken, NJ: Wiley.

Nolan, R. W. 2002. *Development Anthropology: Encounters in the Real World.* Boulder, CO: Westview Press.

Nordstrom, C. 2004. *Shadows of War: Violence, Power, and International Profiteering in the Twenty-First Century.* Berkeley: University of California Press.

Nugent, D., and J. Vincent, eds. 2004. *A Companion to the Anthropology of Politics.* Malden, MA: Blackwell.

Omohundro, J. T. 2001. *Careers in Anthropology,* 2nd ed. New York: McGraw-Hill.

Ong, A. 1987. *Spirits of Resistance and Capitalist Discipline: Factory Women in Malaysia.* Albany: State University of New York Press.

———. 1989. Center, Periphery, and Hierarchy: Gender in Southeast Asia. In *Gender and Anthropology: Critical Reviews for Research and Teaching,* S. Morgen, ed., pp. 294–312. Washington, DC: American Anthropological Association.

Ong, A., and S. J. Collier, eds. 2005. *Global Assemblages: Technology, Politics, and Ethics as Anthropological Problems.* Malden, MA: Blackwell.

———. 2010. *Spirits of Resistance and Capitalist Discipline: Factory Women in Malaysia,* 2nd ed. Albany: State University of New York Press.

Ontario Consultants on Religious Tolerance. 2011. Religions of the World: Number of Adherents of Major Religions, Their Geographical Distribution, Date Founded, and Sacred Texts. http://www.religioustolerance.org/worldrel.htm.

Oriji, J. N. 2000. Igbo Women from 1929–1960. *West Africa Review* 2:1.

Ortner, S. B. 1984. Theory in Anthropology since the Sixties. *Comparative Studies in Society and History* 126(1):126–166.

Paine, R. 2009. *Camps of the Tundra: Politics through Reindeer among Saami Pastoralists.* Oslo: Instituttet for sammenlignende kulturforskning.

Palmer, S. 2001. The Rael Deal. *Religion in the News* 4:2. Hartford, CT: Trinity College. The Leonard E. Greenberg Center for the Study of Religion in Public Life. http://www.trincoll.edu/depts/csrpl/PJNVol4No2/Rael.htm.

Pardo, I., and G. B. Prato, eds. 2012. *Anthropology in the City: Methodology and Theory.* Burlington, VT: Ashgate.

Patterson, F. 1978. Conversations with a Gorilla. *National Geographic,* October, pp. 438–465.

Paulson, T. E. 2005. Chimp, Human DNA Comparison Finds Vast Similarities, Key Differences. *Seattle Post-Intelligencer Reporter,* September 1, 2005. http://seattlepi.nwsource.com/local/238852_chimp01.html.

Peletz, M. 1988. *A Share of the Harvest: Kinship, Property, and Social History among the Malays of Rembau.* Berkeley: University of California Press.

Pelto, P. 1973. *The Snowmobile Revolution: Technology and Social Change in the Arctic.* Menlo Park, CA: Cummings.

Perry, M. A., ed. 2012. *Bioarchaeology and Behavior: The People of the Ancient Near East.* Gainesville: University of Florida Press.

Petraglia-Bahri, D. 1996. Introduction to Postcolonial Studies. http://www.emory.edu/ENGLISH/Bahri/.

Pew Research Center 2011. *The Pew Forum on Religion and Public Life.* http://www.pewforum.org/uploadedFiles/Topics/Religious_Affiliation/Christian/Evangelical_Protestant_Churches/Global%20Survey%20of%20Evan.%20Prot.%20Leaders.pdf.

———. 2012a. *The Global Religious Landscape: A Report on the Size and Distribution of the World's Major Religious Groups as of 2010, Analysis* December 18. http://www.pewforum.org/global-religious-landscape-exec.aspx#src=global-footer.

———. 2012b. *"Nones" on the Rise, One-in-Five Adults Have No Religious Affiliation,* October 9. http://www.pewforum.org/unaffiliated/nones-on-the-rise.aspx

———. 2012a. *The Global Religious Landscape: A Report on the Size and Distribution of the World's Major Religious Groups as of 2010, Analysis* December 18. http://www.pewforum.org/global-religious-landscape-exec.aspx#src=global-footer.

Piddocke, S. 1969. The Potlatch System of the Southern Kwakiutl: A New Perspective. In *Environment and Cultural Behavior,* A. P. Vayda, ed., pp. 130–156. Garden City, NY: Natural History Press.

Podolefsky, A., and P. J. Brown, eds. 1992. *Applying Anthropology: An Introductory Reader,* 2nd ed. Mountain View, CA: Mayfield.

Polanyi, K. 1968. *Primitive, Archaic and Modern Economies: Essays of Karl Polanyi,* G. Dalton, ed., Garden City, NY: Anchor Books.

Pospisil, L. 1963. *The Kapauku Papuans of West New Guinea.* New York: Holt, Rinehart & Winston.

Potash, B., ed. 1986. *Widows in African Societies: Choices and Constraints.* Stanford, CA: Stanford University Press.

Price, R., ed. 1973. *Maroon Societies.* New York: Anchor Press/Doubleday.

Radcliffe-Brown, A. R. 1952 (orig. 1924). The Mother's Brother in South Africa. In A. R. Radcliffe-Brown, *Structure and Function in Primitive Society,* pp. 15–31. London: Routledge & Kegan Paul.

Radcliffe-Brown, A. R. 1965 (orig. 1952). *Structure and Function in Primitive Society.* New York: Free Press.

Ramos, A. R. 1995. *Sanumá Memories: Yanomami Ethnography in Times of Crisis.* Madison: University of Wisconsin Press.

Ranger, T. O. 1996. Postscript. In *Postcolonial Identities,* R. Werbner and T. O. Ranger, eds. London: Zed.

Rappaport, R. A. 1974. Obvious Aspects of Ritual. *Cambridge Anthropology* 2:2–60.

———. 1999. *Holiness and Humanity: Ritual in the Making of Religious Life*. New York: Cambridge University Press.

Rathje, W. L., and C. Murphy 2001. *Rubbish! The Archaeology of Garbage*. Tucson: University of Arizona Press.

Rathus, S. A., J. S. Nevid, and J. Fichner-Rathus 2013. *Human Sexuality in a World of Diversity,* 9th ed. Boston: Pearson/Allyn & Bacon.

Redfield, R. 1941. *The Folk Culture of Yucatan*. Chicago: University of Chicago Press.

Redfield, R., R. Linton, and M. Herskovits 1936. Memorandum on the Study of Acculturation. *American Anthropologist* 38:149–152.

Reese, W. L. 1999. *Dictionary of Philosophy and Religion: Eastern and Western Thought*. Amherst, NY: Humanities Books.

Robbins, Jim 2012. The Ecology of Disease, *New York Times*, July 14, 2012. http://www.nytimes.com/2012/07/15/sunday-review/the-ecology-of-disease.html?pagewanted=all.

Robbins, Joel 2004. The Globalization of Pentecostal and Charismatic Christianity. *Annual Review of Anthropology* 33:17–143.

Robbins, R. H. 2011. *Global Problems and the Culture of Capitalism,* 5th ed. Boston: Pearson/Allyn & Bacon.

Roberts, S., A. Sabar, B. Goodman, and M. Balleza 2007. 51% of Women Are Now Living without Spouse. *New York Times,* January 16. http:www.nytimes.com.

Robson, D. 2013.There Really Are 50 Eskimo Words for Snow. *Washington Post*, January 14. http://articles.washingtonpost.com/2013-01-14/national/36344037_1_eskimo-words-snow-inuit.

Rodseth, L., R. W. Wrangham, A. M. Harrigan, and B. Smuts 1991. The Human Community as a Primate Society. *Current Anthropology* 32:221–254.

Romaine, S. 1999. *Communicating Gender*. Mahwah, NJ: Erlbaum.

———. 2000. *Language in Society: An Introduction to Sociolinguistics,* 2nd ed. New York: Oxford University Press.

Romero, S. 2008. Rain Forest Tribe's Charge of Neglect Is Shrouded by Religion and Politics. *New York Times*, October 7, 2008.

Root, D. 1996. *Cannibal Culture: Art, Appropriation, and the Commodification of Difference*. Boulder, CO: Westview Press.

Rosaldo, M. Z. 1980a. *Knowledge and Passion: Notions of Self and Social Life*. Stanford, CA: Stanford University Press.

———. 1980b. The Use and Abuse of Anthropology: Reflections on Feminism and Cross-Cultural Understanding. *Signs* 5(3):389–417.

Roscoe, W. 1991. *Zuni Man-Woman*. Albuquerque: University of New Mexico Press.

———. 1998. *Changing Ones: Third and Fourth Genders in Native North America*. New York: St. Martin's Press.

Rothstein, E. 2006. Protection for Indian Patrimony That Leads to a Paradox. *New York Times,* March 29.

Rouse, R. 1991. Mexican Migration and the Social Space of Postmodernism. *Diaspora* 1(1):8–23.

Royal Anthropological Institute 1951. *Notes and Queries on Anthropology,* 6th ed. London: Routledge and Kegan Paul.

Ryan, S. 1990. *Ethnic Conflict and International Relations*. Brookfield, MA: Dartmouth.

Ryang, S., and J. Lie 2009. *Diaspora without Homeland: Being Korean in Japan*. Berkeley: University of California Press.

Rylko-Bauer, B., M. Singer, and J. Van Willigen 2006. Reclaiming Applied Anthropology: Its Past, Present, and Future. *American Anthropologist* 108(1):178–190.

Sabloff, J. A. 2008. *Archaeology Matters: Action Archaeology in the Modern World*. Walnut Creek, CA: Left Coast Press.

Sack, K. 2011. In Tough Times, a Boom in Cremations as a Way to Save Money. *New York Times*, December 8. http://www.nytimes.

com/2011/12/09/us/in-economic-downtown-survivors-turning-to-cremations-over-burials. html?scp=1&sq=cremations&st=cse.

Sahlins, M. D. 1968. *Tribesmen*. Englewood Cliffs, NJ: Prentice Hall.

———. 2004. *Stone Age Economics*. New York: Routledge.

Salzman, P. C. 1974. Political Organization among Nomadic Peoples. In *Man in Adaptation: The Cultural Present,* 2nd ed., Y. A. Cohen, ed., pp. 267–284. Chicago: Aldine.

———. 2004. *Pastoralists: Equality, Hierarchy, and the State*. Boulder, CO: Westview Press.

———. 2008. *Culture and Conflict in the Middle East*. Amherst, NY: Humanity Books.

Salzmann, Z. 2012. *Linguistic Anthropology: A Short Introduction*. Prague, Czech Republic: Nezavisle centrum pro studium politiky.

Salzmann, Z., J. M. Stanlaw, and N. Adachi 2012. *Language, Culture, and Society: An Introduction to Linguistic Anthropology*, 5th ed. Boulder, CO: Westview Press.

Sanday, P. R. 1974. Female Status in the Public Domain. In *Woman, Culture, and Society,* M. Z. Rosaldo and L. Lamphere, eds., pp. 189–206. Stanford, CA: Stanford University Press.

———. 2002. *Women at the Center: Life in a Modern Matriarchy*. Ithaca, NY: Cornell University Press.

Sapir, E. 1931. Conceptual Categories in Primitive Languages. *Science* 74:578–584.

———. 1956 (orig 1928). The Meaning of Religion. In *Culture, Language and Personality: Selected Essays,* E. Sapir. Berkeley: University of California Press.

Scheidel, W. 1997. Brother-Sister Marriage in Roman Egypt. *Journal of Biosocial Science* 29(3):361–371.

Schneider, D. M. 1967. Kinship and Culture: Descent and Filiation as Cultural Constructs. *Southwestern Journal of Anthropology* 23:65–73.

Scholte, J. A. 2000. *Globalization: A Critical Introduction*. New York: St. Martin's Press.

Schwartz, M. J., V. W. Turner, and A. Tuden, eds. 2006. *Political Anthropology*. New Brunswick, NJ: Aldine Transaction.

Scott, James C. 1985. *Weapons of the Weak*. New Haven, CT: Yale University Press.

———. 1990. *Domination and the Arts of Resistance*. New Haven, CT: Yale University Press.

Scott, Janny. 2011. *A Singular Woman: The Untold Story of Barack Obama's Mother*. New York: Riverhead Books.

Scudder, T., and E. Colson 1980. *Secondary Education and the Formation of an Elite: The Impact of Education on Gwembe District, Zambia*. London: Academic Press.

Scupin, R. 2012. *Race and Ethnicity: An Anthropological Focus on the United States and the World*, 2nd ed. Upper Saddle River, NJ: Prentice Hall.

Sebeok, T. A., and J. Umiker-Sebeok, eds. 1980. *Speaking of Apes: A Critical Anthropology of Two-Way Communication with Man*. New York: Plenum.

Service, E. R. 1962. *Primitive Social Organization: An Evolutionary Perspective*. New York: McGraw-Hill.

———. 1966. *The Hunters*. Englewood Cliffs, NJ: Prentice Hall.

Shaffer, M. S., ed. 2008. *Public Culture: Diversity, Democracy, and Community in the United States*. Philadelphia: University of Pennsylvania Press.

Shannon, T. R. 1996. *An Introduction to the World-System Perspective,* 2nd ed. Boulder, CO: Westview Press.

Sharma, A., and A. Gupta, eds. 2006. *The Anthropology of the State: A Reader*. Malden, MA: Blackwell.

Shivaram, C. 1996. Where Women Wore the Crown: Kerala's Dissolving Matriarchies Leave a Rich Legacy of Compassionate Family Culture. *Hinduism Today*. http://www.spirit-web.org/HinduismToday/96_02_Women_Wore_Crown.html.

Shore, C., S. Wright, and D. Però, eds. 2011. *Policy Worlds: Anthropology and the Analysis of Contemporary Power*. New York: Berghahn Books.

Shostak, M. 1981. *Nisa: The Life and Words of a !Kung Woman*. Cambridge, MA: Harvard University Press.

Shreeve, J. 1992. The Dating Game: How Old Is the Human Race? *Discover* 13(9):76–83.

Shryock, Andrew 1988. Autonomy, Entanglement, and the Feud: Prestige Structures and Gender Values in Highland Albania. *Anthropological Quarterly* 61(3):113–118.

Silberbauer, G. 1981. *Hunter and Habitat in the Central Kalahari Desert*. New York: Cambridge University Press.

Sillitoe, P., ed. 2007. *Local Science versus Global Science: Approaches to Indigenous Knowledge in International Development*. New York: Berghahn Books.

Singer, M. 2008. *Drugging the Poor: Legal and Illegal Drugs and Social Inequality*. Long Grove, IL: Waveland.

———2012. *Introducing Medical Anthropology: A Discipline in Action*, 2nd ed. Lanham, MD: AltaMira.

Smart, A., and J. Smart 2003. Urbanization and the Global Perspective. *Annual Review of Anthropology* 32:263–285.

Smith, A. T. 2003. *The Political Landscape: Constellations of Authority in Early Complex Polities*. Westport, CT: Praeger.

Smith, M. K., and M. E. Doyle 2002. Globalization. The Encyclopedia of Informal Education. http://www.infed.org/biblio/globalization.htm.

Solway, J., and R. Lee 1990. Foragers, Genuine and Spurious: Situating the Kalahari San in History (with CA Treatment). *Current Anthropology* 31(2):109–146.

Sotomayor, S. 2009 (orig. 2001). A Latina Judge's Voice. Judge Mario G. Olmos Memorial Lecture, University of California, Berkeley School of Law. Reprinted by the *New York Times*, http://www.nytimes.com/2009/05/15/us/politics/15judge.text.html.

Spencer, E. T. 2010. *Sociolinguistics*. Hauppauge, NY: Nova Science.

Spickard, P., ed. 2004. *Race and Nation: Ethnic Systems in the Modern World*. New York: Routledge.

———. 2012. *Race and Immigration in the United States: New Histories*. New York: Routledge.

Spindler, G. D., and L. Hammond, eds. 2006. *Innovations in Educational Ethnography: Theory, Methods, and Results*. Mahwah, NJ: Erlbaum.

Srivastava, J., N. J. H. Smith, and D. A. Forno 1999. *Integrating Biodiversity in Agricultural Intensification. Toward Sound Practices*. Washington, DC: World Bank.

Stack, C. B. 1975. *All Our Kin: Strategies for Survival in a Black Community*. New York: Harper Torchbooks.

Statistical Abstract of the United States. Washington, DC: U.S. Bureau of the Census, U.S. Government Printing Office. *Statistical Abstract of the United States*, 2012. http://www.census.gov/prod/www/statistical-abstract.html.

Statistics Canada 2001. Census. Nation Tables. http://www.statcan.ca/english/census96/nation.htm.

———. 2010. *Study: Projections of the Diversity of the Canadian Population*. http://www.statcan.gc.ca/daily-quotidien/100309/dq100309a-eng.htm.

Stein, R. L., and P. L. Stein, eds. 2011. *The Anthropology of Religion, Magic, and Witchcraft*, 3rd ed. Upper Saddle River, NJ: Pearson Prentice Hall.

Stevens, W. K. 1992. Humanity Confronts Its Handiwork: An Altered Planet. *New York Times,* May 5, pp. B5–B7.

Stevenson, D. 2003. *Cities and Urban Cultures*. Philadelphia: Open University Press.

Stoler, A. L. 1977. Class Structure and Female Autonomy in Rural Java. *Signs* 3:74–89.

Stoler, A. L., C. McGranahan, and P. C. Perdue, eds. 2007. *Imperial Formations*. Santa Fe, NM: School for Advanced Research Press.

Stone, L. S. 2004. Gay Marriage and Anthropology. *Anthropology News* 45(5). http://www.aaanet.org/press/an/0405if-comm4.htm.

———. 2010. *Kinship and Gender: An Introduction*, 4th ed. Boulder, CO: Westview Press.

Strathern, A., and P. J. Stewart 2010. *Kinship in Action: Self and Group.* Boston: Prentice Hall.

Strathern, M. 1988. *Dealing with Inequality: Analysing Gender Relations in Melanesia and Beyond: Essays by Members of the 1983/1984 Anthropological Research Group at the Research School of Pacific Studies, the Australian National University.* New York: Cambridge University Press.

Sullivan, M. 2012. Trouble in Paradise: UCLA Book Enumerates Challenges Faced by Middle-Class L.A. Families, June 19. http://newsroom.ucla.edu/portal/ucla/trouble-in-paradise-new-ucla-book.aspx.

Sunderland, P. L., and R. M. Denny 2007. *Doing Anthropology in Consumer Research.* Walnut Creek, CA: Left Coast Press.

Sunstein, B. S., and Chiseri-Strater, E. 2012. *Fieldworking: Reading and Writing Research,* 4th ed. Upper Saddle River, NJ: Prentice Hall.

Suttles, W. 1960. Affinal Ties, Subsistence, and Prestige among the Coast Salish. *American Anthropologist* 62:296–305.

Swift, M. 1963. Men and Women in Malay Society. In *Women in the New Asia,* B. Ward, ed., pp. 268–286. Paris: UNESCO.

Tanaka, J. 1980. *The San Hunter-Gatherers of the Kalahari.* Tokyo: University of Tokyo Press.

Tannen, D. 1990. *You Just Don't Understand: Women and Men in Conversation.* New York: Ballantine Books.

———. 2005. *Conversational Style: Analyzing Talk among Friends,* new ed. New York: Oxford University Press.

Tannen, D., ed. 1993. *Gender and Conversational Interaction.* New York: Oxford University Press.

Tannen, D., S. Kendall, and C. Gordon., eds. 2007. *Family Talk: Discourse and Identity in Four American Families.* New York: Oxford University Press.

Tannen, D., and A. M. Trester, eds. 2012. *Discourse 2.0: Language and New Media.* Washington, DC: Georgetown University Press.

Tavernise, S. 2012. Whites Account for Under Half of Births in U.S. *New York Times,* May 17. http://www.nytimes.com/2012/05/17/us/whites-account-for-under-half-of-births-in-us.html?pagewanted=all&_r=0.

Taylor, C. 1987. Anthropologist-in-Residence. In *Applied Anthropology in America,* 2nd ed., E. M. Eddy and W. L. Partridge, eds. New York: Columbia University Press.

Taylor, P., M. H. Lopez, J. H. Martínez, and G. Velasco 2012. *When Labels Don't Fit: Hispanics and Their Views of Identity,* Pew Research Hispanic Center, April 4. http://www.pewhispanic.org/2012/04/04/when-labels-dont-fit-hispanics-and-their-views-of-identity/.

Telegraph. 2005. Third Sex Finds a Place on Indian Passport Forms. *The Telegraph,* March 10, 2005. http://infochangeindia.org/human-rights/news/third-sex-finds-a-place-on-indian-passport-forms.html.

Terrace, H. S. 1979. *Nim.* New York: Knopf.

Thomas, L., and S. Wareing, eds. 2004. *Language, Society, and Power: An Introduction.* New York: Routledge.

Thompson, W. 1983. Introduction: World System with and without the Hyphen. In *Contending Approaches to World System Analysis,* W. Thompson, ed., pp. 7–26. Thousand Oaks, CA: Sage.

Tice, K. 1997. Reflections on Teaching Anthropology for Use in the Public and Private Sector. In *The Teaching of Anthropology: Problems, Issues, and Decisions,* C. P. Kottak, J. J. White, R. H. Furlow, and P. C. Rice, eds., pp. 273–284. Mountain View, CA: Mayfield.

Tishkov, V. A. 2004. *Chechnya: Life in a War-Torn Society.* Berkeley: University of California Press.

Titiev, M. 1992. *Old Oraibi: A Study of the Hopi Indians of Third Mesa.* Albuquerque: University of New Mexico Press.

Toner, R. 1992. Los Angeles Riots Are a Warning, Americans Fear. *New York Times,* May 11, pp. A1, A11.

Tougher, S. 2008. *The Eunuch in Byzantine History and Society*. New York: Routledge.

Trevathan, W. R., E. O. Smith, and J. McKenna. 2008. *Evolutionary Medicine and Health*. New York: Oxford University Press.

Trivedi, B. P. 2001. Scientists Identify a Language Gene. *National Geographic News,* October 4. http://news.nationalgeographic.com/news/2001/10/1004_Tvlanguagegene.html.

Trudgill, P. 2000. *Sociolinguistics: An Introduction to Language and Society,* 4th ed. New York: Penguin Books.

———. 2010. *Investigations in Sociohistorical Linguistics: Stories of Colonisation and Contact*. New York: Cambridge University Press.

Turnbull, C. 1965. *Wayward Servants: The Two Worlds of the African Pygmies*. Garden City, NY: Natural History Press.

Turner, V. W. 1974 (orig. 1967). *The Ritual Process*. Harmondsworth, England: Penguin Press.

———. 1995 (orig. 1969). *The Ritual Process*. Hawthorne, NY: Aldine de Gruyter.

Tylor, E. B. 1958 (orig. 1871). *Primitive Culture*. New York: Harper Torchbooks.

Ubelaker, D. H., ed. 2012. *Forensic Science: Current Issues, Future Directions*. Hoboken, NJ: Wiley.

U.S. Census Bureau 2010. http://quickfacts.census.gov/qfd/index.html.

Ulijaszek, S. J., and H. Lofink 2006. Obesity in Biocultural Perspective. *Annual Review of Anthropology* 35:337–360.

Van Allen, J. 1971. *"Aba Riots" or "Women's War"? British Ideology and Eastern Nigerian Women's Political Activism*. Waltham, MA: African Studies Association.

Van Cantfort, T. E., and J. B. Rimpau 1982. Sign Language Studies with Children and Chimpanzees. *Sign Language Studies* 34:15–72.

Vayda, A. P. 1968 (orig. 1961). Economic Systems in Ecological Perspective: The Case of the Northwest Coast. In *Readings in Anthropology,* 2nd ed., volume 2, M. H. Fried, ed., pp. 172–178. New York: Crowell.

Veblen, T. 1934. *The Theory of the Leisure Class: An Economic Study of Institutions*. New York: The Modern Library.

Verdery, K. 1997. *What Was Socialism and What Comes Next?* Princeton, NJ: Princeton University Press.

———. 2001. Socialist Societies: Anthropological Aspects. *International Encyclopedia of the Social & Behavioral Sciences,* pp. 14496–14500. New York: Elsevier.

Vidal, J. 2003. Every Third Person Will Be a Slum Dweller within 30 Years, UN Agency Warns: Biggest Study of World's Cities Finds 940 Million Already Living in Squalor. *The Guardian,* October 4. http://www.guardian.co.uk/international/story/0,3604,1055785,00.html.

Vigil, J. D. 2010. *Gang Redux: A Balanced Anti-Gang Strategy*. Long Grove, IL: Waveland.

———. 2012. *From Indians to Chicanos; The Dynamics of Mexican-American Culture,* 3rd ed. Boulder, CO: Westview Press.

———. 2005. For Gay Men, Different Scent of Attraction. *New York Times,* May 10, late ed.—final, p. A1.

———. 2012. Earliest Americans Arrived in Waves, DNA Study Finds. *New York Times,* July 11. http://www.nytimes.com/2012/07/12/science/earliest-americans-arrived-in-3-waves-not-1-dna-study-finds.html.

Wade, P. 2002. *Race, Nature, and Culture: An Anthropological Perspective*. Sterling, VA: Pluto Press.

———. 2010. *Race and Ethnicity in Latin America,* 2nd ed. New York: Pluto Press.

Wallace, A. F. C. 1966. *Religion: An Anthropological View*. New York: McGraw-Hill.

Wallerstein, I. M. 1982. The Rise and Future Demise of the World Capitalist System: Concepts for Comparative Analysis. In *Introduction to the Sociology of "Developing Societies,"* H. Alavi and T. Shanin, eds., pp. 29–53. New York: Monthly Review Press.

————. 2004. *World-Systems Analysis: An Introduction*. Durham, NC: Duke University Press.

Ward, M. C., and M. Edelstein 2009. *A World Full of Women,* 5th ed. Needham Heights, MA: Allyn & Bacon.

Warms, R., J. Garber, and R. J. McGee, eds. 2009. *Sacred Realms: Readings in the Anthropology of Religion,* 2nd ed. New York: Oxford University Press.

Wasson, C., M. O. Butler, and J. Copeland-Carson, eds. 2012. *Applying Anthropology in the Global Village*. Walnut Creek, CA: Left Coast Press.

Waterston, A. and M. D. Vesperi, eds. 2009. *Anthropology off the Shelf : Anthropologists on Writing*. Malden, MA: Blackwell.

Watzman, H. 2006. The Echoes of Ancient Humans. *Chronicle of Higher Education,* January 27. http://chronicle.com/weekly/v52/i21/21a01601.htm.

Weber, M. 1958 (orig. 1904). *The Protestant Ethic and the Spirit of Capitalism*. New York: Scribner.

————. 1968 (orig. 1922). *Economy and Society*. E. Fischoff et al. (trans.). New York: Bedminster Press.

Webster's New World Encyclopedia 1993. College Edition. Englewood Cliffs, NJ: Prentice Hall.

Weston, K. 1991. *Families We Choose: Lesbians, Gays, Kinship*. New York: Columbia University Press.

White, L. A. 1959. *The Evolution of Culture: The Development of Civilization to the Fall of Rome*. New York: McGraw-Hill.

————. 2009. *Modern Capitalist Culture,* abridged ed. Walnut Creek, CA: Left Coast Press.

Whorf, B. L. 1956. A Linguistic Consideration of Thinking in Primitive Communities. In *Language, Thought, and Reality: Selected Writings of Benjamin Lee Whorf,* J. B. Carroll, ed., pp. 65–86. Cambridge, MA: MIT Press.

Whyte, M. F. 1978. Cross-Cultural Codes Dealing with the Relative Status of Women. *Ethnology* 12(2):203–225.

Wiley, A. S., and J. S. Allen 2012. *Medical Anthropology: A Biocultural Approach,* 2nd ed. New York: Oxford University Press.

Winford, J. 2007b. Fossils Reveal Clues on Human Ancestors. *New York Times,* September 20. www.nytimes.com.

Wilk, R. R., and L. Cliggett 2007. *Economies and Cultures: Foundations of Economic Anthropology,* 2nd ed. Boulder, CO: Westview Press.

Williams, L. M., and D. Finkelhor 1995. Paternal Caregiving and Incest: Test of a Biosocial Model. *American Journal of Orthopsychiatry* 65(1):101–113.

Willie, C. V. 2003. *A New Look at Black Families*. Walnut Creek, CA: AltaMira.

Wilmsen, E. N. 1989. *Land Filled with Flies: A Political Economy of the Kalahari*. Chicago: University of Chicago Press.

Wilson, R., ed. 1996. *Human Rights: Culture and Context: Anthropological Perspectives*. Chicago: Pluto Press.

Winter, R. 2001. Religions of the World: Number of Adherents; Names of Houses of Worship; Names of Leaders; Rates of Growth. http://www.religioustolerance.org/worldrel.htm.

Witt, J. 2011 *Soc,* 2nd ed. Boston: McGraw-Hill.

Wolcott, H. F. 2008. *Ethnography: A Way of Seeing,* 2nd ed. Lanham, MD: AltaMira.

————. 2010. *Ethnography Lessons: A Primer*. Walnut Creek, CA: Left Coast Press.

Wolf, E. R. 1966. *Peasants*. Englewood Cliffs, NJ: Prentice Hall.

————. 1982. *Europe and the People without History*. Berkeley: University of California Press.

Wolf, E. R., with S. Silverman 2001. *Pathways of Power: Building an Anthropology of the Modern World*. Berkeley: University of California Press.

Wolf, M. 1992. *A Thrice-told Tale: Feminism, Postmodernism, and Ethnographic Responsibility*. Stanford, CA: Stanford University Press.

Wolpoff, M., B. Senut, M. Pickford, and J. Hawks 2002. Sahelanthropus or "Sahelpithecus"? *Nature* 419:581–582.

Womack, M. 2010. *The Anthropology of Health and Healing*. Lanham, MD: AltaMira.

Wood, B. 2011. *Human Evolution*. New York: Sterling Books.

Worsley, P. 1985 (orig. 1959). Cargo Cults. In *Readings in Anthropology* 85/86. Guilford, CT: Dushkin.

York, A. 2009. Alaskan Village Stands on Leading Edge of Climate Change. Mother Nature Network, August 19. http://news21.jomc.unc.edu/index.php/stories/alaska.html.

Young, A. 2000. *Women Who Become Men: Albanian Sworn Virgins*. New York: Berg.

Yurchak, A. 2005. *Everything Was Forever until It Was No More: The Last Soviet Generation*. Princeton, NJ: Princeton University Press.

Zaborenko, D. 2012. In U.S., 2012 So Far Is Hottest Year on Record. *Yahoo News*. http://news.yahoo.com/u-2012-far-hottest-record-192659729.html.

Zimmer-Tamakoshi, L. 1997. The Last Big Man: Development and Men's Discontents in the Papua New Guinea Highlands. *Oceania* 68(2):107–122.

Index